MW00856258

PHILIPPIANS

Brazos Theological Commentary on the Bible

PHILIPPIANS

GEORGE HUNSINGER

BrazosPress
a division of Baker Publishing Group
Grand Rapids, Michigan

Published by Brazos Press
a division of Baker Publishing Group
PO Box 6287, Grand Rapids, MI 49516-6287
www.brazospress.com

Printed in the United States of America

Library of Congress Cataloging-in-Publication Data
Names: Hunsinger, George, author.
Title: Philippians / George Hunsinger.
Description: Grand Rapids, Michigan : Brazos Press, a division of Baker Publishing Group, 2020. |
    Series: Brazos theological commentary | Includes bibliographical references and index. | Summary: "A
    respected theologian offers a theological reading of Philippians in this addition to the Brazos Theological
    Commentary on the Bible"—Provided by publisher.
Identifiers: LCCN 2019027596 | ISBN 9781587433740 (cloth)
Subjects: LCSH: Bible. Philippians—Commentaries.
Classification: LCC BS2705.53 .H86 2020 | DDC 227/.607—dc23
LC record available at https://lccn.loc.gov/2019027596

Unless otherwise indicated, the translation of Philippians in this commentary is the author's own, though it generally follows the English Standard Version.

20   21   22   23   24   25   26   7   6   5   4   3   2   1

Head of an Apostle (1508) by Albrecht Dürer

What delights *me* most is the course on *The Epistle to the Philippians* on Wednesdays. . . . *Paul! That's what it is!* Next to him all dogmatics is slime, and ethics too.

—Karl Barth, letter to Eduard Thurneysen, May 18, 1924

CONTENTS

SERIES PREFACE

Near the beginning of his treatise against gnostic interpretations of the Bible, *Against Heresies*, Irenaeus observes that scripture is like a great mosaic depicting a handsome king. It is as if we were owners of a villa in Gaul who had ordered a mosaic from Rome. It arrives, and the beautifully colored tiles need to be taken out of their packaging and put into proper order according to the plan of the artist. The difficulty, of course, is that scripture provides us with the individual pieces, but the order and sequence of various elements are not obvious. The Bible does not come with instructions that would allow interpreters to simply place verses, episodes, images, and parables in order as a worker might follow a schematic drawing in assembling the pieces to depict the handsome king. The mosaic must be puzzled out. This is precisely the work of scriptural interpretation.

Origen has his own image to express the difficulty of working out the proper approach to reading the Bible. When preparing to offer a commentary on the Psalms he tells of a tradition handed down to him by his Hebrew teacher:

> The Hebrew said that the whole divinely inspired scripture may be likened, because of its obscurity, to many locked rooms in our house. By each room is placed a key, but not the one that corresponds to it, so that the keys are scattered about beside the rooms, none of them matching the room by which it is placed. It is a difficult task to find the keys and match them to the rooms that they can open. We therefore know the scriptures that are obscure only by taking the points of departure for understanding them from another place because they have their interpretive principle scattered among them.[1]

1. Fragment from the preface to *Commentary on Psalms 1–25*, preserved in the *Philokalia*, in Trigg, *Origen*, 70–71.

As is the case for Irenaeus, scriptural interpretation is not purely local. The key in Genesis may best fit the door of Isaiah, which in turn opens up the meaning of Matthew. The mosaic must be put together with an eye toward the overall plan.

Irenaeus, Origen, and the great cloud of premodern biblical interpreters assumed that puzzling out the mosaic of scripture must be a communal project. The Bible is vast, heterogeneous, full of confusing passages and obscure words, and difficult to understand. Only a fool would imagine that he or she could work out solutions alone. The way forward must rely upon a tradition of reading that Irenaeus reports has been passed on as the rule or canon of truth that functions as a confession of faith. "Anyone," he says, "who keeps unchangeable in himself the rule of truth received through baptism will recognize the names and sayings and parables of the scriptures."[2] Modern scholars debate the content of the rule on which Irenaeus relies and commends, not the least because the terms and formulations Irenaeus himself uses shift and slide. Nonetheless, Irenaeus assumes that there is a body of apostolic doctrine sustained by a tradition of teaching in the church. This doctrine provides the clarifying principles that guide exegetical judgment toward a coherent overall reading of scripture as a unified witness. Doctrine, then, is the schematic drawing that will allow the reader to organize the vast heterogeneity of the words, images, and stories of the Bible into a readable, coherent whole. It is the rule that guides us toward the proper matching of keys to doors.

If self-consciousness about the role of history in shaping human consciousness makes modern historical-critical study actually critical, then what makes modern study of the Bible actually modern is the consensus that classical Christian doctrine distorts interpretive understanding. Benjamin Jowett, the influential nineteenth-century English classical scholar, is representative. In his programmatic essay "On the Interpretation of Scripture," he exhorts the biblical reader to disengage from doctrine and break its hold over the interpretive imagination. "The simple words of that book," writes Jowett of the modern reader, "he tries to preserve absolutely pure from the refinements or distinctions of later times." The modern interpreter wishes to "clear away the remains of dogmas, systems, controversies, which are encrusted upon" the words of scripture. The disciplines of close philological analysis "would enable us to separate the elements of doctrine and tradition with which the meaning of scripture is encumbered in our own day."[3] The lens of understanding must be wiped clear of the hazy and distorting film of doctrine.

2. *Against Heresies* 9.4.
3. Benjamin Jowett, "On the Interpretation of Scripture," in *Essays and Reviews* (London: Parker, 1860), 338–39.

Postmodernity, in turn, has encouraged us to criticize the critics. Jowett imagined that when he wiped away doctrine he would encounter the biblical text in its purity and uncover what he called "the original spirit and intention of the authors."[4] We are not now so sanguine, and the postmodern mind thinks interpretive frameworks inevitable. Nonetheless, we tend to remain modern in at least one sense. We read Athanasius and think of him stage-managing the diversity of scripture to support his positions against the Arians. We read Bernard of Clairvaux and assume that his monastic ideals structure his reading of the Song of Songs. In the wake of the Reformation, we can see how the doctrinal divisions of the time shaped biblical interpretation. Luther famously described the Epistle of James as a "strawy letter," for, as he said, "it has nothing of the nature of the Gospel about it."[5] In these and many other instances, often written in the heat of ecclesiastical controversy or out of the passion of ascetic commitment, we tend to think Jowett correct: doctrine is a distorting film on the lens of understanding.

However, is what we commonly think actually the case? Are readers naturally perceptive? Do we have an unblemished, reliable aptitude for the divine? Have we no need for disciplines of vision? Do our attention and judgment need to be trained, especially as we seek to read scripture as the living word of God? According to Augustine, we all struggle to journey toward God, who is our rest and peace. Yet our vision is darkened and the fetters of worldly habit corrupt our judgment. We need training and instruction in order to cleanse our minds so that we might find our way toward God.[6] To this end, "the whole temporal dispensation was made by divine Providence for our salvation."[7] The covenant with Israel, the coming of Christ, the gathering of the nations into the church—all these things are gathered up into the rule of faith, and they guide the vision and form of the soul toward the end of fellowship with God. In Augustine's view, the reading of scripture both contributes to and benefits from this divine pedagogy. With countless variations in both exegetical conclusions and theological frameworks, the same pedagogy of a doctrinally ruled reading of scripture characterizes the broad sweep of the Christian tradition from Gregory the Great through Bernard and Bonaventure, continuing across Reformation differences in both John Calvin and Cornelius à Lapide, Patrick Henry and Bishop Bossuet, and on to more recent figures such as Karl Barth and Hans Urs von Balthasar.

4. Jowett, "On the Interpretation of Scripture," 340.
5. *Luther's Works*, vol. 35, ed. E. Theodore Bachmann (Philadelphia: Fortress, 1959), 362.
6. *On Christian Doctrine* 1.10.
7. *On Christian Doctrine* 1.35.

Is doctrine, then, not a moldering scrim of antique prejudice obscuring the Bible, but instead a clarifying agent, an enduring tradition of theological judgments that amplifies the living voice of scripture? And what of the scholarly dispassion advocated by Jowett? Is a noncommitted reading—an interpretation unprejudiced—the way toward objectivity, or does it simply invite the languid intellectual apathy that stands aside to make room for the false truism and easy answers of the age?

This series of biblical commentaries was born out of the conviction that dogma clarifies rather than obscures. The Brazos Theological Commentary on the Bible advances upon the assumption that the Nicene tradition, in all its diversity and controversy, provides the proper basis for the interpretation of the Bible as Christian scripture. God the Father Almighty, who sends his only begotten Son to die for us and for our salvation and who raises the crucified Son in the power of the Holy Spirit so that the baptized may be joined in one body—faith in *this* God with *this* vocation of love for the world is the lens through which to view the heterogeneity and particularity of the biblical texts. Doctrine, then, is not a moldering scrim of antique prejudice obscuring the meaning of the Bible. It is a crucial aspect of the divine pedagogy, a clarifying agent for our minds fogged by self-deceptions, a challenge to our languid intellectual apathy that will too often rest in false truisms and the easy spiritual nostrums of the present age rather than search more deeply and widely for the dispersed keys to the many doors of scripture.

For this reason, the commentators in this series have not been chosen because of their historical or philological expertise. In the main, they are not biblical scholars in the conventional, modern sense of the term. Instead, the commentators were chosen because of their knowledge of and expertise in using the Christian doctrinal tradition. They are qualified by virtue of the doctrinal formation of their mental habits, for it is the conceit of this series of biblical commentaries that theological training in the Nicene tradition prepares one for biblical interpretation, and thus it is to theologians and not biblical scholars that we have turned. "War is too important," it has been said, "to leave to the generals."

We do hope, however, that readers do not draw the wrong impression. The Nicene tradition does not provide a set formula for the solution of exegetical problems. The great tradition of Christian doctrine was not transcribed, bound in folio, and issued in an official, critical edition. We have the Niceno-Constantinopolitan Creed, used for centuries in many traditions of Christian worship. We have ancient baptismal affirmations of faith. The Chalcedonian Definition and the creeds and canons of other church councils have their places in official church documents. Yet the rule of faith cannot be limited to a specific set of words, sentences, and creeds. It is instead a pervasive habit of thought, the animating culture of the church in its intellectual aspect. As Augustine observed, commenting on Jeremiah 31:33, "The creed is learned by listening; it is written, not on stone tablets nor on any material, but on the heart."[8] This is why Irenaeus is able to appeal to the rule of faith more than a century before the first ecumenical council, and this is why we need not itemize the contents of the Nicene tradition in order to appeal to its potency and role in the work of interpretation.

Because doctrine is intrinsically fluid on the margins and most powerful as a habit of mind rather than a list of propositions, this commentary series cannot settle difficult questions of method and content at the outset. The editors of the series impose no particular method of doctrinal interpretation. We cannot say in advance how doctrine helps the Christian reader assemble the mosaic of scripture. We have no clear answer to the question of whether exegesis guided by doctrine is antithetical to or compatible with the now-old modern methods of historical-critical inquiry. Truth—historical, mathematical, or doctrinal—knows no contradiction. But method is a discipline of vision and judgment, and we cannot know in advance what aspects of historical-critical inquiry are functions of modernism that shape the soul to be at odds with Christian discipline. Still further, the editors do not hold the commentators to any particular hermeneutical theory that specifies how to define the plain sense of scripture—or the role this plain sense should play in interpretation. Here the commentary series is tentative and exploratory.

Can we proceed in any other way? European and North American intellectual culture has been de-Christianized. The effect has not been a cessation of Christian activity. Theological work continues. Sermons are preached. Biblical scholars produce monographs. Church leaders have meetings. But each dimension of a formerly unified Christian practice now tends to function independently. It is as if a weakened army has been fragmented, and various corps have retreated to isolated fortresses in order to survive. Theology has lost its competence in exegesis. Scripture scholars function with minimal theological training. Each decade finds new theories of preaching to cover the nakedness of seminary training that provides theology without exegesis and exegesis without theology.

Not the least of the causes of the fragmentation of Christian intellectual practice has been the divisions of the church. Since the Reformation, the role of the

---

8. *Sermon* 212.2.

rule of faith in interpretation has been obscured by polemics and counterpolemics about *sola scriptura* and the necessity of a magisterial teaching authority. The Brazos Theological Commentary on the Bible series is deliberately ecumenical in scope because the editors are convinced that early church fathers were correct: church doctrine does not compete with scripture in a limited economy of epistemic authority. We wish to encourage unashamedly dogmatic interpretation of scripture, confident that the concrete consequences of such a reading will cast far more light on the great divisive questions of the Reformation than either reengaging in old theological polemics or chasing the fantasy of a pure exegesis that will somehow adjudicate between competing theological positions. You shall know the truth of doctrine by its interpretive fruits, and therefore in hopes of contributing to the unity of the church, we have deliberately chosen a wide range of theologians whose commitment to doctrine will allow readers to see real interpretive consequences rather than the shadowboxing of theological concepts.

The Brazos Theological Commentary on the Bible endorses a textual ecumenism that parallels our diversity of ecclesial backgrounds. We do not impose the thankfully modest inclusive-language agenda of the New Revised Standard Version, nor do we insist upon the glories of the Authorized Version, nor do we require our commentators to create a new translation. In our communal worship, in our private devotions, and in our theological scholarship, we use a range of scriptural translations. Precisely as scripture—a living, functioning text in the present life of faith—the Bible is not semantically fixed. Only a modernist, literalist hermeneutic could imagine that this modest fluidity is a liability. Philological precision and stability is a consequence of, not a basis for, exegesis. Judgments about the meaning of a text fix its literal sense, not the other way around. As a result, readers should expect an eclectic use of biblical translations, both across the different volumes of the series and within individual commentaries.

We cannot speak for contemporary biblical scholars, but as theologians we know that we have long been trained to defend our fortresses of theological concepts and formulations. And we have forgotten the skills of interpretation. Like stroke victims, we must rehabilitate our exegetical imaginations, and there are likely to be different strategies of recovery. Readers should expect this reconstructive— not reactionary—series to provide them with experiments in postcritical doctrinal interpretation, not commentaries written according to the settled principles of a well-functioning tradition. Some commentators will follow classical typological and allegorical readings from the premodern tradition; others will draw on contemporary historical study. Some will comment verse by verse; others will highlight passages, even single words that trigger theological analysis of scripture. No reading strategies are proscribed, no interpretive methods foresworn. The central premise in this commentary series is that doctrine provides structure and cogency to scriptural interpretation. We trust in this premise with the hope that the Nicene tradition can guide us, however imperfectly, diversely, and haltingly, toward a reading of scripture in which the right keys open the right doors.

R. R. Reno

AUTHOR'S PREFACE

This commentary is an exercise in ecclesial hermeneutics. It represents my attempt to appropriate some concerns that were important to my teachers. It may help if I frame the discussion by mentioning some mentors who influenced me and the lineage reflected in my commentary.

It seems that the faculty at Yale when I studied there years ago has known few peers before or since. It was an extraordinarily rich academic environment in which to study, and it gave me many things to ponder over a lifetime. My teachers, who did not always agree with one another of course, might not have been entirely pleased with the mosaic I have gone on to construct from them. One does what one can. "The student is not above the teacher, nor a servant above his master" (Matt. 10:24 NIV).

A sketch of what I mean by "ecclesial hermeneutics" can be found in excursus 2. There it pertains to how Phil. 2:5–11 may be related to Ebed Yahweh material in Isaiah, especially Isa. 53—a hotly disputed topic. I take this relationship to be primarily hermeneutical, not narrowly exegetical or philological. The chief figures in my mind as I drafted the excursus were George A. Lindbeck, Brevard S. Childs, and Hans W. Frei.

As a background presence, Lindbeck is more important than may be evident in my text. Although I disagreed with him when he tried to reduce Nicaea to a set of mere rules, I certainly agreed that Nicaea should exercise a strong regulative function in the interpretation of scripture. I also agree with Childs that ecclesial interpretation needs to be done with an eye toward the canon as a whole and toward the abundant network of often loose but crucial intertextual relations within it. Looking for broad literary and conceptual patterns, as opposed to tight philological dependencies, makes it possible to bring the so-called Philippians hymn and Isa. 53 into fruitful convergence for the church.

The question of hermeneutics was central for Frei, to whom I am greatly indebted both personally and academically. Throughout his career he was preoccupied with what he called the "literal sense." Although at first he proceeded as though the literal sense were a property of the text, he eventually changed his mind. In his later years he came to regard the *sensus literalis* as more nearly a matter of the *sensus communalis*—that is, of how the faithful community construes the text. I was initially puzzled by this shift, but an increasing awareness of the ambiguities of scripture pulled me in Frei's direction. I too became convinced that construal is all. More than Frei, however, I came to regard the communal sense as something determined by the ecumenical councils of the undivided church, especially the first four (Nicaea, Constantinople, Ephesus, and Chalcedon). Normatively, therefore, the *sensus communalis* would ultimately come down to the *sensus conciliorum*, with the councils being taken largely as hermeneutical guidelines and not just as doctrinal affirmations (a point that the later Frei would make about Chalcedon). How I think this idea of conciliarity works out becomes evident in the commentary.

My debt to Frei in this commentary is great on at least two other points. First, in his mind three things—realistic narrative, literal sense, and typological interpretation—were always closely interwoven. For Frei, prior to the eighteenth century, narrative unity was provided for the Bible's faithful readers largely by means of typological interpretation. I pick up on this theme when I argue, beyond Frei, that for ecclesial hermeneutics typological interpretation involves "reading backwards." Ecclesial hermeneutics means reading backwards, I suggest, not only from the New Testament to the Old but also from the ecumenical councils to the canonical texts. It is by no means a one-way street, either backwards or forward, but it finally demands something like a complex Möbius strip, or an exegetical/hermeneutical feedback loop, in shaping the Christian *sensus communalis*.

Second, the pattern of exchange was important to Frei. He seems to have adopted it from his early reading of Luther, where it appears in more or less mystical terms as an exchange between bridegroom and bride—that is, between Christ and the church. Although Frei discerned clearly that the saving exchange—or *admirabile commercium*—entails the vicarious identity of Christ with the sinful, he never fully anchored it in the sacrificial religion of Israel. In excursus 5, I attempt to do so. I argue that the mysterious ideas of exchange, substitution, and participation are inseparable for Paul in the *admirabile commercium*, and that for him the atoning significance of Christ's death cannot properly be understood apart from Yom Kippur and apart from Passover as combined with Yom Kippur in the primitive Christian imagination.

Finally, I would like to mention parenthetically that my whole academic career has been shaped by Frei's acute sense as a Jewish refugee of how monumental in importance was Barth's break with liberalism from the 1920s onward, especially in the German church struggle—liberalism not only as familiar in Harnack but also and primarily as familiar in Schleiermacher (see excursus 3).

Other unforgettable instructors and mentors, continually present as I wrote, left traces that appear in this work:

- Robert C. Johnson was an incomparable teacher not only of Barth but also of Luther, Calvin, and Kierkegaard—whom he taught his students not only to read but to love.

- Jaroslav Pelikan, with his magisterial grasp of the Christian tradition, made it impossible to ignore the history of doctrine, though I finally remained closer to Heiko A. Oberman (whom I knew from elsewhere).

- Nils A. Dahl set forth a powerful grasp of New Testament Christology, with an eye toward trinitarian and theological matters, while charting a path toward later creedal formulations. From Dahl I found my way to scholars like Otfried Hofius, Martin Hengel, and Richard Bauckham, as reflected in this commentary.

- David H. Kelsey, with his unequaled analytical acuity, set a high standard for aspiring to clarity in theological and exegetical work.

- Gene Outka, ethicist at Yale, stressed the unique identity of Jesus Christ, which places limits on *imitatio Christi*, and defined *agape* as a self-giving response not to merit but to need—ideas that have informed what this commentary maintains about the primacy of divine mercy for Paul as grounded in Yom Kippur.

- William Sloane Coffin Jr., university chaplain at Yale, collaborated with Martin Luther King Jr. in the civil rights movement, with whom he was often arrested, before becoming a leading voice against the Vietnam War and then an outspoken anti-nuclear activist. I served as his assistant for one year in the Riverside Church Disarmament Program, which he founded after moving to New York.

- Rowan A. Greer, whose books I did not read until later, showed a way to the Greek East from the Latin West. I am increasingly convinced that the Greek fathers, whom Greer revered, are indispensable not only for understanding Paul but also for the ecumenical future.

My appreciation of the Greek fathers also owes a great deal to Thomas F. Torrance, without whose contributions I could not have written this commentary (see excursus 6). As with Barth, so also with Torrance: I have tried to go with him and through him, but also beyond him and against him. To his credit, Torrance pays far more attention to Christ's priestly office than does Barth, who relegates it too much to the shadows. Nevertheless, I distinguish more sharply than does Torrance between priestly/cultic motifs and forensic ones. I do not reject forensic ideas in my interpretation of Paul, but I do try to decenter them and to break their unfortunate dominance in traditional Pauline interpretation. My approach to Phil. 3:9, for example, would not be possible without Torrance, but I do not believe he achieves sufficient clarity about the direction in which he is pointing (see excursus 5).

I hope these remarks about my teachers and mentors will be helpful to readers as a map, or perhaps better, as a series of guideposts, as they make their way through the commentary. It is a theological commentary, not merely an exegetical one. In light of my history as here explained, I offer it as an essay in postliberal biblical interpretation.

ACKNOWLEDGMENTS

I would like to thank the following persons, beginning with some New Testament scholars, for their advice and counsel after reading portions of my manuscript. Although responsibility for the final product is of course my own, I benefited from the critical suggestions (in alphabetical order) of Shane Berg, Lisa M. Bowens, Simon J. Gathercole, Moyer V. Hubbard, George L. Parsenios, and Mark A. Seifrid. I am also indebted to Khaled Anatolios as well as to colleagues in the Yale-Washington Theology Group, especially James J. Buckley, David J. Gouwens, Joseph L. Mangina, Michael Root, Katherine Sonderegger, and William Werpehowski. My friends and former students Han-luen Kantzer Komline and Jeffrey Skaff also made valuable suggestions, as did R. R. Reno, R. David Nelson, and Eric Salo, my editors at Baker. Princeton Seminary allowed me a generous sabbatical leave. Finally, as in all things, I owe more than I can say to my dear wife, Deborah van Deusen Hunsinger. Without support from her, and these my friends, this work would not have been possible.

ABBREVIATIONS

Old Testament

Gen.	Genesis	Song of Sol.	Song of Solomon
Exod.	Exodus	Isa.	Isaiah
Lev.	Leviticus	Jer.	Jeremiah
Num.	Numbers	Lam.	Lamentations
Deut.	Deuteronomy	Ezek.	Ezekiel
Josh.	Joshua	Dan.	Daniel
Judg.	Judges	Hosea	Hosea
Ruth	Ruth	Joel	Joel
1–2 Sam.	1–2 Samuel	Amos	Amos
1–2 Kings	1–2 Kings	Obad.	Obadiah
1–2 Chron.	1–2 Chronicles	Jon.	Jonah
Ezra	Ezra	Mic.	Micah
Neh.	Nehemiah	Nah.	Nahum
Esther	Esther	Hab.	Habakkuk
Job	Job	Zeph.	Zephaniah
Ps. (Pss.)	Psalm (Psalms)	Hag.	Haggai
Prov.	Proverbs	Zech.	Zechariah
Eccles.	Ecclesiastes	Mal.	Malachi

New Testament

Matt.	Matthew	John	John
Mark	Mark	Acts	Acts
Luke	Luke	Rom.	Romans

1–2 Cor.	1–2 Corinthians	Philem.	Philemon
Gal.	Galatians	Heb.	Hebrews
Eph.	Ephesians	Jas.	James
Phil.	Philippians	1–2 Pet.	1–2 Peter
Col.	Colossians	1–3 John	1–3 John
1–2 Thess.	1–2 Thessalonians	Jude	Jude
1–2 Tim.	1–2 Timothy	Rev.	Revelation
Titus	Titus		

PHILIPPIANS 1

1:1 Paul and Timothy, servants of Christ Jesus, to all the saints in Christ Jesus who are at Philippi, with the bishops and deacons. **2**Grace to you and peace from God our Father and the Lord Jesus Christ. **3**I thank my God in all my remembrance of you, **4**always in every prayer of mine for you all making my prayer with joy, **5**because of your partnership in the gospel from the first day until now. **6**And I am sure of this, that he who began a good work in you will bring it to completion at the day of Jesus Christ.

1:1 Paul and Timothy—Christian ministry never takes place in a vacuum. Even when carried out by an individual, it is always a collaborative effort. Not even the original apostles could act on their own as "free agents." Their ministry was always "conciliar" (Acts 15). It was always rooted in the apostolic community and carried out for the sake of the community. Paul's vocation illustrates this point. While he might have written to the Philippians simply in his own name, he included Timothy in the byline as someone responsible for the contents of the letter. We do not know exactly what role Timothy might have played. Did he at least act as the scribe? As Paul's interlocutor and companion, he would probably have been much more than that.

Paul's relationship with Timothy was complex and many layered. We may assume that the letter was discussed carefully between them before being written and sent. Nevertheless, Paul was the mentor while Timothy served as his apprentice. Indeed, the older man was an apostle whose unique office could not be transferred to another, while the younger man (probably converted by Paul's preaching) was being groomed as his emissary and successor. According to later tradition, Timothy would go on to become "bishop" of Ephesus and would die—like his mentor—as a martyr. Their unity-in-difference needs to be noted as carefully as their difference-in-unity.[1]

servants of Christ Jesus—Paul and Timothy's unity is derived from a higher authority. Whatever differences may have existed between an apostle and his successor, they were relativized by a larger consideration. Paul introduced himself and Timothy as being in the same category—namely, "servants" or "slaves" of Christ. Their lives were no longer their own, for they had been claimed in the service of another. They knew themselves to be entirely at Christ's disposal, in life and in death. To be a "servant" (*doulos*) of this Lord meant having been set apart for a special task. As with some of God's servants in the Hebrew scriptures (e.g., Isa. 53), a peculiar authority has been invested in Paul and Timothy that is finally inseparable from suffering and death.[2]

It is of some interest that Paul's phrase "servants of Christ Jesus" echoes the term "servant of Yahweh" in the Old Testament. The name of Jesus seems to have been substituted for the name of the Lord. Any number of Old Testament figures were directly or indirectly depicted as Yahweh's servants, including Moses, Joshua, David, and several of the prophets. By modifying a phrase that would have been familiar to Jewish people, Paul implies (and apparently takes for granted) the assertion that Jesus is somehow equal with God.[3]

1. "The intercourse between Timothy and the Philippian church had been constant and intimate. He had assisted the Apostle in its first foundation. . . . He was there not improbably more than once during the captivity at Caesarea, when the Apostle himself was prevented from seeing them. And now again he was on the eve of another visit, as one whose solicitude for the Philippians had become second nature." Lightfoot, *Philippians*, 79 (slightly modified).

2. The word "slave" (*doulos*) did not necessarily carry the kind of servile implications that would attach to it elsewhere. "Central features that distinguish 1st century slavery from that later practiced in the New World," writes S. Scott Bartchy, "are the following: racial factors played no role; education was greatly encouraged (some slaves were better educated than their owners) and enhanced a slave's value; many slaves carried out sensitive and highly responsible social functions; slaves could own property (including other slaves!); their religious and cultural traditions were the same as those of the freeborn; no laws prohibited public assembly of slaves; and (perhaps above all) the majority of urban and domestic slaves could legitimately anticipate being emancipated by the age of 30." Bartchy, "Slavery (Greco-Roman)," 6:66. For an interesting fictional narrative about the life of a former slave in the first-century church, see Witherington, *Life of Corinth*. Nevertheless, it should not be overlooked that the life of slaves in the Roman Empire could often be very harsh. Seneca acknowledged that Romans treated their slaves cruelly. Some were forced to fight wild beasts in the arena. They were under total domination and submission to their masters. Even those slaves who received manumission, considered "freedmen," continued to be forever in debt to their former masters. In a sense they were never really free of their servitude. See Smith, "Slavery in the Early Church."

3. "It is noticeable how quietly St. Paul steps into the place of the prophets and leaders of the Old Covenant, and how quietly he substitutes the name of his own Master in a connection hitherto reserved for that of Yahweh." Sanday and Headlam, *Epistle to the Romans*, 3 (slightly modified).

to all the saints in Christ Jesus who are at Philippi—For Paul, as this saluta-tion suggests, Jesus Christ is not only the supreme object of loyalty and devotion. He is also the mysterious figure of participation. All who take part "in Christ Jesus" (*en Christō Iēsou*) are for that reason established as "saints" (*pasin tois hagiois*). They are made holy by a holiness not their own.

I would suggest that the phrase "in Christ" has a double aspect. It is, for lack of better terms, at once "mystical" and "apocalyptic." In this verse it is used to suggest a status of holiness through spiritual union with Christ (the mystical side). The mystical interpretation that I suggest includes both personal union with Christ and membership in Christ's body, the church. At the same time this holiness remains ineffable. Despite being real in itself, it is a holiness that still remains hidden apart from the eyes of faith. It is yet to be revealed in glory at the end of all things (the apocalyptic side). (For further discussion of the phrase "in Christ," see excursus 1.)

The faithful do not participate in Christ without being truly holy (and so they are called "saints"),[4] yet their holiness remains hidden with Christ in God. Only at the end of all things, with the resurrection of the dead, will it be unveiled for what it is and has been all along. Until that day their holiness will be displayed only imperfectly on earth. It remains undiminished in Christ while standing in tension with their lesser selves on earth.

Therefore to be "in Christ" while still "at Philippi" does not mean that the "saints" in themselves are perfect, but that they are summoned to a life of continual repentance. They are caught up in an apocalyptic transition effected by Christ's resurrection, a transition from the old eon to the new. Their task is to become ever and again the saints that they already are in Christ.

It should be noted that the status of being "in Christ" as both a "mystical" and an "apocalyptic" condition includes public practices, even though it is not constituted by them. Although it cannot be reduced to a mode of private inwardness, neither can it be grasped merely through the public/private distinction.[5] As a mystical and spiritual matter, it can only be apprehended by faith, transcending anything observable by sight. As something apocalyptic, on the other hand, it is destined to be revealed in glory at the end of all things. Until that day it will remain revealed to faith in the midst of its hiddenness and hidden in the midst of its revelation.

---

4. Although the word "saint" also means being "set apart" for tasks of worship and witness, its connec-tion with the phrase "in Christ" seems here to suggest a different primary, more "ontic," determination: actual holiness before God (*coram Deo*).

5. For a different view see Kelsey, *Eccentric Existence*, 727–33.

with the bishops and deacons—Rudiments of organization within the nascent community come to light with Paul's reference to "bishops and deacons," a phrase as intriguing as it is inconclusive. "Bishops" or "overseers" (in the plural) would most likely have been responsible for the tasks of teaching and worship. If so, they would have been expected to instruct this predominantly Gentile church not only in the gospel of the apostolic faith but also, if possible, in the unfamiliar Hebrew scriptures, apart from which the gospel would be unintelligible, concerning as they did the Savior of the world, who was also the Jews' crucified Messiah.

Presumably the "bishops" (*episkopoi*) would have been responsible for leading worship, and thus for presiding at baptism and the Eucharist. "Deacons" (*diakonoi*) would perhaps have been responsible, as in Acts, to care for the sick and needy. It cannot be ruled out, as intimated later in the letter, that women may have served in these "offices" at that time.[6]

An emerging "church order" seems to be implicit. It apparently runs from the apostle to his coworker Timothy (both as "servants" or "slaves"), to "bishops and deacons," and finally to the "saints." "Egalitarian" and "hierarchical" elements would both seem to be in play, but at this distance they can hardly be sorted out.

At least two further points seem worthy of note. First, in marked contrast to his other letters, Paul does not immediately identify himself as an "apostle." It would seem that his apostolic authority—so contested elsewhere throughout his ministry—is simply not an issue here. The church at Philippi is a community of his loyal supporters, on whose collaboration he could always count.[7] Second, we may wonder why "bishops and deacons" are singled out for special mention at the beginning, again in contrast to other letters. Since Paul is concerned about simmering problems of disunity at Philippi, perhaps these officeholders would be expected to play a role in straightening things out.

1:2 from God our Father and the Lord Jesus Christ[8]—It is not always recognized that Paul's apostolic benedictions, like this one (*apo theou patros hēmōn*

---

6. Regarding bishops and deacons, Chadwick writes, "Although one cannot be sure just what functions the Philippian bishops and deacons had, the subsequent development suggests that the deacons helped on the administrative side, while the spiritual leadership of the community would be in the hands of the 'bishops' with pastoral oversight, subject to Paul himself." Would Euodia and Syntyche (Phil. 4:2–3) perhaps have been numbered among the "bishops," or the "deacons," or neither? See Chadwick, "Episcopacy," 11.

7. "The official title of Apostle is omitted here, as in the Epistles to the Thessalonians. In writing to the Macedonian Churches, with which his relations were so close and affectionate, St. Paul would feel an appeal to his authority to be unnecessary." Lightfoot, *Philippians*, 79.

8. In the comments that follow I first discuss the theological ascription in the latter part of 1:2 before turning to what this ascription provides the foundation for: the blessings Paul invokes in the first part of 1:2.

kai kyriou Iēsou Christou), seem to display an incipient trinitarian structure. In later tradition a typical literary form would run: "*from* the Father, *through* the Son, and *in* the Spirit." This form sheds interesting light on the benediction as formulated here.

First, in contrast to the "from/through" structure that would later become more conventional, what appears here is essentially a structure of "from/from." Because "the Lord Jesus Christ" is placed in apposition to "God our Father," the preposition "from" (*apo*), though appearing only once, would seem to apply equally to both referents. "God our Father" and "the Lord Jesus Christ" are invoked as the twofold source of "grace and peace."

It does not follow, however, that they would each need to be the source in the same way. If "God our Father" is understood as the absolute origin of "grace and peace," then "the Lord Jesus Christ" can be seen as the Mediator through whom "grace and peace" are imparted. In any case, by placing the two in what might be called an apposition of origin, with respect to grace and peace, a certain coequality between them is implied. The deity of the Lord Jesus Christ, as suggested by the word "Lord" (*kyrios*), emerges more than once in the letter.

Second, a veiled reference to the Holy Spirit may perhaps be discerned under the aspect of "grace and peace."[9] In Paul, the Spirit is regularly associated with "peace" (e.g., Gal. 5:22) as well as with God's "gifts" (e.g., 1 Cor. 12:4). The Holy Spirit is at once "object" and "subject," the gift as well as the giver of gifts. A fully candid trinitarian expression might thus affirm that "grace and peace" are given from the Father, through the Son, and in the Spirit. In this light the typical Pauline benedictions, as evidenced here, may be regarded as precursors of later and more explicit trinitarian formulations. It is finally only in and by the Spirit that grace and peace are imparted from the Father through the Son to the community.[10]

9. From the standpoint of later tradition, the idea that grace implies the Holy Spirit would be a natural one, as may be seen, for example, in Edwards: "Grace in the soul is the Holy Ghost acting in the soul." Edwards, "Charity and Its Fruits," in *Works of Jonathan Edwards*, 8:332.

10. Today there is a greater openness than there was a generation ago in New Testament scholarship to the kind of ecclesial reading I am attempting. "To interpret the Bible in light of the doctrine of the Trinity," writes C. Kavin Rowe, "does not, therefore, distort its basic content but penetrates to its core with respect to the reality of the divine identity, the living God outside of the text known truly by Israel and fully in Jesus Christ. Such interpretative liberty does not entail a dismissal of the original sense of the text but instead seeks to illuminate the full breadth of ontological reality about which the biblical text, Old and New Testament together, speaks in its entirety." Rowe, "Biblical Pressure," 311–12. Throughout this commentary I do not argue that such a reading is entirely necessary, but only that it is possible and fitting, and therefore not illicit for the Christian community as grounded in the Nicene faith.

Grace to you and peace—"Grace" (*charis*) is therefore not so much an impersonal spiritual power as it is the powerful spiritual presence of a person. It is Christ's presence to us as "a gift." Athanasius once remarked that the Spirit is always in the Son even as the Son is always in the Father, so that the three are inseparable. Elsewhere he made it clear that the reverse is also true, so that the Son is always in the Spirit while the Father is always in the Son. Therefore, none of them is to be had without the others. If so, we may infer that "grace" is always finally the personal presence of the Son in the power of the Spirit. Or we may say that "grace" is always the gift of the Spirit proceeding from the Father through the Son. Related turns of phrase would also be permissible, each with its own nuance. It would be a mistake (not uncommon) to suppose that the use of one particular idiom automatically excludes others. A directly Christocentric idiom, for example, should not be taken as excluding a more trinitarian or a more pneumatological formulation, and so on.

"Grace" may thus be said to be effectual only insofar as it is Christocentric, trinitarian, and personal. At the same time the spiritual power of grace must be seen against an apocalyptic background. The ascended Christ is never present in the Spirit except in the disruptive power of Christ's own resurrection (resurrection being an apocalyptic event). The presence of Christ by grace is God's contradiction of sin and death. The once-for-all cross of Christ, where God's protest against sin, evil, and death was carried out, becomes effectual in the present by the apocalypse of grace—in the Word and through the Spirit. "For the crucifixion of Christ," writes J. Louis Martyn, "proves to be the centerpiece in God's war on our behalf, the event of his powerful invading grace, in no way contingent on the fulfilling of a single presupposition from our side. . . . On the contrary, the crucifixion is God's revelation of that gift of grace that, not assuming or presupposing faith, calls faith into existence."[11]

Grace always involves an "in spite of" structure. It comes again and again to deliver the faithful from sin and death. It comes, that is, to deliver sinners from what they would otherwise deserve. It is not merely, as is sometimes said, that grace is undeserved. Of course it is undeserved; but more to the point, it is contrary to what is actually deserved. Grace brings mercy and life instead of condemnation and death. Therefore it is always unsettling and new.

"Peace" is also finally an apocalyptic concept. It cannot be separated from conflict. Peace with God means conflict with the world, even as peace with the world means conflict with God. The peace that passes all understanding is a peace

---

11. Martyn, *Theological Issues*, 288.

that remains restless until the end. It is a peace that opposes death and the things that make for death. It is a peace that enters into death and in the midst of death perseveres. It is a peace that has the wisdom to change what can be changed while *refusing* to accept the things that cannot be changed (*pace* Reinhold Niebuhr). It seeks instead to oppose the unacceptable in the mode of a revolutionary patience. It is a peace that transcends every affliction. It is not such a peace as the world gives, nor a serenity indistinguishable from weak resignation. It is a peace that embraces the cross, yet is never without a lively hope. It is the peace of our Lord Jesus Christ, crucified and risen from the dead.

Grounded in the apocalypse of grace, peace necessarily takes its bearings from the end of all things. In the time between the times, grace creates possibilities where there are no possibilities, so that the way of peace might be adopted in witness to Christ, who is himself the death of death, the hope of the poor, the liberation of the afflicted, and the expiation of all our sins. In short, what the apocalypse of grace effects is a radical peace—and this is the apostolic benediction—that is militant, forward looking, and imperturbable as sent by the Father through the Son and in the Spirit.

Note finally that the order is "grace and peace," not "peace and grace." It is not so much peace that leads to grace as grace that issues in peace. Peace arises from grace, even as grace finds its fulfillment in peace. Although peace may include a sense of inner harmony, it is primarily a matter of reconciling the estranged—not only vertically (between God and sinners) but also horizontally (between male and female, slave and free, Jew and Greek). The apocalypse of *grace* means that our warfare is ended, while the apocalypse of *peace* brings the promise of shalom—of well-being, justice, security, and blessing—not just inwardly but for all things. What comes initially to the community and to the believer in the community— grace and peace—is destined to embrace the whole world.

1:3 I thank my God—If prayer is the chief act of the Christian life, as Calvin believed, then giving thanks belongs to the chief acts of prayer. Although Paul speaks to the Philippians about God, he speaks all the more to God about the Philippians. He rejoices that they are committed to "active partnership" (*koinōnia*) with him in the gospel. This *koinōnia* is perhaps for the apostle a gift than which no greater can be conceived. The source of this gift is from above. While the Philippians are praised, all thanks is returned to God.[12] Paul wants them to know that they are constantly remembered ("in all my remembrance of you," *epi pasē tē mneia hymōn*, 1:3), that

---

12. "Paul felt closer to the Philippians than to any other church.... Philippians has the longest thanksgiving section of all the Pauline letters (1:3–11)." Schnelle, *Apostle Paul*, 370.

not one of them is excluded ("for you all," *hyper pantōn hymōn*, 1:4), and that he values their friendship ("your partnership," *epi tē koinōnia*, 1:5) beyond measure.[13]

1:4 making my prayer with joy—Paul makes it a point to stress that his prayers are offered not in sorrow but in joy (*charas*). There is reason to believe not only that he himself is living *in extremis* but also that the Philippians are in dire straits. The apostle's note of joy in the midst of suffering, so prominent in this letter, finds its first expression here.

The joy of which Paul writes, and which he exhibits by his manner of life as well as by his prayer, is inseparable in his mind from the *koinōnia* he has just mentioned. Fellowship with the Philippians in and through Christ, and for the sake of Christ as clothed in the gospel, greatly sustains Paul in the midst of his trials. Joy, fellowship, and perseverance emerge as themes central to the letter.

For Paul, "joy" is a spiritual concept with vertical and horizontal elements. Joy arises, according to Aquinas, from love. It occurs when the person who is loved is present, or else when something good for that person comes to pass. Sorrow, on the other hand, arises from the absence of the beloved person, or else when that person undergoes some form of deprivation or harm.[14]

The joy of loving God, Aquinas continues, arises not only from God's intrinsic goodness but also from his presence to the faithful and their presence to him. They are present to one another in love: "God is love, and those who abide in love abide in God, and God abides in them" (1 John 4:16). This love is accompanied by joy. "These things I have spoken to you, that my joy may be in you, and that your joy may be full" (John 15:11). The mutual presence of God and the faithful to each other in love (*koinōnia*) brings joy.

A similar pattern exists in the case of joy at the more horizontal or mundane level. Especially when the love is spiritual, as grounded in grace through faith, joy again arises from the mutual presence of each to the other. The joy of loving God carries over into joy among the faithful, who not only love one another but also, in and through one another, love God.

Joy is often expressed in the Bible through the imagery of bride and bridegroom.

> I will rejoice greatly in the LORD,
> My soul will exult in my God;
> For He has clothed me with garments of salvation,

---

13. "The thanksgiving in this epistle is more than usually earnest. The Apostle dwells long and fondly on the subject. He repeats words and accumulates clauses in the intensity of his feeling." Lightfoot, *Philippians*, 80.

14. Thomas Aquinas, *Summa Theologiae* II-II.28.

He has wrapped me with a robe of righteousness,
As a bridegroom decks himself with a garland,
And as a bride adorns herself with her jewels. (Isa. 61:10 NASB)

As the bridegroom rejoices over the bride,
    so shall your God rejoice over you. (Isa. 62:5)

As mediated through Christ, the mutuality of love, at both the horizontal and the vertical levels, enables Paul to pray with joy in the midst of affliction.[15]

1:5 because of your partnership in the gospel—Joy is therefore doubly inseparable from *koinōnia*. *Koinōnia* with God through prayer is inseparable from *koinōnia* with coworkers in the gospel. *Koinōnia*, we may note, is a rich term whose semantic range cannot be captured in a single English word. At the lower end it means fellowship, which connotes some sort of alliance, camaraderie, and common interests. Beyond that, and more significantly, it can mean companionship and help, including economic assistance. At the high end, for Paul and the whole apostolic tradition, it means spiritual oneness and loving communion, even finally a kind of spiritual or "mystical" bond of mutual indwelling (Rom. 12:5), as suggested by the phrase "in Christ."

The high form of *koinōnia* as "communion" is grounded in union with Christ while spilling over to embrace all those who know and love him by faith—the *totus Christus*, Christ in and with his people. In the New Testament, communion can be conveyed as mutual indwelling simply by the preposition "in." "On that day you will know that I am *in* my Father, and you *in* me, and I *in* you" (John 14:20, italics added). It also has eucharistic implications. "Whoever feeds on my flesh and drinks my blood abides in me, and I in him" (John 6:56). Communion knits the faithful together into one body. "We, though many, are one body in Christ, and individually members one of another" (Rom. 12:5).[16]

Koinōnia exists eternally in the Holy Trinity as the mutual indwelling (or *perichoresis*) of the three divine "persons" in love. It is a matter of mutual giving and receiving—of self-giving and receiving in love. It is mediated by Christ through the Spirit to the faithful by means of word and sacrament. *Koinōnia* at

---

15. Paul elsewhere also places joy in relation to suffering—for example, when writing to the Thessalonians. You welcomed the gospel, he reminds them, "in much affliction, with the joy of the Holy Spirit" (*en thlipsei pollē meta charas pneumatos hagiou*) (1 Thess. 1:6). The affliction of the end times is overridden by the joy of the promised future in Christ.

16. Cf. Cranmer's great eucharistic "Prayer of Humble Access" as found in the 1979 *Book of Common Prayer*: "Grant us therefore, gracious Lord, so to eat the flesh of thy dear Son Jesus Christ, and to drink his blood, that we may evermore dwell in him, and he in us." *Book of Common Prayer*, 337.

the deepest level stands for ultimate reality itself.[17] It is the beginning and end of all things. Joy arises from *koinōnia*, in its various forms, because of the divine exuberance at the heart of the Holy Trinity.

From the standpoint of later tradition, this is the larger theological background for the term as it comes to expression in this verse. Paul gives thanks for the Philippians in his prayers, because they share a "fellowship" or "partnership" (*koinōnia*) in the gospel. "Here, as the context shows," writes J. B. Lightfoot, "it [*koinōnia*] denotes cooperation in the widest sense—their participation with the Apostle, whether in sympathy or in suffering or in active labor or in any other way."[18] Their mutual fellowship in attesting the gospel is a benefit that no suffering can diminish.

Note that by this use of *koinōnia* Paul may also be alluding to more than just their common vocation. He is perhaps also giving thanks to the Philippians for their repeated gifts to him of material aid. For Paul *koinōnia* can assume an almost sacramental aspect when embodied in the gift of money (2 Cor. 8:4; 9:14).[19] This theme reappears at the end of the letter (Phil. 4:10–19).

from the first day until now—Paul commends the Philippians for their perseverance in remaining true to Christ and the gospel. They have not wavered "from the first day until now" (*apo tēs prōtēs hēmeras achri tou nun*). Their loyalty to Paul, to whom they owed much, remains a source of encouragement to him through all his hardships and afflictions. What Paul is commending is the "perseverance of the saints" as a communal, not just an individual, good.

"Perseverance" (*hypomonē*) is not a word found here, though what it stands for is being commended. It is a specifically biblical virtue that may be usefully compared to the classical virtue of "courage" (*andreia*) (cf. Rom. 5:4). For Aristotle, courage represents the golden mean between cowardice (a deficit of courage) and recklessness (an excess of courage), though it is closer to being reckless. It implies valor, bravery, and (notably) trusting in one's own strength. "Physical courage," or acting fearlessly despite pain, danger, or the threat of death, is distinguished from "moral courage," which means acting rightly despite opposition, shame, or discouragement.[20]

---

17. From this perspective, the "ultimate reality" of God pertains not to an abstract "being itself," as some have argued, but rather to a concrete "being in communion," loving communion, as exemplified by the Holy Trinity. The Trinity can be described as *autokoinōnia*, or Communion itself. *Koinōnia*, in the inner life of God, is the beginning and end of all things.

18. Lightfoot, *Philippians*, 81 (slightly modified).

19. "Their almsgiving was a signal instance of this cooperation [*koinōnia*], and seems to have been foremost in the Apostle's mind." Lightfoot, *Philippians*, 81.

20. See Aristotle, *Nicomachean Ethics* 3.6–7 (Irwin, 71–74).

By contrast, and regardless of any overlaps, for Paul as for all of scripture, the good represented by "perseverance" is oriented not toward human self-reliance but toward God. *Hypomonē* is a profoundly theocentric (and in that sense "eccentric") virtue (or better, gift). Like *koinōnia*, it has no single translation in the English Bible. It is commonly rendered as "patience," "endurance," and "waiting."

Hypomonē essentially means waiting on God, crying out to God in distress, trusting in God's promises, and not ceasing to hope in God for deliverance despite all adversity regardless of how severe.[21] Among its biblical exemplars are Joseph languishing in prison, Job being afflicted in the land of Uz, and Jesus dying in agony on the cross. *Hypomonē* means the confidence of being sustained and the hope of being delivered, not by one's own resources or virtues but by the intervention of divine grace. "Indeed, we felt that we had received the sentence of death so that we would rely not on ourselves but on God who *raises* the dead" (2 Cor. 1:9, italics added; note the present tense).[22]

The ideas of joy, *koinōnia*, and *hypomonē* are closely linked in Paul's mind. While the term *koinōnia* is used in this verse for "active partnership" in the gospel, it pertains also (if only implicitly) to prayer as Paul's communion with God. Paul is filled with thanks and joy toward God for his *koinōnia* with the Philippians, and theirs with him. *Koinōnia* means their joint participation in the same benefits (salvation), the same mission (proclamation of the gospel), and the same sufferings (persecution). The term *hypomonē*, while not appearing here (or anywhere in this letter), is clearly implied by the object of Paul's thanksgiving—namely, the gift of the Philippians' steadfast partnership with him, "from the first day until now," in evangelical fellowship and joy despite all adversity and suffering.

1:6 And I am sure—This verse contains a promise that Paul may have formulated in light of a specific need. Signs of anxiety among the Philippians seem to seep through the edges at various points in the letter. It seems that they are suffering for their convictions, perhaps not so much from direct Roman persecution (though that cannot be ruled out) as from various forms of social ostracism and hostility. Their break with established social networks and cultural-religious bonds may have plunged them into serious economic hardship. Doubts about God's grace have apparently entered the community, and defections are perhaps not unknown.

---

21. In Rom. 15:5 God is described as "the God of patience and comfort" (*ho de theos tēs hypomonēs kai tēs paraklēseōs*).

22. Literally, "having trusted in God, the one raising the dead" (*pepoithotes . . . epi tō theō tō egeironti tous nekrous*). The phrase *tō egeironti* is, remarkably, a present participle in the active voice.

If so, then Paul is encouraging them to live above their circumstances. His attention shifts from their perseverance to its objective ground, from their constancy to its future hope. Paul does not overpromise what they can expect, nor does he scale down the gospel to fit the circumstances. He simply appeals to the faithfulness of God.

The apostle is at least sure of one thing: the faithful should look on their hardships in light of the gospel, not the other way around. This policy is the benchmark of his evangelical realism. It is not their hardships that contradict the gospel, he believes, but the gospel that contradicts their hardships. It is not sin, evil, and death that will sway the future, nor their suffering from shunning, slander, and want.[23]

will bring it to completion—The Father of our Lord Jesus Christ has triumphed over death and the things that make for death. The promise of the gospel is not that the faithful will be spared hardships but that they will be sustained in the midst of their afflictions. Adversity is not a sign that the faithful have been abandoned by God. It serves rather to remind them that Christ's resurrection is greater than any adversity, and that the way of the cross is the common lot of his followers.

Above all, God will not abandon the work of his hands. Though his ways may at times be obscure, they are grounded in resurrection hope. The work of salvation that God has begun in the faithful (*en hymin*, plural) will be completed "at the day of Jesus Christ" (an implicitly apocalyptic concept), and therefore to all eternity.[24]

This verse is sometimes thought to apply not so much to economic and social hardship as to feelings of discouragement arising from a sense of failure. These might be doubts that can afflict someone who has committed a grave moral wrong, someone who has failed despite much effort to overcome a besetting sin, or someone who has simply not made the hoped-for progress in spiritual life. Or again, there may be anxieties that are felt about a loved one—by a believer, for example, about a child who seems to have drifted away, or about any similar circumstance.

The pastoral care offered by this verse is much the same in any such cases. Look not to yourself and your failures, to the failings of another, or to any outward

23. The sufferings of the community at Philippi apparently "sprang," writes Peter Oakes, "from a variety of primary causes: principally abandonment of pagan worship, also suspicion of secretive associations, suspicion of [perceived] Jewish activities, and attempts at evangelism. . . . For almost every group [in the church] the most serious long-term suffering seems likely to have been economic." Oakes, *Philippians*, 91, 96.

24. "Divinely inspired impulses and actions in the Christian life confirm God's faithfulness to God's intent to finish God's salvific purposes begun in believers." Gundry Volf, *Paul and Perseverance*, 270.

afflictions. Anyone who concentrates on his own life or that of another is bound to be stricken at some point with anxieties, as Luther well knew. It is as if Paul were saying, "However great your sins may be, God is greater than your sins, even as he is greater than your afflictions. Your hope should rest never in yourselves but in God. Despite all your failures and weaknesses, or all your adversities and disappointments, the God who has begun a good work in you can be trusted to bring it to completion. All other ground is sinking sand." What Paul says in another connection would apply here as well: "What if some were unfaithful? Will their faithlessness nullify the faithfulness of God? By no means!" (Rom. 3:3–4).

the day of Jesus Christ—Note again that the day of completion is described as "the day of Jesus Christ" (*hēmeras Christou Iēsou*). Three things seem to follow.

First, the ultimate goal Paul writes of is not finally to be found, and therefore not to be sought, under the conditions of this life. The faithful are not to expect perfection, nor perhaps even "progressive sanctification," should there be such a thing. They are called to cling solely to God, in life and in death. Grace comes precisely to lost sinners. Thérèse of Lisieux writes, "In the evening of this life, I shall appear before you with empty hands, for I do not ask you, Lord, to count my works. All our righteousness is blemished in your eyes. I wish, then, to be clothed in your own righteousness and to receive from your love the eternal possession of yourself."[25]

Second, "the day of Jesus Christ" points toward his return in glory, and so not merely to the day of one's death. The good work begun in the faithful stands under the sign of resurrection hope.

Finally, it cannot be insignificant that where the Old Testament refers to Yahweh—"the day of the Lord"—Paul re-mints the phrase christologically to read "the day of Jesus Christ." The lordship of Yahweh is connected with Christ himself. Christ is the hope of the afflicted, the comforter of the discouraged, and the deliverer of the lost. He is not just the source but the content of hope. The faithful are to look not to themselves but to him who is the resurrection and the life (John 11:25).

> [7]It is right for me to feel this way about you all, because I hold you in my heart, for you are all partakers with me of grace, both in my imprisonment and in the defense and confirmation of the gospel. [8]For God is my witness, how I yearn for you all with the affection of Christ Jesus. [9]And it is my prayer that your love may abound more and more, with knowledge and all discernment, [10]so that you may

25. St. Thérèse of Lisieux, *Story of a Soul*, 435.

13

approve what is excellent, and so be pure and blameless for the day of Christ, ¹¹filled with the fruit of righteousness that comes through Jesus Christ, to the glory and praise of God.

1:7 **It is right for me to feel this way**—The *koinōnia* theme returns because Paul's heart is at least as compendious as his mind. To have an "active partnership" (*koinōnia*) in the gospel (1:3), to pray to God with thanksgiving and joy (1:3–4), to have a good work begun in one's community (and in oneself) by God (1:6), to be "partakers" (*synkoinōnous*) with the apostle in grace (1:7)—these are all aspects of what it means to be "in Christ Jesus" (1:1). They are variations on a theme. Paul's relationship to the Philippians, and theirs to him, is mediated through their common bond of union with Christ (*participatio Christi*).

because I hold you in my heart—Paul feels this bond with emotional intensity. He holds the Philippians "in his heart" (*en tē kardia*), every one of them without exception ("you all," *pantōn hymōn*). The bond the Philippians enjoy with Christ is the same bond that joins them to Paul as well as to one another. They are mutual partakers of one grace (*synkoinōnous . . . tēs charitos*), which is Christ's personal intervention for them in the Spirit. That is precisely the spiritual bond that makes the depth of Paul's affection so fitting ("it is right for me to feel this way," *kathōs estin dikaion emoi touto phronein*). He holds the Philippians in his heart, as he also does the Corinthians (2 Cor. 7:3), knowing that they will finally live together and die together, for they are all one body in Christ.

in my imprisonment—It is now disclosed to the reader what the Philippians themselves must have already known—namely, that Paul writes as one imprisoned and in chains. The imprisonment is most likely in Rome,[26] where the trial Paul faces could mean death. The apostle's joy in the midst of incarceration offers a model of the Christian life for the Philippians. He seeks to encourage them, to relieve their anxieties about him, putting all things into spiritual perspective.

and in the defense and confirmation of the gospel—Whether in prison or in the courtroom, whether in chains or in freedom, Paul strives to do one thing above all else. He strives to advance the gospel. By the Word and in the Spirit, Paul strives to let Christ reveal himself to the world through his apostleship.

for you are all partakers with me of grace—The *koinōnia* of the Philippians with Paul in grace (*synkoinōnous*), their oneness with him, extends also to his

---

26. Rome seems to be the best guess. For reasons for this, consult the standard commentaries, such as those by Fee and Bockmuehl. See also my comment below on 4:22.

defense and confirmation of the gospel, even as it extends to his imprisonment. In joy and affliction, in vocation and perseverance, they are called to see themselves as one body in communion.

1:8 how I yearn for you all with the affection of Christ Jesus—Paul endeavors to put first things first, but not at the expense of his love for the Philippians. Not only are they in his heart; they are loved by him with "the affection of Christ Jesus" (*en splanchnois Christou Iēsou*), an affection given from above.[27] The implication is clear. Christ himself loves the Philippians in and through Paul, even as Paul loves them in and through Christ.[28] No deeper affection can be imagined. The two loves—Paul's and Christ's—in their abiding distinction are one. Paul desires that the joy he feels in Christ will be completed by his reunion with his friends. Facing trial and perhaps imminent death, he can state, "I yearn for you with all the affection of Christ Jesus."

1:9 And it is my prayer—Paul prays for the Philippians as whole persons—heart, hand, and mind. The heart in particular is the seat of faith, involving not just the affections but also all spiritual knowledge and discernment. In practice, the heart thus involves perseverance (*hypomonē*) (cf. 1:5) and sincerity (*eilikrineis*) (cf. 1:10).

that your love may abound . . . , with knowledge—Paul knows that love (*agapē*) and knowledge (*epignōsis*) cannot be separated. Knowledge without love can be contentious, while love without knowledge can be naïve. Above all, God cannot be known without also being worshiped and loved. Nor can he be loved and worshiped without also being truly known. That is one reason, perhaps the deepest, why revelation is always necessary. Without the generosity of his self-revelation, God can be neither known nor loved nor worshiped aright.

God is the Lord of his own self-giving in love and of his own self-disclosure in knowledge—and just so is he the source of the world's salvation in Christ. Ultimately, therefore, there can be no such thing as a neutral knowledge of God detached from love (as in some philosophical theologies), nor a true love of God apart from knowledge (as in some "spiritualities"). A God not worshiped with love in true knowledge is no God at all.

abound more and more, with knowledge and all discernment—The "more and more" passages in Paul (*mallon kai mallon*) are a sign that the communities

---

27. J. B. Lightfoot paraphrases this part of 1:8 as follows: "Did I speak of having you in my own heart? I should rather have said that in the heart of Christ Jesus I long for you." He comments, "A powerful metaphor describing perfect union." Lightfoot, *Philippians*, 83.

28. "In Paul it was not Paul who lived but Christ" (cf. Gal. 2:20). Lightfoot, *Philippians*, 83, citing Bengel (in Latin).

to whom he writes require encouragement more than correction. He prays that love among the Philippians—for God and for one another—will increasingly abound. Where love abounds, knowledge (*epignōsis*) and all discernment (*pasē aisthēsei*) will tend toward their proper proportions. They will bear fruit in sound judgment and right action. Whatever is excellent will be recognized and approved, while deceiving appearances will be unmasked and exposed. Perhaps not least, discord and rivalry among the faithful will be held at bay.[29] Love cannot flourish with knowledge and all discernment where the atmosphere is poisoned by discord and rivalry.

1:10 **approve what is excellent, and so be pure and blameless**—The church fathers tended to think that "approve what is excellent" (*to dokimazein . . . ta diapheronta*, "to discern what needs to be distinguished") pertains to distinguishing heresy from true doctrine, while being "pure and blameless" (*eilikrineis kai aproskopoi*) concerns the kind of practices that flow from true beliefs. Modern interpreters, on the other hand, usually read "approve what is excellent" as a matter of wisdom in spiritual or moral discernment. Being "pure and blameless" would then mean putting that discernment into practice. Either way, sound judgment is essential to sincere dispositions (*eilikrineis*) and worthy deeds (*aproskopoi*).

for the day of Christ—Resurrection hope is oriented toward the "day of Christ" (*eis hēmeran Christou*), and for Paul all practices need to be gauged accordingly. On that day the divine judgment of grace will be fulfilled. Only what is "pure and blameless"—or authentic and true—will survive, only the "gold, silver, and precious stones." All else—the "wood, hay, and straw"—will be destroyed as in a consuming fire (1 Cor. 3:12–13). Right practices for the faithful are not a matter of attaining salvation but a matter of receiving the reward earned in response to the salvation given as a free gift (1 Cor. 3:14–15).

1:11 **filled with the fruit of righteousness**—Paul does not pray that the Philippians will become righteous, for by the grace of Christ the "saints" are already righteous in God's sight (cf. 1:1). He prays rather that they will bear "the fruit of righteousness" (*karpon dikaiosynēs*), fulfilling the gift of their calling, and so receive their appointed reward.[30] The fruit of righteousness—the harvest of justice—is peace and the things that make for peace (Jas. 3:18). This fruit therefore comes "through Christ" and means being shaped in conformity to his image, in union

29. "If such love increases among the Philippian Christians, it will remove the threats to their unity of heart and purpose that arise from occasional clashes of personality and temperament." Bruce, *Philippians*, 36.

30. "Righteousness by faith is intimately bound up with the life in Christ: it must in its very nature be fruitful; it is indeed the condition of bearing fruit." Lightfoot, *Philippians*, 85.

and communion with him.[31] The peace grounded in justice, and the justice that bears fruit in peace, will redound through Christ "to the glory and praise of God" (*eis doxan kai epainon theou*).

through Jesus Christ, to the glory and praise of God—A later trinitarian formula is again perhaps anticipated, this time not in benediction but in intercession (1:9). Recall that the benediction (1:2) anticipated the formula "from the Father, through the Son, and in the Spirit." Now in intercession (as seen in the prepositions *dia* and *eis*) the movement is implicitly reversed: "*in* the Spirit, *through* (*dia*) the Son, and *to* (*eis*) the Father."

Reference to the Spirit remains as yet unexpressed. However, the abounding of love, the grace of knowledge and all discernment, the approval of what is excellent, the rejection of whatever mars it, the spiritual authenticity that withstands the fires of judgment, and the harvest of justice as manifest in peace—what are these if not fruits of the Spirit? In the Spirit and through the Son, such fruits glorify and praise the Father, their ultimate origin and source. Paul's intercession for his beloved Philippians reflects a nascent trinitarian sensibility.

> **12**I want you to know, beloved, that what has happened to me has really served to advance the gospel, **13**so that it has become known throughout the whole imperial guard and to all the rest that my imprisonment is for Christ. **14**And most of the brothers and sisters, having become confident in the Lord by my imprisonment, are much more bold to speak the word without fear.

1:12 served to advance the gospel—The fact that God brings good out of evil does not make evil good. The Lord God bends evil to serve his purposes despite itself. In small ways and in large, in ways known and largely unknown, he compels sin, evil, and death to achieve his sovereign purposes of grace and peace. The great reversal from Good Friday to Easter is what grounds the promises of the gospel.

Unexpected deliverances, surprising turns of affairs, providential windfalls— these are echoes of the great reversal.[32] They are portents of the world to come. They occur at times and places of God's own choosing, not subject to our manipulations or control. They represent the divine cunning in history. While their nonoccurrence, when evil prospers, may sometimes overwhelm us with dismay, in the end everything stands or falls with the sign of the great reversal that points to the faithfulness of God—namely, the invincible sign of Easter Day.

31. "Righteousness without Christ cannot be fruitful." Vincent, *Philippians*, 14.
32. Recall that Bunyan's *Pilgrim's Progress* is a narrative depicting such themes.

The divine jujitsu, by which evil is used to defeat itself, finds expression in the imprisonment of Paul. What has happened to him is neither pleasant nor promising. Though he is an emissary of grace and peace, he is incarcerated as a threat to society. His mission as an itinerant preacher has ground to a halt. He is cut off from most of his friends while facing the possibility of an imminent death. The Philippians, we may imagine, are understandably distressed. Paul, however, fixes his eyes on the lodestar. The advance of the gospel is the entire meaning of his existence, and despite his imprisonment, that advancement has not ceased. Indeed, it has taken an unexpected twist that would have been scarcely imaginable.

1:13 throughout the whole imperial guard—We do not know exactly how the gospel has spread throughout "the whole imperial guard," and so presumably into the imperial palace itself. Nor do we know exactly what it is that prompted most of the faithful in Rome to become more confident in the Lord (1:14). But we can well imagine. What else could have sparked these things but Paul's astonishing and indefatigable spirit? He does not focus on his hapless circumstances but seizes the margin of freedom that remains.

my imprisonment is for Christ—Whether inside the prison or outside it, no one is left in doubt that Paul's captivity is "for Christ."[33] Despite his chains, Paul remains free as the slave of a higher Lord. He knows a different captivity than his earthly captivity, one that affords meaning to his earthly captivity by bending it to a higher good. His shackles are the occasion for telling anyone within earshot about the difference between Roman captivity, however dismal, and the joy of belonging to Christ.

1:14 much more bold to speak the word without fear—Paul's boldness in speaking the word has inspired a renewed boldness in others. His fearlessness is not only attention-grabbing but contagious. Because of him, the word continues to advance like a spreading flame. That is what he wants his friends at Philippi to know. He wants them to be encouraged by the providential effects of his imprisonment.

Another New Testament term for "boldness," *parrēsia*, though not used here, conveys much the same sense of "boldness in speaking the word" (e.g., Acts 4:13, 29, 31). It stands in interesting juxtaposition to the term *hypomonē*. The persistent cry for deliverance from suffering (*hypomonē*) represents much the same boldness and confidence in relation to God as proclaiming the gospel without fear (*parrēsia*) represents in relation to others. While *hypomonē* pertains more to the vertical dimension, and *parrēsia* to the horizontal, both are expressions of trust in the transcendent power that governs all things.

---

33. "It had now become clear that Paul was a prisoner, not for any crime he committed, political or otherwise, but simply because he was a Christian." Hawthorne, *Philippians*, 34 (slightly modified).

It may be noted in passing that Paul's description of the community as, in effect, his "siblings"—here translated as "most of the brothers and sisters" (*tous pleionas tōn adelphōn*)—is not merely pious rhetoric. As will be evident as the letter unfolds, the bonds of Christian fellowship run deep. The family of believers is especially important to Paul as a haven in a heartless world.

> **15**Some indeed preach Christ from envy and rivalry, but others from good will. **16**The latter do it out of love, knowing that I am put here for the defense of the gospel. **17**The former proclaim Christ out of rivalry, not sincerely but thinking to afflict me in my imprisonment. **18**What then? Only that in every way, whether in pretense or in truth, Christ is proclaimed, and in that I rejoice.

1:15 Some indeed preach Christ from envy and rivalry—T. S. Eliot once wrote that "the greatest treason" is "to do the right deed for the wrong reason." Paul, it seems, would not entirely agree. Sometimes, he thinks, it is enough for the right deed to be done, even if the motivations are shaky. For him the advance of the gospel is everything, while any possible small-minded interests behind it are almost nothing—so long as Christ is truly proclaimed.

The "envy and rivalry" (*phthonon kai erin*) mentioned here suggests that some preachers are faithful to Christ but unfriendly to Paul. Perhaps they are ashamed that he is in prison or fearful about it. Perhaps they wish to disown him or discredit him because of his embarrassing circumstances or his critical views. Perhaps they want to elevate themselves or their faction at his expense.

In his letter to the Romans, presumably written prior to Philippians, Paul had tried to steer a delicate course between contending parties in the church at Rome. Could it be that he is resented by some of the Jewish Christians, whom he described as the "weak," so that they now strive to undermine him? Or is the animosity perhaps being spread by Gentile Christians (the "strong") who are disgruntled because Paul has not supported their cause more vigorously? Whoever these opponents may have been, they are apparently not above resorting to ad hominem attacks against Paul.

Their breach of *koinōnia* is no doubt painful for Paul. Yet these particular opponents do not seem to have proclaimed a false gospel. Their preaching would indeed have been false if it had set forth a proto-Gnostic *theologia gloriae* (theology of glory), a "prosperity gospel," at the expense of a *theologia crucis* (theology of the cross). No gospel can be valid if it promises cheap grace, as if the faithful can expect to avoid all suffering in their discipleship to Christ, or as if Christian freedom is indistinguishable from license. Again, it would have been false if, in a more "Judaizing" manner, it had tried to subject the community to superseded aspects of the law. The point is that the opponents' preaching is not unacceptable to Paul despite their ill will toward him ("thinking to afflict me," *oiomenoi thlipsin egeirein*, 1:17). Their ill will is just one more burden for him to bear. He takes it as well as he can and tries putting it in the best possible light.

but others from good will—The situation is not without its bright side. There are others proclaiming the gospel in Rome who love Paul and do not malign him. They understand why he is in prison, and they respect his defense of the gospel. They do the right thing in the right way. They preach Christ truly and regard Paul fairly. They live lives worthy of the gospel. They do not undermine the community through envy, rivalry, and strife. They rejoice with Paul, we may presume, for the unexpected surprises of grace.

1:16 out of love—Love for Paul and love for Christ (*ex agapēs*) coalesce in those who preach Christ "from good will" (*di' eudokian*, 1:15). They take a charitable view of his imprisonment, seeing it as a badge of honor, not a source of shame or danger from which they need to distance themselves. They know that Paul is in chains "for the defense of the gospel" (*eis apologian tou euangeliou*). They do not strive to preach Christ at his expense.

1:17 out of rivalry . . . thinking to afflict me—Paul ascribes motives of competition (*eritheias*) and retaliation (*thlipsin egeirein*) to his opponents. They are not pure in heart (*hagnōs*; cf. 1:10). Paul does not respond to them in kind.

1:18 whether in pretense or in truth—Paul is candid with the Philippians. He does not try to gloss over certain tensions as they exist in the church at Rome (and about which the Philippians have perhaps already heard). For him everything depends on one thing, and he directs their attention to that. Perhaps in their own community they have known petty rivalries as well. If so, some sort of resolution needs to be sought. For Paul the overriding consideration that determines all things, whether in Rome or at Philippi, is simply this: that Christ should be truly proclaimed. All perils from without, all discords from within, all sorry motivations are finally of little consequence. No room for discouragement can exist as long as Christ is lifted up. Paul can therefore find reason to rejoice, as he emphasizes doubly by his rhetoric, anchoring his present and his future in joy. "In that"—"Christ *is* proclaimed" (*Christos katangelletai*)—"I rejoice. Yes, and I *will* rejoice" (*en toutō chairō, alla kai charēsomai*).[34]

---

34. "There's no discouragement / Shall make him once relent / His first avowed intent, / To be a pilgrim." "To Be a Pilgrim," a song from *The Pilgrim's Progress*, part 2 (1684), by John Bunyan.

19For I know that through your prayers and the help of the Spirit of Jesus Christ this will turn out for my deliverance, **20**as it is my eager expectation and hope that I will not be at all ashamed, but that with full courage now as always Christ will be honored in my body, whether by life or by death. **21**For to me to live is Christ, and to die is gain.

1:19 this will turn out for my deliverance—It seems that Paul expects to be delivered, but not necessarily from death. He thinks about his death from a center in Christ, even as he also thinks about it in apocalyptic terms. By his resurrection Christ has overcome and renewed the world. By his perfect obedience, as fulfilled in the cross, he has defeated the powers of sin and death. All who trust in him not only have been baptized into his death but also share in the hope of his resurrection. The world has done its worst but not prevailed. Easter joy and Easter hope permeate Paul's outlook on death because his heart is planted in Christ and the gospel.

through your prayers and the help of the Spirit of Jesus Christ—The prayers of his friends and the Spirit of the living Jesus are vital to Paul's resurrection hope. Prayer is the appointed means by which God includes the faithful in his sovereign work. It is through prayers of intercession that they are drawn into *koinōnia* with Christ. Just so, they are drawn into his self-witness and his self-mediation to the world. They can finally be drawn into this intercession only by the Word and in the Spirit. Their prayers and the Spirit's provision are thus correlative terms. The position of prayer is a position of intercession, a mode of receptivity, and a means of consolation. A supply of the Spirit's help is the promise accompanying their prayers. It enlivens their transcendent hope. The two together—their prayers and the Spirit's provision—will somehow eventuate in Paul's deliverance. In effect, using later trinitarian terms, it may be said that their prayers on Paul's behalf are offered to the Father, "with the help of the Spirit" (*kai epichorēgias tou pneumatos*), through the Son.

1:20 hope that I will not be at all ashamed—Paul desires only that he should not be ashamed. Clearly he means not being ashamed before Christ. He wishes only to do what is pleasing in his sight. That is his "eager expectation and hope" (*kata tēn apokaradokian kai elpida*). He knows that he cannot succeed by relying on his own strength. But he confesses that "I can do all things through him who strengthens me" (4:13). His hope is in Christ alone. Through countless trials and ordeals he has learned that Christ is faithful. With death looming at his door, he is indeed full of courage and prepared to act "in all boldness" (*en pasē parrēsia*).

What he wants, "now as always" (*hōs pantote kai nun*), is simply for Christ to be honored ("magnified," *megalynthēsetai*) "in my body" (*en tō sōmati mou*).[35] It is not Paul who is on trial but the gospel. His life is absorbed by his vocation, and his future by the faithfulness of Christ. Whether as an apostle or a martyr, whether in life or in death (*dia zōēs eite dia thanatou*), he wishes to be faithful to Christ as Christ has been faithful to him—and to the world. Whether granted freedom or execution, he will rejoice. His times are in Christ's hands.

1:21 For to me to live is Christ, and to die is gain—This is one of the great declarations in all of Pauline literature, indeed in all of Holy Scripture. It cuts to the very heart of Paul's faith. Nothing could express more powerfully his understanding of life and death. Both are centered wholly in Christ and therefore wholly in the riches of divine mercy and love. Paul has found the treasure hidden in the field, he has found the pearl of great price, and he has sold all to obtain it (3:7–8). For him to live is Christ (*to zēn Christos*), because Christ has loved him and given himself up for him, even to the point of death on the cross (Gal. 2:20; Phil. 2:8). Paul has been crucified with Christ so that it is no longer he who lives but Christ who lives in him. The life he lives in the flesh he lives by faith in the Son of God (Gal. 2:20).[36]

The Christ who lives in him is also the Christ who lives for him. *Koinōnia* with Christ, as given in the present, is laden with promise for the future. While its present form means sharing in Christ's sufferings, the sufferings are not worthy of being compared with the glory that is finally to be unveiled (Rom. 8:18). For Paul it is always one and the same *koinōnia*, one and the same *participatio Christi*, in two different forms: whether hidden or revealed, whether in suffering or in glory, whether in this world or in the age to come. Paul belongs to Christ, and Christ belongs to God (1 Cor. 3:23). Death holds no terrors for him. It means his transition from faith to sight (2 Cor. 5:7). It means nothing but ineffable gain ("to die is gain," *to apothanein kerdos*).

The question is sometimes raised about how this sort of declaration can be squared with Paul's belief in resurrection. Isn't the idea of resurrection at the end of all time incompatible with that of entering into Christ's presence immediately upon one's death? The answer, I suggest, is that "simultaneity" and "sequence" are standpoint-relative.

---

35. "The passive voice of the verb ["to be honored"] allows Paul to make a significant distinction. While it is Paul who might be disgraced, it is Christ who will be magnified in Paul's body whether the apostle lives or dies." Fowl, *Philippians*, 47.

36. I take *pistis Iēsou Christou* to be an objective genitive; see at 3:9.

As we know from Einstein's theory of relativity, events that are simultaneous for one observer will appear in sequence for another. Under certain circumstances a flash of lightning for a passenger on a train traveling at the speed of light will appear at the beginning and end of the train at the same time, but that flash will appear in sequence for an observer on the train platform. Similarly, death and resurrection into Christ's eternal presence may be simultaneous for the person who dies but sequential from the standpoint of those who remain on earth.[37] It is the difference between a first-person and a third-person perspective. As T. F. Torrance has written, "Looked at from the perspective of a new creation there is no time gap between the death of the believer and the *parousia* of Christ, but looked at from the perspective of time that decays and crumbles away, there is a lapse of time between them."[38]

> [22]If I am to live in the flesh, that means fruitful labor for me. Yet which I shall choose I cannot tell. [23]I am hard pressed between the two. My desire is to depart and be with Christ, for that is far better. [24]But to remain in the flesh is more necessary on your account. [25]Convinced of this, I know that I will remain and continue with you all, for your progress and joy in the faith, [26]so that in me you may have ample cause to glory in Christ Jesus, because of my coming to you again.

This portion of the letter has been described as a "reflective soliloquy."[39] If so, it may be useful to compare it with perhaps the most famous soliloquy in the English language. Hamlet's "To be or not to be" stands in an interesting counterpoint to Paul's "If I am to live in the flesh." Below are the two soliloquies—from *Hamlet*, act 3, scene 1, and Phil. 1:22–26—in parallel columns.

There is more than one way to read the Shakespearean soliloquy.[40] I follow those critics who argue that Hamlet is contemplating not suicide but revenge and the likely consequences of taking revenge, both temporal and eternal.[41] On the supposition that his father's ghost commands him to commit a most monstrous deed in the form of blood revenge, Hamlet ponders whether he should resolve to obey his father or to follow his moral conscience (and divine law) instead. As

---

37. "Perhaps the most . . . satisfactory solution is to say that for Paul the dead pass into a kind of time beyond time [in the presence of Christ] while [this mode of existence] is still anticipated on earth." Bockmuehl, *Philippians*, 93.

38. Torrance, *Theology in Reconstruction*, 118.

39. Fee, *Philippians*, 132n24.

40. For a good sense of the complexities and ambiguities of *Hamlet*, see Shapiro, "Question of Hamlet."

41. See especially Prosser, *Hamlet and Revenge*; also Richards, "Meaning of Hamlet's Soliloquy." An extensive bibliography for this line of interpretation may be found in Curran, *"Hamlet,"* 27n31.

much as he detests Claudius for murdering his father and for usurping both his mother and the crown, and as much as he craves a just and bloody retribution, he hesitates. From an earthly perspective, leaving this mortal life behind, should he eventually be caught and executed, as seems quite possible, would perhaps be worth the price—or would it? But all the more, what would such a dark and forbidden action, should he carry it out, mean for his eternal destiny?

Hamlet	Paul
To be, or not to be: that is the question:	If I am to live in the flesh, that means
Whether 'tis nobler in the mind to suffer	fruitful labor for me.
The slings and arrows of outrageous fortune,	Yet which I shall choose I cannot tell.
Or to take arms against a sea of troubles,	I am hard pressed between the two.
And by opposing end them? To die: to sleep;	My desire is to depart and be with
No more; and by a sleep to say we end	Christ, for that is far better.
The heart-ache and the thousand natural shocks	But to remain in the flesh is more
That flesh is heir to, 'tis a consummation	necessary on your account.
Devoutly to be wish'd. To die, to sleep;	Convinced of this, I know that I will
To sleep: perchance to dream: ay, there's the rub;	remain and continue with you all,
For in that sleep of death what dreams may come	for your progress and joy in the
When we have shuffled off this mortal coil,	faith,
Must give us pause: there's the respect	so that in me you may have ample
That makes calamity of so long life;	cause to glory in Christ Jesus,
For who would bear the whips and scorns of time,	because of my coming to you
The oppressor's wrong, the proud man's contumely,	again.
The pangs of despised love, the law's delay,	
The insolence of office and the spurns	
That patient merit of the unworthy takes,	
When he himself might his quietus make	
With a bare bodkin? who would fardels bear,	
To grunt and sweat under a weary life,	
But that the dread of something after death,	
The undiscover'd country from whose bourn	
No traveller returns, puzzles the will	
And makes us rather bear those ills we have	
Than fly to others that we know not of?	
Thus conscience does make cowards of us all;	
And thus the native hue of resolution	
Is sicklied o'er with the pale cast of thought,	
And enterprises of great pith and moment	
With this regard their currents turn awry,	
And lose the name of action. . . .	

Nor does it seem, in turn, that Paul contemplates dying by his own hand.[42] What he ponders is not suicide but martyrdom. As he anticipates his courtroom

42. See Holloway, *Consolation in Philippians*, 112–15.

trial, more than one course of action would be open to him. One the one hand, he could profess his faith in Christ with such boldness and even defiance (*parrēsia*) that his martyrdom would be virtually assured. On the other hand, he might temper his self-defense in a way that could more likely lead to his acquittal (which seems to be what he expects). Left simply to his own devices, a bold course of action might be preferred, but a larger consideration for the good of others is at stake. In any case Paul cannot control the outcome, and the choice is not finally his to make. He is prepared to leave the issue in the hands of the living Christ whom he serves.

Both Hamlet and Paul thus find themselves contemplating death, and both face a choice by which they might live or die. The choice facing Hamlet is apparently between bitter resignation, on the one hand ("to suffer / . . . outrageous fortune"), and, on the other, an active form of bloody retaliation that might well end in his capture and death, even if carried out successfully ("to take arms against a sea of troubles, / And by opposing end them").

The choice before Paul is less clear. He states that he faces a most difficult choice between life and death, and that he is "hard pressed between the two."[43] What would it have meant for him to choose death? Suicide would seem out of the question. Perhaps he is merely speaking hypothetically. Or perhaps he means that in court he might not defend himself at all (a decision that could lead to death) or that he might do so through some bold though dignified gesture that would be likely to end in capital punishment. According to these lines of interpretation, both Hamlet and Paul would be contemplating death at the hands of another as the result of choosing a noble though futile course of action.

Hamlet, however, stands alone as a tragically isolated figure, while Paul enjoys a network of vital relationships regardless of his severe adversities. Deeply estranged from his mother (the "incestuous" Queen Gertrude), his fiancée (the hapless Ophelia), his uncle and stepfather (the usurping King Claudius), and his few remaining friends (e.g., Laertes, who would indeed eventually kill him),[44] Hamlet appears bereft of all meaningful earthly ties.[45]

---

43. "The grammar of the passage reflects the conflict of feeling in the Apostle's mind. He is tossed to and fro between the desire to labor for Christ in life, and the desire to be united with Christ by death. The abrupt and disjointed sentences express this hesitation." Lightfoot, *Philippians*, 90.

44. Laertes, as it happened, was also killed by Hamlet. Mortally wounded, the two forgave one another and were reconciled before they succumbed.

45. The exception would be Horatio, Hamlet's comrade to the bitter end. "Hamlet, as he dies," writes Harold Bloom, "loves nobody—not father or mother, Ophelia or Yorick—but he knows that Horatio loves him." Bloom, *Shakespeare*, 421.

Paul, by contrast, despite being a difficult person, has friends and colleagues, far and near, whom he deeply loves and by whom he is deeply loved in return. Among those mentioned in the letter are Timothy, Epaphroditus, and the Philippians themselves; his other letters could be consulted to extend the list. Paul faces death not alone but in union with both Christ and his community.

Three further points may be noted. First, Hamlet and Paul stand on different sides of the role of a blood-stained avenger. Hamlet looks on it in prospect, while Paul looks back on it in retrospect. Hamlet has no doubts about the desirability of his seeking violent retribution, and indeed of his dark obligation to do so, if Claudius is as guilty as the mysterious paternal ghost has alleged. His deepest doubt is whether the apparition has told the truth or whether it is not actually instead a form taken by the devil. ("The devil hath power / To assume a pleasing shape; yea, and perhaps . . . / Abuses me to damn me.")

Paul, for his part, is an avenger no more. Nevertheless, at that former time when he was in the grip of a murderous passion, few doubts had assailed him about the perfect desirability of vengeance. In that sense, Paul *then* was not unlike Hamlet *now*. "For I am the least of the apostles, unfit to be called an apostle, because I persecuted the church of God" (1 Cor. 15:9). Paul had breathed out "threats and murder" against the disciples of the Lord (Acts 9:1). Having been delivered in spite of himself, Paul could look back: "This is a faithful saying and worthy of all acceptance, that Christ Jesus came into the world to save sinners, of whom I am chief" (1 Tim. 1:15 NKJV). Retribution for Hamlet would be drenched in blood; for Paul, his retribution having been aborted by a power not his own had meant grace abounding to the chief of sinners.

Second, if we shift the frame of reference, Hamlet looks on himself as an outraged victim, whereas Paul sees himself as a forgiven sinner. Both would draw conclusions from the particular to the general. Death, if it did not mean damnation, Hamlet broods, would at least bring an end to the "heart-ache and the thousand natural shocks / That flesh is heir to." Death presents itself, from that angle, as "a consummation / Devoutly to be wish'd." If only one could be sure that it brought no more than the oblivion of "sleep," death would be preferable to the onslaughts of outrageous fate as suffered in this life: "the whips and scorns of time, / The oppressor's wrong, the proud man's contumely, / The pangs of despised love, the law's delay, / The insolence of office and the spurns / That patient merit of the unworthy takes."[46] Hamlet's list seems to express his own personal resentments (as he perceived them) writ large.

---

46. The spurns taken by "patient merit" may pertain to personal humiliations endured at the hands of a disagreeable person ("the unworthy"), or else from someone unfairly rewarded at the expense of oneself.

Though Paul is no stranger to afflictions, he bears them differently. They are not the injuries of outrageous fortune but the appointed trials of faithfulness. Whether or not subject to rectification by human effort, they belong supremely to the context of grace. They pose a choice not between bitter resignation and violent retribution but between loyal endurance (*hypomonē*), when things could not be changed, and "faith working through love," when they can be (Gal. 5:6). Evil is met by the imperatives of faith. "Do not be overcome by evil, but overcome evil with good" (Rom. 12:21). Grace means hope for the godless, who would deserve to die (Rom. 1:32). It means sustenance in affliction and ultimate deliverance. It means justification of the godless and resurrection of the dead. It means dying with Christ in order to rise with him. Death itself means fulfillment in union with Christ, while life means fellowship in his service. Above all, Christ's love for his enemies means hope for the guilty and the lost, as Paul knows only too well from his own case. Paul's deliverances not only in his Damascus Road experience, but then also throughout his postconversion life, profoundly shape his generalizations about endurance (*hypomonē*), fellowship (*koinōnia*), and hope.

Finally, Hamlet and Paul regard hope beyond death from very different spiritual vantage points. The premise behind Hamlet's ruminations seems to be that one is innocent unless one has made oneself guilty. Taking revenge would not even be a stain if the revenge were merited and no one else could take it. The avenging Hamlet would receive confirmation of his being authorized, and so of his innocence ("his quietus make"), if Claudius were indeed guilty of murdering the king, Hamlet's father. In that case the brazen murderer might himself be justifiably dispatched by the thrust of the bereaved son's dagger ("with a bare bodkin"). If the paternal ghost is false, however, and Claudius is not guilty of murder, Hamlet's bloody vengeance would damn his soul forever (though apparently not otherwise). This is Hamlet's uncertainty: "that the dread of something after death, / The undiscover'd country from whose bourn / No traveller returns, puzzles the will / And makes us rather bear those ills we have / Than fly to others that we know not of." Improper vengeance would sully the soul, but proper vengeance would not.[47] Hamlet wants to do what is right, but he also wants to save his own skin. He is concerned about the latter, perhaps, more than the former.

47. Prosser (*Hamlet and Revenge*, 74–94 and passim) argues that bloody personal vengeance (in the context of Shakespeare's times) would have been seen as illicit under any circumstances. For a measured dissent, see Belsey, "Case of Hamlet's Conscience." See also Herbert, "Wings as Swift as Love." Reasonable objections to Prosser can also be found in Bradshaw, "Hamlet and the Art of Grafting," 392–93. As far as I can see, they do not affect my reading of the famous soliloquy.

In the end, Paul is Christocentric where Hamlet is self-absorbed. Paul is pre-occupied not with himself but with Christ—and with those entrusted to him by Christ. His communion with Christ, which sustains him through every trial "in the flesh," would find its fulfillment beyond time. It would thus be far better "to depart and be with Christ."[48] That is the object of Paul's desire. Yet there are times when self-regard, no matter how valid, has to yield to other-regard, when established by Christ. In service to Christ, human life would always mean "fruitful labor," even if it sometimes means swimming in a "sea of troubles." Having indicated uncertainty about what he would "choose," Paul takes an unexpectedly optimistic turn. Wanting to encourage the Philippians in every way, he holds out the hope that they would see him again. He would remain with them and continue with them all. They would therefore have "ample cause to glory in Christ Jesus."[49] While Paul's placing the needs of the Philippians above his own desires may well have been encouraging to them, his expression of optimism about the outcome of his trial may not have been entirely well thought out. It is not certain that his forecast of deliverance, though forgivable, was borne out.[50]

To conclude, the main differences between Hamlet and Paul about the desirability of earthly life can be traced to their different premises about life after death. For Hamlet this life is a "weary life," a "calamity" filled with undeserved woes, while death is fearsome as "the undiscover'd country from whose bourn [territory] / No traveller returns." For Paul, on the other hand, this life means fruitful labor, joy in adversity, grace for the undeserving, and hope for the lost, because a Traveler was known who had returned.

> **27**Only let your manner of life be worthy of the gospel of Christ, so that whether I come and see you or am absent, I may hear of you that you are standing firm in one spirit, with one mind striving side by side for the faith of the gospel, **28**and not frightened in anything by your opponents. This is a clear sign to them of their destruction, but of your salvation, and that from God. **29**For it has been granted to you that for the sake of Christ you should not only believe in him

48. "Paul here expects being with Christ immediately after death." Schnelle, *Apostle Paul*, 371. See my comment on 1:21.

49. Paul's forecast might make more sense if he were imprisoned not in Rome but in Ephesus. Positing an Ephesus imprisonment, however, would generate other imponderables. There is much that we do not know.

50. "How far Paul's confidence in his liberation and future personal intercourse with the Philippians was justified, it is impossible to determine without more knowledge concerning the latter portion of his career." Vincent, *Philippians*, 31.

but also suffer for his sake, ³⁰engaged in the same conflict that you saw I had
and now hear that I still have.

1:27 Only let your manner of life be worthy—For Paul, faith and suffering
are two sides of *koinōnia* with Christ, though it is promised that this suffering will
not occur without a measure of comfort. Knowing Christ means knowing him
in two respects: "the power of his resurrection" and "the fellowship of his sufferings" (Phil. 3:10 NKJV, adapted). It means sharing abundantly in his afflictions,
and through him also abundantly in comfort (2 Cor. 1:5). The point of faith is
not to avoid suffering at all costs but to "let your manner of life be worthy of the
gospel of Christ" (*axiōs tou euangeliou tou Christou politeuesthe*).

Because suffering for the sake of Christ is to be expected, evading it (in the
wrong way or at the wrong time) would be unworthy. Suffering therefore does
not need to be sought. It will arrive in due course—that is, in the normal course
of bearing witness to Christ. Suffering will then be used by grace in spite of itself.
It will be accompanied by spiritual consolation and the hope of deliverance. It
will be used to deepen the soul, fostering spiritual growth and reliance on God.

By the same token, some causes of suffering are to be neither welcomed nor
endured. Ill-advised suffering is no more worthy of the gospel than shameful
avoidance. When a Christian faces suffering because of confessing Christ's name,
it would be wrong to escape by denying Christ. Yet very different causes having
nothing to do with one being a Christian (afflictions like rape, slavery, or domestic
violence) might expose believers to cruelty, injustice, or abuse. Prudence and self-
regard in such cases are not contrary to the gospel. Failure to avoid needless or
unjust suffering can itself mean disloyalty to Christ, as can failing to resist injustice.

The phase translated as "manner of life" (*politeuesthe*) carries political over-
tones. Paul is implicitly contrasting one form of "citizenship" with another. The
citizenship of the Christian community is of a higher order than that of a Roman
citizen in Philippi. "Religion" and "politics"—obligations of Christian worship
and perceived civic duties—were not always easy to sort out. Some form of imperial cult was pervasive. As one historian observes, it was the "capstone of the
ideology which legitimated Roman power," and Roman power would have been
"a massive presence" for most of Paul's contemporaries, impressing itself forcefully
on their minds through festivals, games, statues, calendars, coins, temples, and
"sundry other social phenomena."[51] Paul is not necessarily suggesting a head-on

---

51. Barclay, "Roman Empire," 368.

clash between these two types of citizenship. But he is suggesting that should conflict arise in particular cases, Christian loyalty to Christ and the obligations of heavenly citizenship need to take precedence regardless of the cost.

standing firm in one spirit—Paul wants the Philippians "to stand firm in one spirit" (*stēkete en heni pneumati*)—or, perhaps better, "in the one Spirit." He wants them not only to live at peace among themselves but also to be resolute in their witness to the outside world. His remarks seem to reflect not only a measure of discord from within but also a certain wavering under pressure from the outside. Paul encourages the faithful to be "of one mind" (*mia psychē*), so that they may strive together with him ("side by side") in pursuit of their high common calling ("the faith of the gospel"). He calls them to display a maturity that prevails against their adversities regardless of whether he can come to them personally or must remain absent.

so that whether I come and see you or am absent—Paul here clarifies any possible misunderstanding about whether he regarded his release from captivity, or even from execution, as a sure thing (cf. 1:19).

1:28 and not frightened in anything by your opponents—For the first time we learn that because of opponents near at hand, the Philippians may have been living in the grip of fear (*ptyromenoi*). Paul wishes to help them recover a sense of perspective. If the Philippians stand before demoralizing opponents, those opponents stand in turn, unbeknownst to themselves, before God. Any evident persecution or harassment of the community is a "clear sign" (*endeixis*) that the opponents will come to grief ("their destruction," *apōleias*) while the faithful will be upheld for the good ("your salvation," *hymōn de sōtērias*). The faithful are called to be known by what they stand for, not by any fear of their adversaries.[52]

1:29 For it has been granted to you—Above all, they are encouraged to see that they have received a special grace—the grace not only of faith but also of suffering for the sake of Christ. Moreover, by suffering for Christ, they suffer also in fellowship with Paul. They are engaged "in the same conflict" (*ton auton agōna*, 1:30) as Paul is, a conflict that continues to be his lot in captivity. In and with Christ, the apostle and the faithful at Philippi are forged into a single community of suffering. "If one member suffers, all suffer together" (1 Cor. 12:26).

Suffering for Christ's sake raises a serious question about ultimate allegiances and belonging. From a "secular" point of view, a potentially dangerous idea of citizenship is suggested by the term *politeuesthe* (manner of life, citizenship; 1:27).

---

52. "Paul does not say: *against* the adversaries just mentioned. . . . Christians do not strive against anybody (or for anybody either!), but *for the faith.*" Barth, *Epistle to the Philippians*, 47.

The faithful at Philippi, though they dwell on earth, will be described later as citizens of heaven (3:20). As inhabitants of a Roman military colony—though most would not have been Roman citizens—they are to some degree "resident aliens" who inevitably find themselves at odds with the empire.

By turning to Christ they have broken with Nero. The emperor, though honored, is not to be feared, and certainly not to be worshiped. Prayers may be offered for him but not to him. Christians cannot confess that "Caesar is Lord," because they know a different Lord. They are viewed with suspicion—not just in high places but also perhaps in the highways and byways of local neighborhoods. They are regarded as a potential danger to social stability and political cohesion. From both a Christian and a Roman point of view, it was not clear that the way of Caesar was fully compatible with the way of the cross. A community whose highest loyalties are not to Caesar would pose a perceived threat, whether implicitly or not, to civic duties and perhaps also to national security.[53]

1:30 engaged in the same conflict that you saw I had and now hear that I still have—Again, Paul stresses that the Philippians are not alone in their conflicts. He especially wants them to see that they exist with him in a solidarity of suffering. They share in the same conflict (*ton auton agōna*), because of the same loyalties, and with the same hopes. For they are all bound together in one Lord. Their consolation, both now and forever, is found in Christ alone.

---

53. "The source of their 'same struggle' [shared by Paul and the Philippians] (v. 30) is probably the same, [namely,] perceived disloyalty to the empire." Fee, *Philippians*, 157n9.

PHILIPPIANS 2

2:1 Therefore if there is any benevolence in Christ, any comfort of love, any fellowship in the Spirit, any compassion and mercy, **2**complete my joy by being of the same mind, having the same love, being in full accord and of one mind. **3**Do nothing from rivalry or conceit, but in humility count others more significant than yourselves. **4**Let each of you look not only to his own interests, but also to the interests of others.

2:1 **Therefore if there is any benevolence in Christ**—In his powerful plea to the Philippians for unity, Paul crafts a set of appeals designed to touch their hearts.[1] He sees that there can be no unity in their common life without benevolence or supportiveness (*paraklēsis*),[2] without consolation, without love (mentioned twice), without fellowship (*koinōnia*), without compassion and mercy.[3] But with these elements concord could be restored and unity upheld. Each part of his appeal concerns conduct "worthy of the gospel" (1:27). Each is a matter of grace as rooted in Christ and actualized through the Spirit. Each needs only to be put into practice by word and deed. A life worthy of the gospel demands unity in the ranks.[4]

1. "The appeal is deliberately emotional, both in terms of the rhetorical effect and in much of its vocabulary as well." Bockmuehl, *Philippians*, 105.

2. The word *paraklēsis* is hard to translate in this context. It is commonly rendered as "encouragement" or "consolation," neither of which quite seems to capture Paul's point. If a "paraclete" is an advocate or a supporter of good will, then "benevolence" (kindness) or "support" (assistance) might better convey what Paul has in mind.

3. Some interpreters (e.g., Lightfoot and Vincent) have attempted to divide up this appeal into "principles" and "experiences." It would seem better, however, to regard every factor in the list as a matter of "principle" in one way and of "experience" in another.

4. "The apostle here appeals to the Philippians by all their deepest experiences as Christians, and all their noblest impulses as [human beings], to preserve peace and concord." Lightfoot, *Philippians*, 105.

Mutual respect, cooperation, and humility, as practiced in fellowship and love, thus form the backbone of Paul's exhortation. Together they are a token of the new eon under the conditions of the old, a foretaste of the promised future. Their diametrical opposites mean exactly the reverse, a sorry though unmistakable residue of the old eon despite the inbreaking of the new. Self-assertion, rivalry, and jockeying for power belong to the bygone eon abolished in Christ. If not confronted and rooted out at Philippi, such maladies would undermine the church and its work.

2:2 complete my joy—Paul underscores his appeal by adding a personal note to his list of incentives—namely, loyalty to himself as their spiritual mentor. The Philippians, already worried about Paul's well-being in prison, are reminded of how much a spirit of unity in their common life would mean to him. News of dissension could only add to his burdens, while unity, concord, and peace would serve to "complete [his] joy" (*plērōsate mou tēn charan*).

being in full accord and of one mind—Concord is indispensable not only for the community's own sake but also for its witness and mission. A church divided against itself is impaired and veers toward dysfunction. To underscore this point, Paul summons all the rhetorical power at his disposal.

The benefits of salvation, of Christian love, and of the Holy Spirit are all very much to the fore. Where would the Philippians be without the support received in Christ, the comfort conveyed in love, the *koinōnia* enjoyed through the Spirit, the compassion and kindness extended by God, and through God to one another? How can the gospel bear fruit if the faithful fail to be of one heart and one mind? And how can they be of the same mind if they do not live together in unity, concord, and peace (1 Cor. 1:10)? Not least, how can they really show care for Paul in his captivity if they fail to repair the divisions in their midst?

In short, the Philippian church faces not only hostility from without but also discord from within. For Paul, while external opposition is unavoidable for a church true to its calling, internal discord suggests a church in danger of dissolution or schism. External opponents, he counsels, stand under the sign of divine judgment, while internal opponents manifest the corrosive power of egotism.[5]

in Christ . . . love . . . in the Spirit—It is not always recognized that Paul's appeal to the benefits of grace is phrased in an implicitly trinitarian, or proto-trinitarian, manner here. The formulation of "from the Father, through the Son, and in the Spirit," from later times, may again be recalled as a benchmark. As

---

5. It has been said that while the heretic is brilliantly wrong, the schismatic is obstinately wrong.

seen in 2 Cor. 13:14, Paul himself could adopt the contrasting rhetorical order of Christ, God, and the Holy Spirit: "the grace [*charis*] of our Lord Jesus Christ, the love [*agapē*] of God, and the communion [*koinōnia*] of the Holy Spirit."

That same sequence, in muted or broken form, would seem to be adopted here: Christ, God, Spirit. If so, benevolence or support (*paraklēsis*) is associated with Christ, *agapē* is mentioned but without reference to God, and *koinōnia* is again connected with the Spirit. We might suggest, from this wording, that grace (*charis*) took the form of benevolence (through Christ), that love took the form of comfort (implicitly from God), and that *koinōnia* took the form of compassion and kindness, of mutual giving and receiving (in the Spirit).

No claim need be made that the Philippians would have discerned any such proto-trinitarian structure, nor is it likely to have been greatly present in the mind of Paul. The syntax may be read in retrospect, however, as implying something more than it said. Rivalry and discord in the church were contrary, finally, to the concord and unity of the Holy Trinity.

2:3 Do nothing from rivalry or conceit—Personality conflicts rather than false teachings were apparently behind the discord at Philippi. Personality conflicts had also been known to exist in other churches instructed by Paul. As in Corinth, however, or in Galatia, they were usually entangled with theological errors, whether "proto-Gnostic" or "pro law observance" in nature. It seems important that no such mischief is singled out at Philippi for rebuke. Paul could plead to his readers to strive toward unity mainly on the basis of sound doctrine.

"Rivalry" or "conceit" (*eritheian* or *kenodoxian*) is the toxin to which "humility" (*tapeinophrosynē*) is prescribed as the antidote. The former is a garden-variety specimen of sin; the latter, a significant attribute of the very God who had stooped down from heaven to become incarnate. Rivalry meant arrogating esteem to oneself at the expense of others. It meant overstepping one's limits. Mutual respect is enjoined as the solution. One should avoid looking solely to one's own interests, Paul urges, but each should take seriously the views of others, and each one should be ready to put others above oneself.

Paul's admonitions must always be understood in their context. While he urges humility over against rivalry and conceit, he says nothing here about the importance of withstanding abuse, since that problem is not in view. The contingency of his guidance is important. The parties in dispute whom Paul is addressing are apparently among the "dominants," not the "subordinates," in the community. Whereas the former (the relatively powerful) have an excess of self-regard, in other situations the latter (the rank and file) may sometimes lack enough of it.

Failure to discriminate at points like this has sometimes brought trouble to the church, leading to misfortune in its teaching and pastoral care. Scriptural statements that are meant *secundum quid* ("in a certain respect") can cause harm if taken *simpliciter* ("absolutely")—that is, as if they applied to any and all circumstances without distinction. Not all self-regard would be self-seeking, though all self-seeking would be an excess of self-regard. Humility without valid self-regard would be defective; self-regard without humility would be sin.

> **5**Have this mind among yourselves, which is in Christ Jesus, **6**who, though he was in the form of God, did not count equality with God a thing to be grasped, **7**but emptied himself, taking the form of a slave, being born in the likeness of human beings. **8**And being found in human form, he humbled himself by becoming obedient to the point of death, even death on a cross. **9**Therefore God has highly exalted him and bestowed on him the name that is above every name, **10**so that at the name of Jesus every knee should bow, in heaven and on earth and under the earth, **11**and every tongue confess that Jesus Christ is Lord, to the glory of God the Father.

Much has been written about the possible prehistory of this important passage. Was it composed by Paul, or did it exist in a prior form? If in a prior form, what sources might lie behind it? Were they Persian, Hellenistic, Hebraic? Some combination of these? Something else? If composed by Paul, why do certain themes, such as Christ's resurrection, appear to be missing? While all such questions are interesting, in the end their answers must remain speculative and inconclusive.

The approach taken in this commentary is ecclesial and theological. It attempts to interpret the letter in the context of Holy Scripture taken as a canonical whole. It thus sees the letter as a document to be read intertextually in and for the church. It also attempts to read the epistle theologically by presupposing the church's faith as something that arises from Holy Scripture and is expressed in common worship. It proceeds on the assumption that the faith of the church, as ecumenically defined, finds normative expression in the Niceno-Constantinopolitan Creed and the Chalcedonian Definition. Modern readers unhappy with a high doctrine of the Trinity and with a "two-natures" Christology can expect to be dissatisfied with what follows. It is hoped, however, that the faithful, including bishops, presbyters, and deacons (or their functional equivalents), will find something of value for their life and work.

2:5 Have this mind—As was his common practice, Paul exhorts his readers by moving from the indicative to the imperative. The faithful are to adopt the very mindset (the imperative) that already belongs to them in Christ (the indicative). This is not a move from possibility to actuality, but one from actuality to possibility. The mindset that is already theirs in Christ Jesus needs to be reclaimed ever anew. It encounters them not as an ideal possibility but as a concrete reality—one in which they already participate. It is not something to be constructed but something to be appropriated. It is a gift before it is a task. It means becoming what they already are.[6]

in Christ Jesus—Both "all the saints" (*pantes hoi hagioi*) (1:1) and now a certain "mindset" (*touto phroneite*) (2:5) are said to be found "in Christ Jesus" (*en Christō Iēsou*). This mindset, according to Paul, is to be practiced "among you" (*en hymin*). From these remarks it seems fair to infer that the saints are called to adopt a frame of mind that already belongs to them in Christ. They are to appropriate in practice what is already theirs by grace.

By operating out of rivalry and conceit (2:3), some members of the community have entered into contradiction with *who* they already are in Christ Jesus (saints) and *what* they are called to be in him (humble-minded). The implied contrast, I suggest, is thus not between the possible and the actual, but between the real and the unreal. To live according to grace is to live according to the real. It is therefore to live in accord with the promised future—the future of the only reality that will not pass away but endure. To contradict the real is to revert to sin and therefore to lapse into impossibility. It means reverting to the disorder of the old eon that has already been abolished in Christ.[7]

The "real" is defined not by sin but by grace, not by human self-seeking but by Christ's resurrection from the dead, not by the old defeated eon but by the new eon that in Christ has already broken in and has yet to be universally unveiled. Humble-mindedness is not something to be achieved by the Philippians on the basis of their own unaided efforts. It is something to be received from Christ, partaken of in Christ, and renewed by Christ. It is an ongoing gift, not a possession, a gift that is new each morning. It is therefore not so much a settled disposition as the object of continual prayer with open hands. It involves a life of kindness and generosity in dependence on grace. The Philippians are called to live by a humility not their own, the prior humility of Christ. It is the one humility common to Christ and his church. In loving communion with him,

6. "A moral imperative is contained within a christological indicative. . . . The soteriological reading implies the ethical, and the ethical reading presupposes the soteriological." Migliore, *Philippians*, 96, 81.

7. For such a contrast between the "real" and the "unreal," see Küng, *Church*, 28. Küng apparently derived it from Barth's description of sin as the "impossible possibility" and the "unreal reality."

the humble-mindedness he embodies and imparts is continually to be received day by day.

There can therefore be no conflict between soteriology and ethics. While Christ's saving work is not something that can be reenacted, it is something to be attested and received. While *imitatio Christi* in the narrow sense is ruled out (since his saving work is finished and unique), *conformatio Christi*, whereby believers are conformed to the image of Christ—and his frame of mind—is ruled in.[8]

Christ does not represent the law so much as he represents the gospel. He does not constitute a rigid paradigm, nor is he merely external to the believer. He is rather a living presence—to them, in them, and against them. By the grace of his Spirit, he personally brings those who love him into ever greater union with himself. He can indeed be followed, but only at a distance.[9] Being brought into conformity with his likeness (Rom. 8:29) means being conformed to the pattern established in his humiliation and exaltation. For believers it is a pattern of self-giving, of love and deliverance, of faithful obedience and final vindication, of mortifying pride ("the flesh") while entering into a humble frame of mind ("by the Spirit") (Rom. 12:2).

Koinōnia with Christ, as a fellowship of mutual indwelling, thus establishes a set of "internal relations" with Christ (*conformatio*) that take precedence over merely "external relations" (*imitatio*). Being in him means being conformed to him by grace. No likeness can ever be so great that an infinitely greater unlikeness will not still be in force. The likeness is a matter of participation and reception; the unlikeness, of Christ's saving uniqueness. Humility in the faithful attests to the humility of their Lord. Being conformed to him by grace can never lead to mere equivalence. But it can lead to genuine resemblance.

Although the theme of Christ's humility—as the object of participation, conformation, and witness—is introduced with reference to the disorders at Philippi, it immediately takes on a life of its own. It is as if, having broached the topic, Paul

---

8. Concerning the supposed conflict between soteriology and ethics in Paul: this is a false issue among the commentators. There is no need to choose between a Käsemann and a de Boer. As is often the case, false contrasts can be overcome by asking "In what respect?" "Christ Jesus" is indeed to be imitated in a certain respect (*secundum quid*) but not absolutely (*simpliciter*). I would argue, however, that *imitatio* language (active voice) is best understood, theologically, in the context of *conformatio* language—of being conformed to the image of Christ (passive voice). *Conformatio* points to the work of the Holy Spirit in the life of faith. It is the obverse side of Christ being formed in us (Gal. 4:19).

Being conformed to Christ by the power of the Spirit does not mean that the believer is merely "passive." The believer is moved to cooperate with grace, but it is the Spirit to whom the effectual power of *conformatio Christi* belongs. In this process the believer's active reception is a free gift, not a meritorious work. For background on this discussion, see R. Martin, *Carmen Christi*, 68–74, 84–92.

9. See Outka, "Following at a Distance."

cannot contain himself (whether he wrote the hymn himself or only modified it). When he turns to the supreme act of humility revealed at the heart of the gospel, the discussion leaps to a higher plane. Intending to compare the lesser to the greater, Paul magnifies the greater in itself. Nevertheless, he does so with practical ends in view.[10]

2:6 who, though he was in the form of God—This verse, in accord with the passage it introduces, is more suggestive than technical. The ideas it expresses would be worked out more precisely in theology and church over the course of time and controversy. From that perspective, however, it represents a train of thought whose trajectory is again proto-trinitarian.

The idea of "the form of God" (*morphē theou*) anticipates the later idea of God's "being" (*ousia*). From this point of view, the divine *morphē* is a conceptual precursor for the idea of divine essence or substance.[11] As a suggestive term, *morphē* is seminal while still remaining open and indeterminate. If due care is taken, however, its relation to the later, more technical term *ousia* may be thought of in analogy to that between a seed and its flower. The flower is in some sense in the seed, but the seed is not the flower. In itself the seed would not necessarily tell us just what flower it will become, but that does not mean that a particular flower is not inherent in the seed. Modern theology often proceeds as if the seed were fundamentally indeterminate so that any number of very different flowers might have sprung from it and might still spring from it. Ecumenical theology, on the other hand, as I understand it, is guided by the conciliar history of the church. What at one time may have appeared indeterminate and polysemous developed in a way that became specific and normative. In retrospect it became possible to discern what flower was inherent in the seed.[12]

The divine *ousia*, as a technical term, would eventually come to include the ideas of concreteness, divine simplicity, life, self-existence, self-sufficiency, and divine sovereignty. The term *morphē*, being less technical and more imprecise, could not have conveyed all these aspects in its present context. The two ideas that it approached most closely, however, are those of self-existence and sovereignty.[13]

---

10. "The spiritual and eternal, in deep continuity, descends into the practical." Moule, *Philippians*, 63.

11. See Stead, *Divine Substance*.

12. We may regard this sort of doctrinal or hermeneutical development as the work of the Spirit guiding the church into all truth (John 16:13).

13. T. F. Torrance understands *ousia*, as defined above, in a way that is closely in line with Stead and Prestige. All three scholars emphasize, in particular, that the divine essence is ineffable, and all three agree that it is *not* something "generic." Perhaps more than Stead, Prestige emphasizes that in the patristic tradition, as it developed over time, it became increasingly clear that the divine *ousia* is not some "impersonal stuff," but is rather ineffably living, volitional, and active, though never in abstraction or independence

It would seem that being in the *form* of God means existing in the *nature* of God.[14] If so, then modern discussion has been burdened by a degree of terminological mayhem. This verse really has nothing to do with the unfortunate term "preexistence." Nor is the term "pretemporal existence" much of an improvement. The sooner these terms are laid quietly to rest, the better. A more proper term, if not a perfect one, would be "preincarnate."[15]

God's eternal mode of being is a matter of self-existence, not preexistence. "Preexistence" (when used to interpret this passage) comes too close to suggesting that being in "the form of God" is just a "prelude" to an earthly "existence" that is somehow more basic. Nothing could be more basic, however, than God's self-existent being from and to all eternity. Divine self-existence represents a uniquely sovereign and eternal mode of being. Strictly speaking, it is neither "preexistent" to something else nor merely "pretemporal," as if it were little more than an unaccented syllable. God qua God is eternal, sovereign, and self-existent. "Subsisting" (*hyparchōn*) in the form of God would mean subsisting in this distinctively divine mode of being (*morphē*), according to the line of interpretation followed here.[16]

"Christ Jesus" (2:5), the figure under consideration, is said to be "in the form of God" (2:6). Would the very idea of divine self-existence, as suggested here—thus,

from the three divine *hypostases*. To that extent Torrance is perhaps closer to Prestige. Nevertheless, Stead finally associates *ousia* with the divine love, or with the ground of divine love. All three scholars agree that *ousia* is a word denoting one indivisible and concrete reality of God in three "persons," not three persons in one generic or abstract Godhead. See Torrance, *Christian Doctrine of God*, 112–21. See also Stead, *Divine Substance*, 223–80; Prestige, *God in Patristic Thought*, 219–301.

14. "To be in the form of God is to be in the nature of God." Thomas Aquinas, *Commentary*, 79. Even if "form of God" involves the idea of "visible appearance," as Daniel Fabricatore has argued, that would not rule out the idea of "essence," as Richard Weymouth has rightly observed. "Accepting the Visible Appearance understanding in a primary sense," he writes, "in no way invalidates the Essence view when placed more appropriately as a secondary implication of the text." The visible appearance is a reflection of the underlying nature. See Weymouth, "Christ-Story of Philippians 2:6–11," 412. Cf. Fabricatore, *Form of God*, 141–56, 174–75, 204–14.

15. The "pre" in "preincarnate" is logical and ontological, not temporal. The point to see is that the incarnation is a contingent event. In other words, it is not a necessary aspect of the Son's eternal subsistence. We might say that the divine Son is "non-incarnate" in two respects: (1) his being eternally begotten of the Father and (2) his being of one essence (*homoousion*) with the Father. But he is "preincarnate" with respect to his *assumptio carnis*.

The Son would be the eternal Son even if the incarnation had never occurred. His noncontingent, essential, and eternal properties are not changed by his incarnational and contingent properties into something other than they were before. "Just as God does not change in himself when he created the world, so also the Word of God is not changed into something else when he is made flesh." Chadwick, "Chalcedonian Definition," 103 (slightly modified).

16. It is important to note that the divine being as eternal being is logically and ontologically prior to created being. It subsists independently of created being, whereas created being cannot subsist apart from divine being.

of eternity as a sovereign mode of divine being—have in any sense been available to Paul? At a nontechnical level, it would seem that the answer is yes. He can speak, for example, about God the Creator's "invisible attributes, namely, his eternal power and divine nature" (Rom. 1:20). As "the Lord of heaven and earth," this God has "no need of anything," being essentially self-sufficient (Acts 17:24–25) (if these ideas are rightly ascribed to Paul). Jesus Christ is in any case "the Lord of glory" (*kyrios tēs doxas*) (1 Cor. 2:8) and "the Lord of all things" (*kyrios pantōn*) (Rom. 10:12)—both of which are divine titles that Paul ascribes to Jesus Christ.[17] A glance at two further passages will help support this interpretation.

On 2 Corinthians 8:9. "For you know the grace of our Lord Jesus Christ, who though he was rich, yet for your sake he became poor, so that you by his poverty might become rich." What Paul writes here presupposes the fullness of divine life. It suggests a divine mode of being that is "rich" (*plousios*) or superabundant in itself. The general narrative pattern evident here is much the same as in Phil. 2:6–9: elevation, abasement, deliverance. Three points may be noted.

First, a transition takes place. In 2 Cor. 8:9 it is a transition, for a particular figure, from the glorious plenitude of one mode of being (the divine) to the extreme poverty of another (human shame and fallenness). It is thus a transition from elevation to abasement, from a life that is full and rich to one that is earthly and impoverished.

Second, it is not an imposed transition but one that is chosen—literally "he impoverished himself" (*eptōcheusen*). It is an act of self-abasement undertaken in freedom.

Finally, it takes place for the good of others; indeed it is the very essence of grace. It means abasement for the one who chooses it, but blessing for the many on whose behalf it is undertaken: "that you through his poverty might become rich." It is "the grace of our Lord Jesus Christ."

It is hard to see how this verse would be intelligible without the suggestion of a prior, self-sufficient, and abundant mode of divine being, especially when we recall that the earthly Jesus himself—from his birth in a stable to his death on a cross—was far from rich. Much as in Phil. 2:6, this verse suggests a mysterious figure who, though belonging to the divine, superabundant realm, sets it aside in an act of freedom for the good of others who are destitute.

On 1 Corinthians 8:6. "Yet for us there is one God, the Father, from whom are all things and for whom we exist, and one Lord, Jesus Christ, through whom

17. Hofius, "Fourth Servant Song," 176.

are all things and through whom we exist." Again we have a verse with trinitarian implications, written perhaps no more than twenty-five years after Christ's death.[18] A divine mode of being is again implicitly ascribed to Jesus Christ. With regard to the Creator/creature distinction, Christ is situated (remarkably) on the side of the Creator. He is also identified as "the one Lord." It was hard for the later ecumenical tradition to see how such a figure could be an agent of creation without somehow being ontologically prior to it. As an agent of creation, he would be exercising divine sovereignty.[19] His mode of being is therefore not merely "pretemporal," as if eternal being were not something full and sufficient in itself. What belongs to him somehow is the mode of divine being in eternity.[20]

Although other passages from Paul might be cited,[21] these two verses—2 Cor. 8:9 and 1 Cor. 8:6—suffice to make the point. By way of nontechnical terms (and not without remaining puzzles, countervailing trends, and ambiguities), the apostle is no stranger to the idea of a uniquely divine mode of being. He could use it to approximate aspects of what would later become the trinitarian idea of the eternal divine substance or *ousia*. He seems to have some notion that the

18. "One of the most striking and significant contributions of the New Testament to the creation-affirmation is the effort of Paul and other writers to place Christ in the position of preexistent agent of creation." Hefner, "Creation," 1:289.

19. I assume that the church's later view of creation is anticipated here by Paul. Accordingly, God the Creator is the source of all there is; his creatures are dependent, yet real and good; God creates not only in sovereign freedom but with purpose. See Gilkey, *Maker of Heaven and Earth*.

20. The perplexing eternal status of *Jesus* the human being, as intimated throughout the New Testament, can be interpreted in terms of "prolepsis," which in many ways is a better term than "preexistence": (1) The divine Son is not preexistent but eternally existent. (2) The human Jesus is *not* eternally existent. (3) Jesus the incarnate Son, however, is present "before the foundation of the world" in the will and the foreknowledge of God—and therefore in reality (John 17:24; Eph. 1:4; 1 Pet. 1:20; Rev. 13:8). This presence of Jesus the Word made flesh—or (in Pauline terms) of "Christ Jesus"—at the beginning of all the ways and works of God relative to the world is what is meant by "prolepsis." Prolepsis in this sense points to the mystery of the incarnation's anticipatory reality *coram Deo*, and it should be understood both ontologically and noetically. To put it somewhat baldly, the eternal Son points to what God is *by nature* (triune); the incarnate Son or Christ Jesus points to who God is for the world *by grace* (Lord and Savior). All of God's works in relation to the world begin and end in the person and eternal election of Christ—from creation through reconciliation to final redemption (e.g., John 1:3; 1 Cor. 8:6; 2 Cor. 5:19; Eph. 1:10; 4:10; Phil. 3:21; Col. 1:16–17, 20). From this point of view, Christ Jesus would belong to the divine identity in Paul's "christological monotheism" but not to the logically and ontologically prior eternal Trinity—which is eternally existent in and for itself, and so the prior ground of all God's relations to the world. The "before" (Greek: *prin*) in this statement ("before the foundation of the world") is more nearly logical and ontological than temporal. "As this creature—because this is what God sees and wills—Jesus is before all things, even before the dawn of his own time" (Barth, *Church Dogmatics* IV/2, 33, slightly modified). See Hunsinger, *Reading Barth with Charity*, 62–71. Such counterintuitive ideas are not confined to Paul, as for example in the Johannine statement, "Before Abraham was, I am" (John 8:58).

21. For a careful survey of the most explicit statements in Paul and elsewhere in the New Testament, see Harris, *Jesus as God*.

divine being is rich, sovereign, and glorious in itself. He sees it, by implication, as a self-existent and self-sufficient reality that stands over against the created world. It is an eternal reality whereby God alone is the Lord. Remarkably, it is a reality to which an earthly figure, whose name is Jesus, is thought to belong.[22]

equality with God—Returning to Phil. 2:6, we may say that to be "in the form of God" for Paul means to possess the uniquely divine mode of being. It means being "equal to God" (*einai isa theō*). Equality with God is not a goal still to be attained, nor is it an aspiration to be renounced.[23] It is an inherent status, properly enjoyed. It is the uniquely divine condition. It means being transcendent, glorious, and eternally rich. It means being divinely sovereign in calling forth the creation. However strange it may seem, it is the status ascribed to Christ Jesus.[24]

to be grasped—We turn now to the vexing term "to be grasped" (*harpagmon*), which has generated so much discussion while remaining so obscure.[25] Does it mean "using something for one's own advantage"? Does it mean "clinging" to something or "grasping" at it? Does it mean regarding something as "robbery"? What about "demanding one's own rights"? Or even "retaining something by force"? Based on the interpretation offered here—whereby being "in the form of God" and being "equal to God" are thought to be semantically the same—a paraphrase is suggested.

If what is at stake is a transition from one mode of existence to another— the one glorious, the other ignominious—then the core idea would be that of "relinquishment."[26] Christ Jesus does not consider his glorious mode of existence as

22. For a detailed scholarly work that affirms 1 Cor. 8:6 as including Jesus Christ within the divine identity, see Loke, *Origin of Divine Christology*, 26–32.

23. The idea of an Adam Christology, besides being dubious in itself, has no ecumenical standing in church history. *Pace* Dunn, *Christology in the Making*, 98–128. For a trenchant refutation, see Hofius, *Der Christushymnus*, 113–22. See also the careful technical objections in Fee, *Pauline Christology*, 275–91. Less technically, see Hurtado, *Lord Jesus Christ*, 121–26.

24. "This equality of Christ with God is so to speak the fixed, *ultimate* background from which his road sets out and to which it returns." Barth, *Epistle to the Philippians*, 61 (italics original). Further to this: "The Pauline formulations," writes Schnelle, "can be seen as the beginnings of thinking of God and Christ as equals." On the other hand, Paul could also use language that implies their subordination. Later tradition would posit that although the Father and the Son are *ontologically* equal, the Son (who became incarnate and died on the cross) consents to make himself *functionally* subordinate to the Father in love for the good of others. See Schnelle, *Apostle Paul*, 396. Loke argues that the ontological/functional distinction may be used to elucidate Paul: "Paul regarded Jesus as a truly divine person who is distinct but not separate from God the Father ontologically; they have the same ontological divine status, but the Son chooses to be functionally subordinated to the Father." Loke, *Origin of Divine Christology*, 83.

25. For a survey, see the exhaustive coverage in Wright, *Climax of the Covenant*, 56–91, esp. 81.

26. Holloway agrees that in this text "equality with God" is a status that Christ already enjoys (as opposed to being merely a future aspiration). He interprets *harpagmon* along the lines suggested here as pertaining to a good that can be relinquished if necessary. Christ did not regard equality with God, precious

something that cannot be relinquished. He can relinquish it without ceasing to be who he is. Indeed he is never more fully who he is than in the act of relinquishing it. He relinquishes his glorious mode of existence without ceasing to be God. He does not refuse to act selflessly, at cost to himself, for the good of others. We may say the change to which he subjects himself is "existential" rather than "ontological." Without ceasing to be God, he relinquishes the ordinary exercise and enjoyment of the prerogatives of his divine mode of existence.

The term "to be grasped" (*harpagmon*) thus means that he does not count his glorious *mode* of existence, along with the exercise of its prerogatives—"equality with God"—as something that cannot be relinquished in a particular sense. He relinquishes two things—both his outward glory and the normal exercise of his prerogatives—without surrendering his divine essence. The relinquishment of his prerogatives is thus severe without needing to be absolute.

The term *morphē* comports with this suggestion. Being more nearly informal than technical, it possesses a certain flexibility. While it means something like "outward form," it can also suggest an overlap between "form" and "content." Therefore we may posit that the majestic *content* of the divine being is already actual in glory (*morphē theou*). Nevertheless, the outward *form*—as shared *equally* (from the standpoint of later tradition) by the Father and the Son (*isa theō*)—may be relinquished (as we see in Christ) without compromise to its essential content. In the drastic transition that occurs from glory to humiliation, from wealth to poverty, from heaven to earth, the result is a difference in outward mode without a loss of substance. The Son's outward glorious form, along with the normal exercise of his prerogatives, is relinquished, but the divine essence itself is not.

If the core issue is the fairly simple idea of relinquishment, why does Paul choose such an odd term to express it? One possibility would be polemical. Perhaps he is trying to suggest a pointed contrast between Christ Jesus and those Philippians who are locked in rivalry and conceit. "Look at our Lord Jesus Christ," he is saying. "Unlike some of you, his mindset is *not* one of self-seeking and self-aggrandizement. You, on the other hand, are *grasping* at your own power and prerogatives at the expense of others."

If so, the term is expected to operate on two levels. On the surface it is meant to unsettle the Philippians through a devastating contrast, while at a more latent level

---

though it was, as "a possession he could not part with." Holloway, *Philippians*, 120. I lay aside Holloway's supposition that the whole passage is hyperbolic and mythological. His strained attempt to read Phil. 2:6–11 as an example of "angel Christology" is perhaps the last refuge of historicism. For an argument against positing a background here in angel Christology, see Bauckham, "Devotion to Jesus Christ."

it is meant to commend the humility and generosity of the Lord. This rhetorical strategy, however, if that's what it is, does not particularly work. As it turns out, the underlying content (noble relinquishment) has been overshadowed by the surface-level polemic (vulgar grasping), so that commentators have been flummoxed by the term *harpagmon* ever since.

One last point. The nontechnical ambience of Paul's rhetoric pertains to the relationship between "Christ Jesus" and "God." Later theological reflection tries to state the mystery more precisely by using such terms as *ousia*, *hypostasis*, and *physis*. Two thought forms are apparently in the background: on the one hand, identity-and-difference; on the other, unity-in-distinction. They may be illustrated by turning briefly to the Gospel of John.

On John 1:1. In this verse we read: "In the beginning was the Word, and the Word was with God, and the Word was God." Here we may discern a pattern of identity-and-difference. Difference is established by the phrase "with God"; identity, by the phrase "was God." By means of later terminology, we might gloss this verse to mean that "the Word" and "God" are identical in essence (*ousia*) though otherwise different in their modes of being (*hypostases*). The one concrete *ousia* of God is thereby complex without being composite. Without ceasing to be indivisible, it includes differentiation within itself. Such a gloss brings a measure of analytical clarity to the mystery without dissolving it.

On John 1:18. In this verse, which arguably stands as commentary on John 1:1, we read: "the only Son [*theos*], who is in the bosom of the Father, he has made him known" (RSV). Here we may discern the other pattern of unity-in-distinction. The Son, or "only God" (*monogenēs theos*), is *not* identical with the Father, nor the Father with the Son. Using later terminology, we might say that although both are identical with the divine *ousia*, they are not (and could not possibly be) identical as divine *hypostases*. They retain their distinction from one another while still forming an ineffable unity. The unity is so great that the incarnate Son, who is visible, functions as the normative "exegesis" (*exēgēsato*) of the Father, who is invisible. The relationship at the level of divine *hypostases* (of the Father and the Son) is not one of identity-and-difference but one of unity-in-distinction.

To sum up, I am not attempting a full exposition of these verses. I am merely illustrating two patterns of thought. I am suggesting that the relationship between *logos* and *theos* (1:1) falls into a pattern of identity-and-difference, while that between *monogenēs* and *patros* (1:18) falls into a pattern of unity-in-distinction.

The traditional doctrine of the Trinity asserts that the three divine *hypostases* (the Father, the Son, and the Holy Spirit) are the same in indivisible essence (*homoousia*), though not in their specific modes of being (*tropoi hyparxeōs*). Traditional Christology, for its part, asserts that the incarnate Son, while remaining the same in essence as the Father, also becomes the same in essence as us. He subsists in two natures (*physes*), divine and human, at the same time:[27] "without separation or division" (unity) and "without confusion or change" (distinction). The relation of Christ's deity to his humanity is also necessarily asymmetrical (because of the incommensurability in kind). The christological pattern is thus one of asymmetry, unity, and distinction.

The terms "Christ Jesus" and "God," as used here by Paul, may be read as seeds from which these later, more technical distinctions would sprout forth. Paul, for his part, has to stretch his nontechnical vocabulary to the limit. He has to press it, intuitively and embryonically, into a service it is not always well-equipped to perform.

For example, because the term "Christ Jesus" refers somehow to the incarnate Son, it is not clear how it can also refer to the eternal Son. (This difficulty may lie behind the later ill-starred term "preexistence," as if to suggest, unwittingly, that the Son was not robustly in existence prior to the incarnation.) But Paul has only one term to meet both needs (referring to the incarnate Son as well as to the eternal Son), and in any case his conscious grasp of the technical questions would no doubt have been minimal and inchoate.

Or again, his term "God" also has to cover more than one sort of referent. Used absolutely it refers either to God or the Godhead as such (as here with "in the form of God"), while used relatively it pertains rather to God the Father (as here with "equality with God").

I have been using later tradition as a guide for interpreting this Philippians passage in and for the church. If this line of analysis is on the right track, then 2:5b–6 may be glossed as follows:

> **Christ Jesus** [the incarnate Son], **who being in the form of God** [belonging to the divine *ousia* as the eternal Son] **did not count equality with God a thing to be grasped** [did not regard the outward form of the divine glory, along with the normal exercise of its prerogatives, which he shared equally with God the Father,

27. The term "nature" (*physis*) is perhaps best understood as referring to "defining characteristics." When Chalcedon states that Jesus Christ is "at once complete (*teleion*) in deity (*theoteti*) and complete (*teleion*) in humanity (*anthrōpotēti*)," it means that whatever the defining characteristics of "deity" are, they are present in Jesus Christ completely (without abridgement), and that whatever the defining characteristics of "humanity" are, they are likewise present completely (without abridgement). What exactly counts as "deity" and "humanity" is not specified by the Chalcedonian Definition but left open-ended.

as a fixed mode of existence that could not, in all generosity and humility, be relinquished for the good of others].

In what sense the eternal Son may be thought to have relinquished the outward form of his glory, along with its prerogatives, while retaining the divine essence, is the theme to which we now turn.[28]

2:7 but emptied himself—The term "he emptied himself" (*heauton ekenōsen*) has been almost as difficult to interpret as "to be grasped" (*harpagmon*). In the history of theology there are two basic lines of thought. One holds that the eternal Son needs to divest himself of his deity (or some aspects of it) in order to become incarnate. The other denies that any such divestment takes place. It holds that the Son is free to become incarnate without ceasing to be God. His essential divine attributes, though veiled in the process (or very largely veiled), are not abandoned. The first interpretation arises in the modern period, mainly in Germany (1860–1880) and England (1890–1910). The second appears at least as early as Athanasius and Cyril of Alexandria in the Greek East, while being represented in the Latin West by such interpreters as Augustine, Aquinas, Calvin, and Barth.[29]

In the first line of thought, kenosis (emptying) takes place by subtraction; in the second, by addition. For the first, the incarnation means that the Son divests himself of his divine essence; or if not of his essence, at least some of his divine attributes; or if not of his attributes, at least his ability to exercise those attributes. Divestment is the price of incarnation.

For the second approach, none of these ideas are valid. The incarnate Son retains his divine being, his attributes, and (in some sense) their exercise. His act of relinquishment means his entering into humiliation without divesting

28. We might wonder at this point how the idea of relinquishing the outward form of his divine glory would comport with John 1:14: "and we beheld his glory" (*kai etheasametha tēn doxan*). Several possibilities suggest themselves. It could perhaps be an allusion to the transfiguration scene (not mentioned in John), to his postresurrection appearances, or more likely to a kind of spiritual perception that penetrates beyond mere outward appearances. John 17:24, which seems to suggest a special perceiving of something otherwise hidden, could be read as pointing in the latter direction. By the same token, John 12:23 can be read as associating, paradoxically, "the hour" of glorification with the disfiguration of the cross. Jesus is also said to have "manifested his glory" through miraculous signs that led his disciples to believe in him (John 2:11). Since in Ezekiel the glory of God is associated with dwelling in and departing from the temple (Ezek. 10:1–5; 43:1–4), there may be an allusion here to Jesus as the new temple. If so, the allusion would seem to point to his sacrificial significance, though not necessarily to his being an expiation for sins (cf. 1 John 2:2).

29. For a good summary of the various positions, see Law, "Kenotic Theology." For a survey of recent discussion, see also McGinnis, *Son of God*, 169–75. The view adopted here is in line with Athanasius, Aquinas, and Barth.

himself of his essence and its majesty. The majesty is retained in principle even as the element of humiliation is incorporated.[30] Paradoxical language is the price of articulating this mystery.[31]

The first approach arises to solve three problems. First, Christ cannot be truly human if he does not experience human limitations. Yet how can those limitations be real if he is also truly God? The problem is that of docetism, whereby Christ's humanity is not real but merely an appearance, or else merely a passive instrument in the hands of his divine nature. Second, how can Christ be a unified person if he is at once finite as a human being and yet also infinite as God? For example, if his knowledge of the future is limited, how can he have been divinely omniscient? Again, if as a human being he is limited in power, how can he have been divinely omnipotent? And so on. Finally, in a more psychological vein, would not Christ have been encumbered with two centers of consciousness? Burdened with two sets of attributes at the same time, divine and human, would not his consciousness have been split between them? The proposed solution to all these problems is, in one way or another, to divest Christ of his deity.

The second line of thought argues that a Christ so diminished is a Christ fatally defective. A Christ who is not truly God, while yet also truly human, would be bereft of saving power. Even a Christ who suspends all use of his divine attributes might just as well not have them. (For the second view it is not a matter of suspension but of restraint.) No doubt can exist that Christ is indeed truly human. He is therefore subject to all normal human limitations. Nor can any doubt exist regarding the unity of his divine-human person. He is not some kind of metaphysically split personality.[32] Nor can his divine essence be cleverly redefined, as if human finitude is somehow built into it. A Christ whose deity is diminished cannot be the Christ of the church's gospel. He cannot be the object of worship, nor the incarnate Son who discloses God's triune identity, nor the world's Savior by whom sin and death are destroyed.

For the second approach the solution needs to be sought in a different direction. It is especially Gregory of Nazianzus and Cyril of Alexandria who

---

30. "He remained what he was, and what he was not he assumed." Thomas Aquinas, *Commentary*, 80.

31. Attempts to avoid paradoxical language or dialectical modes of thought with regard to kenosis invariably end up compromising the mystery of the incarnation, if not in one way, then in another. For a recent example, one that tends, by turns, to vacillate oddly between some form of Apollonarianism and some form of Ebionitism, see Loke, *Kryptic Model*. The Chalcedonian mystery can be associated with a line from Shakespeare: "These contraries such unity do hold." Shakespeare, "The Rape of Lucrece," #1558.

32. "The ultimate and reasoned analysis of the unique phenomenon, God and Man, One Christ, *is* as to its actual consciousness, if we may use the word, a matter more for his knowledge than our enquiry." Moule, *Philippians*, 66 (slightly modified).

established the basic line. They had to confront the problem of how God could be involved in Christ's suffering and death. One solution, as mentioned, is to deny Christ's true humanity (docetism), while another is to affirm only a moral union between his humanity and his deity (Nestorianism). Both solutions would be heretical.

Gregory and Cyril believe that Christ really suffers and dies as a single subject, that his human nature is truly united with his divine person (in a hypostatic union), and that his divine nature in itself remains incapable of suffering and death (impassible and immortal).[33] Gregory and Cyril nevertheless insist that the person of the eternal Son undergoes suffering and death in his union with the flesh of Christ. Although God transcends suffering and death, he undergoes them humanly in the flesh. "We see in Christ the strange and rare paradox of Lordship in servant's form, and divine glory in human abasement."[34] "We are saved by the sufferings of the impassible God."[35]

For Gregory and Cyril, all nonparadoxical solutions are worse than allowing the paradoxes to stand. These theologians resort to antithetical formulations for describing what is at stake. Cyril famously states of the incarnate Son that "he suffered impassibly" while also suggesting that "he died immortally."[36] By these statements Cyril means that God, who is incapable of suffering and death by nature, is nonetheless capable of them by grace. They cannot be imposed on God by anything external to himself, but can indeed be accepted by his own free choice. When God freely embraces suffering and death in the incarnation, he does not cease to be impassible and immortal in himself.

For Gregory and Cyril the mystery of this event is beyond full comprehension. Their antitheses stand like a flaming sword guarding a threshold impenetrable to the human mind. Any attempt to resolve the tensions leads only to error. Paradoxical phrases do not represent a "problem" to be solved but a mystery to be adored. The mystery of the incarnation can be described by way of paradox but not explained. God remains the Lord of the paradoxical situation even while subjecting himself to it.

---

33. Gregory may have been more unwavering than Cyril, however, in advancing a "single-subject Christology" according to which suffering was thought to be carried all the way into the impassible Godhead in order for it to be destroyed there as through fire. See Beeley, *Unity of Christ*, 264–71. See also Hunsinger, *Reading Barth with Charity*, 146–56, 166–67. For a contrary view that the Godhead in itself could in no way be touched by Christ's suffering on the cross (with an appeal to Aquinas), see Weinandy, *Does God Suffer?*

34. Cyril of Alexandria, *On the Unity of Christ*, 101.

35. Gregory of Nazianzus, *On God and Christ*, 101 (slightly modified).

36. See Prestige, *Fathers and Heretics*, 169.

In Christology it is a rule that statements beginning "I don't see how . . ." are often headed for trouble. Examples might be: "I don't see how a God incapable of suffering could suffer in the flesh." "I don't see how a God who is immortal could die on the cross." "I don't see how a God whose power remained omnipotent could truly be powerless." "I don't see how a God who continued to be glorious could suffer disgrace." And not least: "I don't see how a God who is truly holy could allow himself to be made to be sin." And so on.

The mistake in each case is the premise that we should expect to see "how." As has been shown repeatedly in the history of Christology, explaining "how" these things could be can only be carried out by eliminating one or another of the essential terms. It happens either that one of Christ's natures (divine or human) is abridged or that their union with one another is compromised. The Chalcedonian Definition, however, as I understand it, is not explanatory but descriptive. It offers a second-order conceptual device for making explicit the terms of this ineffable mystery.[37] The task of Christology is not to explain the mystery away but to comprehend the incomprehensible in its incomprehensibility.[38] It is the gospel narrative, or the life history of Jesus, that holds the conjunction of opposites together without explaining it.[39]

When the eternal Son "empties himself" to become human, entering into humiliation and death, he does not cease to be God. He is free to conceal his glory and majesty, along with restraining his prerogatives, without absolutely relinquishing them.[40] What he relinquishes is possessing his majesty in only one modality, or in only its heavenly form. His eternal glory is upheld, but ineffably, in a complex and inconceivable way. It is retained in the midst of earthly abasement. God's glory becomes ignominious without ceasing to be glorious. God is

37. In Christian theology the Chalcedonian Definition and the Nicene doctrine of the Trinity may be regarded, from a logical point of view, as unanalyzable and primitive. They are unanalyzable in the sense that, as ineffable mysteries, they represent the furthest possible extent of analysis; and they are primitive in the sense that, once derived, they are axiomatic in status and thus properly basic to the rest of Christian doctrine.

38. "There are more things in heaven and earth, Horatio, / Than are dreamt of in your philosophy." Shakespeare, *Hamlet* (1.5.187–88).

39. Contrary to some modern interpreters, Chalcedon in itself entailed no strong technical "metaphysical" commitments, such as "impassibility." Apart from its brevity and relative formality, the terms it employed (such as *physis*) had no agreed upon meanings at the time. It was as much a formal device for reading scripture as it was a set of substantive christological claims. See Coakley, "What Chalcedon Solved."

40. It is sometimes proposed that Christ did not empty himself of anything but simply "poured himself out." However, this idea does not seem to take seriously enough that in his self-abasement he divested himself, in some sense, "of the glories, of the prerogatives of Deity." Lightfoot, *Philippians*, 110. Kenosis was not just a metaphor for self-sacrifice. Contra Fee, *Philippians*, 210.

glorious in abasement while also remaining high above it. In assuming flesh to himself, the Son assumes the cross and its shame into his very person. His glory does not cease but is secretly present under the form of its opposite. It is not the shame that diminishes his glory, but his glory that is augmented by the shame, which abolishes it. The *assumptio* of abasement is real, but the glory prevails. God's power is made perfect in weakness.[41]

the form of a slave . . . the likeness of human beings—In emptying himself, the eternal Son takes "the form of a servant," or probably better "the form of a slave" (*morphē doulou labōn*).[42] He adds a new, inglorious mode of existence to himself. He undergoes extreme abasement by assuming it, through his humanity, into ineffable union with his divine person. He does this by being "born in the likeness of human beings" (*homoiōmati anthrōpōn genomenos*).[43]

"Likeness" does not mean something merely partial. But it does mean identity and difference. The eternal Son becomes identical with human beings in essence while remaining different from them in at least two respects. Unlike them he not only (a) lives a true human life without sinning (*ton mē gnonta hamartian*) (2 Cor. 5:21; cf. Heb. 4:15; 1 John 3:5) but also (b) lives it as the one who is God over all (*ho ōn epi pantōn theos*) (Rom. 9:5). It is an assumed likeness in the midst of an infinitely greater unlikeness.

The "likeness" (*homoiōmati*) of a human being is thereby distinguished from the "form" (*morphē*) of a slave. The vocabulary again remains nontechnical and enigmatic. "Likeness" allows for identity and difference in ways that have been suggested. It indicates a true human being who is sinless yet who is also mysteriously God. "Form," however, is another matter. It has just been used to suggest that "being in the *morphē* of God" means "being in the divine essence." If "being

---

41. "God is always God," writes Barth, "even in his humiliation. The divine being does not suffer any change, any diminution, any transformation into something else, any admixture with something else, let alone any cessation. The deity of Christ is the one unaltered, because unalterable, deity of God. . . . He humbled himself, but he did not do it by ceasing to be who he is. He went into a strange land, but even there, and especially there, he never became a stranger to himself." Barth, *Church Dogmatics* IV/1, 179–80.

42. Reasons for preferring the translation "slave" may be found in Harris, *Slave of Christ*, 183–91. As always, it is theologically necessary to read backwards here. Language about *doulos* as the type needs to be read backwards from a center in Christ as the antitype. In loving obedience to God, Christ assumes our plight of bondage to sin and death in order to remove it in mercy by his sacrificial death. "Assuming the form of a *doulos*" and "taking to himself our abject plight so as to remove it" are one and the same. Secondarily, of course, he also enters into profound solidarity with all who are needy and oppressed. See Hunsinger, "The Sinner and the Victim."

43. Here as elsewhere, the line of interpretation adopted in this commentary shows similarities to the views of Proclus of Constantinople (fifth century), who interpreted Phil. 2:7 in connection with John 1:14 and thus effectively in accord with the Councils of Nicaea and Chalcedon. See Constas, *Proclus of Constantinople*, 364–71. I owe this point to George Parsenios.

in human essence" is an idea now effectively conveyed by *homoiōmati*, then the term *morphē* is not needed to make that point.

If *morphē* means possessing the "defining characteristics" of something, then what shifted is the application. First it is used to mean that Jesus somehow possesses the "essential or defining characteristics" of God. Beyond that, it now means that he also possesses the "defining characteristics" of a slave. His being in "the form of a slave" thus compounds the accumulating mysteries. If the word "form" embraces both "ontological" and "ethical" characteristics, then we may say that Christ displays the "ethical" side of God's nature—God's merciful heart—by taking the form of a slave for the good of others.[44]

Many have wondered whether the Ebed Yahweh material in Isa. 52:13–53:12 is in the background for the statements that he "emptied himself" and took "the form of a *doulos*." Certainly there is no direct correspondence with this Christ hymn.[45] Isaiah's "suffering servant" is a figure who is exalted after dying in humiliation, but it is not clear that his death is depicted as obedient. Nor does he divest himself of any prerogatives and majesty, whether by descending from heaven to earth or in some other way. Other differences are evident as well.

Nevertheless, there seems to be no good reason for denying the broad typological significance of the parallels. The humiliation/exaltation scheme is striking in Isaiah.

> *Humiliation*: "He had no form or majesty that we should look on him. . . . He was despised and rejected by men" (Isa. 53:2–3). "He poured out his soul to death" (Isa. 53:12).

> *Exaltation*: "Behold, my servant . . . shall be high and lifted up, and shall be exalted" (Isa. 52:13).

Emphasis also falls on the idea that this death is for the good of others (Isa. 53:8, 12). In the early Christian tradition, Jesus's death is regularly interpreted through the lens of these Isaianic verses—a practice that may have begun with Jesus himself.[46] No good reason seems to exist for denying that in Phil. 2:6–11

---

44. "He displayed the nature (or form) of God in the nature (or form) of a servant." Bruce, *Philippians*, 70.

45. I recognize that on technical grounds Phil. 2:6–11 is not metrical and would therefore not qualify as a "hymn." (It might better be described as an encomium.) I use the word simply for the sake of convenience. Nothing in my commentary hangs on it one way or another.

46. "Mark 10:45 . . . [is] an authentic word of Jesus. It interprets Jesus' mission and suffering from the perspective of Isaiah 43:3–4 and 53:11–12. . . . According to this logion, Jesus understood himself

Jesus is set forth, indirectly, as their fulfillment.[47] (For further reflections on ecclesial hermeneutics, see excursus 2.)

taking . . . being born—The word order here is interesting. "Taking" (*labōn*) the form of a slave (*morphēn doulou*) is oddly mentioned prior to his "being born" (*genomenos*). Are these phrases in apposition? Or does Paul mean to suggest that the decision "to take" (or perhaps even to "elect") such an abject *form* occurs from all eternity—not only before he was born but even "from before the foundation of the world" (*pro katabolēs kosmou*) (Eph. 1:4)? If so, is his "being born" the means by which a prior decision to take the "form of a slave" is fulfilled (or perhaps inaugurated)?

The verb used here for "to take" (*lambanō*) means "actively to lay hold of." It can even mean taking what is available in a forceful manner. It connotes the volition or assertiveness of the actor. Its meaning is thus not far from "electing" or "actively choosing."[48]

The other verb used (*ginomai*) suggests a shift to something more passive. However, it does not necessarily mean "being born" (an essentially passive process), but can simply mean "to become." It can also indicate a change of condition or place. Elsewhere in the New Testament (2 Pet. 1:4), it is used for God's actions as originating from eternity and emerging in time and space.[49] If so, the eternal Son's "being born" would attest his true humanity ("being found in human form") while also fulfilling his prior decision to "empty himself" by taking the form of a slave and so to "change his condition" from one of glory (as the eternal Son) to one of abasement (in the form of a slave).

In any case the sequence runs from "relinquishing" (blessedness as God), to "emptying" (prerogatives), to "taking a new status" (of a slave), to "being born" (in human nature), while then continuing from being "found in human likeness" to "humbling himself," and "becoming obedient unto death," even "death on a cross" (2:8). More simply, it proceeds from "relinquishing" (eternal act) (2:6), to "taking a slave's status" (manifestation of the eternal act) (2:7), to "becoming

---

as the 'man,' or Son of Man, whom God had sent to save Israel, and whose life he had designated as a 'ransom' to redeem the existence of 'the many' from the final judgment, since their existence was forfeited by their guilt." Stuhlmacher, "Isaiah 53," 151 (slightly modified).

47. "It would be a mistake," writes Stephen Pardue, "to overlook legitimate *conceptual* similarities [between Isaiah's servant passages and Phil. 2:5–11] merely because of the absence of philologically verifiable parallels." Pardue, *Mind of Christ*, 57 (italics added). A list of possible correspondences between Isa. 52:13–53:12 and Phil. 2:6–11 may be found in the writings of Bockmuehl and Bauckham. See the measured comments of Bockmuehl, *Philippians*, 135–36; and Bauckham, *Jesus and the God of Israel*, 43–44.

48. Bauer, Danker, Arndt, and Gingrich, *Greek-English Lexicon*, 583–85.

49. Bauer, Danker, Arndt, and Gingrich, *Greek-English Lexicon*, 196–99.

obedient to the point of crucifixion" (telos) (2:8). It is a staggering transition from the heights to the depths.

When all is said and done, however, this line of interpretation for 2:7 (from the active to the passive, or from eternal election to earthly manifestation) is perhaps too clever by half. None of the fathers (or anyone else) seems to have adopted it. The verse may be glossed as follows:

> **But emptied himself** [the eternal Son, in becoming flesh, divested himself of the outward trappings of his divine glory as well as of the normal exercise of his divine prerogatives], **taking the form of a slave** [fulfilling his act of self-emptying in a correspondingly radical act of self-abnegation as the incarnate Son], **being born in the likeness of human beings** [the eternal Son, having assumed Jesus's human nature into hypostatic *union* with himself—without separation or division, without confusion or change—*by the power* of the Holy Spirit (*conceptus de Spiritu Sancto*), was *born* like any other human being, yet of the Virgin Mary (*natus ex Maria Virgine*), so that in his humanity he was *like* us in all respects except without sinning].[50]

2:8 And being found in human form, he humbled himself—Here Christ's humanity is doubly expressed. In appearance or "human form" (*schēmati*) he in no way differs from the rest of humankind.[51] But that is not all. While as God he *empties* himself, as a human being he "*humbles* himself" (*etapeinōsen heauton*).[52] The voluntary aspect of his passion comes to the fore. It is a matter of one divine-human action under two aspects: self-emptying (from the divine side) and self-abnegating (from the human side).[53] His earthly self-humbling itself falls into two parts: being born and dying on a cross. He freely chooses to humble himself, not clinging to his prerogatives—in apparent contrast to the contentious Philippian leaders. He does so by way of his obedience.

What the rest of this verse suggests about "Christ Jesus" can be laid out under three terms: Son, Lord, and servant. (1) As the Son, he is obedient to the Father.

---

50. I am not suggesting that these latter ideas, as drawn from the Chalcedonian Definition and the Apostles' Creed, would have been evident either to Paul or to the Philippians. I am proposing, however, that the humiliation theme that ends on the cross begins in the womb. Whether or not the eternal God could subject himself to such a humiliation was at stake in the early Theotokos debates. The ecumenical Councils of Ephesus (431) and Chalcedon (451) decided in the affirmative, against the Nestorians. Just as the eternal Son received his divine nature from God the Father, so he received his human nature from his mother.

51. So Calvin, "The Epistle to the Philippians," in *Calvin's New Testament Commentaries*, 11:249.

52. Paraphrasing Fee, *Philippians*, 214n1.

53. The phrase "he humbled himself" stands "in chiastic relation" to the phrase "he emptied himself." O'Brien, *Philippians*, 227. I have chosen to continue to interact with O'Brien's *Philippians* commentary as a helpful resource.

(2) As the Lord, his glory is concealed. (3) In the form of a servant or a slave, he yields to death on a cross.

becoming obedient—Obedience for Paul is always to God, though it can be routed through various intermediaries, the most important of which is the law. Obedience to the law means obedience to God, which leads to life, while disobedience means death. Despite its being "chiseled in letters on stone tablets" (2 Cor. 3:7), and despite its having come "in glory" (2 Cor. 3:7), so as to be "holy" in itself (Rom. 7:12), the law in the form of the Decalogue accomplishes "the ministry of death" (2 Cor. 3:7) because of human perversity and willfulness.

Philippians 2:8 does not tell us to whom or to what Christ is "obedient,"[54] but in light of scripture and tradition we may gather two points: first, as the incarnate Son his obedience is to the Father; and second, his obedience involves death as wrought by the law.[55] Indeed an inference has been drawn from ancient times (at least since Irenaeus) that Christ's human obedience as referred to in 2:8 has something to do with reversing the disobedience of Adam. "For as by the one man's disobedience the many were made sinners, so by the one man's obedience the many will be made righteous" (Rom. 5:19). "For as in Adam all die, so also in Christ shall all be made alive" (1 Cor. 15:22). This reversal takes place in various ways through his obedience.

It seems plausible to suppose that his obedience has a saving purpose. Although no soteriology is stated, that does not mean that none is in the background. It is an obedience to God for the good of others. Otherwise the transition from heaven to earth, from transcendent glory to abasement and shame, makes little sense.

to the point of death—We may thereby posit that the obedience of Christ pertains, in a certain respect, to the death of Adam.[56] Death is undone, sin removed, Satan defeated, and all things are made new—by the obedience of the incarnate Son. He not only reverses Adam's disobedience; he also bears its terrible consequences in himself and carries them away. "For he would not have been one

54. "Jesus saw himself as the 'man,' or Son of Man, whom God in his love willed to deliver up for Israel's salvation, and the *hupakoē* or 'obedience' of Jesus praised in Philippians 2:8 consisted of his submitting to this will of God." Stuhlmacher, "Isaiah 53," 150–51.

55. He was "obedient," writes H. G. C. Moule, "to the Father's will that he should suffer (cf. Isa. 53:10). . . . The utterance of Gethsemane was but the amazing summary and crown of his whole sacred course as the Man of Sorrows." Moule, *Philippians*, 67. In a traditional move Moule rightly points to Isa. 53. Note that the Philippians hymn mentions "obedience" without referring to the divine will (2:8), whereas Isa. 53 mentions the "divine will" or "good pleasure" (Isa. 53:10) without referring to obedience. Within these limits, the Philippians hymn may be read as *alluding*, in important respects, to Isa. 53.

56. I mean this with regard to the eternal Son's *assumptio carnis*, and thus the death of Adam, not the disobedient and grasping creature's *eritis sicut Deus*.

truly possessing flesh and blood, by which he redeemed us, unless he had summed up in himself the ancient formation of Adam."[57] In the obedience of Christ to the point of death, the death of Adam is recapitulated, reversed, and overcome.

The phrase "the form of a slave" (*morphēn doulou*) can be read as pertaining to two poles: the Godhead and humankind, or, more fully, to being in "the form of God" (*morphē theou*) and "being found in human likeness" (*schēmati heuretheis hōs anthrōpos*). The glory and lordship intrinsic to "the form of God" are eclipsed by their appearing in "the form of a slave." When the eternal Son takes human flesh, he enters into a state of abasement. The form of God, belonging to him by nature, is a mode of blessedness; the form of a slave involves, by contrast, the experience of suffering and death. His lordship and glory are veiled under the aspects of powerlessness and shame.

For Paul, Adam is the primal sinner through whom death gains a grip on humankind (1 Cor. 15:21–22). He is the original human (*henos anthrōpou*) by whom utter calamity—sin, condemnation, and doom—has entered the world (Rom. 5:12–21). It is through his disobedience that "the many" are made to be sinners (Rom. 5:19). Being found "in human likeness" (*schēmati . . . hōs anthrōpos*) means, in some important sense, that Christ subjects himself to Adam's plight. It means his entering into the misery of fallen humankind. It means his having made the condition of our sorry race his own.

even death on a cross—Christ does not merely exist "in human likeness." Beyond that, he exists in "the form of a slave." He assumes the plight of the primal sinner in order to overcome it from within. He is "a man of sorrows and acquainted with grief" (Isa. 53:3). It is in his flesh that sin is condemned (Rom. 8:3). "He was wounded for our transgressions; he was crushed for our iniquities; upon him was the chastisement that brought us peace, and with his stripes we are healed" (Isa. 53:5). These ideas from Isaiah are echoed in Paul.[58]

The form of a slave means embracing the death of Adam so that Adam's guilt might be reversed and overcome. For these reasons Christ humbles himself, being obedient to the point of dying on a cross—which he "endured . . . scorning its shame" (Heb. 12:2). "To bind a Roman citizen is a crime; to flog him is an

---

57. Irenaeus, *Against Heresies* 5.1.2.

58. Echoes of Isaiah often occur when Paul discusses Christ's death in its saving significance. For example, according to J. Ross Wagner, "it appears that Paul's notion of Jesus being 'handed over for us/for our transgressions' (Rom. 4:25; 8:32) echoes Isaiah 53:6, 11–12." Wagner even suggests that Paul may have been the originator of a christological reading of Isa. 53. The connection of the Isaianic servant with Christ seems to be "a virtually unavoidable implication of Paul's larger reading of Isaiah." See Wagner, *Heralds of the Good News*, 334–35.

abomination; to slay him is almost an act of murder; to crucify him is—what? There is no fitting word that can possibly describe so horrible a deed" (Cicero).[59]

For Paul (elsewhere in his letters), the mercy enacted in Christ in the form of a slave cannot be understood apart from the concepts of participation and substitution.[60] A single example will have to suffice. In a key verse Paul writes "that one died for all, therefore all died" (2 Cor. 5:14 NASB). The verbs here (*apethanen/apethanon*) are both found in the aorist, which suggests a completed, effectual, and one-time action. The second clause—"*therefore* all died"—is, technically, a non sequitur. If one died for all, it does not follow that all died. The verse seems to mean that in this particular case, the death of all is somehow entailed. All died in the death of this one (*coram Deo*) by a real, divinely appointed *participation*.

At the same time participation is accompanied by elements of *representation* and *substitution*, since the death of the one is actual, while the death of all, without failing somehow to be actual (cf. the double aorist),[61] is evidently all-inclusive and vicarious. A *substitute* dies so that others do not; he dies so that they do not have to. A *representative*, on the other hand, may include others in his death, by acting on their behalf, so that when he dies, they are implicated with him. I see both these elements at play in 2 Cor. 5:14. Christ dies the death of all. He dies in their place (vicariously) and for their sakes (representatively). By including them in his death, he spares them from the consequences of their sin.[62]

Just as all are implicated in the death of Adam, so are all implicated in its saving recapitulation. The significance of Christ's death in the form of a slave is thereby established. It means not only the death of all in the death of the one, but also the death of the one in the stead of all. It means the death of death in the death

59. Quoted in Fee, *Philippians*, 217n13. Jesus, of course, was not a Roman citizen, but one gets the point.

60. The idea of substitution seems to have had some roots in Isaiah. "Paul does not merely wish to express 'the vicarious character of the death of Jesus,' . . . but also the fact that Christ died for God's 'enemies' (Rom. 5:10) and took upon himself the fatal consequence of their 'enmity against God' (Rom. 8:7). *This* could not have been said without a citation from Isaiah 53." Hofius, "Fourth Servant Song," 176.

61. Whether the death of Christ is merely "sufficient" for all (as Lombard and many after him like Aquinas would teach) or whether it is actually somehow "efficacious" for all (as apparently Athanasius and Barth would suggest) is beyond the scope of this commentary. See my reflections in Hunsinger, *Beatitudes*, 64–67, 122–24.

62. Representation and substitution are not incompatible. As a representative, Christ represents God to us and us to God. As a substitute, he represents us to God in our sinful condition that he might remove it by his vicarious death for our sakes. "Paul did what no one else was able to do: effect a powerful merging of the political/heroic theme of substitutionary death with the mystery theme of representative death, and attach them to sturdy Jewish monotheism." Finlan, *Paul's Cultic Atonement Metaphors*, 220.

of Christ. The recapitulation is not like the original, because by virtue of Christ's death on the cross—undertaken in humility and obedience—Adam's primal misdeed is superseded and undone.

In Phil. 2:8, Paul writes only that Christ was "obedient to the point of death." It would be a mistake to suppose that because no soteriology is stated, none is at stake. The Philippians cannot be hearing about the death of Christ from Paul for the first time. This is the same Paul who reminds the Corinthians that "I decided to know nothing among you except Jesus Christ and him crucified" (1 Cor. 2:2). It is also the Paul who insists that "Christ crucified" is the content of his preaching (1 Cor. 1:23), and who charges the faithful to "proclaim the Lord's death [in weekly eucharistic worship] until he comes" (1 Cor. 11:26). At the heart of his preaching—which he "received" and regards "as of first importance"—is the message "that Christ died for our sins in accordance with the Scriptures" (1 Cor. 15:3). Accordingly, he can proclaim that "while we were still sinners, Christ died for us" (Rom. 5:8), and that "while we were enemies we were reconciled to God by the death of his Son" (Rom. 5:10). That for Paul the death of Christ is of supreme importance for our salvation would be no less familiar to the Philippians than to any of his other churches—or to any of his readers today. No argument from silence can supplant this point.

Philippians 2:8 may therefore be glossed as follows:

> **And being found in human form** [the form of Adam], **he** [the incarnate Son] **humbled himself** [putting the interests of others ahead of his own] **by becoming obedient** [as the suffering servant] **to the point of death** [for our sakes and in our place], **even death on a cross** [in the shameful form of a crucified slave, by which his divine glory and lordship were concealed].

It is a fair comment that Phil. 2:6–11 concentrates more on what humble obedience meant "for Christ" than on what it might mean "for us and our salvation."[63] Nevertheless, in the end the two cannot be separated. In this bare-bones yet evocative passage, the soteriology remains tacit rather than openly expressed. It cannot be derived directly from the text, but only from related material in Paul and from earlier and later traditions of interpretation. For Christ, obedience means humiliation for the good of others. But the good of others—the undoing of sin and death—is in view all along. His obedience is hollow if its saving significance is discounted. For Paul, the saving death of Christ stands at the

---

63. O'Brien, *Philippians*, 232.

heart of all Christian preaching and worship. "This is my body, given for you" (1 Cor. 11:24).[64]

2:9 Therefore—The importance of the word "therefore" (*dio*) should not be overlooked. It is another sign that soteriology is at stake in what has gone before (2:6–8). Why indeed would Christ "empty himself," why would he assume the incognito form of a slave, why would he so humble himself *in extremis*, why would he be so obedient even to the point of death on a cross? The word "therefore" suggests that this course of action is not undertaken for its own sake. It enacts the good of others. Christ puts the interests of others ahead of his own, and he does so at cost to himself. He subjects himself to a form of extreme degradation so that others might be delivered from theirs.

Theologically, the implicit foreground of divine command and messianic obedience needs to be placed against a background of mutual collaboration, which in turn needs to be seen from a trinitarian vantage point. In his act of humility and self-emptying, the Son makes himself obedient to the Father. In that sense a functional subordination in love can be ascribed to the Son vis-à-vis the Father. At the same time, however, this very action is jointly determined and freely chosen by the Father and the Son as coeternal equals to meet a particular purpose. From the standpoint of later tradition, the foreground of voluntary subordination cannot be understood apart from the background of ontological equality and mutual collaboration between the Father and the Son.

This point is well made by Barth and Anselm. "The Son of God determined to give himself from all eternity," writes Barth. "With the Father and the Holy Spirit he chose to unite himself with the lost human race."[65] "Absolute and true obedience," explains Anselm, "is that which occurs when a rational being, not under compulsion but voluntarily, keeps to a desire which has been received from God."[66] "Since no one else could perform the deed, . . . the Son was willing to die for the sake of the world."[67] "The subject of this decision," Barth states, "is the triune God—the Son of God no less than the Father and the Holy Spirit."[68] "The human race," Anselm observes, "could not have been saved by any other means than by his death. . . . He died not under any compulsion but of his own

---

64. For an argument connecting the Isaianic suffering servant with the historical institution of the Eucharist, see Pitre, *Jesus and the Last Supper.*

65. Barth, *Church Dogmatics* II/2, 158 (slightly modified).

66. Anselm, *Why God Became Man* 1.9 (Evans and Davies, *Anselm of Canterbury*, 280).

67. Anselm, *Why God Became Man* 1.9 (Evans and Davies, *Anselm of Canterbury*, 278–79).

68. Barth, *Church Dogmatics* II/2, 110.

free will."[69] For Barth and Anselm, as for the great ecumenical tradition, Christ's humble obedience to the point of death represents a trinitarian transaction of consent between the Father and the Son in the Holy Spirit—a transaction that is grounded in eternity, fulfilled in history, and elevated back again into eternity.

The reason why the incarnate Son is vindicated by the Father is that he fulfilled the role that was mutually determined between them from all eternity. He fulfilled it in faithful obedience. "God was in Christ reconciling the world to himself" (2 Cor. 5:19). Calvin glosses this statement to mean "that the Father was in the Son, in agreement with John 10:38, 'I am in the Father and the Father in me.'"[70] Thus, Calvin continues, whoever has the Son has the Father also. What the Son does in obedience to the Father, the Father does, in his own way, in and through the Son. The work by which the world is saved from ruin needs to be regarded from the standpoint of a divine, trinitarian reciprocity.

In submitting to death, the Son undoes the power of death. By overturning the fateful deed of Adam, whose disobedience made him the primal sinner, the incarnate Son bears and bears away the ancient curse of Adam's guilt, thereby reversing it from death to life. He does so at untold cost to himself, in order that Adam's race might be rescued from the edge of doom. The Son gives himself up in obedience to the Father (Phil. 2:8), even as the Father does not spare his only Son but gives him up for us all (Rom. 8:32).

Salvation occurs through the great exchange (*admirabile commercium*). "He made him to be sin who knew no sin, so that in him we might become the righteousness of God" (2 Cor. 5:21). The guilt of the guilty is transferred to the one who is innocent, even as in him the guilty are made innocent (or righteous) by an innocence not their own. Because of the incarnate Son, who is obedient in their place and for their sakes, the guilty do not perish but have eternal life. Both now and in the age to come, they are called to live no longer for themselves but for him who for their sakes died and was raised (2 Cor. 5:15).

It may be noted that the great atoning mysteries—such as "substitution," the "double transfer" (of our sin to Christ and of his righteousness to us), and our "objective participation" in him—do not go unrecognized by the Greek fathers, sometimes in an especially striking way. A case in point is Gregory of Nazianzus:

> The one who releases me from the curse was called "curse" because of me (Gal. 3:13); the one who takes away the world's sin was called sin (2 Cor. 5:21). (*Or.* 30)

69. Anselm, *Why God Became Man* 1.9 (Evans and Davies, *Anselm of Canterbury*, 281).
70. Calvin, on 2 Cor. 5:19, in *Calvin's New Testament Commentaries*, 10:78.

He dies, but he vivifies (John 5:21) and by death destroyed death (1 Cor. 15:26). (*Or.* 29)

He delivers us from the power of sin (Rom. 6:17) by giving himself in our stead as a ransom (Mark 10:45) which cleanses the whole world (1 John 2:2). (*Or.* 30.20)

On the cross ... he occupied our own position. ... He saved us by his sufferings, for he made our sins his own (1 Cor. 15:3; 2 Cor. 5:21). (*Or.* 30.5)

He became sin itself and the curse itself [*autoamartia kai autokatara*] (2 Cor. 5:21; Gal. 3:13). (*Or.* 37.1) [This is a remarkably radical statement.]

He carries us bodily in himself with all that is in us (1 Pet. 2:24); he is the leaven mixed with our paste in order to transform it entirely (Rom. 6:5). (*Or.* 30.6)[71] [Note the suggestion here of our objective participation in Christ.]

None of this content, of course, is made explicit in the Philippians hymn. But it represents the kind of rich elaboration without which the reversal from humiliation to exaltation makes little sense. Without some such soteriological premise, it is difficult to see how the extremity of Christ's self-emptying and self-humiliation could be of any great consequence for others. But according to this passage, the final outcome is no less extraordinary, if not more so, than the path that ended on the cross. It is an outcome of universal significance.

In short, the word "therefore" in 2:9 means "for this reason." The incarnate Son's obedience in love to the Father—*Thy will be done*—is reciprocated by the Father's act of love in return. The Son's obedience—the central concept here—is validated and approved from above. Having glorified the Father by his death, the Son is glorified by the Father in return (John 17:1). "I glorified you on earth, having accomplished the work that you gave me to do. And now, Father, glorify me in your own presence with the glory that I had with you before the world was made" (John 17:4–5). The word "therefore" in Phil. 2:9 points to the way in which that prayer is answered. "Now is the Son of Man glorified, and God is glorified in him" (John 13:31).

God has highly exalted him—It is on account of his saving obedience—a work of substitution, drastic reversal, and objective inclusion, a work of wondrous

---

71. The first two citations are from Gregory of Nazianzus, *On God and Christ*. The rest are from Rivière, *Doctrine of the Atonement*, 1:207–8. I have inserted references to the relevant scripture verses to which Gregory alludes. I do not mean to suggest that this is the only line that Gregory takes regarding the saving significance of Christ's death, nor even that it is the most prominent line, only that it is an important line.

exchange (*admirabile commercium*), a work undertaken in love by the innocent one on behalf of the guilty many—that "God has highly exalted him" (*ho theos auton hyperypsōsen*).

The formal pattern is essentially up-down-up. It runs from the eternal Son, to the crucified Son, to the exalted Son. It is, in a sense, a pattern of thesis, antithesis, synthesis. It proceeds from position, to negation, and finally to the negation of the negation. The process runs as follows. The eternal Son is in the form of God and equal with God. He empties himself of his divine lordship and glory by subjecting them to concealment and restraint. He does not regard the precious blessedness he knows in eternity as something that cannot be laid aside. In accord with the Father, for purposes of love, he places the interests of many, regardless of how lost and undeserving, above his own.

Without ceasing to be who and what he is as God, he assumes a human form. It is the form of a servant, the form of a slave, and indeed the form of Adam. He humbles himself in obedience to the point of a terrible death. His majesty is concealed. By his obedience Adam's disobedience is revoked; by his death Adam's death is undone; and by his submission to the cross, the condemnation of the primal sinner, and so of the whole human race, is reversed and overturned. As Calvin notes, "Christ is much more powerful to save, than Adam was to destroy."[72]

After this great work is concluded, it is vindicated by God. The incarnate Son is exalted to a summit than which no greater can be conceived. The majesty that belonged to him in eternity is returned to him in his new assumed form. Exaltation is now accorded to him in his humanity (*schēmati hōs anthrōpos*, 2:7). It is based on the salvation that has taken place in him. It negates (in the sense of overcoming) all that he has suffered for the sake of the world. It restores him to his proper place in the Godhead, but without leaving his assumed humanity behind. It is something like the incarnation in reverse. Just as God crosses over into sin and death without ceasing to be God, so now in union with the Son, the assumed human nature, designated by the name of Jesus, is elevated to divine majesty without ceasing to be human.[73]

Is this act of exaltation a "reward"? Does it perhaps involve a scheme of "merit" and "obligation"? Or is it instead a "free gift"? None of these ideas quite seem to work. It is not a "reward" (though that cannot be entirely ruled out) because it does not involve mere compensation or desert. Nor is it a matter of merit, according to

---

72. Calvin, on Rom. 5:15, in *Calvin's New Testament Commentaries*, 8:114–15.

73. Again, both the kenosis and the exaltation took place, in various ways, by addition and not by subtraction.

which the Son places the Father under some sort of obligation. The exaltation of the incarnate Son falls outside what can be captured by the metaphors of a financial or a legal transaction. Yet neither does the idea of a "free gift" seem correct, as if the exaltation is undeserved. Being a matter neither of external necessity nor of undeserved grace, the only category left seems to be what is ontologically fitting in love. His exaltation is the free response of love to love—of love freely given by the Father to the love freely offered in obedience by the Son.

It is not possible for the incarnate Son to be held by the bonds of death (Acts 2:24). It is not he who is swallowed up by death, but death that is swallowed up by him. How can he who is the very essence of Life be conceived as succumbing to its negation?[74] The incarnate Son cannot *not* have been exalted by the Father, not because of some external necessity or unmerited grace but because of what is intrinsically fitting in love. The negation cannot fail to be negated, simply because God is God, and God is love. In Christ, God is the one who negates our fatal negations out of love. *How* God chooses to do so may be discretionary (for God is infinitely resourceful), but *that* he should do so belongs to his essential nature as the one who loves in freedom.[75]

God does not tolerate sin and evil, nor does he compromise with them, nor does he call them good. Whatever enters into conflict with God, under the forms of sin and death, can have no future. The appointed means of their abolition is the person of the incarnate Son. When his work of saving obedience is fulfilled in his death, he is restored to the form of his eternal power and glory. How can it have been otherwise? But—and this is key—by virtue of the permanence of the hypostatic union, the Son brings his assumed humanity, designated by the name of Jesus, with him in his elevation.

Philippians 2:9 marks a transition in the narrative. The first part focuses on what the Son does in obedience to the Father (2:6–8); the second part, on what the Father does in vindication of the Son (2:9–11). The career of the Son runs from glory through humiliation to exaltation. The glory belongs to him by nature, the humiliation by free consent, and the exaltation by fittingness or propriety.

No mention is made of the process by which the exaltation takes place. It is the brute fact of the exaltation, not the means by which it occurred, that is of interest to the narrative. Nevertheless, from the standpoint of ecclesial interpretation, just

---

74. "How can he who constitutes the very definition of life be conceived of as the opposite of what he defines? To think of him as dead is the equivalent of not thinking of him at all." Frei, *Identity of Jesus Christ*, 148.

75. See Barth, *Church Dogmatics* II/1, 257–321.

as the narrative implies trinitarian relations between the Father and the Son, so it also implies Jesus's bodily resurrection and ascension. Otherwise, it is hard to see how this exaltation could be ascribed so pointedly to "Jesus," on whom the remainder of the narrative turns. An exalted but disembodied Jesus would be no Jesus at all.

the name that is above every name—What is accorded to Jesus in his "exaltation" or "super-exaltation" (*hyperypsōsen*) is said to be "the name above every name" (*to onoma to hyper pan onoma*). This is the name that can belong only to God. The divine name and the divine essence are one. They do not belong to Jesus by his human nature, but rather by the union of that nature with the person of the eternal Son.[76] As the eternal Son is abased in the crucifixion, so the human Jesus is exalted in the vindication. The abyss of the cross is surpassed only by the summit that succeeds it. In humiliation as in exaltation, the eternal Son and the human Jesus are one. Just as the form of Adam, the primal sinner, is given to the Son in his oneness with the crucified Jesus, so the form of God and the name of God are given to the exalted Jesus in his oneness with the eternal Son. Henceforth the Son's glory and sovereignty are invested in Jesus, for the two, Jesus and the Son, are one. As this faith unfolds over the course of time, God himself (the God of Israel) is named by way of Jesus as the Father, the Son, and the Holy Spirit.

---

76. "Jesus is given the divine name," writes Richard Bauckham, "because he *participates* in the divine sovereignty." See Bauckham, "Worship of Jesus," 131 (italics added). Note that Bauckham's repeated use of the term "participation" is well-intended but unfortunate. From the standpoint of later tradition, Jesus does not "participate" in the Godhead. It rather belongs to him by virtue of the hypostatic union. His oneness with the eternal Son, as Bauckham rightly suggests, makes him properly the object of worship. The hypostatic union means, however, that the human nature of Jesus has no independent hypostasis of its own, which it would need if Jesus's relation to the Godhead were merely one of "participation." Although Jesus does not lose his human essence, the divine essence actually belongs to him by virtue of the hypostatic union.

Bauckham is on stronger ground when he avoids the term "participation" by speaking about Jesus's being "included in the divine identity" (132). The relative indeterminacy of the terms "inclusion" and "divine identity" seems exactly right for this early, nascent stage of christological understanding. In light of other relevant passages such as Phil. 2:6 (*morphē theou*) and 1 Cor. 8:6 (*heis kyrios . . . di' hou*), these interpretive terms are open-textured enough not to say too much while also not saying too little. They point to what would eventually be seen as the mystery of the divine essence (*homoousion*) belonging to the divine-human person of Jesus Christ (one *prosopon* having one *hypostasis* in two natures, *en duo physesin*).

"Participation" is, in any case, not the right term to describe Jesus's relationship to the divine essence, which would make him both independent and inferior. Again, the human nature of Jesus has no *hypostasis* other than that of the eternal Son. Strictly speaking, the relation is a matter of "having been assumed," not of "participating." "The essence of the one God is simple and undivided. . . . It belongs to the Father, the Son, and the Spirit." Calvin, *Institutes* 1.13.22 (trans. Battles, slightly modified), 147. In short, the exalted Jesus does not "participate" in the divine essence; the divine essence "belongs" to him by the hypostatic union.

2:10 the name of Jesus—Having been invested with the divine name, and having been elevated in his oneness with the eternal Son, Jesus now bears the name above every name. "The name of Jesus" (*to onoma Iēsou*) and the divine name (*to onoma to hyper pan onoma*) are conjoined. It is at the name of *Jesus* that "every knee should bow" (*pan gonu kampsē*).[77] His obedience is met with a double response: he is not only vindicated by the Father but also acclaimed for who he is—the Lord (*kyrios*)—by all creation.[78]

In Jewish religious practice, no mere creature may be worshiped.[79] Worship marks the absolute difference between God and everything else. While a creature may be venerated, worship belongs to God alone. It signals God's utter uniqueness. God alone is the Creator of all things. God alone is the Lord. God alone is the Judge of heaven and earth. In worship God is acknowledged, thanked, feared, and praised in his distinctive identity as Creator, Lord, and Judge.

God is also the God of the eternal covenant with Israel. It is to Israel as the people of the covenant that God not only reveals his holy name (YHWH) but also promises to renew all things through them. In early Christian worship—beginning apparently in Jewish Palestine—the revealed name and the divine promise are invested, remarkably, in Jesus. In him the divine name is made humanly concrete, even as in him the promise of divine blessing is confirmed, extended, and renewed. The refraction of Jewish monotheism by the worship of Jesus is rooted in "the earliest post-Easter christology." "Philippians 2:9–11 is the earliest extant text in which the worship of Jesus is depicted," and it is a very early text indeed.[80]

The worship of Jesus, with its trinitarian implications, has served as a stumbling block ever since. It is regarded as a scandal by some (e.g., Jews) and as foolishness by others (e.g., Gentiles) (1 Cor. 1:23). Everything depends on whether the eternal Son

77. "It seems clear from the context that 'the name of Jesus' is not only the medium but the object of adoration.... The bending of the knee is an act of reverence *to* Jesus, and not only to God *through* him." Lightfoot, *Philippians*, 112.

78. I do not mean to suggest a direct or simple identity between the ineffable divine name and the name of Jesus. The divine name belongs to the human Jesus in and through the mystery of the incarnation. That is, it belongs to him by virtue of the hypostatic union of his human nature with the eternal Son. The ineffable divine name as revealed in the Old Testament is YHWH. In the New Testament it is revealed as the no less ineffable name of the Father, the Son, and the Holy Spirit. According to the faith of the church, these are names for one and the same God, one and the same sovereign Lord. In the Philippians hymn, the ineffable divine name is bestowed on the obedient, crucified, and exalted Jesus by virtue of his union, the union of his human nature, with the person of the eternal Son. Jesus is therefore properly set forth as the object of his worship.

79. "However diverse Judaism may have been in many other respects, this was common: only the God of Israel is worthy of worship because he is sole Creator of all things and sole Ruler of all things." Bauckham, *Jesus and the God of Israel*, 9.

80. Bauckham, "Worship of Jesus," 128.

in fact became incarnate in Jesus, and thus on whether the incarnate Son—Jesus, God and human—underwent humiliation and exaltation for the sake of the world.

In the history of Christology, both ancient and modern, there have always been those who could not give the worship of Jesus their unqualified support. Some ancient theologians held, for example, that while worship is proper with respect to the eternal Son, the human Jesus for his part deserves only the highest veneration, but no more than that, because of his "close union" with the Son. Where Jesus and the Son are two separate "persons" (concrete acting subjects), and where their oneness is volitional but not hypostatic, the human Jesus as such cannot rightly be the object of worship.[81] A Nicene view of the Trinity is not always matched by an adequate view of the incarnation. To that extent, the saving significance of Jesus tends to move in a semi-Pelagian and exemplarist direction.

Much modern Christology also hesitates to affirm the propriety of worshiping Jesus.[82] While typically continuing in the tradition of (a watered-down) Antiochene Christology, it tends to abandon a Nicene view of the Trinity, which in combination with rejecting a high view of the incarnation, as well as a properly kenotic Christology, makes it difficult for Jesus to be affirmed as the proper object of worship.[83] Many things can be ascribed to him. He can be the object of devotion and loyalty. He can be the source of transforming spiritual power. He can serve as an inspiring moral example. But he cannot be worshiped as the one in whom the divine name and the divine prerogatives are invested as revealed to faith.

Only where Christ's divine and human natures are distinctly maintained within the context of their inseparable unity in one *hypostasis* can a single act of worship be directed to Jesus as the incarnate Son. For Nicene orthodoxy, the eternal Word does not do any work in heaven or on earth, or receive any worship, apart from his assumed flesh. Withholding worship from Jesus means departing from the Nicene faith.[84]

81. Theognis of Nicaea, a supporter of Arius, insisted that only the Father was to be worshiped, while the Son was merely venerated. A similar position seems to have belonged to Paul of Samosata. Gregory of Nazianzus anathematized those who did not worship the Crucified. Whether any such theologians existed, however, is another matter. It should be noted that even within the Antiochene school it was not impossible for the two natures to be distinguished while still uniting the worship, because the natures were regarded as united in one person.

82. This hesitation is implicit and sometimes explicit in such modern theologians as Schleiermacher, Troeltsch, Tillich, Bultmann, the Niebuhrs, Gustafson, Kaufman, Ruether, McFague, Cone, and many others.

83. See the incisive discussion in Law, *Kierkegaard's Kenotic Christology*, 130–54.

84. "Therefore, the true worship of God is to kiss the Son: that is, to adore him, and to see nothing . . . apart from him, nor trust in anything besides him, according to the first commandment." Luther, commenting on Ps. 2:12, in *Commentary on the First Twenty-Two Psalms*, 547 (slightly modified).

every knee . . . in heaven and on earth and under the earth—Nevertheless, according to this verse, the divine/human Jesus, worshiped at first by only a tiny community, will one day be confessed by all the world. At the end of all things (at his parousia), it is "every knee" (*pan gonu*) that shall bow[85] "in heaven and on earth and under the earth" (*epouraniōn kai epigeiōn kai katachthoniōn*). The universalistic note here is as remarkable as the distinctions by which it is expressed. No explanation is offered for what "in heaven," "on earth," and "under the earth" might mean. Does it mean angels (in heaven), those who have not died (on earth), and those who have died (under the earth)? But does not the church triumphant already worship with the angels "in heaven"? If so, are the distinctions somehow pointing to the church triumphant, the church militant, and even those who have died outside the church's fellowship? Moreover, in what spirit do they all worship? Is the adoration offered gladly and spontaneously by all (regardless of location), or is it sometimes grudging and coerced (for those "under the earth")?

The universalistic note is sounded more clearly than the precise meaning of the three distinctions. Nevertheless it remains as intriguing as it is indeterminate. Among the four main views in the history of Christian theology—eternal torment, annihilationism, universal salvation, and reverent agnosticism—regarding those who do not attain to faith and repentance in this life,[86] perhaps any one of them could, in a pinch, be made to square with this verse. If the New Testament, taken as a whole, remains without closure on this question, however, then the better part of wisdom might be to leave the matter open in hope. As for Paul himself, before breaking off into doxology, perhaps his most definitive word on the subject, while still enigmatic, could be construed as pointing in a hopeful direction: "For God has consigned all to disobedience, that he may have mercy on all" (Rom. 11:32).[87]

---

85. The verbs *kampsē* ("should bow") and *exomologēsētai* ("should confess") are both in the active voice and both are aorist subjunctives, which gives them a future orientation in this usage. The direct allusion to Isa. 45:23 indicates that divine status has been accorded to Jesus. A more uncertain allusion may be to what is reported in the Mishnah about Yom Kippur. It is said that whenever the high priest pronounced aloud the ineffable divine name (YHWH)—which was otherwise never done—the congregation fell on their faces and cried, "Blessed be the Name of the glory of His kingdom forever and ever." Whether this practice stands in the background of Phil. 2:10 is uncertain. But if it does, there would be a link, even if a remote one, between the Day of Atonement and the primitive Christian confession of Jesus Christ as Lord, as reflected in the Philippians hymn. See Mishnah, tractate *Yoma* 6.2, in Danby, *Mishnah*, 169.

86. See Hunsinger, "Hellfire and Damnation: Four Ancient and Modern Views," in *Disruptive Grace*, 226–49.

87. For a measured discussion, see Hillert, *Limited and Universal Salvation*. Hillert concludes that for Paul the limited and universal aspects of salvation stand in unresolved tension, but possibly with a tilt toward universal hope. Cf. Porphyrios: "You are unable to be saved alone, if all others are not also

2:11 and every tongue confess that Jesus Christ is Lord—The bowing of "every knee" is accompanied by the confession of "every tongue" (*pasa glōssa*). While the bowing of the knee might be reluctant, it seems harder to regard the tongue's confession in that light. "No one can say 'Jesus is Lord' except by the Holy Spirit" (1 Cor. 12:3). "If you confess with your mouth that Jesus is Lord and believe in your heart that God raised him from the dead, you will be saved" (Rom. 10:9). Confessing is not a neutral act. It is a gift of the Holy Spirit. For those in the three locations, including those "under the earth," the tenor seems to be promising. All things in heaven and earth will finally be one in acclaiming Christ for who he is (Eph. 1:10).

to the glory of God the Father—Here the trinitarian faith is suggested in outline. The Father is "glorified" when Jesus is confessed, a confession that cannot occur except by the Holy Spirit. For Paul, this same "glory" has raised Jesus from the dead (Rom. 6:4). Unrecognized for a while as "the Lord of glory" (1 Cor. 2:8), the Crucified is raised up for the sake of the world. The glory of Easter Day means that God chooses not to be God without us. It means that God is not glorified in Christ apart from the redemption of the world. It means that through the Son and in the Spirit, God appoints creaturely worship as the end of all things. Confessing Jesus as Lord redounds "to the glory of God the Father" (*eis doxan theou patros*). A later liturgical formula is adumbrated, as the whole creation will pray: "Through Jesus Christ our Lord, who lives and reigns with you and the Holy Spirit, one God, for ever and ever. Amen."

Just as modern liberal theology finds it difficult to regard Jesus as the proper object of worship, so it also hesitates to affirm him as the Lord. In their major works, for example, neither Schleiermacher nor Tillich ascribes the term "Lord" to Jesus. He might be for them the Redeemer. He might be the bearer of the New Being. He might be the vehicle of God-consciousness or of transforming spiritual power. But he is not, for such theologians, the incarnate Son. Therefore he is not properly worshiped, nor is he confessed as the Lord. Ecumenical theology can only appropriate such teachings with a measure of restraint. Modern christological insights need to be assimilated in a context informed by the Nicene faith. Only where Jesus is confessed as Lord, by the power of the Holy Spirit, is the Father glorified for who he is—namely, the delight of all his creatures, the fountain of all goodness, and the source of every blessing. (For further comments on Jesus as Lord, see excursus 3.)

---

saved. It is a mistake for one to pray only for oneself, for one's own salvation. We must pray for the entire world, so that not one is lost. . . . I am not afraid of hell and I do not think about Paradise. I only ask God to have mercy on the entire world and on me as well." Elder Porphyrios, "Counsels," 168.

At Philippi, to confess Jesus as Lord was a subversive act. It represented a break with the allegiances of the surrounding culture. It involved a transvaluation of all values. It meant the subversion of every conventional idea of what it meant to be "in the form of God." The mighty had been cast down from their thrones; dignity had been restored to those of low degree; the rich were sent away empty; the hungry were filled with good things (Luke 1:46–56). The most potent symbol of shame had been transposed into an emblem of glory. The Lord who submitted to death on a cross, only to be vindicated against his enemies, and even on their behalf, had been invested with the name above every name. Those who lived by the power of that name, and who confessed him as Lord, could not, in turn, confess Caesar as Lord. Nor could they expect to avoid all suffering for their allegiance to Christ. But they cherished a hope that neither their worship nor their witness would be in vain.

The final section of the hymn (2:9–11) may be glossed as follows:

> **Therefore** [for this reason, i.e., on account of his faithful obedience in love] **God** [the Father] **has highly exalted him** [the incarnate, crucified Son] **and bestowed on him the name that is above every name** [the ineffable divine name], **so that at the name of Jesus** [now equal to the ineffable name] **every knee should bow** [in a supreme act of worship], **in heaven and on earth and under the earth** [in a way that is universal in scope], **and every tongue confess** [by the power of the Holy Spirit] **that Jesus Christ is Lord** [one of the earliest Christian confessions],[88] **to the glory of God the Father** [because the Father is not glorified without the Son, nor is the Son glorified without the Father].

Throughout the Philippians hymn, Paul has only one term for the figure who undergoes such drastic transitions as "self-emptying," "obedience to the point of death," and being "highly exalted" so as to receive "the name above every name." That single term is "Christ Jesus." Later tradition introduces other terms, not yet available to Paul, like "the eternal Son," "the incarnate Son," and "the exalted Son." Without some such distinctions it is difficult to read the hymn rightly. Remarkably, in 2:10 the wording shifts away from "Christ Jesus" to "the name of Jesus." In light of later terminology, this is a shift away from the "eternal Son" (2:5–7) and the "incarnate Son" (2:8–9) to the Son under the particular aspect of his "assumed humanity" (2:10–11).

It is not the incarnate Son but the preincarnate, eternal Son who empties himself. When he takes the form of a slave and is found in human form, through

88. See Harris, *Slave of Christ*, 87–90.

an act of self-abnegation, the eternal Son has already assumed Jesus's human nature into hypostatic union with himself ("being born in the likeness of human beings"). The puzzle of how the eternal Son can later be exalted and receive the name above every name, if he has never renounced his deity (being in the form of God and being equal with God), can be explained on these terms.

By becoming incarnate, the eternal Son relinquishes the manifestation of his divine glory as well as the normal use of his divine prerogatives, yet without ceasing to be God. He appears *in extremis* under the form of his opposite. He does this not only in loving obedience to God the Father but also in collaboration with him. The Son's gift of himself to God, for the good of all others ("in heaven and on earth and under the earth"), is met by the Father's gift of love in return. The crucified Son is vindicated and acclaimed. His exaltation (through resurrection and ascension) to a pinnacle than which no greater can be conceived reveals that divinity is conferred on Jesus.[89]

Without losing his true human nature, Jesus is one with the eternal Son—by virtue of the hypostatic union. It is in and as Jesus that the Son is not only obedient to the point of death but also "highly exalted" by the Father. The human Jesus is acknowledged as the Lord of glory—even as the eternal Son is, and had always been, the Lord of glory. Jesus is revealed as the proper object of worship. He is invested with divine status—not by losing his human nature but by virtue of his ineffable union with the eternal Son.[90]

In conclusion, that is how I suggest the Philippians hymn appears from the standpoint of ecclesial hermeneutics. No claim is made that it was evident in this form to either Paul or his original readers. It required theological reflection, taking shape over a long period, and culminating in the ecumenical councils of the undivided church—especially Nicaea, Constantinople, Ephesus, and Chalcedon—under the guidance of the Holy Spirit. Ecclesial hermeneutics intends to make explicit what is implicit in the apostolic witness to Christ. It is shaped by authoritative readers, including ancient church fathers and bishops. It is a reading that attempts to go beyond, but not against, what the hymn would have meant in its

89. Again, to be clear, for the Nicene faith, the human nature of Jesus has no mode of existence (*anhypostasis*) apart from his union with the *hypostasis* of the eternal Son. His human nature exists in and only in his union with the second *hypostasis* of the Trinity (*enhypostasis*).

90. Martin Hengel has emphasized, as a point of history, how little time elapsed between the death of Jesus and the flowering of ecclesial devotion to him—including his corporate worship as Lord—by followers who were initially Jews. "One is tempted to say," he remarks, "that more happened [christologically] in this period of less than two decades [ca. 30–50 CE] than in the whole of the next seven centuries." Hengel, *Son of God*, 2.

original setting. It depends on making use of a complex exegetical/hermeneutical feedback loop. It proceeds from a center in Christ, reading backwards from the new to the old as well as from tradition as informed by scripture to scripture as illuminated by tradition. It reads biblical types in light of Christ as the antitype. Many enigmatic words in Phil. 2:6–11 need to be deciphered before such a reading can be offered in accord with scripture as interpreted by the Nicene faith.

> **12**So then, my beloved, as you have always obeyed, so now, not only as in my presence but much more in my absence, work out your own salvation with fear and trembling, **13**for it is God who works in you, both to will and to work for his good pleasure.

At least three background beliefs are needed to understand these verses: (1) salvation has three tenses; (2) two (or more) acting subjects are involved, but there is only one Saving Agent; (3) quantitative modes of thought are not fitting, or more precisely, they represent a category mistake.[91]

Paul writes here about the present tense of salvation. Its past and future tenses are presupposed but not explicated. In its future tense God will be all in all. What is already real in Christ will be revealed and actualized in glory. In its past tense—or, perhaps better, its perfect tense—salvation is a finished and perfect work. It has been accomplished once and for all. It has been realized apart from us in Christ and by Christ (*extra nos*). It is identical with him in the unity of his person and work, for—and this is crucial—his person is in his work and his work is in his person. The key result is that Christ himself just *is* our salvation. As Luther never tired of insisting, Christ is our righteousness and our life. He is our righteousness, sanctification, wisdom, and redemption (1 Cor. 1:30).[92] He himself is the reality and content of salvation, not only its external source. The faithful are called not to seek anything in Christ other than Christ himself.[93]

---

91. What follows is a basic template constructed from a theological point of view as informed largely by the Reformation. The eschatology of salvation in Christ, as Paul understood it, is subject to more variations and complications than can be considered here. For further discussion see Tappenden, *Resurrection in Paul*; Schnelle, *Apostle Paul*, 577–97; Dunn, *Theology of Paul the Apostle*, 461–98.

92. This verse, 1 Cor. 1:30, was arguably more seminal for the outbreak of the Reformation than even Rom. 1:17.

93. I am thinking of the idea of the "perfect tense" as found in Koine Greek, which indicates a past and completed action with ongoing effects into the present—something like a timed-release capsule. As Barth remarks on the Latin phrase *Deus dixit*, "I have chosen the Latin *Deus dixit* not least because of the Latin perfect tense (*dixit*), which expresses something that the translations do not. To be sure, we have here a remarkable and unique perfect. What is denoted is an eternal perfect. But in the first instance it takes the form of the usual perfect, and the meaning cannot be separated from this form. . . .

Salvation in the present tense mediates between its past and its future. On the one hand, its present form is secondary and derivative; on the other, it is anticipatory and provisional. What is already real in Christ (Col. 3:3)[94] needs to be actualized in the lives of the faithful. This occurrence does not mean adding new content to a salvation that is somehow less than perfect in itself. It means receiving the gift of salvation for what it is here and now. This reception takes place under three aspects: (1) once for all, (2) again and again, and (3) more and more.

(1) When Christ is acknowledged and received, through Word and Spirit, he preserves the faithful in salvation in a way that cannot be undone. They are united with him, and he with them, irrevocably.[95] Baptism—which is not something to be repeated—is the sacramental form of this present-tense occurrence (*once for all*). "All of us who have been baptized into Christ Jesus have been baptized into his death" (Rom. 6:3 NASB).

(2) Under another aspect, the grace of Christ is offered and received whole and entire, not in a piecemeal fashion.[96] Like manna, it is new each morning. The faithful turn to God with empty hands. They are continually dependent on grace in their ongoing neediness, having daily recourse to prayer. The Eucharist—which is something to be repeated—is the sacramental form by which Christ and his salvation[97] are offered and received on a regular basis (*again and again*).[98] "This is my body which is broken for you. Do this in remembrance of me" (1 Cor. 11:24).

(3) Under a third aspect, the faithful receive salvation over time by degrees.[99] They may expect to grow in knowledge and love.[100] The gift of Christ includes

---

Deus dixit [God has spoken once for all, in a way that continues to speak] indicates a special, once-for-all, contingent event to which these particular writings [in the New Testament], rather than any other possible writings, bear witness." Barth, *Göttingen Dogmatics*, 1:59. The continuation does not add to the original, but it does attest it and mediate it under certain aspects.

94. "For you have died, and your life is hidden with Christ in God" (Col. 3:3).

95. "I give them eternal life, and they will never perish, and no one will snatch them out of my hand" (John 10:28). "He will establish you until the end, so that you may be blameless on the day of our Lord Jesus Christ" (1 Cor. 1:8). "For the gifts and the calling of God are irrevocable" (Rom. 11:29).

96. "God's grace is not divided into bits and pieces, . . . but . . . takes us up completely into God's favor for the sake of Christ." Luther, "Preface," 56. For Luther grace is always an indivisible whole.

97. Or better, Christ in and with his salvation. As T. F. Torrance liked to emphasize, we are saved not by the work of Christ but by the person of Christ in his work.

98. "I am the living bread that came down from heaven. If anyone eats of this bread, he will live forever. And the bread that I will give for the life of the world is my flesh" (John 6:51).

99. "Finally, brothers and sisters, we ask and urge you in the Lord Jesus that, as you learned from us how you ought to live and to please God (as, in fact, you are doing), you should do so more and more" (1 Thess. 4:1 NRSV).

100. What grows is not the grace but its faithful appropriation. Salvation is a complex matter. It is already complete on one level (in Christ) while in process of appropriation on another (in us).

gradual sanctification (*conformatio Christi*). For some traditions, this process involves the sacrament of penance.[101] For others, growth comes more through an ongoing encounter with God's Word in its twofold form as written and preached.[102] This diversity of means (kerygmatic and sacramental) involves various particulars that are not mutually exclusive (*more and more*). "But grow in the grace and knowledge of our Lord and Savior Jesus Christ" (2 Pet. 3:18).

Whether regarded under the aspect of the past, the present, or the future, salvation is effected, as the Reformation recognized, by God alone. It is God who performs the work of salvation—apart from us (*extra nos*), in us (*in nobis*), against us (*contra nos*), and beyond us (*supra nos*). What God has done in Christ in the perfect tense (*extra nos*), and will be revealed universally in the future tense (*supra nos*), requires no "secondary causation" or "auxiliary contribution" from others in the present tense (*in nobis*), not even when they are numbered among the faithful. Only God can save souls from sin, only God can destroy death, and only God can make all things new. This is what has been effected, and continues to be effected, in Christ.

In the present tense, while there is only one Saving Agent, there is more than one acting subject. God operates in the faithful, even as they also "cooperate" with his saving work, but only God, not the faithful, actualizes the grace of salvation. They cooperate with this grace by actively receiving or partaking of it, as well as by attesting and mediating it, but they do nothing to constitute or deserve it or even to make it possible. They are active in appropriating, but not in effecting, this grace. Every act of appropriation is itself a gift. God acts in and through the faithful, even as they act in and through him. But the status of their respective actions is not the same. While the faithful may be subsidiary acting subjects, cooperating with grace under grace, God alone is the Saving Agent by whom grace is made effectual. In the present tense he performs his work of grace in the faithful by moving them through their free consent "in all spiritual wisdom and understanding" (Col. 1:9).

The participation of the faithful in Christ—sacramentally enacted in baptism, renewed in the Eucharist, and grounded in God's Word—is a pure gift. There

---

101. "In the life of the spirit a man is sick on account of sin; thus he needs medicine that he may be restored to health. This grace is bestowed in the sacrament of penance." Thomas Aquinas, *Aquinas Catechism*, 86.

102. "The soul can do without anything except the Word of God, and where the Word of God is missing there is no help at all for the soul." Luther, "Freedom of a Christian," in *Luther's Works*, 31:345. There is a sense in which salvation in Christ is received once for all through faith in the Word of God, as well as again and again, and, in another sense, also more and more.

is no *participatio Christi* without partaking of the salvation that Christ imparts by imparting himself. What is objectively real, hidden, and complete in him (the perfect tense) is fulfilled by being made actual in the faithful in a continual *and* gradual way on another, more "existential" plane (the present tense). At the same time, their appropriation of Christ will always be imperfect until the end. It is a gift to be sought continually with empty hands. "We are more perfectly in Christ than he is in us."[103]

These matters have been historically vexing, and quantitative modes of thought have been the bane of trying to sort them out. Quantitative thinking is ill-suited to grasp the mystery at stake. What is required is a form of spiritual thinking. Salvation in Christ is an indivisible whole. It can assume different aspects, but it cannot be divided into parts. It is not as though one part of it is realized in the perfect tense, another part in the present tense, and the last part eventually in the future tense. It is always an indivisible whole to be received under various aspects.

It is just as whole and entire under the present aspect as it was when accomplished perfectly by Christ in the past and will be when revealed to the world in the future. For the time being, as mentioned, it needs to be seen as real, hidden, and yet to come. "Jesus Christ is the same, yesterday and today and forever" (Heb. 13:8). Salvation is always a matter of the one Jesus Christ in three temporal forms. These forms—"yesterday and today and forever"—are coinherent, so that they participate in one another even as they dynamically (and variously) anticipate, reiterate, and fulfill one another. These three aspects of salvation can no more be conceived in quantitative terms than can the three *hypostases* of the Holy Trinity.

There is no division of labor in the present tense between Christ and the faithful. Christ shares his unique work of salvation with no other (*solo Christo*). There is no "inferior" cause, whether great or small, from elsewhere. Causal thinking, whether overt or subtle, which divides the work of salvation between Christ and another, is a form of "quantitative" thinking that is not suited to grasping this mystery. "For by grace you have been saved through faith. And this is not your own doing; it is the gift of God, not a result of works, so that no one may boast. For we are his workmanship, created in Christ Jesus for good works, which God prepared beforehand, that we should walk in them" (Eph. 2:8–10). Good works are the consequence, not the cause, of this salvation.[104]

---

103. Peter Martyr Vermigli, *Defensio doctrinae veteris et apostolicae de sacrosancto Eucharistia . . . adversus Stephani Gardineri*, #752 (1559), quoted in McLelland, *Visible Words of God*, 148.

104. Every clause in these verses (which arguably summarize the argument of Romans and Galatians) is important. Individually and together, they serve to underscore the sole efficacy of grace in

2:12 So then, my beloved—With these words (*hōste agapētoi mou*) Paul returns to his concern that divisiveness be uprooted from the community. Obedience (*hypakoē*) is the theme that links the hymn just finished to the exhortation now resumed.[105] The Philippians are not merely Paul's "converts." They are his "beloved friends" (*agapētoi*).[106] He wishes he could visit them, freed from his chains, even as they long to see him too. If he were present in person, perhaps he could help straighten things out. Yet for the time being he has to be absent, with no guarantee that he will ever see them again. He urges them to be as diligent in resolving their quarrels as if he were on hand to help. Alluding to Christ's exemplary obedience, surpassing and grounding their own, he exhorts them to be obedient from the heart just as, he adds in encouragement, they have always been obedient.[107] It is a matter of faithfulness, not to him but to God. It is a matter of being true to the gift of their salvation.

work out your own salvation—The Philippians are urged to work out (*katergazesthe*) a salvation (*sōtēria*) that already belongs to them.[108] They need to call on God's grace and cooperate with it. They need to do what they can from their side—in continual prayer and fasting, as it were—to make this salvation their own. Since they have already received it by grace through faith, it is not something dependent on their obedience. It is rather a matter of receiving anew what has already been given. They need to do what they can to appropriate it concretely here and now. "'Work out your salvation' does not mean that Christians themselves have the task of securing their own eternal welfare, but that they are active in the

---

the occurrence of salvation. Good works do not lead to salvation, but salvation leads to good works; otherwise it is not salvation.

Again: "For *by grace* you *have been* saved through faith. And this is *not* your own doing; it is the *gift* of God, *not* a result of works, so that *no one* may boast. For we are *his workmanship, created* in Christ Jesus for good works, which *God* prepared *beforehand*, that we should walk in them" (Eph. 2:8–10, italics added). Consider Calvin on these verses: "Faith, then, brings us empty to God, that we may be filled with the blessings of Christ. And so Paul adds, 'not of yourselves,' that claiming nothing for themselves, they may acknowledge God *alone* as the author of their salvation.... Works themselves are a part of grace.... We do not *in any way* procure salvation for ourselves but obtain it freely from God.... We are what we are *completely* by the grace of God.... In our own strength we are not able to lead a holy life, but only so far as we are adapted and formed by the hand of God." Calvin, "The Epistle to the Ephesians," in *Calvin's New Testament Commentaries*, 11:144–47 (slightly modified; italics added).

105. "Paul frequently uses *hupakouō* [to obey] to refer to obedience to Christ, the gospel and apostolic teaching." McAuley, *Paul's Covert Use of Scripture*, 178n64.

106. "*Agapētos* [beloved] is a favorite of Paul's ... to introduce earnest appeals to his readers.... The implication may be twofold: 'You are a people especially loved by God, but also by me.'" Hellerman, *Philippians*, 128.

107. "He commends their previous obedience, that he may encourage them the more to persevere." Calvin, "The Epistle to the Philippians," in *Calvin's New Testament Commentaries*, 11:253.

108. "Salvation is not only a gift but also a task to be worked out communally." Reumann, *Philippians*, 411.

appropriation of the salvation which God has accomplished for them."[109] Their salvation in Christ is already whole and entire, while its appropriation takes place over time in ever new forms (again and again) and also by degrees (more and more).

with fear and trembling—The word order, which places this phrase first, is emphatic. It is with "fear and trembling" (*meta phobou kai tromou*) that the faithful are enjoined to work out their salvation. What is Paul commending here, and why? Is he thinking about reverence toward God (the vertical), respect toward others (the horizontal), or perhaps both? Moreover, is he thinking about conduct within the community, in the outside world, or again perhaps both?[110]

To take Jesus Christ as a spiritual paradigm has to mean at least two things: not only acting in obedience out of love but also relinquishing self-interest to the point, if need be, of suffering loss. "Fear and trembling" points to a spiritual disposition of holy awe. It is not self-centered but "eccentric."[111] It is focused not on self-interest but on serving God and the community. It is a commitment not to dishonor or disgrace either the one or the other under pressure. The results can at times be costly. "When Christ calls us," wrote Bonhoeffer, "he bids us to come and die."[112]

It seems that "fear and trembling" here mostly means honoring God within the community (2:3–4). Nevertheless, the picture might be expanded to include the context of tensions between citizenship in heaven and citizenship on earth (3:20). In the end, there would be little point in pitting the vertical against the horizontal, or in forcing a choice between the community's internal and external affairs. Appropriating the gift of salvation with "fear and trembling," through reverent obedience to God, with a readiness for hardship and loss, and with forbearance toward one another in love, would cover every base.

2:13 for it is God who works in you—Paul views God and the faithful as subjects of a single operation. He articulates the paradox of grace. Jonathan Edwards describes this paradox well: "We are not merely passive in it, nor yet does God do some and we do the rest, but God does all and we do all. God produces all and we act all. For that is what he produces, our own acts. . . . We are in different

---

109. Gundry Volf, *Paul and Perseverance*, 269n47 (slightly modified).

110. "Not of tormenting misgiving, but of profound reverence and wakeful conscience." Moule, *Philippians*, 72.

111. "True piety dreads to offend God more than to die." Calvin, *Instruction in Faith*, 22 (slightly modified). "Even if there were no hell, the pious mind would still shudder at offending him alone." Calvin, *Institutes* 1.2.2 (trans. Battles, slightly modified), 45.

112. Bonhoeffer, *Cost of Discipleship*, 99 (slightly modified). Further to this: "Thus the call to follow Christ always means a call to share the work of forgiving others their sins. Forgiveness is the Christlike suffering which it is the Christian's duty to share" (100, slightly modified). "If we refuse to take up our cross and submit to suffering and rejection at the hands of others, we forfeit our fellowship with Christ and have ceased to follow him" (101, slightly modified).

respects wholly passive and wholly active."[113] The two factors—God's sovereignty and human responsibility—are allowed to coexist in unresolved tension.[114] They operate ineffably together.[115] Neither human obedience in love nor a readiness to suffer hardship for the gospel would be possible without the priority of grace. Only the will moved by grace is free to appropriate the gift of salvation with the necessary fear and trembling.[116]

The human will, as moved by grace, is not merely passive. Pointing to this verse, Augustine remarks, "We are acted upon so that we may act, not so that we may do nothing."[117] According to Aquinas, four views are ruled out: (1) that we can be saved by our own free will apart from the operation of grace (Pelagianism), (2) that free will plays no part but is merely manipulated by grace (determinism), (3) that grace merely prepares human freedom to act in its own strength (semi-Pelagianism), and (4) that grace accomplishes the good in us according to our merits rather than according to God's good pleasure (works righteousness).[118] What is free will if not completely a gift of grace at every point?

Grace operates in and through the faithful, even as they operate in and through grace. Yet the faithful, working by faith through love, remain earthen vessels to show that the transcendent power belongs to God and not to them (2 Cor. 4:7). Augustine explains, "The grace of God, which both begins a person's faith and which enables it to persevere until the end, is not given according to our merits, but is given according to his own most secret and at the same time most righteous, wise, and beneficent will. . . . We therefore will, but God works in us to will also. We therefore work, but God works in us to work also for his good pleasure."[119]

---

113. Edwards, "Efficacious Grace, Book III," in *Works of Jonathan Edwards*, 21:251. "I sought the Lord, and afterward I knew / He moved my soul to seek him, seeking me; / It was not I that found, O Savior true; / No, I was found of thee." Anonymous hymn (1878).

114. "God's work and the believer's efforts are coextensive, thereby excluding, as non-Pauline, any kind of synergism whereby some 'division of labor' might come into play between God and the Philippians." Hellerman, *Philippians*, 132. "For there is only one form of free will, and that is obedience to the leading of the Spirit." Martyn, *Theological Issues*, 264n28.

115. God effectually calls the faithful "by renewing their wills." He draws them to Jesus Christ in such a way that they come most freely, "being made willing by his grace." Westminster Confession of Faith (1646), chap. 10, "Of Effectual Calling," in *Book of Confessions*, 226.

116. "Here one of the deepest mysteries of grace is touched upon. On the one hand is the will of the Christian—real, personal, and in full exercise. . . . On the other hand, beneath it, as cause beneath result . . . is seen God's working, God 'effecting.' A true theology will recognize with equal reverence . . . both these great parallels of truth." Moule, *Philippians*, 73 (slightly modified).

117. Augustine, "On Rebuke and Grace" 4 (*NPNF*[1] 5:473, slightly modified).

118. Thomas Aquinas, *Commentary*, 87–88.

119. Augustine, "On the Gift of Perseverance" 33 (*NPNF*[1] 5:538, slightly modified). "God works in us all our good works," wrote Francis Turretin, "as far as they have any goodness in them." Turretin, *Institutes of Elenctic Theology*, 2:709.

Quantitative modes of thought (*partim/partim*) are ruled out because they are incapable of grasping this mystery. The same holds true for schemes that would posit the operation of two separate "causes" (*superior/inferior*).[120] Grace and freedom work mysteriously as one, in accord with the Chalcedonian pattern: without separation or division, without confusion or change, and with absolute priority and precedence belonging to grace (*totus/totus*). It is a pattern of inseparable unity, abiding distinction, and asymmetrical order. Free will is never free except in total dependence on grace.[121]

both to will and to work for his good pleasure—"To will" (*to thelein*) means that God's grace is prevenient; "to work" (*to energein*), that his cooperation is effectual;[122] and "for his good pleasure" (*hyper tēs eudokias*), that his purposes are gracious.[123] Grace is, in short, prevenient, effectual, and beneficent. Marvin Vincent sees this beneficence as finding fulfillment in the final salvation of the faithful,[124] while J. B. Lightfoot goes so far as to associate it with God's desire that all human beings should be saved (1 Tim. 2:4).[125] In any case grace operates in the hearts of the faithful (*en hymin*) in such a way that they appropriate God's effectual willing and working in and with their own receptive willing and working.[126] Grace, as Paul sees it, enables them not only to overcome all rivalry and conceit among themselves but also to withstand any persecution from the outside world. It frees them for love and obedience in times of adversity, even as Christ was loving and obedient in adversity, not only for their sakes but also for the sake of the world.

[14]Do all things without grumbling and questioning, [15]that you may be blameless and innocent, children of God without blemish in the midst of a crooked and twisted generation, among whom you shine as lights in the world, [16]holding fast to the word of life, so that in the day of Christ I may be proud that I did not run in vain or labor in vain. [17]Even if I am to be poured out as a drink offering upon the sacrificial offering of your faith, I am glad and rejoice with you all. [18]Likewise you also should be glad and rejoice with me.

120. Human freedom might be regarded as an "instrumental cause" as long as no "efficient causality" is ascribed to it, whether openly or secretly.
121. "Make me a captive, Lord, and then I shall be free." Matheson, *Sacred Songs*, 1890.
122. The verb "to work" connotes the idea of "effectual working." Vincent, *Philippians*, 66.
123. Lightfoot, *Philippians*, 114.
124. Vincent, *Philippians*, 66.
125. Lightfoot, *Philippians*, 114.
126. Vincent, *Philippians*, 66.

2:14 without grumbling and questioning—Paul continues his steep descent from the lofty heights (the great Christ hymn), to the craggy foothills (free will grounded in absolute dependence), on down to the rocky plains (murmuring among the faithful). Did not Christ empty himself to the point of death before being exalted by God? This same God, benevolent and mysterious, is now at work in believing hearts, liberating them from the powers of sin and death. The faithful, however, are in danger of lapsing into "grumbling and questioning" like the children of Israel wandering through the desert for forty years.

"Grumbling and questioning" (*gongysmōn kai dialogismōn*) seems very far from the "fear and trembling" that Paul has just commended. Fear and trembling presupposes an act of gratitude toward God and a desire to submit to him obediently in love. Grumbling and questioning, on the other hand, or "murmuring and disputing," or "complaining and arguing," represents a different spirit altogether. Paul wants the Philippians to keep their focus on the Lord. Embarking on a path of fear and trembling is like stepping out onto the waves, as Peter did from the boat at the bidding of Jesus (Matt. 14:28–31). When the disciple took his eyes off the Lord, gazing at his peril over the gloomy deep, he began to sink. When the Philippians, in turn, take their eyes off the Lord, dwelling on their hardships, they are in danger of sinking down into grumbling and questioning. Although Lightfoot may be correct that "murmuring or grumbling" is a moral failure while "arguing or questioning" is an intellectual one, the basic problem would seem to be neither moral nor intellectual but spiritual.[127]

2:15 blameless and innocent, children of God without blemish—Imagery from the sacrificial cultus is now joined with imagery from the covenant. Being "blameless and innocent" (*amemptoi kai akeraioi*) and also "without blemish" (*amōma*) evokes a cultic milieu, while being "children of God" (*tekna theou*) suggests a covenantal status as grounded in election.

The imperative—"do all things" (*panta poiete*, 2:14)—is explicit, while its premise remains hidden or presupposed. Nevertheless, only one is blameless and innocent, and only one is truly without blemish: the Lamb of God who takes away the sin of the world (John 1:29). Sacrificial practices like Passover and Yom Kippur come to their fulfillment in him (1 Cor. 5:7). Only in Christ can the faithful be blameless and innocent without blemish. The apostle calls them, once again, to put their identity into practice by becoming who they are in Christ.

127. Lightfoot, *Philippians*, 115.

Much the same applies to the exhortation that they are to behave as "children of God"—something they already are. They cannot fulfill their identity as God's children if they fail to work out their salvation with fear and trembling. They cannot live in accord with their calling while bogged down in strife and contentiousness. Only Christ is God's Son by nature, but they are God's children by grace (Rom. 8:15). They are called to be steadfast for him, as he has been steadfast for them. They are called to devote themselves from the heart, as he has done, to living out their lives in obedience and love.

in the midst of a crooked and twisted generation—The faithful are set apart from the world—one of the chief biblical marks of holiness—for the sake of obedience to Christ. They are not to be conformed to this world, but to be transformed by the renewing of their minds (Rom. 12:2). Unjust and immoral wars, economic exploitation, racial oppression, the subjugation and demeaning of women, the trafficking of children, their stomach-churning sexual abuse by clergy, the normalizing of abortion, the persecution of the Jews, the worshiping of the nation, the institutionalizing of greed, the condoning of torture, the despoliation of the earth, and much more would be indications today of "a crooked and twisted generation" (*geneas skolias kai diestrammenēs*). The faithful, whether then or now, have no need to "believe" in original sin. They will have seen it with their own eyes by living "in its midst" (*meson*). They are faced, every day, with an existential choice. Again, peace with Christ means conflict with the world, and peace with the world means conflict with Christ. A crooked and twisted church—condoning the world's corruptions, or even repeating them—will have nothing to offer a crooked and twisted generation.[128]

among whom you shine as lights in the world—The faithful are expected to stand for a different way of life. They are expected to order their affairs—both within and without—by a new calculus of generosity and freedom. They are to

---

128. Let judgment begin "with the household of God" (1 Pet. 4:17). Note that Gerald Hawthorne's association of the phrase "wicked and crooked generation" with Judaism is reprehensible. Hawthorne, *Philippians*, 102. Relevant here also would be Gandhi's "Seven Social Sins":

Wealth without work.
Pleasure without conscience.
Knowledge without character.
Commerce without morality.
Science without humanity.
Worship without sacrifice.
Politics without principle.

See Woolever, *Gandhi's List of Social Sins*. The list was first published in Gandhi's weekly newspaper *Young India* (October 22, 1925).

shine as "lights in the world" (*hōs phōstēres en kosmō*).[129] They are to break with crooked and twisted ways, including, as suggested, a vast array of social disorders and immoral practices. They are expected to let their lights shine in the world. And they are to do so as a countercultural community—evangelical, eucharistic, and humane—not just as isolated individuals.[130]

In principle, according to Paul, they already do so. In principle (and sometimes in fact) the light of Christ cannot help but shine through them. Are they not already partakers of him who is "the light of the world" (John 8:12)? Have they not been grafted into Israel, God's everlasting people (Rom. 11:17), established as a "light to the nations" (Isa. 49:6)? By sharing in the grace of this radiance— engrafted into Christ and Israel—how can they fail to be radiant in their own way, becoming "the light of the world" (Matt. 5:14), as Jesus has named them? Despite individual and social failings, they will shine forth—because of Christ and the gospel—as lights in the world.[131]

2:16 holding fast to the word of life—The light of the world, Jesus Christ, is also in himself the word of life. The faithful, through whom his light is destined to shine, know themselves as upheld by a life force not their own. The apostle urges them to "hold fast" (*epechontes*) to that power—namely, to the living Christ as present to them in his word (*logon zōēs*).[132]

In the midst of a wicked generation, to whom else can they turn? Jesus not only has the words of eternal life (John 6:68); he is also eternal life in himself (John 11:25). "The free gift of God," Paul would write, "is eternal life in Christ Jesus our Lord" (Rom. 6:23). The word proclaimed to them, and which they in turn proclaim to the world, is the word of life. Through it Christ's life-giving power is spread abroad. By it the faithful are corrected and sustained. Apart from it they can do nothing. With it they can lead lives worthy of the gospel (Phil. 1:27), even though besieged on all sides. To be faithful in a difficult world, everything depends on holding fast to the word of life.[133]

---

129. "The most basic New Testament incentive to holy living is an emphasis on what we already are." Silva, *Philippians*, 127.

130. Once again the "you" in this passage is plural.

131. "Paul's point . . . is clear: the Philippians shine among their pagan neighbors [as] stars shine in the sky." Hellerman, *Philippians*, 136. They will do so in their better selves by grace despite their lesser selves. The line from Luther's "A Mighty Fortress" comes to mind: "*Das Wort sie sollen lassen stahn / Und kein'n Dank dazu haben*" (That Word above all earthly powers, / No thanks to them, abideth).

132. The "word of life" is not only "a word which has life in itself" but also a word "which leads to life." Vincent, *Philippians*, 69. Both aspects are centered in Christ.

133. From the context, I presume that "holding fast" means "steadfastness in faith," not merely proclamation. See Reumann, *Philippians*, 394. Cf. O'Brien, *Philippians*, 297: "standing firm in the faith against the attacks of external opponents."

the day of Christ—The day of Christ (*hēmeran christou*) is an apocalyptic idea pointing to the judgment of grace. It means the inbreaking of "the end of all things" (*pantōn to telos*) (1 Pet. 4:7). It will come like a thief in the night. It will leave nothing unscathed. What is true about every life will be unveiled—to consternation or welcome surprise. On that day Christ the Center will be made known—in judgment and grace—for who he is.

proud that I did not run in vain or labor in vain—The metaphor "run in vain" (*eis kenon edramon*) is an athletic one, while "labor in vain" (*eis kenon ekopiasa*) is more work related, but they both tend toward a grand finale that is juridical. The apostle contemplates what verdict might befall him on the last day.[134] "For we must all appear before the judgment seat of Christ, so that each one may receive what is due for what he has done in the body" (2 Cor. 5:10). He appeals to his beloved Philippians—beleaguered as he knows they are—in hope. He views their destiny as intertwined with his own. He believes that if they stand firm to the end, they will be revealed as gold, silver, and precious stones. "Now if anyone builds on the foundation with gold, silver, precious stones, wood, hay, straw—each one's work will become manifest, for the Day will disclose it, because it will be revealed by fire" (1 Cor. 3:12–13).

The apostle's ministry will also be tested in judgment as through fire. If what he has built on Christ survives, he will meet with a fitting reward. If his work is burned up like straw, he will suffer loss, though he himself will be saved (1 Cor. 3:14–15). He hopes to be able to "boast" (*kauchēma*) in the Philippians—"boast" in the good sense of being justifiably proud. Just as he regards them as bound up with his destiny, so he wants them to see their destiny as bound up with his. Not only their love for Christ but also their devotion to the apostle should give them an incentive to persevere in repentance and faithfulness until the end.

2:17 poured out as a drink offering—At this point the metaphors are piling up quickly and getting increasingly mixed. In rapid succession they have evoked spheres as diverse as athletics and hard labor before moving on to cultic sacrifice. Having just depicted himself as a runner and a worker, the apostle unexpectedly portrays himself as a libation.[135] It is, in effect, a shift from the active to the passive voice.

---

134. "*Hēmeran christou* marks the day of 'final judgment,' when Paul must stand before the tribunal of Christ (2 Cor. 5:10), not to discover his eternal destiny but to give an account of his stewardship to his Lord (1 Cor. 4:1–5). . . . Paul anticipated a final eschatological testing of all mission work (1 Cor. 3:10–15)." Hellerman, *Philippians*, 138, 139.

135. "In the ancient world sacrifices, both pagan and Jewish, were usually accompanied and completed by a libation." Hawthorne, *Philippians*, 105.

In this metaphor the Philippians are the acting subjects in relation to whom Paul assumes the role of a passive object.[136] Their active faith (*tēs pisteōs hymōn*)—their total positive relationship to Christ—is portrayed as their "sacrificial offering" (*tē thysia kai leitourgia*). Paul will, potentially, serve as a libation "poured out" (*spendomai*) to ratify their offering.[137]

Whether the cultic background here is Jewish or pagan doesn't greatly matter, though the many non-Jews in the congregation could easily have read this language through a pagan lens. Paul's rhetorical intention is for them to imagine themselves as leading lives of sacrificial faithfulness. Their loyalty to Christ, costly though it may be, will be received by God as a liturgical offering. Moreover, should Paul be tried and executed, their "offering" will be ratified by his death (the "libation"). At the same time his ministry will also be validated. Paul is encouraging them to remain constant even if he is martyred. His death will be a "drink offering" poured out on their behalf. In turn their sacrificial lives will bring honor to his martyrdom. Paul is encouraging them not to lose heart.

I am glad and rejoice with you all—Despite not hiding a sober realism about his possible martyrdom, Paul does not give it the last word. Because Christ is risen, there can be no sorrow unmitigated by gladness, no martyrdom untempered by joy. The shadow of the cross is cast by the light of resurrection hope. It is a hope known to all the faithful ("you all," *pasin hymin*).[138] Paul can share joy and gladness with them because the new eon has been inaugurated in Christ.[139] *Media mortis in vita sumus*—in the midst of death we are in life. The traditional *media vita in morte sumus* has it exactly backwards.

> **19**I hope in the Lord Jesus to send Timothy to you soon, so that I too may be cheered by news of you. **20**For I have no one like him, who will be genuinely concerned for your welfare. **21**For they all seek their own interests, not those of Jesus Christ. **22**But you know Timothy's proven worth, how as a son with a father he has served with me in the gospel. **23**I hope therefore to send him just as soon as I see how it will go with me, **24**and I trust in the Lord that shortly I myself will come also.

136. "The Philippians offer the main sacrifice. Paul's death would add but a modest drink offering to their *thusia* [sacrifice]." Hellerman, *Philippians*, 142.

137. It seems clear that Paul is alluding to his death. "The verb's cultic associations made it suitable for use with reference to martyrdom." Silva, *Philippians*, 128.

138. "His willing death for Christ, viewed as a last contribution to their spiritual good, a last aid in their life of believing self-consecration, would be a personal joy to him, and an occasion of joy with them." Moule, *Philippians*, 76.

139. "Nowhere else in his letters does Paul so pointedly emphasize joy in the midst of suffering for the gospel." Hellerman, *Philippians*, 143.

2:19 **I hope in the Lord Jesus to send Timothy**[140]—Paul turns from perseverance and possible martyrdom to happier themes of fellowship and friendship. Timothy, his coworker (1:1), has been commissioned to be his ambassador. Paul will send him to the Philippians, hoping that he will come back with good news. If the Philippians wish to lift Paul's spirits, as he hopes to do for them, they will remedy the rifts in their community. Paul wants to inspire them, from his end, by "practicing resurrection"[141]—with his unflagging spirit of hope[142]—while they could cheer him (*kagō eupsychō*) by "practicing reconciliation."

2:20 **For I have no one like him**—Paul was not always an easy person for people to like, whether in his day or ours. His early troubles with Barnabas display one side of his personality, while his closeness to Timothy shows another. A charitable view would be that his virtues outweighed his flaws. What he ascribes to Timothy would apply to himself as well. Like Timothy, he is greatly concerned for the welfare of others (*gnēsiōs ta peri hymōn merimnēsei*), especially those in the household of faith (Gal. 6:10). Like Timothy, he seeks not his own interests but (as he states in Phil. 2:21) those of Christ Jesus (*heautōn zētousin / ta Christou Iēsou*). When it comes to loyalty toward Christ—at remarkable cost to himself (2 Cor. 11:24–27)—it would be hard to find anyone who surpasses him. Paul's friendship with Timothy speaks well of the younger man. Paul is known by the people who walk beside him. In sending Timothy to the Philippians, he is sending his very best.

2:21 **For they all seek their own interests**[143]—Timothy stands out because there are so few like him. The apostle apparently has reason to be disappointed in others. The details behind his allusion to "those who seek their own interests" (*hoi pantes gar ta heautōn zētousin*)[144] remain obscure.[145] His comment suggests, however, that self-seeking is not absent in the community at Rome. "St. Paul

140. "In the Lord Jesus" (*en kyriō Iēsou*) is not just a pious phrase. All Paul's hopes and plans are subject to his faith in the lordship of Christ.

141. "As soon as the generals and the politicos / can predict the motions of your mind, / lose it. Leave it as a sign / to mark the false trail, the way / you didn't go. . . . / Practice resurrection." Wendell Berry, "Manifesto: The Mad Farmer Liberation Front," in *Country of Marriage*, 17.

142. "The proof that God raised Jesus from the dead is not only the empty tomb, but the full hearts of his transformed disciples. The crowning evidence that he lives is not a vacant grave, but a spirit-filled fellowship. Not a rolled-away stone, but a carried-away church." Jordan, *Substance of Faith*, 26 (slightly modified).

143. "Clearly he cannot mean this in an absolute sense. . . . Paul uses a measure of hyperbole here." Silva, *Philippians*, 140.

144. "These persons . . . were so warm in pursuing their own interests that they were cold in the work of the Lord." Calvin, *Philippians*, in *Calvin's New Testament Commentaries*, 11:261.

145. Paul may be thinking of those mentioned in Phil. 1:15 and 17.

must have suffered grave disappointments where he had a special right to expect ready help."[146]

2:22 But you know Timothy's proven worth—Timothy is no stranger to the Philippians. They know at first hand how able he could be.[147] They know what a sacrifice it will be for Paul to send him, and what a blessing it will be to receive him.

as a son with a father—Timothy has succeeded where John Mark had failed (Acts 15:36–38). He has proven himself ready to undergo hardships for the progress of the gospel. Mentored by the apostle, Timothy has gone on to make him proud. A bond, as between a father and a son, has grown up between them.

served with me in the gospel—The verb "served" connotes serving as a slave (*edouleusen*). Paul and Timothy are "slaves of Christ" (1:1)—just as Christ became a "slave" for others (2:7). Being conformed to him in this service, they live out the "downward mobility" of the gospel.

2:23 just as soon as I see how it will go with me—Paul writes from a situation of uncertainty. Languishing in chains, he does not know his fate, whether it will be execution or freedom. Timothy will not be sent until the matter is settled.

2:24 that shortly I myself will come also—As the letter unfolds, Paul appears to vacillate about whether he expects to live or die. At this point he seems relatively optimistic—stating that he will come to them "shortly" (*taxeōs*)—whereas elsewhere he sounds a more doubtful note (1:20–23; 2:17). Perhaps the letter was not written all in one sitting, but dictated in fits and starts, with intervals in between. If so, minor glitches like this one might be explained as well as larger anomalies that will appear later. In any case, Paul wants the Philippians to know that his decision to send Timothy does not mean that he has abandoned hope of coming himself.[148]

> [25]I have thought it necessary to send to you Epaphroditus my brother and fellow worker and fellow soldier, and your messenger and minister to my need, [26]for he has been longing for you all and has been distressed because you heard that he was ill. [27]Indeed he was ill, near to death. But God had mercy on him, and not only on him but on me also, lest I should have sorrow upon sorrow. [28]I am the more eager to send him, therefore, that you may rejoice at seeing him again, and that I may be less anxious. [29]So receive him in the Lord with all joy,

146. Moule, *Philippians*, 78.
147. Timothy had apparently worked for the gospel in Philippi, either when the church was first planted or else during a later visit. Hellerman, *Philippians*, 146.
148. "It needs no very subtle psychology to see the possibility of the presence, in the same person, of certainties and uncertainties about the same event." Moule, *Philippians*, 79.

and honor such men, **30**for he nearly died for the work of Christ, risking his life to complete what was lacking in your service to me.

2:25 necessary to send to you Epaphroditus[149]—Since Epaphroditus would apparently be dispatched first and Timothy only later, we might wonder why Paul chooses to mention them in reverse order. Perhaps he reckoned that because the Philippians are especially anxious to hear about their emissary, mentioning him first might have detracted from the matter of Timothy and Paul himself, rendering news of their projected visits anticlimactic. Paul has postponed this point of high interest until last.[150]

my brother and fellow worker—Paul could be warm in his affections just as he could be severe in his rebukes. Epaphroditus is praised highly.[151] He is described in glowing terms as Paul's brother, fellow worker, and fellow soldier.[152] He has not only supported the apostle but has ministered to him when others dropped away. He has honored the Philippians not only as their messenger[153] but also as Paul's companion in need.[154]

2:26 for he has been longing for you all—Paul displays pastoral sensitivity toward Epaphroditus.[155] He explains to the Philippians that their emissary was worried about their reaction when they found out about his illness. Worried about his friends, Epaphroditus longs to go home.

2:27 Indeed he was ill, near to death—There was good reason for the Philippians to be concerned. Epaphroditus had nearly died of a fatal illness.[156] We are

149. "I deemed it necessary" (*Anankaion de hēgēsamēn*). "If this is the epistolary aorist, as is probable, it points to Epaphroditus as the bearer of the letter." Vincent, *Philippians*, 75.

150. Or perhaps it is the other way around. "The Philippians did not expect to see Epaphroditus so soon—they wanted Timothy." Silva, *Philippians*, 141. Everything here can only remain speculative, but perhaps the most natural line of interpretation would be to suppose that Epaphroditus's near-fatal illness had aroused a desire in both him and his Philippian friends for a timely reunion.

151. "The commendation of Epaphroditus . . . should be taken at face value." Hellerman, *Philippians*, 161.

152. "The three words are arranged in an ascending scale: common sympathy, common work, common danger in toil and suffering." Lightfoot, *Philippians*, 121.

153. "Epaphroditus was the bearer of the contributions from Philippi (4:18) which just below are designated as 'service' (v. 30)." Lightfoot, *Philippians*, 121. Epaphroditus had been sent by the Philippians to deliver material aid to Paul; Paul now sends him back to reassure them and to deliver his letter.

154. Insinuations that relations between Epaphroditus and the Philippians are difficult would seem to be a strained interpretation.

155. It is "very likely," according to Reumann, that Epaphroditus was "patron or head of one of the house churches." Reumann, *Philippians*, 444. Maybe. He is in any case a respected member of the community.

156. He may have fallen ill in the course of his journey from Philippi to Rome. Bruce, *Philippians*, 96. However, while this view is possible, it remains speculative.

not told what it was, or how long it lasted, or by what medical means, if any, it was treated.[157]

But God had mercy on him, and not only on him but on me—We gain another glimpse into Paul's character.[158] He not only teaches that believers are members one of another (Rom. 12:5; 1 Cor. 12:27); he lives it out in practice. Epaphroditus is close to his heart. As long as his companion was afflicted, Paul was afflicted with him.[159] When God had mercy on him,[160] God had mercy on Paul as well. Such is the fellowship of believers, their *koinōnia* in Christ, as Paul knew it.[161]

lest I should have sorrow upon sorrow—The theme of rejoicing would have less credibility if the element of sorrow were suppressed. Paul encourages his readers to rejoice despite every adversity. Living joyfully in Christ does not exclude living with loss. Paul gives thanks to God for his having been spared this particular grief. No suffering supplants the apostle's remarkable resiliency of spirit.

The phrase "sorrow upon sorrow" (*lypēn epi lypēn*) may allude to the death of another coworker. If so, the loss of Epaphroditus would have been a new grief added to a first. "Is this Paul's way of referring," wonders Peter Walker, "to the death of his great travelling companion, the 'beloved doctor' Luke?" Walker continues, "If so, Luke's slightly unsatisfactory ending to the book of Acts would make eminent sense. He did not proceed to give details about Paul's trial (let alone his martyrdom), because he, Luke, *died before Paul*. What he had written, he had written, and no one had the temerity to add to his brilliant work, which was his unique bequest to the church."[162] This suggestion is intriguing, though of course it must again remain speculative.

2:28 that you may rejoice—To give the Philippians reason for rejoicing would lift a burden from their hearts. Paul is eager to send Epaphroditus to them, because he senses they are anxious to see him. The apostle is a person of empathy who weeps with those who weep and rejoices with those who rejoice.

---

157. "This passage, among others (e.g., 2 Tim. 4:10), shows that the mysterious 'gift of healing' used by St. Paul at Melita (Acts 28:8), was not at the *absolute* disposal of even the faith of its recipient." Moule, *Philippians*, 81.

158. "This short paragraph shows Paul to be a man of great tenderness who writes warmly, even glowingly, of his friend and colleague from Philippi." O'Brien, *Philippians*, 329.

159. "Here, as so often in St. Paul, a heart glowing with holy and generous affection expresses itself in a recognition of the importance of his friends to him." Moule, *Philippians*, 81.

160. "Surviving a life-threatening illness was uncommon in antiquity." Hellerman, *Philippians*, 160.

161. "Paul acknowledges that the death of Epaphroditus would have been bitter to him, and he recognizes that God spares him [Paul] in restoring him [Epaphroditus] to health." Calvin, *Philippians*, in *Calvin's New Testament Commentaries*, 11:264.

162. Walker, *In the Steps of Saint Paul*, 192.

2:29 So receive him in the Lord with all joy—The Lord (*kyriō*) remains central to all Paul's thoughts. It is he who delivered Epaphroditus from death, and it is he in whom the joy should be shared. The Lord is indeed the source of "all joy" (*pasēs charas*). There is no comfort like his in life and in death.

As Markus Bockmuehl remarks, "By saying that it is people like Epaphroditus whom the Philippians should 'hold in honor' (*entimous*), Paul at once contradicts Graeco-Roman society's pervasive culture of rewarding the upwardly mobile quest for prestige and public recognition (*philotima*). The church instead will prize and value those who aspire to 'the mind of Christ' (Phil. 2:6–11)."[163]

2:30 risking his life—Paul does not ask more from his coworkers than he is prepared to ask of himself. Since he expects everything of himself, he asks nothing less from them. Working in service to Christ means risking one's life on a daily basis (1 Cor. 15:30). Epaphroditus came close to paying the ultimate price. The risks he had taken were described under the rubric of "completing what was lacking" (*anaplērōsē to . . . hysterēma*)—a Pauline metaphor that appears elsewhere in another context (Col. 1:24). In neither case, it seems, is it meant to be taken in a merely quantitative way.

Paul's own sufferings no more compensate for a quantitative "insufficiency" (*ta hysterēmata*) in the sufferings of Christ (Col. 1:24) than the risks undertaken by Epaphroditus compensate for an "insufficiency" on the part of the Philippians. It would be a mistake to suppose that Paul believes Epaphroditus fills up something "lacking" (*to hysterēma*) in that sense.

As with Paul so also with Epaphroditus, it is a matter of something already established fully in the past in a way that is newly actualized and attested in the present. Just as Christ's sufferings are in a certain sense actualized and attested at second hand in the sufferings of Paul, so also is the service of the Philippians actualized and attested, at one remove, by the devotion of Epaphroditus, nearly to the point of death. The phrase "completing what was lacking" means attesting and renewing at one remove—in a costly way, and as the delegate of another—something already fully established and sufficient in itself. It means fulfilling in the present (*anaplērōsē*) what the other would have done if the other had been present but was not (*to hysterēma*).[164]

---

163. Bockmuehl, *Philippians*, 174.

164. Cf. Col. 1:24. "Completing what is lacking" in Col. 1:24 is implicitly an *applicatio* of the "perfect tense," in which something completed once for all, and therefore in full sufficiency without defect, continues to actualize itself in certain secondary and dependent forms thereafter, without quantitative addition to itself. See note 93 above.

In Col. 1:24 the sufferings of the apostle not only stand in an "indirect correspondence" to the afflictions of Christ, as a witness (so Barth, *Church Dogmatics* IV/2, 601), but also serve to manifest them in a

To conclude, in this section three figures—Paul, Timothy, and Epaphroditus—all emerge as exemplary. A remark by F. F. Bruce will round out our discussion.

Paul did not set out deliberately to present three examples of the same self-renouncing attitude "as that of Christ Jesus" [Phil. 2:5]. But in fact this is what he has done. His own readiness to have his martyrdom credited to the spiritual account of his Philippian friends, Timothy's unselfish service to Paul and genuine concern for other Christians, Epaphroditus's devotion to his mission at great risk to his health and (as it might have been) to his life—all these display the unself-conscious care for others enjoined at the beginning of this chapter and reinforced by the powerful example of Christ's self-emptying.[165]

---

derivative form, as a secondary "re-presentation." Paul's sufferings correspond to the afflictions of Christ on a new and different plane, even as Christ's afflictions, though on a higher plane, are coinherent with his. The afflictions, writes Bauckham, "are not the redemptive sufferings of Christ (for which *thlipsis* is never used), but those subsequent afflictions of the Church through which the new age is being brought to birth. They are 'deficient' so long as the work of suffering witness is incomplete, i.e. until the parousia, but Paul sees himself as playing a large part in making up the deficiency by virtue of his apostolic ministry." Bauckham, "Colossians 1:24 Again," 170. Perhaps we may posit that these "subsequent afflictions" arise primarily in the form of martyrdom and persecution.

The fellowship in suffering occurs because Christ is inseparable from his church (*totus Christus*). The relation of unity-in-distinction is asymmetrical, nonquantitative, and noncompetitive. The perfect aspect of salvation in Christ, through his passion and death, is attested by its imperfect, dependent manifestation in Paul, through his corresponding afflictions. "Fill up" (*antanaplērō*) therefore means "attesting" and "re-presenting" what is already complete in Christ but is still being worked out and manifested on the plane of history, in a secondary and dependent way, under the aspects of witness and mediation. We might say that the perfect is attested and re-presented in the imperfect. "As, therefore, Christ has suffered once in his own person, so he suffers daily in his members, and in this way there are filled up those sufferings which the Father hath appointed for his body by his decree." Calvin, on Col. 1:24, in *Calvin's New Testament Commentaries*, 11:318 (slightly modified).

165. Bruce, *Philippians*, 98.

PHILIPPIANS 3

3:1 Finally, my brothers and sisters, rejoice in the Lord. To write the same things to you is no trouble to me and is safe for you. **2**Look out for the dogs, look out for the workers of evil, look out for those who mutilate the flesh. **3**For we are the circumcision, who worship by the Spirit of God and glory in Christ Jesus and put no confidence in the flesh—**4a**though I myself have reason for confidence in the flesh also.

No reader can fail to be struck by the break in the argument here. Either fragments of originally different letters are being stitched together, or else it is the same letter being resumed again, perhaps after a lapse of time. No conclusive answer has been found. Nevertheless, sufficient unity exists for the letter to be read, in its final canonical form, as a loosely unified whole.[1]

3:1 my brothers and sisters—By addressing his readers as "brothers and sisters," Paul is not resorting to pious rhetoric. These brothers and sisters have forfeited other social bonds. Their new kinship in Christ comes at a cost. For those who have turned to Christ, family ties could be frayed, old religious connections terminated, and former loyalties diminished. With their countercultural profile, Christians were not always welcomed with favor, not least by existing authorities concerned about social cohesion. Suspicion and ostracism could be acute, even if falling short of persecution. Unlike other citizens in Roman-administered Philippi, Christians would not always take part in ceremonies sanctioned by civil religion. As brothers and sisters in Christ, they have embarked on a way of life that relativizes everything else. Their community in Christ is a refuge in an unfriendly world.[2]

---

1. See Childs, *New Testament as Canon*, 335–37.
2. For the difficult social situation in Philippi, see Oakes, *Philippians*, 77–102.

rejoice in the Lord—Rejoicing in the Lord is Paul's default position. It is the first and last thing to be said. Behind it is his personal encounter with the risen Lord (1 Cor. 15:8).[3] Paul does not view Easter as an isolated occurrence. It has been followed by little "resurrections" from that day onward. He can even refer in the present tense to "the God who *raises* the dead" (*epi tō theō tō egeironti tous nekrous*) (2 Cor. 1:9).[4] Deliverances were known to occur in the teeth of dire circumstances. Paul has experienced them more than once at first hand, as when he and his coworkers had "the sentence of death in themselves" (*en heautois to apokrima tou thanatou eschēkamen*) (2 Cor. 1:9). The trials of the Christian life are mitigated by a larger joy. Paul summons his readers to rejoice in the Lord (*en kyriō*), risen from the dead, exalted into heaven, and alive in their midst to comfort and save.

More broadly, we may say that Paul's remarkable ability to rejoice in the midst of affliction is grounded in three core convictions—namely, that God is perfect in love, infinite in wisdom, and supreme in power. For Paul, God's perfect love is revealed in the cross (Rom. 5:8), his great wisdom is beyond all understanding (Rom. 11:33), and his supreme power, as strangely made perfect in weakness (1 Cor. 1:25), is revealed in Christ's resurrection from the dead (1 Cor. 15:20–24). The God of Jesus Christ—the God of perfect love, infinite wisdom, and supreme power—has equipped the apostle to rejoice in the midst of his adversities. This God can be trusted in life and in death.

To write the same things to you is no trouble to me—Why this remark should appear here is not clear. Paul suggests that he is repeating himself, but how? If "the same things" (*ta auta*) refers to the theme of "rejoicing in the Lord," the consequence is twofold: it is "wholesome" or "safe" (*asphales*) to write about it for the Philippians while not being "irksome" (*oknēron*) for Paul. Rejoicing, for him, can occur with an eye toward adversity, and no adversity can be unmixed with hope. Resurrection, not the shadow of the cross, has the last word.

3:2 Look out for the dogs—The contrast with the previous verse is striking. Without warning, the wording shifts from "Rejoice in the Lord" to "Look out for the dogs." It is a change in both tone and content. Whether something has been spliced in from another letter, now lost, or whether Paul has just received distressing news, or something else, is impossible to tell. His ire has been aroused against zealous Jewish Christians, or circumcisers, who wish to compel Gentile Christians "to live like Jews" (*ioudaizein*) (Gal. 2:14) and who once again threaten to undo his life's work. His central message is under attack.

---

3. See Kim, *Origin of Paul's Gospel*, 51–138.
4. Again, the term *tō egeironti* ("the one raising") is a present participle in the active voice.

It is intriguing to wonder where this language comes from. Is Paul taking over rhetoric from his opponents and throwing it back at them? The term "dogs" (*kynas*) could sometimes be used by Jews to disparage Gentiles. Are these Jewish Christians maligning Gentile converts as "dogs"? For die-hard traditionalists, the difference between Jews and Gentiles was the difference between "the clean" and "the unclean" ("dogs"). Without submitting to circumcision, even Gentile Christians would be unclean. Paul implies that the real "dogs" are his "law-obsessed" opponents, not his "law-free" converts.[5]

look out for the workers of evil—Apparently Paul is still turning the tables on his adversaries. If the zealous Jewish Christians insist that Gentile believers should be subjected to "works of the law" (circumcision), are they not the real doers of "harm" (*tous kakous ergatas*)? By imposing "law observance" on Gentiles, are they not contradicting the grace of the gospel? Claiming to be pure, are they not misguided? Paul warns: Watch out for them! Don't be deceived by such "works-oriented" people (*ergatas*) and their teachings about law observance!

look out for those who mutilate the flesh—It becomes clear that circumcision—as the means to ritual purity and bona fide membership in the covenant—is at stake. The zealous Jewish Christians want to subject Gentile believers to the blade of circumcision. The latter are told that otherwise they will be cut off from God's people, not sharing in the blessings of the covenant. They will be excluded by reason of impurity. In return, Paul replies sarcastically by mutilating the term "circumcision." He chops it down to the unheard-of neologism "concision," which in effect means "mutilation." The zealous Jewish Christians are not "circumcisers" but "mutilators." Claiming to bring purity, they destroy evangelical freedom and bring ruin.

3:3 For we are the circumcision—Paul makes a second retort, this time not of sarcasm but of expropriation. He co-opts the term "circumcision" from his adversaries and reclaims it for his own purposes. The covenantal community finds its true fulfillment in the free grace of Christ. Gentile converts do not need outward circumcision, for in Christ they have received the only circumcision that matters, the circumcision of the heart (cf. Rom. 2:29). "For in Christ Jesus neither circumcision nor uncircumcision counts for anything, but only faith working through love" (Gal. 5:6). Older measures of ritual purity have been rendered superfluous by the apocalyptic advent of Christ, who has ushered in the new

5. "St. Paul retorts upon the Judaizers the term of reproach by which they stigmatized the Gentiles as impure." Lightfoot, *Philippians*, 141.

eon.[6] "For neither circumcision counts for anything, nor uncircumcision, but a new creation" (Gal. 6:15).

In Christ, physical circumcision has become a matter of indifference, one way or the other. As a ritual of purification, circumcision can now be seen as having prefigured baptism. Baptism is a kind of symbolic resurrection with Christ. It is the true purification that matters. "In him also you were circumcised with a circumcision made without hands, by putting off the body of the flesh, by the circumcision of Christ, having been buried with him in baptism, in which you were also raised with him through faith in the powerful working of God, who raised him from the dead" (Col. 2:11–12). The community of baptized Jews and Gentiles—who were cleansed when they died and rose again with Christ—are themselves the true circumcision and its fulfillment.[7]

who worship by the Spirit of God and glory in Christ Jesus—This verse is not "implicitly trinitarian" in itself. But from a retrospective, "ecclesial" perspective, it might be described as "proto-trinitarian." The seeds of the future are germinating. The Father would be worshiped in the Spirit through the Son.[8]

Worship or service (*latreuontes*, "we who worship") can be taken in both a narrow and an expansive sense. More narrowly, it pertains to worship strictly speaking—that is, to the early Christian cultus, which includes the Eucharist, baptism, communal prayer, preaching, scripture reading, and music.[9] In effect, the faithful are integrated "by the Spirit" into what T. F. Torrance has called the incarnate Son's vicarious worship of the Father.[10] More expansively, worship or

6. "He is not saying that uncircumcised Christians are the 'true' (allegorical) circumcision and Jews are not," writes Bockmuehl, "or that Christianity has replaced and invalidated Judaism." On the contrary, he is saying that covenant membership is determined by faith in Christ and not by works of the law. "Christ places Gentile believers on the same footing before God as Jewish believers." Bockmuehl, *Philippians*, 191.

7. "We are the *true* circumcision; we who have put off the impurity of the heart and have put on Christ, whether by belonging to the outward circumcision, as I do, or to the outward *un*circumcision, as you do." Lightfoot, *Philippians*, 142–43 (slightly modified).

8. The wording of verse 3 prefigures, embryonically, the *Phos hilaron*, from the late third or early fourth century:

Joyous Light of the holy glory of the immortal Father,
Heavenly, holy, blessed Jesus Christ:
Coming to the setting of the sun, seeing the evening light,
We hymn Father, Son, and Holy Spirit, God.
It is right for You at all times to be praised with blessed voices,
Son of God, the Giver of Life. Therefore, the cosmos glorifies You.

See McGowan, *Ancient Christian Worship*, 126.

9. McGowan, *Ancient Christian Worship*.

10. See Torrance, "Mind of Christ in Worship": worship is "essentially a participation in the heavenly worship beyond, where Christ ever lives . . . , for it is worship in the one Spirit through whom we have access through Christ to the Father" (139–40).

service (*latreia*) pertains to practicing a faithful way of life in the world. Here, too, it does not take place except "by the Spirit of God" (*pneumati theou*).

Either way, the *latreia* is "eccentric," centered in Christ. Just as Gentiles can no longer be disparaged as "dogs," so zealous Jewish Christians can no longer be exalted through a misguided sense of "religious purity." "Circumcision" in Christ means election to humility and service, not to pride. "Every valley shall be lifted up, and every mountain and hill be made low; the uneven ground shall become level, and the rough places a plain" (Isa. 40:4).

The true "circumcision" is now established for Jew and Gentile alike. The haughty are brought down, even as the disparaged are lifted up. "There is neither Jew nor Greek, there is neither slave nor free, there is no male and female, for you are all one in Christ Jesus" (Gal. 3:28). There can be neither elitists nor deplorables in Christ, neither "the legally pure" nor "dogs." Those who glory must glory in the Lord (1 Cor. 1:31).

and put no confidence in the flesh—The word "flesh" has a double meaning. It pertains not only to literal circumcision as a sign of religious status but also to any special earthly status by which one might lord it over another. Distinctions based on religion, ethnicity, class, nationality, gender, academic attainments, and so on would fall into this latter category (*sarx*). Those who glory in Christ are called to glory in him alone. They can "put no confidence in the flesh" (*ouk en sarki pepoithotes*). They can allow nothing but Christ to be their ultimate validation. As Luther teaches in his *Large Catechism*, whatever your heart clings to, that properly is your god. Placing false confidence in any earthly status, whether religious or worldly, is a violation of the first commandment. When circumcision becomes an emblem of group superiority, it has decayed into a false god.

3:4a though I myself have reason—From a Jewish standpoint, Paul speaks from a position of strength. If his opponents would claim religious superiority, he is not to be outdone. He outbids them in order to undermine them. He has every reason to exalt in his heritage. He can easily have placed "confidence in the flesh" (*pepoithēsan en sarki*), and he does not hesitate to explain why.

> **4b**If anyone else thinks he has reason for confidence in the flesh, I have more: **5**circumcised on the eighth day, of the people of Israel, of the tribe of Benjamin, a Hebrew of Hebrews; as to the law, a Pharisee; **6**as to zeal, a persecutor of the church; as to righteousness under the law, blameless.

3:4b I have more—Recent sociology distinguishes three categories of social status. *Ascribed status* involves a position that is inherited or received. It cannot be changed by personal effort. *Achieved status* is enjoyed by virtue of personal accomplishments. Finally, *master status* is uppermost and surpasses the other two.[11] These distinctions are useful in sorting out the kinds of "confidence" Paul claims that he might have placed "in the flesh." He commands an outstanding degree of status in each category.

3:5 circumcised on the eighth day, of the people of Israel, of the tribe of Benjamin, a Hebrew of Hebrews—The first four descriptions fall into the category of ascribed status. None of them is achieved by personal effort. Nor could they have been relinquished even if Paul had wished. They are ascriptions received at birth, and they function as markers of prestige. The apostle was born, we might say, with a religious silver spoon in his mouth. He begins by mentioning his superior form of circumcision and ends with his distinctive cultural rank. His references ascend upward from one degree of distinction to another, each one higher than the one before. Yet Paul lists them only to undermine his adversaries, who are pressuring Gentile converts to embrace what he sees as a dubious religious standing by outward, ceremonial means.

circumcised on the eighth day—Not all circumcisions are created equal. Paul wasn't circumcised merely in his thirteenth year like the Ishmaelites. Nor was he like a convert circumcised at a mature age. He enjoys a first-rate status. Circumcised on the eighth day (*oktaēmeros*), in strict conformity with the law, he has belonged to the covenant people from his birth.[12]

of the people of Israel—Paul was never anything other than an ethnic member of Israel (*ek genous Israēl*). In other words, he is neither a proselyte nor a second-class practitioner. And unlike the Ishmaelites or the Edomites, he is descended not only from Abraham and Isaac but beyond that from Jacob as well. Any status pertaining to ethnicity has belonged to him at the highest level from birth.[13]

of the tribe of Benjamin—Furthermore, not only is Paul an Israelite, but he also comes from perhaps the most prestigious of tribes.[14] Despite its shadow side,[15] it has supplied kings, garnered military honors, and remained loyal to the

11. See Scott and Marshall, *Dictionary of Sociology*. I am unaware of any commentary that uses the category "master status" here, though some have employed the distinction between "ascribed" and "achieved."

12. "Paul leads with this particular item, not with the next two, for obvious contextual reasons." Fee, *Philippians*, 306.

13. "Paul was an insider by descent." Bockmuehl, *Philippians*, 196.

14. "The tribe of Benjamin stood high in Jewish estimation—it had within its borders the city of Jerusalem and with it the temple (Judg. 1:21)—and so it was regarded a special privilege to belong to it." O'Brien, *Philippians*, 371.

15. See Hellerman, *Philippians*, 177.

house of David through times of crisis and trial. Paul is more than just an ethnic Israelite. As an Israelite, his tribal background as a Benjaminite is distinguished.

a Hebrew of Hebrews—Not all Israelites speak Hebrew, not all maintain a close connection with Palestine, and not all conform to Hebraic habits of culture and life.[16] Some have assimilated to the customs of a surrounding Gentile culture, in Paul's case a culture like that of Tarsus. Assimilation easily correlates with the shriveling of cultural roots through a loss of the ancestral tongue. As a "Hebrew of Hebrews," Paul has been reared in a strictly observant, unassimilated family. It has maintained not only Hebrew literacy but also strong ties with the homeland. This upbringing has instilled in him a loyalty to the ways of the fathers. "He belonged to the purest and most loyal type of Jews, the Hebrews."[17] In short, from whatever standpoint—law-observant, ethnic, tribal, or cultural—Paul commands the highest "ascriptive status."

as to the law, a Pharisee—Paul's commitments as a Pharisee are not mainly ascriptive but elective. They are not so much inherited as chosen. Although he may have been "a son of Pharisees" (Acts 23:6), he has made this sect his own. It represents, as he is quoted as saying, "the strictest party of our religion" (Acts 26:5). The Pharisees are concerned to maintain the most demanding standards of purity and to separate themselves from all that is unclean.[18] Paul's circumcising opponents, who (as we have seen) are apparently urging Gentile Christians to turn from being "unclean" ("dogs"), may have been Pharisees themselves. They have nothing over Paul, who has been just as committed as they are to observing the law (*kata nomon*) in every detail of life—not only the Mosaic law but also the almost endless regulations of the oral law. Paul's claim to be a Pharisee is "deliberate and well-placed" and confirms "his unassailable Jewish credentials in the face of his Judaizing opponents."[19] His achieved status is no less imposing than his ascriptive status.

3:6 as to zeal, a persecutor of the church—And yet Paul's religious credentials surpass even his being a Pharisee. He has not only separated himself from all that is unclean, but in his zeal (*kata zēlos*) he has attempted to eradicate uncleanness

---

16. Although born outside of Palestine in Tarsus, Paul "was yet brought up under a great Hebrew teacher [Gamaliel] in the Hebrew metropolis [Jerusalem]. He spoke the 'Hebrew' language fluently [probably Aramaic along with Greek], and he quotes frequently from the Hebrew Scriptures, which he translates for himself, thus contrasting with [some of his illustrious Jewish] contemporaries [like Philo]." Lightfoot, *Philippians*, 145 (slightly modified).

17. Robertson, *Paul's Joy in Christ*, 183.

18. "For this reason Pharisees needed to distance themselves from 'unclean' persons like non-observant Jews or Gentiles, and to maintain exclusive table fellowship." Bockmuehl, *Philippians*, 197.

19. Bockmuehl, *Philippians*, 198.

wherever he found it, particularly with regard to that most recent outrage, the church. As a Pharisee he would surely have looked on the idea of a crucified Messiah as an unspeakable offense.[20] It was a scandal that provoked him to launch a personal campaign of terror. "I persecuted the church of God violently and attempted to destroy it" (Gal. 1:13). Paul has exceeded his zealous opponents even when it comes to harassing the church.

as to righteousness under the law, blameless—I take this point to involve Paul's master status over against the other forms. "Righteousness under the law" (*dikaiosynēn tēn en nomō*) was for him the supreme status that had exceeded all others in importance. "Righteousness," whether before or after his conversion to Christ, represents the essential spiritual condition as seen by the eyes of God (*coram Deo*). It includes deeds and yet cannot be reduced to deeds. It is at once the ground, the goal, and the result of deeds undertaken in accord with the law. Without a spiritual condition of righteousness, no one can have access to God. Nevertheless, by claiming that he is "blameless" (*amemptos*) with regard to the law, Paul is not laying claim to spiritual perfection.[21] He means, rather, that he has been scrupulous in observing all of the law's external prescriptions.[22]

> [7]But whatever gains I had, I counted as loss for the sake of Christ. [8]What is more, I count everything as loss because of the surpassing worth of knowing Christ Jesus my Lord. For his sake I have suffered the loss of all things and count them as rubbish, in order that I may gain Christ [9]and be found in him, not having a righteousness of my own derived from the law, but that which is through faith in Christ, the righteousness that comes from God on the basis of faith—[10]that I may know him and the power of his resurrection and the fellowship of his sufferings, being conformed to his death, [11]in order that I may attain to the resurrection from the dead.

3:7 But whatever gains I had—Paul does not turn his back on the blessings he has known as a Jew. In some sense his markers of ascribed status—ritual, ethnic, tribal, and cultural—can still be regarded as "advantages" or "gains" (*kerdē*). Even select aspects of his achieved status are not utterly without value.[23] In certain

---

20. Other provocations may have concerned the church's inclusion of Gentiles and its criticism of the temple. Bockmuehl, *Philippians*, 200.

21. "A blameless observance of the law involved using the means of atonement for sin." Thielman, *Paul and the Law*, 154–55.

22. "He means 'I omitted no observance however trivial.'" Lightfoot, *Philippians*, 146.

23. "Then what advantage has the Jew? Or what is the value of circumcision? Much in every way. To begin with, the Jews were entrusted with the oracles of God. What if some were unfaithful? Does their faithlessness nullify the faithfulness of God? By no means! Let God be true though every one were a

respects, even as a Christian he seems to have remained an observant Jew.[24] A nuanced judgment needs to be made here. Nevertheless, Paul's world has been turned upside down.

I counted as loss for the sake of Christ—The apostle no longer places confidence "in the flesh" (3:3). Every element in his former life has been called into question. "Righteousness" through ritual observance—his master status—most especially has taken a hit. All his old advantages have become as nothing to him "for the sake of Christ" (*dia ton Christon*). Although law observance is not excluded for Jewish Christians, it ought not to be imposed on Gentile Christians.

Law observance no longer marks the difference between the clean and the unclean. That religious distinction—as well as any between superior and inferior (dogs)—has been toppled by the cross. Christ has emptied law observance—with all its accumulated externalities, exclusions, and ritual purities—of saving significance. Whereas Paul's zealous Jewish Christian opponents would in some sense subordinate Christ to the law, Paul subordinates the law to Christ. His old markers of status are now empty. Whether they be ascribed, achieved, or master, Paul counts them as loss (*zēmian*).[25] They have paled into insignificance because of Christ.

3:8 What is more—Paul intensifies his point (*alla menounge kai*). The loss column is expanded to include not only his advantages as a Jew but "all things" (*ta panta*). He counts not just some things but all things as loss because of Christ.

the surpassing worth of knowing Christ Jesus my Lord—Every alternative means of salvation is reduced to nothing. Only one thing matters: a love supreme, "knowing Christ Jesus" (*tēs gnōseōs Christou Iēsou*),[26] and a personal confession,

---

liar" (Rom. 3:1–4). "They are Israelites, and to them belong the adoption, the glory, the covenants, the giving of the law, the worship, and the promises. To them belong the patriarchs, and from their race, according to the flesh, is the Christ" (Rom. 9:4–5).

24. "Acts and (to a certain extent) the Epistles offer hints that he continued to regard himself, in some meaningful sense and in important contexts, as observant." Bockmuehl, *Philippians*, 202. Whereas Sechrest posits a sharp break for Paul from Judaism, Bird argues that being "in Christ" for him "does not negate his Jewish origins, but it does transcend it and even relativizes it in relation to a new Christ-given and Spirit-endowed identity. That new identity is continuous with his Israelite ancestry, but also consciously distinct from it in some regards." Rudolph points out that Paul stated it as a rule for all the churches that Jews believing in Christ were to remain Jews (1 Cor. 7:17–24). See Sechrest, *Former Jew*, 105–9, 164; Bird, *Anomalous Jew*, 51; Rudolph, *Jew to the Jews*, 33n43.

25. "The several gains were massed in one loss." Vincent, *Philippians*, 99. They were, in effect, not simply a zero but a deficit (*zēmian*).

26. "Knowledge of Christ Jesus" is not merely "intellectual knowledge" but knowledge based on "personal experience" and lived out in "intimate relationship." Fee, *Philippians*, 318. "Paul speaks here in terms of *knowledge* rather than *love* of Christ, but from the Jewish perspective love for God implies knowledge of God, and vice versa." Bockmuehl, *Philippians*, 206.

"my Lord" (*tou kyriou mou*).[27] On that basis religious observances and external distinctions can then in certain respects be reinstated.[28] The worth of knowing Christ Jesus is beyond measure (*to hyperechon*). While we were yet lost sinners, he died that we might live. In Christ the God who owes us nothing has given us everything. "Love so amazing, so divine, demands my soul, my life, my all" (Isaac Watts).

For his sake I have suffered the loss of all things—Having devoted himself to Christ, Paul has suffered the loss of all things (*ta panta ezēmiōthēn*). He does not specify what that entailed, but it may have included his being disinherited by his family; a corresponding loss in property; alienation from friends, teachers, associates, and perhaps even from a Jewish wife.[29] Certainly, it would have meant his loss of status in Judaism at points that were previously dear to him.[30] All in all, he has lost "religious advantages, status, material benefits, honor, comforts."[31] Such advantages have been relinquished for the sake of Christ.

and count them as rubbish—The factors that his adversaries are extolling, Paul—who has known them all—brushes aside as "rubbish" (*skybala*). What is being demanded for the sake of religious purity, he dismisses bluntly as "a pile of refuse." Gordon Fee is probably right that "Paul was taking a parting shot at the 'dogs.'" "It is hard," Fee continues, "to imagine a more pejorative epithet than this one now hurled at what the Judaizers would promote as advantages. Paul saw them strictly as disadvantages, as total loss, indeed as 'foul-smelling street garbage' fit only for 'dogs.'"[32] Paul wants to shock his Gentile readers away from yielding to false demands. It is not they who are "dogs" (unclean) but those who would shame them into submitting to works of the law.

in order that I may gain Christ—For Paul, to "gain Christ" (*Christon kerdēsō*) involves three temporal aspects: it is a gift once received and now presently enjoyed, but it also stands out as the future goal. The gift once given is continually renewed day by day. Note that along with the giving side, there is also a receiving side. Paul does not take his reception of the gift for granted. Ongoing faithfulness is required

---

27. "Here and here alone in his writings do we find the intensely personal *Christ Jesus my Lord*; and it would be a dull reader indeed who did not mark the warm and deep devotion which breathes through every phrase." F. W. Beare, quoted in O'Brien, *Philippians*, 388.

28. Ritual observances: e.g., baptism and the Lord's Supper. External distinctions: e.g., Eph. 4:7, 11.

29. It is not known whether Paul ever had a wife, but if he did, perhaps she left him "when he became a Christian: that when he 'suffered the loss of all things' for the sake of Christ he lost his wife too." Bruce, *Paul*, 270.

30. Hellerman, *Philippians*, 184.

31. Fee, *Philippians*, 317.

32. Fee, *Philippians*, 319 (slightly modified).

of him. His devotion to Christ needs to be continually renewed. Only so can Christ be "gained" on the last day insofar as it involves the apostle's human response. The apostle is moved by grace to receive the gift of Christ by faith ever anew. His gaining of Christ is the purpose of his renouncing so forcefully any possible status of righteousness—ascribed, achieved, and master—as may be derived from the law.

3:9 and be found in him—The voice of the verb "be found" (*heurethō*) suggests a divine passive.[33] Paul's faithfulness to Christ is tantamount to his relationship with God. The high Christology of 2:5–11 is reflected indirectly in 3:2–11.[34] The lordship of Christ; his surpassing worth; the excellency of knowing him; his reduction of all other means of salvation to insignificance, including the outward, exclusionary markers of the law; the appropriateness of relinquishing all else because of him; and the suffering of loss for his sake—all these indicate that the humiliated and exalted Jesus, who bears the name above every name, and to which every knee shall bow, is more than a mere human being. By means of his resurrection, he has become, through his Spirit, the world's Contemporary, especially to those who acknowledge him and receive him by faith.[35]

Borrowing from later thought forms, we may say that Paul hopes to be found in union with the Son (*en autō*), by the judgment of the Father, through the power of the Spirit. To gain Christ (3:8), to be found in him (3:9), and to know him (3:10) are three ways of indicating the same thing. They are diverse aspects of a single gift. Paul's hope is "to know Christ fully, to gain him completely, and to be found in him perfectly."[36] Paul hopes to gain Christ, whose presence is new each morning, and he hopes to be found in him on the last day. Otherwise he would be bereft of saving righteousness *coram Deo*.

33. "The passive voice here refers to divine not human assessment." Hellerman, *Philippians*, 185.

34. See Koperski, *Knowledge of Christ Jesus My Lord*. For an interesting discussion of possible parallels and disjunctions between Phil. 2:5–11 and Phil. 3:2–11, see Bertschmann, "Is There a Kenosis in This Text?" "The issue is not obedient kenosis," Bertschmann argues, "but the earth-shattering encounter with Christ, who deconstructs and reconstructs Paul's identity" (253).

35. Note that the link between "resurrection" and "justification" can be explained on this basis (Rom. 4:24–25): the sinless Christ (*Christus vicarius*) who removed our sins by his blood (Rom. 3:25) is the present Christ (*Christus praesens*) who communicates his perfect righteousness by grace to faith. Without his resurrection, there would be no *Christus praesens*; therefore no communication of his righteousness could occur, and no justification would be possible. His present activity here and now applies and communicates the result of the perfect work as accomplished in his atoning sacrifice there and then. With reference to Rom. 4:25, Seifrid writes, "The risen Lord is the vehicle of God's grace, through which God has granted us righteousness and life. . . . Christ *is* God's grace and righteousness, and not merely their cause. . . . Righteousness . . . is the reality of the resurrection as it has entered the world in Christ." Seifrid, "Paul's Turn to Christ," 20, 21, 24n20 (italics added). Righteousness as a spiritual condition is akin to blamelessness and holiness; it is thus more than mere *iustitia* narrowly conceived.

36. O'Brien, *Philippians*, 391–92.

not having a righteousness of my own derived from the law—"Righteousness" (*dikaiosynē*), for Paul, is the sine qua non of salvation. It is the indispensable spiritual predicate. Without it no one can attain access to God.[37] The opposite of "righteousness" is "sinfulness."

God's commandment reveals that humans have become "sinful beyond measure" (*kath' hyperbolēn hamartōlos*) (Rom. 7:13). Sinfulness is a radical corruption that affects the whole person. It involves both guilt and bondage. For salvation to take place, not only does sin's guilt need to be both forgiven and removed, but its bondage needs to be broken. It would not be enough for the guilt to be removed while the bondage remained in force. That would be justification without sanctification. Nor would it be enough for sin's bondage to be broken while sin's guilt was not taken away. That would be sanctification without justification. Righteousness, and therefore access to God, cannot be had unless sinfulness is overcome in both its relevant aspects of bondage and guilt.[38]

The righteousness required for access to God cannot be merely partial. It needs to accord with God's attributes of holiness and righteousness. Human righteousness cannot be effectual without being whole and entire.[39] Paul realizes, in light of Christ, that the decisive requirement of perfect righteousness cannot be met by sinful human beings in themselves. Atonement for sin might be provided by the existing Hebrew cultus, but not perfectly. Nor can sin's power be broken by even the most zealous obedience to the law, as shown by the recurring need, under the law, for atonement and repentance. In his divine forbearance God has passed over former sins (Rom. 3:25). But not until the death and resurrection of Christ could that righteousness be obtained which removes sin's condemnation (guilt) (Rom. 8:1), breaks its power (bondage) (Rom. 6:14), and provides full and unending access to God (Rom. 5:2).

37. The question of "righteousness" (*dikaiosynē*) is "the question as to the proper, just, correct condition of the human being—namely, before God." Barth, *Epistle to the Philippians*, 99 (slightly modified).

38. In principle Paul is no less concerned about sin as guilt (sins in the plural) than about sin as an enslaving power (sin in the singular). Unfortunately, recent New Testament scholarship (e.g., Käsemann, Martyn, and their followers) has sometimes focused on the element of bondage at the expense of guilt. For an important corrective, see Gathercole, "'Sins' in Paul."

39. "You therefore must be perfect, as your heavenly Father is perfect" (Matt. 5:48). This saying from Jesus presupposes the received Jewish idea of God. Cf. Lev. 19:2 and Deut. 18:13 LXX. The location of this saying in the Sermon on the Mount points toward enemy love as a key indicator of "perfection" or "completeness." God's essential attribute of "perfection" is a matter of holiness, impartiality, and goodness. In his works *ad extra*, God includes all in his holiness precisely by including the excluded. See Tannehill, *Shape of the Gospel*, 130; Massey, *Sermon on the Mount*, 52–56; Du Plessis, *Teleios*. "In wider Greek usage this word [*teleios*] could denote the quality of sacrificial victims, entire and without blemish, and is so used of the Passover lamb in Exod. 12:5." Dunn, *Epistles to the Colossians and to Philemon*, 125. The Passover associations of *teleios* would have indirect implications for the great exchange (*admirabile commercium*).

but that which is through faith in Christ, the righteousness that comes from God on the basis of faith—The phrase *pisteōs Christou*, translated here as "faith in Christ," is notoriously difficult. Should it be taken as an objective genitive, "faith *in* Christ," or else, as some contend, as a subjective genitive, "faith *of* Christ"?[40] The respective translations, I want to stress, are finally less important than the assumptions that lie behind them. It seems that, generally speaking, neither side of the translation dispute operates with an entirely satisfactory conception of salvation in Christ. The position adopted here is as follows.

Salvation in Christ is, for Paul, God's solution to the plight of human sin. What human beings need is to be delivered from sinfulness into righteousness. No saving righteousness exists apart from Christ, because God, having sent him for that reason, made him to be our righteousness in himself (1 Cor. 1:30). He became our righteousness by his obedience (Rom. 5:19). It is his obedience that removes sin's guilt (Rom. 3:25) while also destroying its power (Rom. 6:6). His saving work is seen to occur in two ways, first of all apart from us (*extra nos*) and then, on that basis, within us (*in nobis*).

What the Reformation calls Christ's "passive obedience," as correlated with his "passive righteousness," refers primarily to his having borne and removed the guilt of our sins on the cross.[41] Although he was without sin—in the bold phrase of the Greek fathers, he was Righteousness itself (*autodikaiosynē*)[42]—he died the death of the sinner—that is, the death that would otherwise have been ours. He did so freely, for our sakes and in our place. He made our sin to be his own, in an act of supreme intercession, by taking it to himself. Sin was condemned, vicariously, in his flesh (Rom. 8:3). Out of his unfathomable mercy and grace, he consented to die on the cross, so that a double transfer might occur. He took our sin and death to himself, that in him we might receive a share in his righteousness and life (2 Cor. 5:21). Note well that this double transfer—from us to Christ (sin and death) and from Christ to us (righteousness and

40. Among the distinguished exegetes who, rightly in my opinion, construe the phrase *pistis Christou* as an objective genitive ("faith *in* Christ") are John M. G. Barclay, C. E. B. Cranfield, James D. G. Dunn, Grant Macaskill, R. Barry Matlock, Douglas J. Moo, Udo Schnelle, and Francis Watson. The disputed passages are Gal. 2:16, 20; Rom. 3:22, 26; Phil. 3:9; and Eph. 3:12. In discussing Rom. 3:22 and 3:26 below, I assume the objective genitive.

41. "Passive *obedience*" refers to a form of *activity*; "passive *righteousness*," to a corresponding *condition* or state of being.

42. The term *autodikaiosynē* was used by Origen. "For he is the king of heaven, and as such he is *autosophia* [Wisdom itself], and *autodikaiosunē* [Righteousness itself], and *autoaletheia* [Truth itself], is he not also therefore *autobasileia* [the Kingdom itself]?" Origen, *Commentary on Matthew* 14.7, quoted in Kalantzis, *Caesar and the Lamb*, 59 (slightly modified).

life)—cannot be accounted for within the forensic logic of the courtroom, nor yet within that of common morality. It can finally only make sense, as I will argue, when typological allowances are made, within the logic of the ritual sacrifices as practiced in the religion of Israel,[43] most especially in Yom Kippur.[44] (For reflections on Kant's rejection of cultic atonement on the grounds of rational morality, see excursus 4.)

In the mind of Paul, a judicial end (the just condemnation of sin) (Rom. 8:3) has been accomplished by ritual means (Rom. 3:25). It is, we might say, accomplished "sacramentally" (symbolically), and therefore "effectually," by Christ in our place, so that, without compromise to God's righteousness, divine mercy toward lost sinners can prevail.[45] The double transfer is thought to involve a ritual "exchange" (*admirabile commercium*). Two things happen at once. The innocent one takes the place of the guilty many ("substitution"), while the sins of the many are removed ("expiated") by the blood (the "atoning sacrifice") of the innocent one. The many are thus made "innocent" by an innocence not their own. They receive this innocence (or "righteousness") in union with Christ by grace through faith, apart from their merit or works.[46]

43. Cf. Stökl Ben Ezra, *Impact of Yom Kippur*; Finlan, *Paul's Cultic Atonement Metaphors*; Hasel, "Day of Atonement."

44. Along with the centrality (as I will argue) of Rom. 3:21–26, I assume that the following passages as indicated by Finlan are seminal for understanding Phil. 3:9—the verse that is here under consideration. "In at least two passages (2 Cor. 5:21 and Gal. 3:13) and probably in three more (Rom. 6:6, 7:4, 8:3), Paul pictures the salvific death of Christ with the scapegoat image: Christ the sin-bearer or curse-bearer, the 'body of Christ' as victim that brings deliverance to others." Finlan, *Paul's Cultic Atonement Metaphors*, 120. Stökl Ben Ezra agrees about Gal. 3:13 but not about 2 Cor. 5:21, because of philological considerations. Stökl Ben Ezra, *Impact of Yom Kippur*, 173. Finlan argues, on the other hand, rightly in my view, on the basis of broader conceptual patterns and ritual themes.

45. In other words, the blood of Christ effects what it symbolizes and symbolizes what it effects. It fulfills the cultic atonement rituals as established in the religion of Israel. It atones for and removes the guilt of sin. It takes away the sin of the world, and therefore the wrath of God at the same time. For Paul, Christ's blood is the means by which our salvation is secured (Rom. 3:25; 5:9; Eph. 1:7; 2:13; Col. 1:20). Note that there is only one blood of Christ. The same blood that was shed on Good Friday is the blood that is offered to the faithful in the Eucharist in sacramental form. "Love is that liquor sweet and most divine, / Which my God feels as blood; but I, as wine" (George Herbert). One way that the faithful participate in Christ and his saving righteousness is through the sacrament. Cf. Hunsinger, *Eucharist and Ecumenism*.

46. Cf. Hooker, "Interchange in Christ"; Hooker, "Interchange and Atonement." Hooker offers many fine insights into the pattern of exchange in Paul's understanding of the atonement. Nevertheless, her work, as I see it, contains at least one basic flaw. She posits, wrongly in my view, that "participation" and "substitution" are mutually exclusive. By overlooking the significance of Paul's cultic atonement metaphors, she not only rejects substitution as a key element in Paul's Christocentric doctrine of salvation ("interchange"), but is also forced to ground the interchange in "experience" rather than more objectively, as argued in this commentary, in God's mercy and grace as informed by the sacrificial religion of Israel—principally Yom Kippur, and Passover as "recombined" with Yom Kippur. These sacrificial elements are adapted to the cross of Christ in the primitive Christian imagination through word and sacrament.

As in Passover and Yom Kippur, which stand in the background, the whole point of this strange transaction is to avert punishment while freely extending mercy. The condemnation is carried out vicariously so that mercy can prevail. Markus Tiwald, for example, regards Rom. 3:25 as an allusion to Yom Kippur, outlined in Lev. 16:13–15.[47] He also regards Rom. 3:21–26 "as among the most influential verses not only of Paul, but of the whole New Testament. . . . Indeed, they can be seen as the architectonic and theological center of the Letter to the Romans. . . . The sentences in these verses carry axiomatic significance"[48]—a significance that carries over into Phil. 3:9. Daniel Stökl Ben Ezra agrees that Yom Kippur, as set forth in Leviticus, forms the background to Rom. 3:24–26, which therefore requires a cultic interpretation. "The allusion to the *hilastērion* in the holy of holies according to usage in the Greek Torah must have been clear not only to Paul but to everybody familiar with the Greek Torah. . . . Jesus is inaugurated as *hilastērion and* he atones as such. . . . Romans proposes a sacrificial conception of atonement."[49] "Righteousness" in Phil. 3:9 cannot be understood apart from Rom. 3:21–26.

Here is a suggestion for how Rom. 3:21–26 might be analyzed.

A. *The Self-Revelation of God*

But now the *righteousness* of God has been *manifested* apart from the law [forensic/cultic], although the Law and the Prophets [the scriptures] bear witness to it. (3:21)

B. *The Christ-Centered Solution*

the *righteousness* of God through *faith in Jesus Christ* for all who believe. (3:22)

C. *The Universal Plight*

For there is no distinction: for *all have sinned* and fall short of the glory of God. (3:23)

47. The same cultic atonement "pattern of exchange" in the background is noted by Bell: "The Israelite through the laying on of hands is identified with the sacrificial animal to such an extent that the death of the animal is the death of the Israelite and by passing through this judgement of death, the Israelite is able, via the blood rite, to have fellowship with God." Note that the vicarious identification or transfer is thus carried out in the service of mercy. Bell, "Sacrifice and Christology in Paul," 4. From this point of view, the difference between "identification" and the more nearly retrospective idea of "transfer of sins" in light of Christ is arguably not great. At this point my argument about Paul in such passages as Rom. 3:25; 8:3; and 2 Cor. 5:21 does not require a tight, point-for-point fit between Yom Kippur and the cross. It depends more on reading backwards from the cross than forward from Yom Kippur, so that with modifications Paul interprets the type in light of the antitype.

48. Tiwald, "Christ as *Hilastērion*," 189 (slightly modified). For a different view, see Campbell, *Rhetoric of Righteousness*.

49. Stökl Ben Ezra, *Impact of Yom Kippur*, 201, 203 (italics original). Stökl Ben Ezra supports the objective interpretation of *pistis Christou* (204).

B'. The Christ-Centered Solution Elaborated

and are *justified* by his grace as a gift [forensic], through the *redemption* that is *in Christ Jesus* [financial/social], whom God put forward as an *expiation* [*hilastērion*] by his blood [priestly/cultic], to be *received by faith* [personal/communal]. (3:24–25a)

A'. The Self-Revelation of God Elaborated

This was *to show* God's *righteousness*, because in his divine *forbearance* [mercy] he had passed over former sins. It was *to show* his *righteousness* at the present time, so *that he might be just* [the divine integrity] *and the justifier* of the one who has faith in Jesus [the divine mercy]. (3:25b–26)

The chiastic structure as proposed here is more conceptual than verbal. The A-elements at the beginning and the end pertain to God's self-revelation in Christ as a God who chooses not to be righteous in himself without also being merciful to his creatures.[50] God is a God of mercy who determines to be true to his fallen creatures despite their sins without entering into contradiction with himself. The B-elements indicate the Christ-centered solution to how mercy can be extended to the ungodly and the wicked (Rom. 1:18) without compromise to the divine integrity. The C-element indicates the universal plight encompassing the whole human race, both Jew and Gentile, to which the solution pertains.

Of special interest is the B'-element that elaborates on the solution. In this element (3:24–25a), diverse metaphors are juxtaposed in quick succession: the forensic, the financial/social, the priestly/cultic, and the personal/communal. Paul reasons from the outside in, so to speak, or from the ends to the means. The forensic aspect (acquittal) and the financial/social aspect (redemption from slavery) designate the ends for which the priestly/cultic aspect at the center (expiation by Christ's blood) serves as the ground of salvation (objectively) in league with faith as the instrument of its personal and communal reception (subjectively). Both justification (acquittal) and redemption (liberation) emanate from the centrality of Christ as the "mercy seat" or the place of sacrifice (*hilastērion*), where sin—the irreversible human catastrophe—has been covered, blotted out, and removed by Christ's sacrificial blood (*en tō autou haimati*).

This short passage, according to C. E. B. Cranfield, "is the center and heart of the whole of Rom. 1:16b–15:13."[51] It suggests not only the "cultic" as the

---

50. Again, I presuppose that although the term "righteous" can often carry connotations of mercy, "righteousness" and "mercy" nevertheless remain distinct so that neither can be reduced to the other.

51. Cranfield, *Epistle to the Romans*, 1:199.

basis of the "forensic" in Pauline soteriology, but also the person of Christ in his atoning sacrifice as the object and content of faith. His sacrificial blood is not only the price by which "redemption" (*apolytrōsis*) is secured for those in bondage to sin, but also the ground on which "justification" (*dikaiosynē*) is afforded to the guilty who are otherwise lost in their sins and condemned. Without the removal of sin by the atoning blood of Christ, neither redemption nor justification would be possible.

The "faithfulness *of* Christ" translation for *pisteōs Christou* is problematic, because it regards the person of Christ mainly as faith's pattern as opposed to faith's object and content. Although not entirely wrong, this proposal mistakes the part for the whole, while missing the essential element. As Barth suggests, it runs the risk of introducing a new legalism: "If we operate too much here with trust, confidence, faithfulness, etc., on the human side towards God, then we almost inevitably come imminently near to the very thing that Paul wanted his concept [of faith in Christ] to abrogate and replace—the human being's own 'righteousness from the Law'—and fail to understand the sharpness of the opposition he maintains toward it."[52]

Moreover, what the "faith *of* Christ" option overlooks (or minimizes), most especially, are the cultic modes of thought at the heart of Paul's concept of salvation. Christ is the *object* of faith no less in Phil. 3:9 than in Rom. 3:22 and 3:26—verses where a form of *pistis Christou* appears. Nevertheless, at the same time, the cultic atonement background is also underappreciated, to a significant extent, by proponents of the "faith *in* Christ" translation, who are often overly influenced by forensic modes of thought. I will discuss the forensic issue more fully in due course.

It cannot be urged too strongly that, for Paul, Christ is our righteousness (*dikaiosynē*) (1 Cor. 1:30) precisely because he is the expiation (*hilastērion*) for our sins (Rom. 3:25). (I assume that, for Paul, these three—who Christ was, what he did, and why he has saving significance—are all in apposition.) Christ makes us to be righteous at the cost of his blood, by which our sins are removed (Rom. 5:9). He takes our place on the cross, that we might be restored to new life. In Christ we have "access" (*prosagōgēn*) to God (Rom. 5:2), a priestly idea, because "in him" (*en autō*) we receive the essential condition—righteousness— that we would otherwise lack (2 Cor. 5:21). Access to God, based on the gift of righteousness in and through Christ, is the solution to the human dilemma. The

52. Barth, *Epistle to the Philippians*, 101 (slightly modified).

highest good of human beings is to be united with God, but this good is impossible without righteousness.

For Paul, it is not a righteousness based "on the law" (*ek nomou*) but one that comes "through faith in Christ" (*dia pisteōs Christou*) (Phil. 3:9).[53] It is an "alien righteousness" whose source and ground is to be sought "apart from us" (*extra nos*) in the vicarious obedience of Christ (Rom. 5:19). It is given as a gift, whole and entire, by grace through faith. It is not an "inherent righteousness," a righteousness of one's own (*mē echōn emēn dikaiosynēn*) acquired piecemeal from following the law (*tēn ek nomou*) (Phil. 3:9), regardless of whether the law is conceived ceremonially or morally or both.[54] It is a "passive righteousness" in the sense that it can only be received as a gift (Rom. 5:17). It has been constituted by Christ apart from us—for our sakes and in our place (Rom. 5:19).[55] Because saving righteousness is constituted *extra nos* and then communicated to the faithful as a free gift, it forms, as Heiko Oberman suggests, "the stable *basis* and not the uncertain *goal* of the life of sanctification, of the true Christian life."[56]

"Faith in Christ" (*pistis Christou*) means union with him. It means fellowship here and now with the one who died in our place there and then. It means that the one who removed our sins by his blood gives us a share in his perfect righteousness. This is what Paul means by "the righteousness that comes from God on the basis of faith" (*tēn ek theou dikaiosynēn epi tē pistei*) (Phil. 3:9). It is a righteousness that cannot be separated from participation in Christ (*en autō*). Faith is no mere embracing of a pattern ("faithfulness"). It is the means by which Christ is confessed, the instrument by which he is received, the bond that establishes

---

53. "Faith is only the means, not the source, of justification." Lightfoot, *Philippians*, 148.

54. If Paul has no righteousness of his own derived from the law, it goes without saying that he has none on any other basis than the self-giving of Christ in and with his righteousness to faith (1 Cor. 1:30). No one, not even the most perfect saints, will be justified by the righteousness that is in them. Cf. Origen, *Commentary on John* 2.11. For a balanced discussion of what Paul means by "works of the law," see Hultgren, "Paul and the Law," 202–15.

55. From this point of view, the righteousness of Christ is the "formal cause" of our salvation, not simply its "material cause." The righteousness by which we are righteous before God is not a righteousness of our own (Phil. 3:9). It is the righteousness of Another, accomplished vicariously apart from us (Rom. 3:25; 5:19), and communicated whole and entire to the faithful by grace in the context of union with Christ (2 Cor. 5:21).

"Formal cause," writes C. F. Allison, "was agreed upon by all sides [in the seventeenth century] as the central problem in a discussion of justification. The form—or formal cause—of a thing is 'that by which a thing is what it is.' . . . It was . . . the formal cause ('by which') of our justification that separated Roman Catholic from Reformed theologians." Allison, *Rise of Moralism*, 6. The saving righteousness by which we are righteous before God (*coram Deo*) is the perfect righteousness of Christ, given to us freely as a gift, not a righteousness of our own based on works of the law—or works of any other kind.

56. Oberman, *Dawn of the Reformation*, 124 (italics original).

communion with him, and the channel through which he communicates to the faithful a share in his righteousness and life. Although, like Paul, we have no righteousness of our own, Christ is our righteousness as a free gift. (For a discussion of righteousness as grounded in "merciful substitution," see excursus 5.)

Note that in its essence the concept of substitution is not forensic but sacrificial, not declaratory but expiatory, and not penal but merciful, though these elements are surely mixed together.[57] The ritual transaction in the background means that just as the offence of sin is mercifully removed ("expiation"), so also is the No of God's wrath toward sin removed along with it ("propitiation"). God demonstrates his righteousness in Christ, which cannot condone sin, in such a way that his mercy prevails (Rom. 3:25; 11:32; 15:9; Eph. 2:4, etc.). Mercy triumphs over judgment even as righteousness receives its full due. In the cross, God's mercy is revealed as a severe mercy, his grace as a costly grace, and his love as a harsh and dreadful love. This divine manifestation of mercy-cum-righteousness is unlike any other we know.

How Christ broke the power of sin through his "active righteousness" (*extra nos*), and how he was thought to actualize by his Spirit here and now (*in nobis*) the salvation he accomplished there and then (*extra nos*), cannot be explored here. (They are touched on elsewhere in this commentary.) What is pertinent to understanding Phil. 3:9 is the implicit relationship posited that joins Christ, faith, and righteousness.

For Paul, Christ is what he enacted, and he enacted what he is. From one point of view, what he enacted in his obedience is essentially his righteousness (Rom. 5:19). He enacted it in mercy not only to deliver us from death but also to remove our sins by his blood. He bore our plight in his flesh in order to bear it away (Rom. 8:3). He made himself one with us in humiliation, that we might be made one with him in exaltation. Union with Christ by faith is the appointed means of salvation.[58]

Union with Christ takes place under two aspects: objectively by grace and subjectively through faith. The incarnate Son was made to be Sin itself (*autoamartia*) for our sakes (Gregory of Nazianzus). He is to that extent exclusively unique and

57. They are basically mixed together as ground and consequence. The ground is priestly/cultic (removal) while the consequence is forensic (acquittal) and existential (liberation from bondage).

58. "This is the way we should see Christ. He is our friend, our brother; He is whatever is good and beautiful. He is everything. Yet, He is still a friend and He shouts it out, 'You're my friends, don't you understand? We're brothers. I don't hold hell in my hands. I am not threatening you. I love you. I want you to enjoy life together with me.' Christ is Everything. He is joy, He is life, He is light. He is the true light who makes man joyful, makes him soar with happiness; makes him see everything, everybody; makes him feel for everyone, to want everyone with him, everyone with Christ." Elder Porphyrios, "Counsels," 165.

so not a pattern to be imitated. In his divine-human person he is and remains *at the same time* Righteousness itself (*autodikaiosynē*) and Life itself (*autozōē*).[59] He is made to be Sin itself without ceasing to be Righteousness itself.[60] He has done something for us that could not have been done by any other. As a unique divine-human person, he has accomplished a unique saving work—one that is finished, perfect, and unrepeatable. He is essentially faith's object and content while only secondarily its pattern.

Those who acknowledge and receive Christ by faith obtain a share in his perfect righteousness and life. He gives salvation to faith precisely by giving himself. Again, he is the object and content of faith, not merely its pattern. From this standpoint, the translation of *pistis Christou* is not "faith *of* Christ" but "faith *in* Christ."[61] Nevertheless, it is important to see that the "faith *of* Christ" translation is not necessarily incompatible with seeing Christ as the object and content of faith. Christ, through his perfect faithfulness, can be seen as causing believers to place their trust in him. To that extent his faithfulness is efficacious for the bestowal of righteousness. It is a transformative event that brings justification, righteousness, and salvation to the world. Everything depends, however, on seeing Christ's faithfulness (or vicarious obedience) as a pure gift carried out in our place and for our sakes. Everything depends on seeing it as a pure gift that we live out of, like his righteousness and life, before it can be a pattern that we live into. Everything depends on seeing that all our saving "faithfulness" before God is found outside of us in Christ (*extra nos*), and that we share in its efficacy solely by grace through faith. As with *saving* righteousness, so also with *saving* faithfulness, we have none of our own. Apart from Christ (*remoto Christo*), all our

59. The term *autodikaiosynē* was used by Origen (see note 42 above). The term *autozōē* was used by Athanasius, *De Incarnatione* 20–22.

60. So Gregory of Nyssa: "Why did the divine being descend to such humiliation? Our faith staggers at the thought that God, the infinite, inconceivable and ineffable reality, who transcends all glory and majesty, should be clothed with the defiled nature of man, so that his sublime activities are abased through being united with what is so degraded" (*Catechetical Oration* 14). Nyssa again, if possible even more strongly: "Although Christ took our filth upon himself, nevertheless he is not himself defiled by the pollution, but in own self he cleanses the filth, for it says, the Light shone in darkness, but the darkness did not overpower it" (*Refutation of the Views of Apolinarius* 26). So also Athanasius (or pseudo-Athanasius): "If sinlessness had not been seen in the nature which had sinned, how could sin have been condemned in the flesh, when that flesh had no capacity for action, and the Godhead knew not sin?" (*On the Incarnation against Apollinaris* 2:6). These passages are cited by Torrance, *Trinitarian Faith*, 153, 162, 161n53.

61. Christ brings justification and sanctification simultaneously, in their unity, order, and distinction—not merely sanctification without justification (as the subjective genitive translation seems to imply). Justification is the ground of which sanctification is the consequence, even as sanctification is the telos of which justification is the precondition. Barth, *Church Dogmatics* IV/2, 508.

faithfulness is as filthy rags (Isa. 64:6). (For further discussion of *pistis Christou* as a vicarious term, see excursus 6.)

Only where Christ is seen in decisively priestly/cultic terms, along with ideas drawn from other metaphorical domains, can various soteriological pitfalls be avoided. Only on the basis of his vicarious saving work can it be seen that

- divine mercy is the leading concept (Eph. 2:4);

- substitution (Rom. 3:25) cannot be separated from *participatio Christi* (and vice versa) (2 Cor. 5:21);

- our salvation is based on a real exchange of predicates between Christ and us (*admirabile commercium*) (2 Cor. 5:21);[62]

- participation in a "pattern" is not enough, and by itself can only lead to sanctification without justification, and so in effect to a new law (cf. Rom. 3:20);

- for Paul the forensic rests squarely on the cultic, so that we have been "justified" not only subjectively "by faith" (*dikaiousthai pistei*) (Rom. 3:28) but also objectively "by his blood" (*dikaiōthentes en tō haimati autou*) (Rom. 5:9); and

- salvation is finally at least as cosmic, corporate, and communal in scope as it is personal and individualistic (2 Cor. 5:19; Phil. 3:21; Col. 1:20; Rev. 21:1).

Although none of these priestly or cultic atonement themes are explicit in Paul's letter to the Philippians, they are arguably presupposed when he states in Phil. 3:9 that he hopes to be found *in Christ* (*en autō*), that he has no righteousness *of his own* as based on the law (*mē echōn dikaiosynēn tēn ek nomou*), and that his righteousness comes "through faith *in* Christ" (*dia pisteōs Christou*)—namely, "the righteousness that comes from God *on the basis of* faith" (*tēn ek theou dikaiosynēn epi tē pistei*)—with Christ our Passover as its *object* (1 Cor. 5:7).[63] Righteousness is therefore given as *a free gift* (*tēs dōreas tēs dikaiosynēs*)

---

62. It is a mistake to suppose, as is sometimes said, under the influence of an undue forensicism, that our righteousness in Christ is merely "positional" or merely a "legal status." On the contrary, it is already real even though it remains hidden. Our righteousness, like our life, is "hidden with Christ in God" (Col. 3:3). Although embedded in a complex eschatology of "already" and "not yet," it does not become real only in the future while remaining merely virtual or prospective in the present. It is already perfect in Christ, though not yet perfect in us. *Simul iustus et peccator.* See excursus 8.

63. If we take "imaginary" as a technical term denoting a prior set of symbols, values, and conventions common to a particular religious consciousness, then we may posit, with Jeffrey Siker, that in the primitive Christian "imaginary," three things—Passover, Yom Kippur, and the Akedah (sacrifice of Isaac in Gen. 22)—were all being associated and intermingled at a theopoetic level (as opposed to a technical level). Whereas Passover was apotropaic, Yom Kippur cathartic, and the Akedah an act of divine mercy, in primitive Christianity they were all being seen, in some sense, as expiatory. In a similar vein, Morris

(Rom. 5:17). It is given for what it is: the righteousness of the Christ who died mercifully *in our stead* (Rom. 3:25) and *for our sakes* (Rom. 5:19). A *perfect* righteousness is then communicated to us in union with *the risen Christ* by grace through faith (Rom. 4:24–25). Being *found* in him (*en autō*) (Phil. 3:9) and being *made righteous* in him (*en autō*) (2 Cor. 5:21) amount to essentially the same thing. Christ our Passover and Christ our Righteousness are one. (See excursus 7 for more on the pattern of exchange. See excursus 8 for further discussion of this complex eschatology.)

In conclusion, the table below is a schematic representation of some conceptual issues discussed above (and elaborated in the excurses). As observed, it seems that both juridical/forensic and priestly/cultic elements are present in Paul. It also seems, however, that the former are tempered by the latter in such a way that the latter tend to be logically prior (and so teleologically ultimate). Mercy and judgment in God are related without separation or division, without confusion or change, and with the priority and precedence belonging to the divine mercy. It is a pattern of asymmetrical unity-in-distinction.

The Mercy and Judgment of God: Two Soteriological Motifs

Mode of thought	Priestly/Cultic	Juridical/Forensic
Function	Removal (separation of the sin from the sinner)	Condemnation (rejection of the sinner with the sin)
Means	Vicarious Death (wondrous exchange) (substitution)	Death Penalty (consequence of indelible guilt) (punishment)
Purpose	Restorative (mercy)	Retributive (justice)
Focus	Corporate	Individualistic
Relations	Internal/Participatory	External

3:10 that I may know him and the power of his resurrection—For Paul, knowing Christ (3:8), gaining Christ (3:8), and being found in him (3:9) are three aspects of a single reality. Knowing Christ is the pearl of great price, gaining him is worthy of every sacrifice, and being found in him is the condition for the

---

presents evidence that by the close of the Old Testament period, all sacrifices were regarded as expiatory in some way. On these grounds it is possible that the saving significance of Passover and Yom Kippur as applied to the sacrifice of Jesus would not have been sharply distinct in Paul's mind. See Siker, *Jesus, Sin, and Perfection*, 246; Morris, *Gospel according to John*, 127.

possibility of salvation. After discussing the free gift of righteousness (3:9)—the gift that means access to God—the theme of knowing Christ (*tou gnōnai auton*) returns to Paul's thoughts. He links it to a theology of glory (*theologia gloriae*), though not in disconnection from a theology of the cross (*theologia crucis*). Knowing Christ means knowing his resurrection power (*tēn dynamin tēs anataseōs autou*), as given in fellowship with his sufferings, and not apart from them.[64] It is a power made perfect in weakness.

To know Christ is to taste the promised future—"the power of his resurrection"—but to taste it in the sufferings of the present time. By his resurrection the crucified Christ is made the world's Contemporary in the midst of suffering. He is present in power to the faithful as a comfort in every affliction (2 Cor. 1:4). Although the sufferings of the present may be severe, they are not the last word. "For I consider that the sufferings of this present time are not worthy to be compared with the glory that is to be revealed to us" (Rom. 8:18). The resurrection of Christ introduces a hope that transfigures every affliction.

For Paul, union and communion with Christ does not mean cheap grace. Nor does knowing him mean escape from the world. It means entering into "communion with him in his sufferings" (*koinōnian pathēmatōn autou*) and "being conformed to him in his death" (*symmorphizomenos tō thanatō autou*). Christ is the power of life in the midst of death. It is precisely by his resurrection and its power that the faithful are being conformed, for their and the world's salvation, to his afflictions.[65]

The passive voice is important here. *Participatio Christi* is less a matter of *imitatio Christi* than of *conformatio Christi*.[66] Again, the God who has begun a good work in the faithful will bring it to completion at the day of Jesus Christ (Phil. 1:16). In the meantime they are called to work out their salvation with fear and trembling; for it is God who operates within them, both to will and to work for his good pleasure (2:12–13). The divine passive of the verb "being conformed" (*symmorphizomenos*) means that their sufferings are being turned by God to their salvation. Just as *participatio Christi* means justification (3:9), so *conformatio Christi* means sanctification (3:10). Sanctification proceeds through

64. "To know Easter means to be implicated in the events of Good Friday." Barth, *Epistle to the Philippians*, 103.

65. "The Lord's death as the supreme expression of his love and of his holiness, and the supreme act of surrender to the Father's will, draws the soul of the Apostle with spiritual magnetic force to desire, and to experience, assimilation to the character of him who endured it." Moule, *Philippians*, 96.

66. "The 'imitation' of Christ depends on union with him, and is a question of being conformed to his image, not of copying an external pattern." Hooker, *From Adam to Christ*, 7. Hooker rightly links "imitation" with a prior "participation" and "conformation."

loving communion with Christ in his sufferings and through being conformed to him in his death.[67]

3:11 in order that I may attain to the resurrection from the dead—The trajectory of Paul's thinking moves from justification (3:9), through sanctification (3:10), to glorification (3:11).[68] Paul strives to work out his salvation with fear and trembling as the power of God operates within him (2:12–13). The work of God and the response of faith are noncompetitive, though their relationship is mysterious, beyond full understanding. Faithfulness to Christ does not mean complacency. It means striving to live in accord with the grace that is given and received anew each day. It means living a life of gratitude in free response to what has been so wondrously given.

Seen from above, God will bring the work he has begun to completion. Seen from below, the faithful need to strive toward the goal day by day.[69] Paul therefore endeavors to gain Christ (3:8), to be found in him (3:9), to know him in the power of his resurrection (3:10), and to be conformed to him in his sufferings and death (3:10), that he may attain at last to the resurrection of the dead (*ei pōs katantēsō eis tēn exanastasin tēn ek nekrōn*) (3:11). Easter contains within itself not only the promise that many will rise with Christ, but also the mandate to put Easter hope into action. "Attaining to the resurrection" means living and working in hope until the end of all things.

> [12]Not that I have already obtained [this] or am already perfect, but I press on to make it my own, because Christ Jesus has made me his own. [13]Brothers and sisters, I do not consider that I have made it my own. But one thing I do: forgetting what lies behind and straining forward to what lies ahead, [14]I press on toward the goal for the prize of the upward call of God in Christ Jesus. [15]All of us, then, who are mature should take such a view of things. And if on some point you think differently, that too God will make clear to you. [16]Only let us live up to what we have already attained. [17]Join together in following my example, brothers and sisters, and just as you have us as a model, keep your eyes on those who live as we do.

67. "The conformity with the sufferings of Christ implies not only the endurance of persecution for his name, but all pangs and all afflictions undergone in the struggle against sin either within or without." Lightfoot, *Philippians*, 149.

68. "*Resurrection* he puts for the completion of redemption, so that it also involves within it the idea of death." Calvin, *Philippians*, in *Calvin's New Testament Commentaries*, 11:275.

69. "Weiss remarks that while on the human side, the attainment of the goal may be regarded as doubtful, or at least conditioned upon humble self-estimate, on the side of the working of divine grace it appears certain." Vincent, *Philippians*, 106.

3:12 Not that I have already obtained [this] or am already perfect—The situation Paul describes about his reception of salvation is not without complexity. What has been obtained is being obtained and is yet to be obtained. Interpretation is difficult here, among other things, because the verb *elabon* ("obtained") appears with no object. I will assume that Paul is referring to the goal of obtaining the saving benefits of Christ in that perfect form which he expects to know in eternal life. What he thinks those benefits are in particular remains somewhat unclear.

Salvation in Christ, as we have seen, has three temporal aspects. From one point of view, what has already been obtained is called "justification" (*in Christo*), what is now being obtained is called "sanctification" (*in nobis*), and what is yet to be obtained is called "glorification" (resolving the tension between *in Christo* and *in nobis*). More broadly, it may be inferred that what Paul has not yet "obtained" is "resurrection from the dead" (*tēn exanastasin tēn nekrōn*) (3:11). Obtaining it will mean receiving the saving benefits of Christ under the aspect of final perfection.

The perfection of righteousness in Christ involves, we may say, a Christocentric eschatology of participation. In Christ, perfect righteousness is real, hidden, and yet to come. The hiddenness of its perfection under one aspect does not mean that it is not already real for the believer under another aspect, nor does it mean that perfect righteousness does not need to be actualized and revealed on the last day in its future aspect. Although righteousness in Christ involves these several dimensions, its hiddenness in the present is not a matter of simple imperfection. Nevertheless, we may say (with Vermigli) that for the time being we are more perfectly in Christ than Christ is in us.[70]

From another point of view, Paul might be saying that although he already *knows* Christ, he does not yet know him perfectly; that although he has already *gained* Christ, he has not yet gained him perfectly; and that although he is already *in Christ*, he is not yet to be found in him perfectly (at the level of lived experience). Whereas this way of resolving the ambiguities focuses more on the saving benefits of Christ *in nobis*, the former way focuses more on our possession of them *extra nos*. In any case, Paul's saving relationship to Christ is such that he knows Christ, enjoys him, and partakes of him under an eschatological (or apocalyptic) proviso. Christ and his benefits are known under a very different aspect here and now than they will be there and then in eternal life.

I should perhaps note here my agreement with the recent work of Will Timmins, who argues that in the disputed passage of Rom. 7:14–25, Paul

70. Peter Martyr Vermigli, *Defensio doctrinae veteris et apostolicae de sacrosancto Eucharistia . . . adversus Stephani Gardineri*, #752 (1559), cited in McLelland, *Visible Words of God*, 148.

portrays the character of Christian existence here and now, not pre-Christian existence. The *egō* of Rom. 7, Timmins argues, exists simultaneously in two eons at once (the old and the new), although in different respects. "As Romans 7:25 makes clear," he writes, "*egō continues* to experience the division to which Adamic humanity is subject *after* having experienced deliverance through Jesus Christ. . . . Although no longer 'in the flesh,' *egō* is still 'fleshly,' which is why the life of the new aeon will only come to fruition in him if he serves God 'in newness of the Spirit.'" "The fundamental distinction," he continues, "that has come to light in our study is the difference between the *egō*'s ontological identity as a person in Christ and his anthropological condition as someone who remains 'fleshly' for as long as he inhabits the Adamic body of death."[71] This interpretation is supported by Mark Seifrid. "The apostle can hardly *exclude* himself from fallen humanity," Seifrid writes. "Adam's experience is also Paul's experience. . . . The experience and identity of the 'I' whom Paul describes throughout the chapter [Rom. 7] remains his own."[72] In the eschatological interim, the *egō* of Rom. 7, who is written about in the present tense, exists mysteriously on two levels at the same time. (For more on the idea of two levels, see excursus 8.)

I press on to make it my own—As long as the discrepancy between salvation's present tense and its future fulfillment persists, with regard to apprehending Christ and his benefits, Paul, who makes no claim to perfection, will strive to live in accord with the final goal. "I press on to make it my own" (*diōkō de ei kai katalabō*). (There are further difficulties here, on which I do not comment, because the objects of some verbs are again missing in the Greek.)

because Christ Jesus has made me his own—In any case it is clear that, for Paul, salvation's future fulfillment rests entirely on the initiative of Christ. The clause rendered as "Christ Jesus has made me his own" might be translated more literally as "I was laid hold of by Christ Jesus" (*katelēmphthēn hypo Christou Iēsou*).[73] For Paul the only fitting response is "laying hold" (of Christ)—"if indeed I may lay hold" (*ei kai katalabō*). His being "apprehended by Christ" (passive voice) is followed by his resolve to "apprehend Christ" in turn (active voice). We may say, more fully, that the active response to grace is gratitude, to mercy is repentance, and to love is a resolve to love in return. It is a matter of apprehending Christ as one has been apprehended by him.

71. Timmins, *Romans 7 and Christian Identity*, 180, 205 (slightly modified).
72. Seifrid, "Romans 7," 113–14.
73. Some would discern an allusion here to Paul's encounter with Christ on the Damascus Road.

It is not clear why Paul thinks the twofold emphasis in this verse is necessary. On the one hand, he stresses his lack of perfection in himself, and on the other, he accentuates his energetic striving toward perfection as the goal. Is Paul opposing a faction that insists that perfection can already be obtained this side of the eschaton? Would they have been his circumcising opponents? Or would they have been Hellenistic "gnostics" or proto-gnostics? Or is Paul attempting to counteract a faction of "antinomians" or perhaps even "libertines"? Would they have contended that no striving toward the goal of spiritual or moral perfection is necessary, so that all things are permissible? While some such factions appear in the background of other Pauline letters, it is unclear whether the apostle thinks they are a threat to the Philippians.

3:13 forgetting what lies behind—Whatever Paul precisely means by "laying hold" (without an object), and presumably it means laying hold perfectly of Christ—"I do not reckon myself to have laid hold" (*egō emauton ou logizomai kateilēphenai*)—he returns to the theme of "straining forward" (*epekteinomenos*) toward the goal, while again rejecting any false perception (*logizomai*) of having arrived. His direct address ("brothers and sisters") regarding "the one thing [I do]" (*hen de*) adds earnestness to his appeal.

What is new in this verse is the idea of "forgetting what lies behind" (*ta men opisō epilanthanomenos*)—literally, "the things that lie behind" (*ta opisō*).[74] Is Paul thinking of his inglorious past as a persecutor? Might he also be thinking, more broadly, of what he previously regarded as his religious status—ascribed, achieved, and master—based on "works of the law," the status he now regards as worthless when it comes to obtaining salvation? Or, as seems rather less likely, is he merely thinking about his past accomplishments as an apostle?

In any case we may posit that Paul looks on his entire sinful past as having been blotted out and removed by the blood of Christ. His sinful past is therefore no impediment to the future. In Christ it is as good as gone. All anxiety about the past, whatever it may include, is done away with. It is spiritually irrelevant. The remembrance of past guilt can no longer be crippling. "The things that lie behind" might, of course, also include adversities and traumas. In any case, for Paul, the old has passed away, and the new has come (2 Cor. 5:17).

straining forward to what lies ahead—With the term "straining forward" (*epekteinomenos*), an athletic metaphor is again introduced (cf. Phil. 2:16). Paul wants to encourage the Philippians as they race toward the finish line of the

---

74. The plural seems important here. Paul is referring to real impediments and adversities, not just "the portion of the course already traversed," which wouldn't require the plural. *Pace* Lightfoot, *Philippians*, 150.

promised future. Again he seems concerned to dissuade them from discouragement or complacency. The usual paradox reappears. The gift that has already been
given is a goal still to be attained. Whatever failures or adversities the Philippians
have experienced—or may yet experience—they have no reason to lose heart.

Seen from above, the gift of salvation is secure because the Giver and the Gift—
Christ himself—are one. Christ will see the Philippians through. Discouragement
is therefore ruled out. Seen from below, the goal still has to be attained, and the
race has yet to be won. Every possible effort is needed. Anything less would be
ingratitude. In the power of his resurrection, Christ will preserve them—in their
fellowship with his sufferings and their conformity with his death—until the
end. Inaction or defection is therefore also ruled out. Paul depicts himself as an
athlete who is neither encumbered by the past nor unmoved by the future. He
is straining every nerve to reach the goal, and so should they.

3:14 I press on toward the goal—The athletic metaphor continues. Along
with the unique calling of an apostle, Paul shares the common lot of all Christians.
He is a long-distance runner racing toward the finish line (*kata skopon diōkō eis
to brabeion*). Straining every nerve, he keeps his eye on "the prize" (*to brabeion*),
while not forgetting the "upward call" (*tēs anō klēseōs*). The forward look does
not exclude the upward look. Heaven above and the promised future are one.

The Philippians are urged to continue in their common vocation. They are to
heed the same call as Paul by persevering with him in the race. Together they will
obtain the one thing that really matters: "the prize of the upward call of God in
Christ Jesus" (*to brabeion tēs anō klēseōs tou theou en Christō Iēsou*).

3:15 All of us, then, who are mature—This enigmatic verse is not easy to construe. I have borrowed a translation from the Greek that makes the rough places
plain.[75] Paul now turns, so to speak, to direct discourse. In the previous verses
(3:7–14) he has spoken in the first person as a means of rhetorical exhortation.
He has set himself forward as an example. Beginning with 3:15 he begins to make
explicit what has already been implicit. In 3:17 he will tell the Philippians to follow
his example. In 3:15–16 he turns from first-person discourse to direct address.

The word translated as "mature" (*teleioi*) involves guesswork to decide on a
rendering (cf. 1 Cor. 2:6). Almost in the same breath Paul states that he is not
yet "perfected" (*teteleiōmai*) (Phil. 3:12). He seems to be engaged in wordplay.
Many have followed John Chrysostom in interpreting what Paul means—namely,
that Christian perfection means acknowledging Christian imperfection, as if

---

75. Hansen, *Letter to the Philippians*, 257. I use Hansen's translation for 3:15–21.

he were saying, "Let those who are mature recognize that they are not perfect." If so, taking the "mature" view is a matter of humility. The phrase "let us take such a view of things" (*touto phronōmen*) (3:15) lines up rather nicely with the exhortation in Phil. 2:5 to "let this mind be in you" (*touto phroneite*). Both places find Paul commending a "mindset" of humility and perseverance in the midst of affliction for the sake of love. The mindset found in Christ Jesus is reflected in the mindset of Paul.

And if on some point—"Such a view of things" seems to involve certain convictions that are beyond dispute. The imperatives of being "conformed to Christ," for example, or of straining toward "the goal" despite all adversities do not seem controversial. What the "lesser matters" may be on which some might "think differently" (*ei ti heterōs*) is not specified.[76] They cannot have been unimportant, or else Paul would not have expected them to be clarified eventually by divine illumination:[77] "God will make it clear to you" (*ho theos hymin apokalypsei*). Therefore Paul may be saying, "Let us agree in essentials, and if there are disagreements in lesser matters, they will eventually be clarified by God." "If you are sound at the core, God will remove the superficial blemishes."[78]

3:16 Only let us live up—Paul encourages the Philippians to conduct their lives in accord with the truth they have received. Since they have been turned in a certain direction, Paul urges them to continue in it, according to the allotted measure of their wisdom. It is as if he were saying, "Even if there are points of disagreement, we have all already attained to Christ (*ho ephthasamen*); therefore, let us conform to the pattern he displays (*tō autō stoichein*)."

3:17 Join together in following my example—Paul continues to address the Philippians as "brothers and sisters." He now describes them, remarkably, as "fellow imitators of me" (*symmimētai mou*). The way of conformity to Christ runs through imitating the apostle, and the way of imitating the apostle runs through walking in the way of those individuals in their community who follow Christ in conformity with Paul and his coworkers (*tous houtō peripatountas kathōs echete typon hēmas*). Just as Christ is a model for Paul, so also are Paul and his coworkers (such as Timothy and Epaphroditus) a model for the rest.[79] "Those who live

76. "Paul was assured as to his doctrine, but he allows those who could not yet receive it time to make progress, and he does not cease on that account to regard them as brothers and sisters." Calvin, *Philippians*, in *Calvin's New Testament Commentaries*, 11:279 (slightly modified).

77. "Divine revelation would be unnecessary to solve minor disagreements." Hellerman, *Philippians*, 208.

78. Lightfoot, *Philippians*, 151.

79. "The earliest Christians, coming out of paganism and lacking an easily accessible body of sacred literature, relied for ethical direction upon the living examples of those who brought them

as we do" (*tous houtō peripatountas*) may have included not just Paul's coworkers but also, as suggested, his close followers in the community.[80]

> **18**For, as I have often told you before and now tell you again even with tears, many live as enemies of the cross of Christ. **19**Their destiny is destruction, their god is their stomach, and their glory is in their shame. Their mind is set on earthly things.

3:18 many live as enemies of the cross of Christ—There are some close at hand who are not worthy of imitation but rather, more tragically, of tears. The existence of these people cannot be news to the Philippians, because Paul has often talked about them. They are not to be imitated but rejected because of their way of life. They are still a present danger, Paul must have felt, because he is moved to warn about them again. Their lifestyle stands in flagrant contradiction to the gospel. They live "as enemies of the cross of Christ" (*tous echthrous tou staurou tou Christou*).

Who are these "many" (*polloi*)? It seems that they are not members of the Pauline community, though they claim to be Christians. Their posing as Christians is what makes Paul weep.[81] Nor are they likely to have been his Jewish Christian opponents, for that group would not be living an indulgent lifestyle. The problem with the offending group seems to be its lifestyle, not its teaching.[82] They are not strict adherents of the law, but seem more like antinomians or libertines who "degraded the true doctrine of Christian liberty,"[83] perhaps not unlike some at Corinth (1 Cor. 5–6). They are a peril to themselves and an obstacle to the progress of the gospel. They do not accept suffering, should it come, as integral to the Christian life. They want a theology of glory without a theology of the cross. "They make use of Christ's name, but do not follow his example"; instead they live "a life of self-indulgence."[84]

Contemporary Christians in the global North, who not uncommonly have affluent lifestyles, and whose tables may be laden with wholesome food and fine

---

the gospel." Hellerman, *Philippians*, 213. It may be worth remembering here, to some degree over against Hellerman, that during this time Christianity was seen not as a different religion but as a sect of Judaism. Thus, the Hebrew scriptures were the Gentile Christians' sacred texts. Paul assumes that his congregations are familiar with these scriptures, as indicated by the numerous quotations of the Old Testament in his letters, including Philippians.

80. If so, perhaps they included some who had come out of Judaism.

81. "Though his words are harsh, his heart is broken." Hansen, *Letter to the Philippians*, 265.

82. Although they are targets of Paul's criticism, they ought not to be described as his "opponents," since they are not actively contending against him. The search for "opponents" here is a red herring.

83. Lightfoot, *Philippians*, 153.

84. Lightfoot, *Philippians*, 153 (slightly modified).

wine, might not wish to regard themselves as "belly worshippers."[85] Perhaps
they do not give much thought to starving children,[86] refugees of war (not least
unjust and immoral wars perpetrated by their own country),[87] or persecuted
Christians[88] in other parts of the globe. They might not wish to see themselves as
self-indulgent Epicureans whose lives stand in contradiction to the gospel. One
wonders whether Paul, who languished in prison and took "the view from below,"
would agree. Who might he have seen today as "enemies of the cross of Christ"?[89]

3:19 Their destiny is destruction—Philippians 3:19–21 suggests a vivid coun-
terimage to the Christ hymn of Phil. 2:5–11.[90] By indulging themselves with
little heed, there are Christians whose lifestyle contradicts the way of Christ.
For Christ Jesus, though he was rich, "yet for your sake became poor" (2 Cor.
8:9). By contrast, "Epicurean Christians," who fill themselves with good things,
making the belly their god, have departed from Christ. Recall that though Christ
was in the form of God, he emptied himself, dying in the form of a slave on the
cross. For their part, truly faithful Christians would take the high road, straining like trained athletes toward "the prize of the upward call of God in Christ
Jesus" (Phil. 3:14). Self-indulgent Christians, on the other hand, opt for the low
road, setting their softened minds "on earthly things" (*ta epigeia*) (3:19). For
Paul the shame of the truly faithful is their glory, while the worldly glory of the
self-indulgent is their shame.

Contrasting lifestyles are in view. On the one hand are the faithful, who have
fixed their minds on the things that are above. Like athletes, they drive their
bodies toward the goal. Like Christ, they are not self-centered, but prepared
for suffering and death. Their hope is in the resurrection. When Christ who is
their life appears, they will appear with him in glory (Col. 3:4). On the other
hand are the "gourmet Christians," who have set their minds on earthly things.
They are consumed by a life of self-indulgence, perhaps especially regarding food

85. See Sandnes, *Belly and Body*, 136–64.

86. "Approximately 3.1 million children die from undernutrition each year. Hunger and undernutrition contribute to more than half of global child deaths." World Hunger Education Service, "World
Child Hunger Facts," updated July 2018, https://www.worldhunger.org/world-child-hunger-facts.

87. According to World Vision, "68.5 million people around the world have been forced to flee
their homes due to violent conflict." "Forced to Flee: Top Countries Refugees Are Coming From,"
World Vision, June 26, 2018, https://www.worldvision.org/refugees-news-stories/forced-to-flee-top
-countries-refugees-coming-from.

88. The average number of Christian martyrs around the globe in 2017 was 90,000, up from 34,400
in 1900, and headed toward 100,000 in 2050. Johnson et al., "Christianity 2017."

89. See Hunsinger, *Beatitudes*; Sider, *Rich Christians*; Gollwitzer, *Rich Christians*.

90. D. Martin, *Slavery as Salvation*, 130–32.

and sensual pleasures. They avoid persecution through social conformity. Paul condemns them as "enemies of Christ's cross." Their destiny is not a happy one.[91]

The perils of prosperity in Paul's warnings strike a familiar biblical note. "But woe to you who are rich, for you have received your consolation" (Luke 6:24). "I will strike the winter house along with the summer house, and the houses of ivory shall perish, and the great houses shall come to an end" (Amos 3:15). "He has cast down the mighty from their thrones, and exalted those of low degree; he has filled the hungry with good things, and the rich he has sent empty away" (Luke 1:52–53). "When the disciples heard this, they were greatly astonished, saying, 'Who then can be saved?'" (Matt. 19:25).

> **20**But our citizenship is in heaven, and from it we await a Savior, the Lord Jesus Christ, **21**who will transform our lowly body to be like his glorious body, by the power that enables him even to subject all things to himself.

3:20 But our citizenship is in heaven—The Philippians face two main perils: dissension from within and disdain (if not worse) from without. "Fellowship" (*koinōnia*) is Paul's solution to the first difficulty, while a concept of "citizenship" (*politeuma*) is his solution to the second. Although bolstering fellowship within the community is his main concern, he does not overlook challenges from the external world. Pressures exist in Philippi for Christians to yield to pagan forms of worship, and in particular to the practices of a civil religion that exalt the emperor as the object of supreme allegiance.

Those who "set their minds on earthly things" (*epigeia*) (3:19) are inclined, we may suppose, not only toward gastronomic self-indulgence but also toward social conformity, including compromises with pagan religious practices. They are concerned not only with the pleasures of the table but also with social advantages. They have taken pride in their high social position and are averse to any loss in social standing. Paul's phrase "earthly things" would thus include social and economic status as well as sensual pleasures.

Paul has already shown that in "emptying himself" (kenosis) Christ underwent a steep drop in status (2:6–7). The apostle himself has followed suit. In becoming a Christian he has surrendered his privileges (3:7–9), been willing to suffer (3:10), and shown determination to press on toward the goal (3:12–14).[92] The Christian way of life involves suffering for the sake of higher loyalties. True Christians

91. Sandnes, *Belly and Body*, 142–43.
92. Oakes, *Philippians*, 196, 105.

cannot set their minds on Christ without relinquishing "earthly things," which cannot be their ultimate concern.

In *Philippians: From People to Letter*, Peter Oakes casts light on the social and economic circumstances in which the Philippian Christians lived out their lives. He singles out a variety of reasons for their tribulations. The "primary causes" for their being looked on with suspicion by their neighbors would have been "principally abandonment of pagan worship, also suspicion of secretive associations, suspicion of Jewish activities, and attempts at evangelism. When [the Christians] were met with violence, this disturbance acted as a secondary cause of further trouble, namely, being taken before the magistrates. Association in the magistrates' mind with other troublesome Christians" could further contribute to being punished.[93]

Oakes suggests that the most serious long-term sufferings inflicted on the Philippians would probably have been economic. The forms of possible ostracism were varied: "withdrawal of facilities by fellow crafts-people; withdrawal of custom [habitual buying of goods]; violence; summary justice from magistrates; cancellation of tenancy; foreclosure of debt; breaking patron-client relationships; withdrawal of financial assistance; divorce; repudiation by family; withdrawal of opportunities to earn *peculium* [a kind of stipend]; being sold."[94]

According to Oakes, it is not likely that the Philippians' troubles stemmed primarily from their abandoning the emperor cult. Most of them, he thinks, were probably not Roman citizens, and in any case it would be only "one cult among many that they might be seen to abandon."[95] Nevertheless, Oakes depicts the Philippians as a "threatened minority" who were "externally beleaguered."[96]

Some scholars have argued that there was "no such thing as '*the* imperial cult,'" but only various decentralized provincial or municipal "imperial cults," under different emperors, in different places, at different times.[97] In any case, two points seem to be significant.

First, by abstaining from pagan worship, including the imperial cult, Philippian Christians would have been perceived as a threat to civic unity. They were a suspect religious minority. Oakes regards their religious nonconformity as the principal cause of their being ostracized.

93. Oakes, *Philippians*, 91 (slightly modified).
94. Oakes, *Philippians*, 96.
95. Oakes, *Philippians*, 137. Oakes in effect disagrees with the opposite position as taken, for example, by Fee, *Philippians*, 197.
96. Oakes, *Philippians*, 83.
97. See Beard, North, and Price, *Religions of Rome*, 1:348.

Second, some Christians, perhaps especially those of higher social status, may have "set their minds on earthly things" by compromising with pagan worship. "If *koilia* (stomach) (v. 19) means the stomach as the seat of hunger," writes Oakes, "and *aischunē* (shame) is a euphemism for idols, then the 'enemies of the cross' could be those who return to (or stay with) idolatrous worship to escape economic suffering."[98]

In this context, our appreciation for what *politeuma* may have meant for Paul and his Philippian readers has been enhanced through a recent study by Gennadi A. Sergienko.[99] Since in some ways Sergienko seems more extensive than careful in his argument, he is perhaps best read as a supplement to, not a substitute for, Oakes. Nevertheless, Sergienko has done extensive analysis of the archeological, literary, and inscriptional evidence for what he calls "voluntary associations" in Philippi at the time of Paul. These include both civic and religious associations, though the lines between the two, as the author indicates, could be blurred. Since the Philippian church is not necessarily well described as merely a "voluntary association," however, perhaps a better and more neutral term would be "civic association."

As depicted by Sergienko, these associations combined patriotism, social status, and religious observances with regular festivities and banqueting. They would therefore be a plausible *Sitz im Leben* where various forms of idolatry, social conformity, and excessive sensuality might be practiced—all of which were possibly at stake in Paul's denunciation of those "whose god is their belly" and who "set their mind on earthly things." While Sergienko believes that at least some elements of an emperor cult may often have been woven into the religious observances of these associations, he also assumes that something called *the* emperor cult was a stand-alone institution as well, which Oakes and others give us reason to doubt.

A fair conclusion from Sergienko's study would be that allegiance to one's political "homeland" could be intermingled with participation in one of these quasi-religious "civic" associations. The author provides a very detailed list of what these associations may have been.[100] The disputed term *politeuma* would therefore carry the double connotation of "homeland" and "civic association" (not the one, I think, without the other).

from it we await a Savior—Paul insists on a radically different way of life: "Our *politeuma* is in heaven" (3:20). The question of "citizenship" involves at least

98. Oakes, *Philippians*, 106n3.
99. Sergienko, *Our Politeuma Is in Heaven!*
100. Sergienko, *Our Politeuma Is in Heaven!*, 187–90.

three things for the Philippian believers: (1) a different homeland, (2) a different schedule of allegiances, and (3) a different source of protection and deliverance.

(1) The Philippian Christians are citizens of a different commonwealth.[101] They live on earth as though they are in exile.[102] They are not first of all Roman citizens while only incidentally belonging to another homeland. Their heavenly membership is primary, while their earthly membership is less normative. Any penultimate *politeuma* is relativized by the ultimate one, not the other way around. The values of the heavenly *politeuma* take precedence. Their hidden commonwealth is the one to which they really belong. They are to set their minds on it, not on "earthly things." They are called to live in accord with a promised homeland centered in Christ and toward which they are homeward bound.

(2) The Philippian Christians have a different schedule of allegiances. Because Christ is their supreme object of loyalty, their allegiance to any other is limited. What Paul states in 3:20 clearly hearkens back to 2:9–11, in which Jesus himself is acclaimed as the Lord to which every knee shall bow. Living in a Roman context, the Philippians "would hear 2:9–11 as in some sense involving a grant of authority to Jesus that eclipsed the authority of the Emperor."[103] They are expected to infer that, if necessary, in loyalty to Jesus, "they should be willing to lose status and suffer faithfully."[104] Allegiance to Christ may well mean suffering in this world or at least sitting loosely with it.[105] Allegiance to Christ may mean relinquishment and downward mobility.

(3) The Philippian Christians look to a different source of protection and deliverance. In Roman society the emperor was praised as "savior." In the emperor cult he was sometimes acclaimed as savior or deliverer for the whole world. For Christians, however, far from being a savior or deliverer, the emperor might well be a vicious tormentor.[106] Their expectation of Christ as "Savior" meant that they were to look to him alone for their protection and deliverance. Above all, they

---

101. "Just as Philippi was a colony of Rome, whose citizens thereby exemplified the life of Rome in the province of Macedonia, so the citizens of the 'heavenly commonwealth' were to function as a colony of heaven in that outpost of Rome." Fee, *Philippians*, 379.

102. They are "living as a community in exile while belonging to another country." Bockmuehl, *Philippians*, 233. Both "commonwealth" and "homeland" capture different nuances of *politeuma* (*pace* O'Brien, *Philippians*). Following Sergienko, "civic membership" would probably also need to be thrown into the mix. It would be a mistake to suppose that *politeuma* can be rendered by a single English term.

103. Oakes, *Philippians*, 150.

104. Oakes, *Philippians*, 208.

105. "In seeking the protective status of an earthly *politeuma*, they [the compromised Christians] betray their ultimate allegiance to a different *kyrios* and *sōtēr*." Sergienko, *Our Politeuma Is in Heaven!*, 162.

106. "Comparison with Caligula would indeed have been a live issue in Paul's day, especially for a Jewish writer." Oakes, *Philippians*, 131.

were to look to him for their vindication. Just as he himself was vindicated from above after dying ingloriously on the cross, so beleaguered Christians will be vindicated when he returns from heaven in glory. They await their vindication from him with "eager expectation" (*apekdechometha*). Paul sets up "a polemical parallelism, contrasting Christ and Caesar, in order to establish Christ as the only true *kyrios* and *sōtēr*."[107]

Vindication—an apocalyptic theme (especially with respect to martyrdom)—is a major topic in Philippians. For the faithful, the day of Christ (1:6, 10; 2:16) will be a day of vindication. Christ is not only a pattern to which they conform. He is the Lord of glory who has made them his own (3:12). Because they live as "saints in him" by grace though faith (1:1), they will also be "found in him" (3:9) on the last day, when they are vindicated as blameless and righteous before the throne of God (1:10; 2:15; 3:6, 9). Union with Christ is the basis for their sharing not only in his sufferings (3:10) but also in his final vindication (3:21); thus, it is the basis for being conformed to the image of his apocalyptic pattern, whether it means exaltation in heaven or humiliation on earth.

3:21 who will transform our lowly body—Fellowship with Christ (3:10) means union with him in his final exaltation (3:11). Being conformed to him in his death (3:10) means final glorification (3:11)—beyond justification (3:9) and sanctification (3:10). Just as his mangled body has been transformed into his glorious body, so will the "humiliated" bodies of the faithful (*to sōma tēs tapeinōseōs hēmōn*) be "conformed to his body in glory" (*symmorphon tō sōmati tēs doxēs autou*). Having been made one with him in lowliness, they will also be made one with him in splendor. Although the dishonor visited upon the faithful may be severe, it will not be their ultimate fate. Their shame will be turned into glory, even as the glory of Epicurean Christians will collapse into shame. For Paul, whether the mind is set on heavenly things or on earthly things makes a difference.

The "humiliated bodies" of the faithful has a twofold reference. It is broadly existential as well as social and political. Although commentators have generally been more inclined to catch the former connotation than the latter, both are present in the text. Lightfoot, for example, interprets "the body of our humiliation" as referring to "the body which we bear in our present low estate, which is exposed to all the passions, sufferings and indignities of this life."[108] That is the broadly existential aspect. All will undergo "the thousand natural shocks that flesh is heir to" (*Hamlet*, act 3, scene 1) regardless of their social situation. Resurrection hope

---

107. Sergienko, *Our Politeuma Is in Heaven!*, 171.
108. Lightfoot, *Philippians*, 154–55.

is nevertheless a hope for cosmic transformation as well as for final vindication. It is a hope that pertains to the community as well as to the individual. It is a hope whose cosmic scope involves a social and political dimension.

to subject all things to himself—The Christ at whose name every knee shall bow (2:10) is the same Lord who will subject "all things" (*ta panta*) to himself (1 Cor. 15:27–28). Indeed his power not only surpasses that of any earthly ruler, including the emperor; it is tantamount to the power of God. Two points in particular may be noted.

First, in so many words Paul once again ascribes deity to Christ. He uses language here that he elsewhere applies only to God the Father.[109] "It serves as a confirmation of Paul's high christology that the equivalent act of subjugation was in 2:9–11 ascribed to God. . . . Here it is by the power of the exalted Christ himself."[110] "The will of the Father takes effect through the will of the Son, One with him."[111]

Second, the idea that Christ will subject "all things" (*ta panta*) to himself by wielding his resurrection power (*kata tēn energian tou dynasthai*) is, here as elsewhere, an idea fraught with apocalyptic resonance. When the new arises from the abolition of the old, Christ will be revealed as the Pantocrator. Although his power in the present age is still veiled (and on the cross was concealed under the form of its opposite), it will be manifested in glory on "the day of Christ." It will be revealed that the Crucified One has triumphed over all the rampant idolatry and wickedness of the present evil age. By his power his followers, too, will not only be vindicated but also transformed into glory, as he subjects his enemies—most especially the cosmic forces of sin, death, and corruption (*phthora*)—to himself (Rom. 8:21; cf. 1 Cor. 15:25–26). Apocalyptic vindication, final glorification, and cosmic triumph in Christ the Lord go hand in hand.

109. Fee, *Philippians*, 383–84.
110. Bockmuehl, *Philippians*, 236.
111. Moule, *Philippians*, 108. Once again we have an implicit pattern of unity-in-distinction between the Father and the Son.

PHILIPPIANS 4

4:1 Therefore, my brothers and sisters, whom I love and long for, my joy and crown, stand firm thus in the Lord, my beloved.

This verse is a kind of hinge between what came before and what comes next. The appeal to remain "steadfast" connects it to the previous theme of competing loyalties. It pertains to duties in the world ("citizenship") more than to bonds in the community ("fellowship")—more to withstanding external pressures than to healing internal conflicts and divisions (although both are of course involved).

4:1 **Therefore ... stand firm**—"Stand firm in the Lord" (*stēkete en kyriō*) means, in light of external social pressures, "Do not succumb to compromise." The sorry example of the Epicurean Christians must have been tempting to not a few. Otherwise, why would Paul have spoken about them so often and wept about them so openly (3:18)? Having set their minds on earthly things, such Christians capitulate to the ways of the world. Despite all present allurements and hardships, Paul encourages his readers not to go down that path. He calls them to the same kind of resiliency that he exemplifies in his own life.[1]

Standing firm "in the Lord" (*en kyriō*) means living in active union with Christ. Christ is the Lord who will see them through. He is at once their sustaining power as well as their goal and deliverer. As the one who will transform their humiliated bodies into glory, while subjecting all things to himself (3:21), he will not abandon them in their current struggles. As he has remained true to them, so they are called to remain true to him until the end.

my brothers and sisters, whom I love and long for—The tone of this verse is affectionate. Not only are the Philippians his brothers and sisters, not only does

---

1. Bockmuehl, *Philippians*, 238.

he love and long for them, not only are they even his joy and crown, but above all they are simply his beloved. Not for nothing has the epistle been described as a "hortatory letter of friendship."[2]

my joy and crown—Paul returns to the metaphor of athletic striving. Earlier he has said that Christ is the prize toward which he strains like a long-distance runner (3:14). Now he says that his Philippian friends will be his "joy and crown" (*chara kai stephanos*) at the finish line. They will be the victor's wreath laid on his head when his course has been completed with joy.

> [2]I entreat Euodia and I entreat Syntyche to agree in the Lord. [3]Yes, I ask you also, loyal Syzygus, help these women, who have labored side by side with me in the gospel together with Clement and the rest of my fellow workers, whose names are in the book of life.

4:2 I entreat—With the introduction of a striking admonition, the argument now turns from citizenship to fellowship. It is carefully prepared and skillfully delivered. Paul addresses the two women separately and yet also together ("I entreat . . . I entreat," *parakalō . . . parakalō*),[3] and he mentions them boldly by name. He calls them out without embarrassing them. His entreaty is prefaced by heartfelt words of affection for the community, not by a note of consternation or dismay.

He accentuates the positive before turning to the negative. He addresses the women with respect while also expressing his concern. Dissension between leaders, especially in a community as hard-pressed as theirs, will serve neither the cause of Christ nor the progress of the gospel. Fellowship has to be restored so that heavenly citizenship can be sustained. Having the same mind "in the Lord" (*en kyriō*) (4:2) is essential to standing fast "in the Lord" (*en kyriō*) (4:1).

to agree—Literally, "to have the same mind" (*to auto phronein*). Paul seems to think that the conflict is more a matter of attitude than of thorny differences regarding policy. The theme of adopting a proper "mindset" has been prominent throughout the letter, especially in 2:5. Perhaps Paul has been laying the groundwork for his appeal to Euodia and Syntyche all along.

Stand fast "in one spirit" (*en heni pneumati*), he urges, and strive together with "one mind" (*mia psychē*) (1:27). Fulfill my joy by being of "one mind" (*to auto phroneite*), he reiterates (2:2). Above all, have "the same frame of mind" (*touto*

---

2. Fee, *Philippians*, 385.
3. "The word choice and the repetition underscore the earnestness of the appeal." Hellerman, *Philippians*, 229.

phroneite) as was in Christ Jesus—that of humility and of a readiness to relin-quish power and privilege for the good of others (2:5). Let us be "likeminded" (*touto phronōmen*), he has pleaded, but if that is not yet possible, and some "think otherwise" (*heterōs phroneite*), let them wait for a revelation from the Lord (3:15). Let not your "minds be set on earthly things" (*ta epigeia phronountes*) (3:19), he cautions. Having the proper "mindset" is of prime importance throughout. Are Euodia and Syntyche locked in a power struggle?[4]

4:3 I ask you also, loyal Syzygus—Paul does not usually mention people by name. Having just made an exception with Euodia and Syntyche, would he immediately revert to type? It is not impossible, of course, that he resorts to an anonymous address. In that case his words mean something like "true yoke-fellow" (*gnēsie syzyge*), as if it is obvious whom he means.[5] But it would be a nice Dickensian touch, probably too good to be true, if there were actually a comrade named Syzygus in the community to whom Paul could appeal.[6]

The apostle seems to believe that a respected mediator might do the trick in helping (*syllambanou*) these worthy women work through their differences.[7] Having risked calling them out by name, he immediately proceeds to commend them. They have "labored side by side" with him in the gospel (*en tō euangeliō synēthlēsan moi*).[8] They are esteemed colleagues ensnarled in a tangle that a third party might help to straighten out. The spotlight is quickly shifted from their conflict, however, in another tactful move. Along with a certain Clement and the rest of Paul's coworkers, their names are said to be "written in the book of life" (*ta onomata en biblō zōēs*).[9] Pains are taken to single out the antagonists by name while surrounding them with rhetorical bonhomie.

[4]Rejoice in the Lord always; again I will say, rejoice. [5]Let your forbearance be known to everyone. The Lord is at hand. [6]Do not be anxious about anything, but

4. Euodia and Syntyche appear to have been women of rank who play a leading role in the Philippian church. Lightfoot, *Philippians*, 156. Some have wondered whether they might have been rival patrons of house churches, an ingenious speculation for which there is unfortunately no evidence. Perhaps they are vying over how the church's funds should be administered, another plausible speculation with no evidential support.
5. Fee suggests that the anonymous term refers to a mediator who might have been Luke. Bruce agrees. Fee, *Philippians*, 392–94; Bruce, *Paul*, 221. If so, why not appeal to him by name?
6. "It is quite simply a male proper name, whose bearer to be sure is as unknown to us as the two women he is to help." Barth, *Epistle to the Philippians*, 119. There is no evidence that this term was ever a name.
7. Paul does not take sides. Bockmuehl, *Philippians*, 239.
8. The verb suggests not only "a united struggle in preaching the gospel" but also "a sharing in the suffering" that results from it. Hellerman, *Philippians*, 232.
9. "'Book of life' imagery became common in apocalyptic literature to denote those who are admitted to eternal life." Hellerman, *Philippians*, 233.

in everything by prayer and supplication with thanksgiving let your requests be made known to God. ⁷And the peace of God, which passes all understanding, will keep your hearts and your minds in Christ Jesus.

We come to a series of largely disconnected maxims. Their coherence is not easy to discern. "There must have been a completely concrete link," suggests Barth, "which we lack the power to reconstruct." He continues, "It is a handful of requests, hints, observations and encouragements that Paul throws down before addressing himself to his last theme in verses 10ff. The passage is for that reason one of the liveliest and most allusive in Paul, or anywhere at all in the New Testament."[10]

4:4 **Rejoice in the Lord always**—The trials of the present, however severe, are overshadowed by joy because of Easter. If Paul, the Roman prisoner, languishing in chains and facing possible execution, can call on the Philippians to rejoice, how can they fail to do so? Joy has its reasons that reason knows not of, for, as the liturgy has it, Christ is risen from the dead, trampling out death by death, and bestowing life on those in the tombs. Not only Paul's admonition to be steadfast "in the Lord" (*en kyriō*) (4:1), but also his exhortation to be of one mind "in the Lord" (*en kyriō*) (4:2), has rejoicing "in the Lord" (*en kyriō*) at its very heart (4:4).[11] The Philippians will find harmony among themselves through mutual rejoicing. It is a rejoicing fit for all occasions (*pantote*), in season or out of season. Their rejoicing should be continually renewed: "again I will say, rejoice" (*palin erō, chairete*). It is not a matter of elation but of resilience. Nor is it basically introspective but Christocentric.

4:5 **Let your forbearance be known**—Forbearance (*epieikes*) is the test of grace under pressure.[12] Faced with social pressures and enticements to apostasy, a community that can maintain forbearance is a community whose existence is secure. It is a community that will know how to live above its circumstances. The Philippians will not be known for their complaining and capitulation. They will be known for their dignity. Forbearance is the disposition by which others can sense their Easter joy. Martin Luther King Jr.: "For we know that sacrifice is involved, that brutality will be faced, that savage conduct will need to be endured,

10. Barth, *Epistle to the Philippians*, 118.

11. The repeated phrase "in the Lord" again points to being in union and loving communion with the risen Christ.

12. The word *epieikes* can be translated differently. For example, it can mean "patience" or "gentleness." Taking the suffering of the Philippians into account, I opt for "forbearance," but this is a judgment call. It all comes to the same thing in the end. In any case, Lightfoot opts for "forbearance": "the opposite to a spirit of contention and self-seeking." Lightfoot, *Philippians*, 158.

that slick trickery will need to be overcome, but we are resolutely prepared for all of this. We are prepared to meet whatever comes with love, with firmness and with unyielding nonviolence."[13]

The Lord is at hand—Again we have the "already" and the "not yet." Christ is present to them as the Lord (*ho kyrios*). He is both the Lord who is soon to come and the Lord who is already present. He is "near at hand" (*engys*). The Philippians are not alone in their trials. They already live in the midst of their coming Deliverer, who will vindicate them. Since they suffer at the hands of enemies who acclaim Caesar as Lord,[14] Paul invokes their hope in a greater Lord. Their coming vindication is nigh. Martin Luther King Jr.:

> I come to say to you this afternoon, however difficult the moment, however frustrating the hour, it will not be long, because "truth crushed to earth will rise again."
> How long? Not long, because "no lie can live forever."
> How long? Not long, because "you shall reap what you sow."
> How long? Not long:
>
> > Truth forever on the scaffold,
> > Wrong forever on the throne,
> > Yet that scaffold sways the future,
> > And, behind the dim unknown,
> > Standeth God within the shadow,
> > Keeping watch above his own.
>
> How long? Not long, because the arc of the moral universe is long, but it bends toward justice.[15]

4:6 Do not be anxious about anything—Faith as the antidote to anxiety is a familiar biblical theme. To live without anxiety in the midst of suffering is an ongoing challenge of the Christian (or any other) life. The difficult circumstances facing the Philippians give Paul's admonition a special point. Peace of mind is a gift from above to be received by faith ever anew. Martin Luther King Jr.:

> Abnormal fears and phobias that are expressed in neurotic anxiety may be cured by psychiatry; but the fear of death, nonbeing, and nothingness, expressed in existential anxiety, may be cured only by a positive religious faith.

13. King, "Philosophy," in *Testament of Hope*, 92.
14. Fee, *Philippians*, 408.
15. King, "Our God Is Marching On," in *Testament of Hope*, 227–30.

A positive religious faith does not offer an illusion that we shall be exempt from pain and suffering, nor does it imbue us with the idea that life is a drama of unalloyed comfort and untroubled ease. Rather, it instills us with the inner equilibrium needed to face strains, burdens, and fears that inevitably come, and assures us that the universe is trustworthy and that God is concerned.[16]

but in everything by prayer and supplication with thanksgiving—If faith is the antidote to anxiety, prayer is the antidote to despair. To allow anxiety to fester while treating prayer with neglect is tantamount to practical atheism. "Supplication" (*deēsei*) is not merely the expression of a "wish" but a confident appeal by the faithful that their needs should be supplied.[17]

Absolutely dependent on grace, they turn to the Lord. Their petitions are not to be made without "thanksgiving" (*eucharistias*). Thanksgiving without supplication is empty, while supplication without thanksgiving is blind. Prayer makes the needs of the community "known to God" (*gnōrizesthō pros ton theon*). Prayer is the appointed means by which God will fulfill his purposes. Martin Luther King Jr.:

> In a world in which most men attempt to defend their highest values by the accumulation of weapons of mass destruction, it is morally refreshing to hear five thousand Negroes in Montgomery shout "Amen" and "Hallelujah" when they are exhorted to "pray for those who oppose you," or pray "Oh Lord, give us strength of body to keep walking for freedom," and conclude each meeting with: "Let us pray that God shall give us strength to remain nonviolent though we may face death."[18]

4:7 And the peace of God—God's peace (*hē eirēnē tou theou*) is a present reality attached to a future promise. It is communal as well as individual in scope. It is that shalom in which well-being reigns on earth. It has broken into history on Easter Day, bringing a foretaste of many good things. It is a mystery that surpasses all understanding (*hē hyperechousa panta noun*). It is the peace that produces a peaceable people.[19]

16. King, "The Strength to Love," in *Testament of Hope*, 515.
17. The reduction of petitionary prayer to the mere expression of a "wish" is trivializing. New Testament scholarship would do well to abandon the term "prayer-wish."
18. King, "Philosophy," in *Testament of Hope*, 80.
19. For Athanasius, the "peace of God" means that the peace of Christ has accomplished a great reversal in human affairs. Warfare is linked in his mind with dispositions and worship. Those whose dispositions are brutal are the very ones who worship demonic powers. They rage against each other "and could not bear to be a single hour without weapons." It is to "barbarians" such as these, he writes, that the gospel comes. "When they hear the teaching of Christ, they immediately turn from war to farming, and instead of arming their hands with swords they lift them up in prayer; and, in a word, instead of waging war

keep your hearts and your minds—The verb "keep" (*phourēsei*) has a double connotation. It suggests both "preservation" and "protection."[20] The divine peace is present in the "hearts and minds" of the faithful (*tas kardias hymōn kai ta noēmata hymōn*). What is begun in them will not end until God's shalom has covered the earth as the waters cover the sea (cf. Isa. 11:9; Rom. 8:21). It does not reach its final fulfillment until they are transformed into glory (Phil. 3:21). Until that time the peace of God keeps their hearts and minds "in Christ Jesus" (*en Christō Iēsou*), the risen Lord of the heavenly *politeuma*. Despite the cross of present reality, this peace protects and preserves them to the end. Jonathan Edwards: "How rational a ground of peace have they that have their sins pardoned and that have God, who has all things in his hands, for their assured friend! What rest may such considerations well yield to the soul! It is 'peace that passes all understanding.'"[21]

> [8]Finally, brothers and sisters, whatever is true, whatever is honorable, whatever is just, whatever is pure, whatever is lovely, whatever is commendable, if there is any excellence, if there be anything worthy of praise, think about these things. [9]What you have learned and received and heard and seen in me—practice these things, and the God of peace will be with you.

4:8 Finally, . . . think about these things—As in 3:1, where he also writes the word "finally" (*to loipon*), Paul offers a change in topic more than a conclusion to the letter.[22]

The apostle turns his attention to marks of excellence (cf. 1:10). While to his mind they are mainly anthropological in significance, they are indirectly

---

among themselves, from now on they take up arms against the devil and the demons, subduing them by their self-command and integrity of soul."

What this reversal shows, according to Athanasius, is the Savior's Godhead. "What human beings were unable to learn from idols they have learned from him." Christ's followers have ceased from mutual fighting. By their renewed lives and peaceable hearts, they stand opposed to demonic powers. "When they are insulted, they are patient, when robbed they make light of it, and most amazingly, they scorn death in order to become martyrs of Christ." Believers are those who would prefer to die "rather than deny their faith in Christ." In this way they show their love for him who "by his own love underwent all things for the world's salvation." They practice on earth the peace they have received and await from heaven. Athanasius, *On the Incarnation* 52, 27, in *Athanasius on the Incarnation*, 90–91 (slightly modified).

20. The image is a military one. It depicts God's peace "as a detachment of soldiers 'standing guard over' . . . a city so as to protect it from attack." Hawthorne, *Philippians*, 184.

21. Edwards, "Honey from the Rock," in *Works of Jonathan Edwards*, 17:135.

22. The adverb "finally" "does not mark the end of the letter, . . . but introduces the last in a series of imperatives that describe how the Philippians are to 'stand firm in the Lord'" (4:1). Hellerman, *Philippians*, 244.

christological and eschatological as well. The apostle wants to do more than shape the moral dispositions of the faithful.[23] He wants to deepen their faith in Christ and quicken their hope in the future.[24]

The marks of excellence are gifts that God bestows. They reflect attributes of God's own being.[25] Each is somehow revealed in Christ and mediated to the faithful by the Spirit (through word and sacrament). Each also describes an aspect of the promised future. Finally, each pertains to the whole community, not only to the individual believer.

When Paul calls the Philippians to "think about these things" (*tauta logizesthe*), he is not restricting them to a set of received cultural meanings. He expects them to ponder these matters from an evangelical standpoint. They are things that need to be weighed theologically in light of Christ and the gospel. The cross and resurrection of Christ are central to any Christian estimation of their meaning and significance.[26]

What would it be like to "think on these things" from a center in Christ? In principle a Christocentric interpretation would need to keep matters like the Trinity, Christology, ecclesiology, the Christian life, and eschatology in view. In practice the mix would vary according to context. What follows is an extended meditation on these marks of excellence in light of Christ and the Trinity.

whatever is true—In Christian understanding God is conceived as Light, so that "in him is no darkness at all" (1 John 1:5). The Holy Trinity, as a luminous fellowship of Light, is necessarily the repository of all truth.[27] God is the source

23. Here I depart from most commentators.

24. Lightfoot reads the list as referring to the nature of actions and qualities. "Speaking roughly, the words may be said to be arranged in a descending scale. The first four describe the character of the actions themselves: the first two, 'true' (*alēthē*) and 'honorable' (*semna*), being absolute; the second two, 'just' (*dikaia*) and 'pure' (*hagna*), relative; the fifth and sixth, 'lovely' (*prosphilē*) and 'commendable' (*euphēma*), point to the moral approbation which they conciliate [acquire from a state of hostility]; while the seventh and eighth, 'excellence' (*aretē*) and 'praiseworthy' (*epanos*), . . . are thrown in as an afterthought, that no motive may be omitted." Lightfoot, *Philippians*, 159 (slightly modified).

25. Over against Lightfoot, I take each of them to be, in different respects, both "absolute" (first) and "relative" (second).

26. In what follows I depart from the commentaries, which tend to regard these qualities as merely "moral" and as pertaining mainly to the individual believer. Even if that is largely "what it meant," it would no longer suffice for "what it means." In any case, the qualities are not merely "moral" but also—and primarily—"spiritual." They pertain to the vertical dimension first, and only on that basis to the horizontal. They are "Godward" before they are "humanward," "dispositional," or "interpersonal."

27. "Whenever we meet with heathen writers, let us learn from that light of truth which is admirably displayed in their works, that the human mind, fallen as it is, and corrupted from its integrity, is yet invested and adorned by God with excellent talents. If we believe that the Spirit of God is the only fountain of truth, we shall neither reject nor despise the truth itself, wherever it shall appear, unless we wish to insult the Spirit of God." Calvin, *Institutes* 3.2.15 (trans. Allen, 1:246–47). Cf. Aquinas: "Every

and ground of all truth in the world (*verum externum Dei*), just because God's being is the compendium of all truth in itself (*verum internum Dei*). Ultimately, the call to meditate on "whatever is true" (*hosa estin alēthē*) means reflecting on the person of Christ in his role as Mediator. For he is the light of God that has come into the world (John 1:4), and he is the incarnation of divine truth (John 14:6). "The truth is in Jesus" (Eph. 4:21).[28] "I am the light of the world" (John 8:12).

For the faithful, God has made Christ to be not only their righteousness but also their wisdom (1 Cor. 1:30). They are given eyes to see the Crucified for who he is—that is, the "secret and hidden wisdom of God" (1 Cor. 2:7). They are being renewed "in the spirit of their minds" (Eph. 4:23), and they strive to put away "the deceitfulness of sin" (Heb. 3:13). They no longer love "the darkness rather than the light" (John 3:19). They have renounced "disgraceful, underhanded ways" (2 Cor. 4:2). With Paul they refuse "to practice cunning or to tamper with God's word, but by the open statement of the truth" they commend themselves "to everyone's conscience in the sight of God" (2 Cor. 4:2). They are installed as witnesses to the truth they have received.

Truth is something to be practiced as well as something to be known. It involves not just the word but the deed. The faithful are called "to speak the truth in love." Just so, they "grow up in every way into him who is the head, even Christ" (Eph. 4:15). Speaking the truth in love involves unmasking the culture of death. "Take no part in the unfruitful works of darkness, but instead expose them" (Eph. 5:11). Nor can the light of Christ be separated from love for the neighbor. "Whoever says he is in the light and hates his brother or sister is still in darkness" (1 John 2:9). In Christ there can be no truth without love, and no love without truth. "Whatever is true" in Christ means that nothing can be true if it stands in contradiction to God's love.

Eschatologically, the truth of Christ is invincible. As Truth itself (*autoaletheia*) in the flesh, Christ is the presence of the promised future. Just so, he is the future of every true belief and every loving deed. Darkness has no ultimate reality, for in his truth Christ is destined to prevail, even as he is destined to triumph in his love. "For we cannot do anything against the truth, but only for the truth" (2 Cor.

truth by whomsoever spoken is from the Holy Spirit as bestowing the natural light" (*Summa Theologiae* I-II.109.1, ad. 1).

28. "And in order that the mind might walk more confidently towards the truth, the Truth itself, God, God's son, assuming humanity without putting aside his Godhead, established and founded this faith, that man might find a way to man's God through God made man." Augustine, *City of God* 11.3 (Dyson, 451).

13:8). Paul knows that truth crushed to earth will rise again.[29] The triune God, the incarnation of Christ, a life of love, resurrection hope—all these set the terms for reflecting on "whatever is true."

whatever is honorable—For Paul, God's glory is beyond all measure. God is glorious in himself (*interna Dei gloria*). Yet God both hides and reveals his glory in his Son, Jesus Christ (*externa Dei gloria*). He does so most drastically when Christ "empties himself," taking the form of a slave on our behalf. Christ dies in shame that we might be delivered from the dishonor of our sin.[30] Meditating on "whatever is honorable" (*hosa semna*) means reflecting on "the glory of God in the face of Jesus Christ" (2 Cor. 4:6). In the crucified flesh of Christ, the divine glory is at once hidden and revealed.

So vast are the riches of God's glory (Eph. 3:16) that they can withstand the shame of the cross. "None of the rulers of this age understood this, for if they had, they would not have crucified the Lord of glory" (1 Cor. 2:8). "But God chose what is foolish in the world to shame the wise; God chose what is weak in the world to shame the strong" (1 Cor. 1:27). "He disarmed the rulers and authorities and put them to open shame, by triumphing over them in him" (Col. 2:15). Everything is turned upside down. Too often, what the world regards as shameful is glorious, while what the world regards as glorious is shameful (Rom. 1:32).

How to relate this paradox to daily life is not an easy matter. A hermeneutic of suspicion is in order, but that is not enough. Not everything the world might regard as honorable is dishonorable, just as not everything it regards as shameful is mistaken. Beyond suspicion, a hermeneutic of retrieval—critical retrieval—is needed. One thing is clear. Nothing can be affirmed as honorable if it is incompatible with the love of God as revealed in Jesus Christ, but that leaves a wide vista open for discernment. Precisely here Paul's call for *communal* reflection is pertinent.[31]

The faithful can expect to be dishonored in some measure for Christ's sake (Matt. 5:11). Nevertheless their sufferings are grounded in Christ and therefore in joy. "But we have this treasure in earthen vessels, to show that the transcendent

---

29. "Christ came to show us the way. Men love darkness rather than the light, and they crucified him, and there on Good Friday on the cross it was still dark, but then Easter came, and Easter is an eternal reminder of the fact that the truth crushed to earth will rise again (Bryant). Easter justifies Carlyle in saying, 'No lie can live forever.' And so this is our faith, as we continue to hope for peace on earth and good will toward men: let us know that in the process we have cosmic companionship." King, "A Christmas Sermon on Peace," in *Testament of Hope*, 257 (slightly modified).

30. See my commentary at 2:7–9.

31. The imperative to "think on these things" (*tauta logizesthe*) appears in the second person plural.

power belongs to God and not to us. We are afflicted in every way, but not crushed; perplexed, but not driven to despair; persecuted, but not forsaken; struck down, but not destroyed; always carrying in the body the death of Jesus, so that the life of Jesus may also be manifested in our bodies" (2 Cor. 4:7–10). "Then they left the presence of the council, rejoicing that they were counted worthy to suffer dishonor for the name" (Acts 5:41).[32]

Faced with dishonor and shame, the faithful can still rejoice, as Paul shows from prison, for the sufferings of the present time are not worth comparing with the glory that will be revealed to them (Rom. 8:18).[33] What once possessed glory has proven "to have no glory at all, because of the glory that surpasses it" (2 Cor. 3:10). The faithful live by the promise that no one who calls on the name of the Lord will be put to shame (Rom. 9:3). Though their bodies might be sown in dishonor, they will be raised in glory (1 Cor. 15:43). Through Christ the faithful have learned to rejoice "in the hope of the glory of God" (Rom. 5:2). In Christ God has made his glory inseparable from their own. They yearn to enter into "the freedom of the glory of the children of God" (Rom. 8:21). Dishonor on earth does not kill their hope of sharing in the honor that triumphs over bitter shame and the grave (Col. 2:15).

At the name of Jesus their knees, too, will bow, along with all the rest (2:10). The faithful will join in the universal acclamation with rejoicing. They will praise the honor, once hidden but now revealed, by which every true honor is confirmed and sanctified from above. "Whatever is honorable" is forever stamped with a cruciform seal. "Worthy is the Lamb who was slain, to receive power and wealth and wisdom and might and honor and glory and blessing!" (Rev. 5:12). The final vindication of the Crucified means vindication for the faithful as well. Whatever is honorable is made honorable in him. No one believing in him will end in disgrace (1 Pet. 3:16).

whatever is just—Because "whatever is just" (*hosa dikaia*)—like all the other marks of excellence—finds its center in Christ, it cannot be considered apart from his mercy. In him justice is reconciled with mercy, and mercy prevails.

32. "Don't despair if you are condemned and persecuted for righteousness' sake. Whenever you take a stand for truth and justice, you are liable to scorn. Often you will be called an impractical idealist or a dangerous radical. Sometimes it might mean going to jail. If such is the case you must honorably grace the jail with your presence. It might even mean physical death. But if physical death is the price some must pay to free their children from a permanent life of psychological death, then nothing could be more Christian." King, "The Most Durable Power," in *Testament of Hope*, 10.

33. "Human creatures can be honorable and have their glory only in pure thankfulness, in the deepest humility, and—we say it openly—in free humor." Barth, *Church Dogmatics* III/4, 664.

Mercy triumphs even as sin is justly condemned and abolished. Mercy ensures that justice will be meted out for the good of all. Although there can be no justice without mercy, and no mercy without justice, in Christ the priority belongs to mercy.[34] "Mercy triumphs over judgment" (Jas. 2:13).

God's essence is righteous in itself. "God is just," writes Calvin, "not indeed as one among many, but as one who contains in himself alone all the fullness of righteousness."[35] God's righteousness is his perfect harmony with himself. It determines the integrity of his will. God's righteousness toward humankind (*externa Dei iustitia*) is grounded in the righteousness of his eternal being (*interna Dei iustitia*).[36] God does not merely act righteously. He acts righteously because he is righteous. God is himself the righteousness by which he acts righteously.[37] In him there can be no separation of being from act. God's being is in his righteous action, and his action is in his righteous being. The God who is eternally righteous in himself (*ad intra*) reiterates his righteousness in the world (*ad extra*).

If God's mercy failed to be righteous, it would not be the mercy of God. God does not have to compromise his righteousness one whit in order to show mercy

34. "The quality of mercy is not strained; / It droppeth as the gentle rain from heaven. . . . It is an attribute to God himself; / And earthly power doth then show likest God's / When mercy seasons justice. . . . In the course of justice, none of us / Should see salvation: we do pray for mercy; / And that same prayer doth teach us all to render / The deeds of mercy." William Shakespeare, *The Merchant of Venice*, act 4, scene 1. See also Hunsinger, "Blessed Are the Merciful," in *Beatitudes*, 61–71.

35. Calvin, on Rom. 3:26, in *Calvin's New Testament Commentaries*, 8:77.

36. In line with Anselm I follow this pattern throughout. "God is the life by which He lives, and similarly for similar [attributes]. . . . But, surely, whatever You are You are through no other than through Yourself. Therefore, You are the life by which You live, the wisdom by which You are wise, the goodness by which You are good, both to those who are good and to those who are evil." Anselm, *Proslogion* 12, in Hopkins, *St. Anselm's Monologion and Proslogion*, 241.

37. New Testament scholarship goes astray insofar as it regards "righteous" as simply a predicate of God's actions to the neglect of his essence or being. Although Käsemann emphasizes its application to God's activity, he acknowledges only in passing, and with hesitations, that it pertains to God's nature as well. "The widely-held view that God's righteousness is simply a property of the divine nature can now be rejected as misleading," writes Käsemann. "*Dikaiosunē theou* is for Paul, as it is for the Old Testament and Judaism in general, a phrase expressing divine activity, treating not of the self-subsistent, but of the self-consistent revealing God." Nevertheless, God's saving righteousness is said to express his "nature" as "true" in the sense of being self-consistent. See Ernst Käsemann, "The Righteousness of God in Paul," in *New Testament Questions of Today*, 168–82, esp. 174. A still useful survey of the range of scholarly views may be found in S. Williams, "'Righteousness of God' in Romans." "I sense that, in their attempt to avoid giving the impression that the biblical understanding of God is the end result of a speculative process," Williams writes, "biblical scholars sometimes shy away from talk about God's being or nature, concentrating almost exclusively on the divine acts" (261n64). He believes there can be no doubt that the word "righteousness" in Paul points to an aspect of the divine nature (261). Michael Bird concurs. "To speak of the *dikaiosunē theou* is to say something about the righteousness of God's character and how he demonstrates his character. . . . [It] is the character of God embodied and enacted in his saving actions." Bird, *Saving Righteousness of God*, 15.

to lost sinners. In the life and death of Jesus, God's righteousness and mercy are enacted at the same time. The righteousness of God's mercy, and the mercy of his righteousness, are fulfilled on Good Friday and revealed on Easter Day.

The cross of Christ demonstrates the divine righteousness because it fulfills God's condemnation of sin. At the same time, it reveals the richness of God's mercy because it expiates that sin by Christ's blood. The sin is separated from the sinner and transferred vicariously to another, so that God's mercy toward the sinner can prevail. In the mystery of the cross, sin is condemned (righteously), borne (vicariously), and removed (mercifully). God remains true to himself in righteousness while remaining true to his creature in mercy. God reveals himself in a harsh and dreadful love unlike any other that we know.

Here Jesus Christ is the one great answer. He is the answer to all our questions about God and to all God's questions about us. He is above all the answer to God's questions about us in our sinfulness, but also to our questions about God in his mercy and righteousness. Jesus lives a perfectly sinless life, the life that we fail to live. He does so vicariously, for our sakes and in our place (*obedientia activa*). Negatively, he demonstrates God's righteousness, as our sin is condemned in his flesh (*obedientia passiva*).[38] Positively, he reveals God's mercy through the expiation of our sins by his blood (*misericordia Dei*). The paradox of merciful righteousness (*iustitia misericora*) is displayed in his life and death. On the cross he removes our sin (Rom. 3:25a) while upholding the righteousness of God (3:25b).

The faithful are summoned to treat others as God in Christ has treated them (2 Cor. 5:14). The divine mercy confronts them with a special obligation. As reconciled sinners, once lost beyond hope, they cannot be unmerciful to others without contradicting the mercy they have received. Nevertheless, neither can they condone the reality of sin, evil, and the things that make for death, which are subject to necessary judgments of justice, divine and human. The faithful are called to extend mercy in such a way that justice is neither unmitigated nor diminished.[39]

"Walk in love, *as* [*kathōs*] Christ loved us and gave himself up for us, a fragrant offering and sacrifice to God" (Eph. 5:2). The Christ of the evangelical "as" (*kathōs*) represents not so much a model to be followed as a person to be

38. For the distinction between active and passive obedience, see Turretin, *Institutes of Elenctic Theology*, 2:140.

39. Reconciling mercy with justice is not without well-known, often intractable, dilemmas in practice. See Van Zyl, "Dilemmas of Transitional Justice." See also Minow, *Between Vengeance and Forgiveness*; Murphy, *Conceptual Foundations of Transitional Justice*. These can only serve as examples; the literature is vast.

received in power.[40] The faithful are called to live from Christ's mercy as well as into it, to be conformed to it by his Spirit. His sacrificial death is the ground of all mercy on earth. At the same time, it upholds and governs all righteousness. Mercy without righteousness is nothing, while righteousness without mercy is worse than nothing. The faithful are called to live out their lives in this tension. It is a tension between righteousness as tempered by mercy and mercy as fortified by righteousness. Only through a special gift of wisdom can this tension be worked out in practice.[41]

Saving righteousness has three tenses. In Christ the faithful are righteous, they are being made righteous, and they await the coming of their righteousness.[42] The promise of final righteousness is the hope by which they live and die. "For through the Spirit, by faith, we ourselves eagerly wait for the hope of righteousness" (Gal. 5:5). It is a hope to be anticipated with joy. "For the kingdom of God is not a matter of eating and drinking but of righteousness and peace and joy in the Holy Spirit" (Rom. 14:17). It is a hope in which mercy and righteousness embrace. "As it is written, 'He has distributed freely, he has given to the poor; his righteousness endures forever'" (2 Cor. 9:9). On the day of the Lord, the tension between compassion and justice is dissolved. "Mercy and truth are met together; righteousness and peace have kissed each other. Truth shall spring out of the earth; and righteousness shall look down from heaven" (Ps. 85:10–11 KJV).

As with the other marks of excellence, "whatever is righteous" (*hosa dikaia*) is a category that extends from the Trinity through Christ to the faithful while also defining the promised future.

whatever is pure—"Whatever is pure" (*hosa hagna*) is grounded in the purity of God. As with his other attributes, God's purity is contained in his eternal essence (*interna Dei puritas*). It forms the basis for the purity of every work he undertakes outside himself (*externa Dei puritas*). Despite the creature's lapse into an odious impurity—the impurity of idolatry and wickedness—God has determined to renew all things by his purifying work in Christ and through the Spirit.

---

40. For a discussion of the "evangelical as," see Hunsinger, "Karl Barth and Human Rights," in *Conversational Theology*, 169–75.

41. For a suggestive example, see Prejean, *Dead Man Walking*.

42. Each tense is governed by the three aspects of salvation mentioned above as "background beliefs" in the comment at Phil. 2:12–13—namely, once for all, again and again, and more and more. The past tense of righteousness is governed mainly by the once-for-all aspect; its present tense, mainly by the again-and-again and the more-and-more aspects, depending on the perspective; and its future tense, apparently by the again-and-again aspect. The righteousness given in Christ by grace to faith is received once for all, and then, on that basis, not only again and again but more and more until the end.

An idea closely related to purity is "holiness" (*hagiōsynē*). As is the case with his other attributes, God is himself the holiness by which he acts with holiness in the world. Perhaps somewhat more explicitly than righteousness, however, holiness is associated with the Holy Trinity, and therefore with the mystery of three "persons" in one God. The Trinity is essentially a holy fellowship of mutual giving and receiving in love (*koinōnia*). The Trinity reveals itself in the world for the sake of establishing and restoring all that is wholesome. The work of God in holiness, through Christ and in the Spirit, will sanctify every relation.[43]

Holiness involves several aspects, including separation for the sake of (1) integrity, (2) universality, and (3) judgment.

(1) Holiness means separation for the sake of integrity. God separates himself from all that is unholy and impure. He is "of purer eyes than to behold evil and cannot look on iniquity" (Hab. 1:13). For that reason he separates Israel from the nations, that he might establish a people suitable for himself. "You shall be holy to me, for I the LORD am holy and have separated you from the peoples, that you should be mine" (Lev. 20:26). God promises to fashion the sort of people he requires. "You shall therefore be holy, for I am holy" (Lev. 11:45). Through the covenant of their election, the people of God receive the holy law that they might worship God rightly and serve him truly.[44] In pure, unbounded mercy God also institutes a complex scheme of sacrificial religion—principally Passover and Yom Kippur—that the people might be chastened, purified, and protected from the terrible consequences of their sins.

(2) Holiness also means separation for the sake of universality. It is a separation of the *pars pro toto*. The universal prospect of God's sanctifying grace invalidates at the outset any tendency toward group supremacism.[45] The inaugural election of Abraham is instituted for the sake of all. "I will bless those who bless you, and him who dishonors you I will curse, and in you all the families of the earth shall be blessed" (Gen. 12:3).[46] God sanctifies his people with the gift of holy

43. "God's holiness is the majestic incomparability, difference and purity which he is in himself as Father, Son and Holy Spirit, and which is manifest and operative in the economy of his works in the love with which he elects, reconciles and perfects human partners for fellowship with himself." Webster, "Holiness and Love of God," 249.

44. "The law is holy, and the commandment is holy and righteous and good" (Rom. 7:12). "The law of the LORD is perfect, reviving the soul" (Ps. 19:7). "Oh how I love your law! It is my meditation all the day" (Ps. 119:97). "But his delight is in the law of the LORD, and on his law he meditates day and night" (Ps. 1:2).

45. Group supremacism is a constant danger in any doctrine of election. This is true whether in Geneva, New England, Pretoria, Tel Aviv, or any such place.

46. Here Abraham prefigures Christ. "Christ was properly that seed in whom all the nations were to be blessed." Calvin, *Institutes* 2.6.2 (trans. Battles), 343. For a nonsupersessionist (or soft supersessionist) approach to such matters, see Hunsinger, "After Barth," 60–74.

light, that it might radiate outward through them to the world (Isa. 49:6). God promises that all the nations, from whom Israel is separated by election, will finally be drawn to them. "And nations shall come to your light, and kings to the brightness of your rising" (Isa. 60:3). It is precisely through the tiny particularity of Israel—"the fewest of all peoples" (Deut. 7:7)—that "the earth shall be full of the knowledge of the LORD, as the waters cover the sea" (Isa. 11:9). Israel is sanctified as a particular people for the sake of a universal blessing.

(3) Holiness also means purification through divine judgment. The holiness of God is fearsome to behold. Unrepentant sinners and inveterate idolaters cannot stand in the presence of the Holy. They must perish. The common sins of humanity only serve to corrupt fellowship, rendering it utterly impossible to sustain—both vertically (with God) and horizontally (with one another). Lost sinners are impotent to restore themselves to God and so to receive new life. The gruesome blood poured out on Israel's altars, day by day, year after year, points to God's holiness in its appalling paradox—uncompromising destruction and merciful restoration. In Israel the blood of ritual sacrifice represents, paradoxically, new life through judgment and death. (For further discussion of destruction and restoration, see excursus 9.)

In a famous passage, with an unexpected sacrificial twist, the prophet Isaiah sets forth several aspects of the paradoxical divine holiness (Isa. 6:3–7). The Lord God is initially worshiped in the splendor of holiness. "Holy, holy, holy, is the LORD of hosts: the whole earth is full of his glory" (6:3 KJV). There then comes a dreadful shaking of the foundations. "And the foundations of the thresholds shook at the voice of him who called, and the house was filled with smoke" (6:4). The unbearable presence of the Lord is more than the humble prophet can withstand. "Then said I, 'Woe is me! for I am undone; because I am a man of unclean lips, and I dwell in the midst of a people of unclean lips: for my eyes have seen the King, the LORD of hosts'" (6:5). The withering presence of God's holiness can portend only ruin. But an angel of the Lord intervenes. "Then flew one of the seraphim to me, having a live coal in his hand, which he had taken with the tongs from off the altar" (6:6). The altar is an allusion to the sacrificial religion of Israel and the atoning purification it accomplishes, apart from any merit in Israel and despite the full gravity of their sins.[47] "And he laid it upon my mouth, and said, 'Behold, this has touched your lips; and your iniquity is taken

47. "Ah, sinful nation, a people laden with iniquity, offspring of evildoers, children who deal corruptly! They have forsaken the LORD, they have despised the Holy One of Israel, they are utterly estranged" (Isa. 1:4).

away, and your sin purged" (6:7). In an unexpected turn, the holiness of God effects the purging of uncleanness. Fire and cleansing, destruction and restoration, are combined. The Lord God makes the unholy holy through the scorching fire of his love. He imparts the holiness that the prophet cries out that he lacks. Purification is accomplished through two things: the altar (prefiguring Calvary) and the burning coal (prefiguring the Holy Spirit). The altar prefigures Christ's atoning blood while the burning coal foreshadows its application to sinners by the uncanny power, which is terrifying, of the Holy Ghost.

The holiness of God is made incarnate in the person of Jesus. He is described as "the Holy and Righteous One" (Acts 3:14), whom God will not allow to see corruption (Acts 2:27), despite his being "mocked and shamefully treated and spit upon." He is "delivered over" to pitiless Gentiles, who put him to an appalling death (Luke 18:32). At their hands he "endured the cross, despising the shame" (Heb. 12:2). In his holiness he subjects himself to unholiness to save the unholy from their sins. God "made him to be sin who knew no sin, so that in him we might become the righteousness of God" (2 Cor. 5:21). Jesus is associated— enigmatically—with Yom Kippur. "So Jesus also suffered outside the gate in order to sanctify the people through his own blood" (Heb. 13:12).[48] His blood is shed "outside the gate"—the site of exile, carnage, and filth. "And the bull for the sin offering and the goat for the sin offering, whose blood was brought in to make atonement in the Holy Place [on Yom Kippur], shall be carried outside the camp. Their skin and their flesh and their dung shall be burned up with fire" (Lev. 16:27). In a heady and dreamlike conflation of images, Jesus, having been likened to the bull and the goat whose sacrificial blood makes atonement in the Holy Place, is also the goat not slaughtered on Yom Kippur but driven out "into the wilderness" ("outside the camp") with the sins of the people laid on his head (Lev. 16:21). "The goat shall bear all their iniquities on itself to a remote area, and he shall let the goat go free in the wilderness" (Lev. 16:22). In dying "outside

48. In Hebrews, Jesus's atoning death as the antitype does not perfectly correspond to Yom Kippur as the type. Hebrews takes up elements from the type and freely reconfigures them to suit the case—the uniqueness of what has taken place in the atoning mystery of Jesus's death (see note 6 in excursus 2). In a manner that is without precedent, Jesus himself is both the high priest and the appointed sacrifice in its triple aspect (two goats and a bull), though the focus in Hebrews is primarily on the goat that is slaughtered as a sin offering. His saving significance occurs in two phases: his once-for-all death on the cross and his continual intercession in eternity. His death is an unrepeatable event, while his intercession is its ongoing consequence. Note that the cross does not first become efficacious in eternity. It is already efficacious in itself and therefore has eternal significance. For this way of interpreting Hebrews, see Cockerill, *Epistle to the Hebrews*, 393–96, 410–11; Compton, *Psalm 110*, 117–41; O'Brien, *God Has Spoken in His Son*, 219–28. For related ideas in Paul, see Finlan, *Paul's Cultic Atonement Metaphors*, 213–21.

the camp," Jesus gathers up in himself all the sacrifices for sin, fulfilling them in his person once for all, thus bringing exile and bloody sacrifice to an end.

In Jesus grace and holiness are one. He is the Holy One who dies in unholiness that in him the unholy might be sanctified and live. He is the divine purity who enters into impurity, that by him the impure might be purified. He is the only begotten who journeys into the far country, that through him the condemned might be restored to fellowship with the God from whom they are estranged. The appalling paradox of destruction and restoration is fulfilled in his bloody death. Unholiness is destroyed, restoration procured, and exile overcome as he is crucified—in a desolate spot outside the city called the Place of the Skull (Golgotha) (Mark 15:22). In sum, he is the purity who purifies through impurity, the holiness who sanctifies through unholiness, and the only begotten who restores fellowship through forsakenness. In this way Jesus, "the Holy One of God," recognized initially only by demons—"What have you to do with us?" (Mark 1:24)—takes on the form of unholiness, that the unholy might be made holy by his blood. He dies "outside the camp" in an unspeakable act of judgment and grace.

In union and loving communion with Christ, the faithful are restored to purity before God. By grace through faith they are made one with Christ in his sanctifying death. By the Holy Spirit they encounter Christ through preaching, that they might be "made holy by the word of God and prayer" (1 Tim. 4:5). By the same Spirit they are cleansed in Holy Baptism of their sins (Acts 22:16). By that Spirit they are offered the "blood of Jesus" in the Holy Eucharist, receiving it in sacramental form as the blood that "cleanses us from all sin" (1 John 1:7). Word and sacrament are the appointed means by which the Spirit delivers the faithful from impurity to sanctification in Christ Jesus, who was crucified outside the camp and raised again to new, unending life with God.[49]

In Christ their sanctification, like their righteousness, has three tenses. It is something already accomplished, something still being accomplished, and something yet to be revealed.[50] It is a sanctification already accomplished once for all in the sacrificial death of Christ. "We *have been sanctified* (*hēgiasmenoi*) [perfect tense] through the offering of the body of Jesus Christ once for all" (Heb. 10:10).[51]

---

49. "We, who are in ourselves unholy by nature, are born again by his Spirit into holiness, that we may serve God. . . . In other words, [we] must be born anew by his Spirit to blamelessness and purity of life." Calvin, on 1 Cor. 1:30, in *Calvin's New Testament Commentaries*, 9:46.

50. Again, sanctification is also governed by the three aspects: once for all, again and again, more and more (and not one of these without the others). See note 42 above.

51. "By offering himself Christ fulfilled the command of the Father, and thus we have been sanctified." Calvin, on Heb. 10:10, in *Calvin's New Testament Commentaries*, 12:137. "Our sanctification is

Yet in almost the same breath, it can be described under another aspect as an ongoing process for "those who *are being sanctified (tous hagiazomenous)* [present tense]" (Heb. 10:14).[52] Moreover, while the holiness of the faithful is a gift, it is also a task.[53] "Since we have these promises, beloved, let us cleanse ourselves from every defilement of body and spirit, bringing holiness to completion in the fear of God" (2 Cor. 7:1).[54] Under still another aspect their holiness remains an object of hope.[55] Sanctification can be called the goal of righteousness, even as righteousness is the ground "leading to sanctification" (Rom. 6:19). Righteousness in Christ brings "sanctification and its end, eternal life" (Rom. 6:22). The great hope of the faithful lies in the future advent of Christ, their heavenly Bridegroom, who will "present the church to himself in splendor, without spot or wrinkle or any such thing, that she might be holy and without blemish" (Eph. 5:27). In sum, sanctification in Christ is at once a gift, a process, a task, and a promise whose fulfillment is eagerly awaited in the future. "And everyone who thus hopes in him purifies himself as he is pure" (1 John 3:3).

It has been assumed here and throughout this commentary that "what it meant" and "what it means," although intertwined, are not the same. When Paul admonishes the Philippians to "think about these things," what he has in view is the spiritual integrity of faithful persons. That does not mean, however, that ecclesial interpretation must restrict itself narrowly to that sphere. The theme of "purity" and "holiness" extends well beyond the dispositions of the individual and the community to embrace Christ, the Trinity, salvation, and the promised future. The church cannot finally consider "whatever is pure" (*hosa hagna*) without taking this larger scope into account.

---

wrought, effected, accomplished by the offering of the body of Christ." Owen, on Heb. 10:10, in *Epistle to the Hebrews*, 480.

52. "So that how much soever any man hath attained, or in how high a degree soever he is perfect, he hath still need to 'grow in grace' and daily to advance in the knowledge and love of God his savior." Wesley, "Christian Perfection," in *Sermons II*, 104. "We are not in a state of perfection. No, we are in a state of becoming. . . . After being sanctified we are still being sanctified." Luther, "Lectures on Genesis, Chs. 45–50," in *Luther's Works*, 8:267.

53. "It will even be legitimate and possible for him [the believer] to derive confidence, and the assurance of his freedom *and therefore his holiness*, from the fact that he lives cheerfully and gaily strides to work as one whom God has endowed with freedom." Barth, *Church Dogmatics* IV/2, 595 (italics added).

54. "Be killing sin or it will be killing you." Owen, "Of the Mortification of Sin in Believers" [1656], in *Epistle to the Hebrews*, 9.

55. "The church's holiness is not yet complete. The church is holy, then, in the sense that it is daily advancing and is not yet perfect: it makes progress from day to day but has not yet reached its goal of holiness." Calvin, *Institutes* 4.1.17 (trans. Battles), 1031.

whatever is lovely—To think about "whatever is lovely" (*hosa prosphilē*) is to be reminded that God is beautiful in his holiness.[56] A related term for the divine beauty is "glory" (*doxa*). From a biblical point of view, glory is actually the leading concept, whereas beauty is a secondary aspect. "We speak of God's beauty only in explanation of his glory."[57] As with righteousness and holiness, God is glorious in himself (*interna Dei gloria*).[58] He is himself the glory by which he acts gloriously in the world (*externa Dei gloria*).[59] It is a glory intrinsic to his eternal essence as the Holy Trinity. The God who is glorious in himself acts, in Christ and through the Spirit, to bring all things to himself in glory as their final goal.

God dwells in "unapproachable light" (1 Tim. 6:16). This light is his eternal glory as the Holy Trinity. Trinitarian doctrine, with its blinding array of paradoxes, corresponds at the conceptual level to the glory of the eternal Trinity at the objective level. The mystery of the Holy Trinity is the mystery of God's unapproachable light. As Augustine once remarked, if it is comprehensible, it is not God; and if it is God, it is not comprehensible.[60] The Holy Trinity is high above us. We cannot attain it (Ps. 139:6). It is incomprehensible in thought and unapproachable in splendor. It is also unsurpassed in beauty, with a loveliness that transports the soul. "The love of so glorious a Being is infinitely valuable," writes Edwards, "and the discoveries of it are capable of ravishing the soul above all other loves."[61] The doctrine of the Holy Trinity is arguably the most beautiful of all Christian doctrines.

From one perspective God's self-knowledge has a double aspect. It is, as Barth explains, a truthful self-knowing[62] while also being, as Edwards adds, an affectionate self-knowing.[63] The Father knows the Son not only in truth but also with

---

56. "Holiness is in a peculiar manner the beauty of the divine nature. Hence we often read of the beauty of holiness (Ps. 29:2, Ps. 96:9, and 110:3). This renders all his other attributes glorious and lovely." Edwards, "Concerning Religious Affections," in *Works of Jonathan Edwards*, 2:257.

57. Barth, *Church Dogmatics* II/1, 653.

58. "There is an infinite fullness of all possible good in God, a fullness of every perfection, *of all excellency and beauty*, and of infinite happiness." Edwards, "Concerning the End for which God Created the World," in *Works of Jonathan Edwards*, 8:432–33 (italics added).

59. "The glory of God is his essential majesty, by which it is understood that . . . he declares himself to be such [glorious] in all his works. In brief, the powers existing in God and reflected in his works are the essential glory of God." Amandus Polanus, *Syntagma Theologiae Christianae*, 1609, col. 1213, quoted in Barth, *Church Dogmatics* II/1, 643 (translated from the Latin).

60. *Si comprehendis, non est Deus.* Augustine, *Sermo* 117.3.5. See Fitzgerald, *Augustine through the Ages*, 387. The task of Christian theology is not to explain the Trinity away but to comprehend the incomprehensibility of God in its incomprehensibility.

61. Edwards, "The Pure in Heart Blessed," in *Works of Jonathan Edwards*, 17:67.

62. This is Barth's great insight. See *Church Dogmatics* II/1, 16, 51, etc.

63. This is Edwards's great insight. See Crisp and Strobel, *Jonathan Edwards*, chap. 2, "God of Beauty and Glory."

delight. The Son likewise knows the Father not only in truth but with eternal delight. "I was beside him, like a master workman, and I was daily his delight, rejoicing before him always" (Prov. 8:30). The Holy Spirit is the joyful communion between them, "flowing out and breathing forth in infinitely sweet and vigorous affection."[64] "For their love and joy is mutual, in mutually loving and delighting in each other."[65] This mutual delight, this mutual self-giving and receiving in love, suggests Edwards, occurs in the Holy Spirit. As the Father delights in the Son, his love flows out to the Son, and then from the Son back again to himself, in the communion of the Holy Spirit.[66] This communion represents God's "immanent joyfulness."[67] It is "the infinite exultation in the depth of his divine being."[68] The Holy Trinity is an eternal cycle of joy and mutual delight—*perichoresis*!—in ineffable self-giving and receiving. It is beautiful as the joyful communion of love and freedom between the Father and the Son in the Holy Spirit.

God's joyfulness is capable of entering into the depths of human misery and anguish. God is free to lay aside his glory, to enter into the depths, and then to take it up again for the sake of the world. The incarnation cannot be understood apart from the abyss of the cross, nor can the cross be understood apart from the kenotic mystery of incarnation; nor can either be understood apart from Christ's glorious resurrection from the dead. In the person of Christ, the divine glory enters into the world incognito. It is a glory veiled by its advent in an unclean stable full of livestock, only to be eclipsed by its concealment in a place of filth outside the camp. On Good Friday the glory of God is obscured, the holiness of God is dishonored, and the beauty of God is disfigured. Jesus Christ is the glory of God in human flesh, but apart from the revelation of Easter Day his glory remains obscured.

Jesus Christ incarnates the beauty of God. As Augustine states, he is beautiful in every aspect. "He is beautiful as God, *the Word with God*. . . . He then is beautiful in heaven, beautiful on earth; beautiful in the womb, beautiful in his parents' arms; beautiful in his miracles; beautiful under the scourge; beautiful when inviting to life; beautiful also when not regarding death; beautiful in laying down his life; beautiful in taking it up again; beautiful on the cross; beautiful in the sepulchre; beautiful in heaven."[69] The nagging question, however, persists: How can he be

---

64. Edwards, "Discourse on the Trinity," in *Works of Jonathan Edwards*, 21:122.
65. Edwards, "Discourse on the Trinity," in *Works of Jonathan Edwards*, 21:121.
66. Edwards, "Discourse on the Trinity," in *Works of Jonathan Edwards*, 21:143.
67. Barth, *Church Dogmatics* II/1, 648.
68. Barth, *Church Dogmatics* II/1, 647–48.
69. Augustine on Ps. 45; *Enarrationes in Psalmos* 44.3. See *Expositions on the Book of Psalms*, 2:230 (slightly modified).

beautiful under the scourge, beautiful on the cross, beautiful in the sepulchre? Isn't this way of speaking intolerable? Doesn't it verge on the grotesque?[70]

> He had no form or comeliness that we should look on him,
>   and no beauty that we should desire him.
> He was despised and rejected by others;
>   a man of sorrows, and acquainted with grief;
> and as one from whom people turn their faces,
>   he was despised, and we esteemed him as being of no account. (Isa. 53:2–3)

The glory of God is revealed, in an inexpressible conjunction of opposites, on the cross. God does the unthinkable by concealing the loveliness of his beauty in hideous form—"the most unsightly thing humanly imaginable."[71] Nevertheless, the beauty of the cross, though imperceptible, hides the beauty of self-giving love. Holiness "beautifies and adorns that which in itself is vile and has no comeliness."[72] "What is it that we love in Christ—his crucified limbs, his pierced side, or his love? When we hear that he suffered for us, what do we love? Love is loved. He loved us, that we might in turn love him. And that we might return his love he has given us his Spirit."[73]

God is so glorious that he takes the form of the inglorious without ceasing to be glorious, that those who are inglorious might be glorified in the crucified Christ, the incarnate Son. On the cross the force of his strength is revealed in *this* weakness, the summit of his honor in *this* shame, and the brilliance of his splendor in *this* violence. It is not the cross that obliterates God's glory. It is the violence, the cruelty, and the godlessness that are obliterated by the cross. "For the foolishness of God is wiser than human wisdom, and the weakness of God is stronger than human strength" (1 Cor. 1:25 NIV).

To repeat: the fact that God brings good out of evil does not make evil good. The evil of unjust suffering is neither sacralized nor legitimated by the cross. God

---

70. "'*The hour has come for the Son of Man to be glorified*,' says Jesus [John 12:23]. How can this be? Being glorified on a cross? Is that like being enthroned on an electric chair? Is it like being honored by a firing squad? Glory in the cross of Jesus Christ sounds almost grotesque." Nevertheless, "the Gospel wants us to find glory in this disaster, and we want to know what this mysterious glory is, and why we should see it in Jesus' terrible suffering." Plantinga, "Deep Wisdom," 151–52.

71. Garrett, *God's Beauty-in-Act*, 74. I am indebted to Garrett for pointing to certain quotations from Augustine, Moltmann, and Plantinga.

72. Edwards, "Sermon on Heb. 6:7," in *Works of Jonathan Edwards*, 11:139n8.

73. Augustine on Ps. 128; *Enarrationes in Psalmos* 127. See *Expositions on the Book of Psalms*, 6:38–39 (slightly modified).

turns evil against itself by a secret and subversive grace, that the evilness of evil might be bent to his saving purposes. Recall that the cross is the divine jujitsu. It is the beauty of a love that absorbs all death has to offer while evil is reduced to nothing in the process. It is a love "that empties itself without losing itself" and "that forgives without giving itself away."[74] It is a love that becomes inglorious in death, that it might return with an invincible radiance. The reversal of disfigurement into glory is the beauty of Christ's suffering love for our sakes.

The veiled beauty of the cross introduces a new way of life. The faithful are called to take up their cross and lose themselves, to forget their selfish ways. They are heirs of the riches of Christ, "provided," states Paul, "we suffer with him in order that we may also be glorified with him" (Rom. 8:17). The disfigured Christ who was raised from the dead "by the glory of the Father" (Rom. 6:4), and who exists in glory "at God's right hand" (Acts 7:55), is the very Christ who imparts his glory to those who receive him by faith (John 17:22). Their "momentary afflictions" are slight, preparing them for "an eternal weight of glory beyond all comparison" (2 Cor. 4:17).[75] "For I consider that the sufferings of this present time are not worthy to be compared with the glory that is to be revealed to us" (Rom. 8:18). "And we all, with unveiled face, beholding the glory of the Lord, are being transformed into the same image from one degree of glory to another. For this comes from the Lord who is the Spirit" (2 Cor. 3:18).

Christ promises the faithful that they will share in the splendor of his beauty. Thus Edwards says:

> The saints in heaven, who have all remainders of pride taken away, do yet rejoice to see themselves made excellent by God and appearing beautiful with holiness. . . . If they delight to see the loveliness of Jesus Christ, it must needs be a matter of delight to see that Christ has communicated of his loveliness to their souls.[76]

> Surely if God loves and accepts the head for its holiness and amiableness, he won't separate head and members; but he will accept of and delight in the members for the sake of the excellency of the head. That is our great encouragement. . . . We are accepted and beloved because we are in him who is beloved. Christ is more than our head, he is as the whole body. And we are not only joined to him as the members to the head, but he covers us all over. He is as clothing to us. We are commanded

74. Moltmann, *Theology and Joy*, 60.
75. "The present glory of the church, paradoxically and parallel to the experience of its Lord prior to his resurrection, is veiled by affliction and adversity." Gaffin, "Glory, Glorification," 349.
76. Edwards, "The Pleasantness of Religion," in *Works of Jonathan Edwards*, 14:108 (slightly modified).

to put him on, so that our deformity don't appear. Because we are clothed with him who is so beautiful, and because of his beauty with which we are clothed, we are accepted and loved.[77]

More might be said about "whatever is lovely." A distinction might be made between created and uncreated loveliness, and within the former category all loveliness that is corporeal might be distinguished from that which is spiritual. Uncreated beauty in the life of the Holy Trinity is the source and norm, the archetype, of all that is lovely in the world. The divine loveliness in itself, inaccessible to frail human minds, is made accessible through the mediation of Christ. By partaking of his grace, the faithful are being prepared for the *visio Dei*.[78] They will see "the glory of God in the face of Jesus Christ" (2 Cor. 4:6). They will behold the glory of the Father through the eyes of the Son. This beholding will be their delight in the state of glory (*status glorificationis*). Created forms of beauty on earth can in turn be perceived as images and shadows of divine things, as "sacramental" signs of the loveliness to be revealed in the life to come.

When the paradox of the cross is considered—with its *coniunctio oppositorum* involving glory as subjected to disfigurement for the sake of love—a further point may be considered. Certainly all *corporeal* beauty anticipates the divine loveliness as it will be revealed in eternal life. Even more is all *spiritual* beauty on earth a worldly intimation of the divine, whether in music, painting, poetry, or any such thing.

What the paradox of the cross would suggest, however, are cases where loveliness is hidden under the form of its opposite, as under the aspect of an outward lack of beauty. Any number of examples might be considered. But if spiritual discernment involves a sense for moral beauty as manifest under contrary aspects, then perhaps Mother Teresa of Calcutta comes most readily to mind. It would not be easy to find a more palpable case where moral beauty is manifested in so humble an enactment of sacrificial love. When it comes to "whatever is lovely," Mother Teresa's work among the poor and the destitute would stand out as a luminous moment.[79] Whatever is lovely in her person and work points to the loveliness of Christ.

---

77. Edwards, "Christ's Righteousness," in *Works of Jonathan Edwards*, 13:454 (slightly modified). The word "because" in this final sentence would best be regarded as a "final cause," not as the sole ground.

78. As suggested by Thérèse of Lisieux in her "little way," Christ is not a stairway to be ascended, but an elevator, as it were, who comes down to take us up by his grace. "Jesus, your arms are the elevator which will lift me to heaven." St. Thérèse of Lisieux, *Story of a Soul*, 329.

79. Mother Teresa is of course a complex figure. She need not be enlarged beyond her frailties, as some perceive them, in order to make my point.

whatever is commendable—"Whatever is commendable" or "well spoken of" (*hosa euphēma*) is informed, very largely, by the previous five items on Paul's list—whatever is true, whatever is honorable, whatever is just, whatever is pure, whatever is lovely. However, whatever is commendable or praiseworthy, as a new category, can perhaps be elucidated more broadly in terms of the good, the beautiful, and the true—the so-called transcendentals. Each is grounded in the inner life of God, and thus in God's own self-knowledge.

Following Calvin, we might say that God knows himself as the essence of all goodness. There is an "infinitude of good," Calvin writes, that "resides in God" (*in Deo residet bonorum infinitas*).[80] It flows to us from him (*ab ipso fluat*), because he is "the fountain of all goodness" (*fontem omnium bonorum*).[81] As the essence of the Good (*autoagathos*), God is the ground and source of all goodness.

Following Edwards, we might then say that God knows himself as the essence of all beauty. "God is God, and distinguished from all other beings, and exalted above them, chiefly by his divine beauty, which is infinitely diverse from all other beauty."[82] As the essence of the Beautiful (*autokalos*), God is the ground and source of all beauty.

Finally, following Barth, we might say that God knows himself as the essence of all truth. "God is the truth, not merely in himself, but also for us."[83] As the essence of the True (*autoaletheia*), God is the ground and source of all truth.

The Holy Trinity is thus, in a profound sense, the archetype of all that is good, beautiful, and true. God is himself the goodness, the beauty, and the truth (*internum Dei bonum, pulchritudo, et veritas*) by which he acts accordingly in the world (*externum Dei bonum, pulchritudo, et veritas*). This holy God is therefore the ground and source of all that is "well spoken of," and the object of unending praise. "And now we thank you, our God, and praise your glorious name" (1 Chron. 29:13). "We will give thanks to your name forever" (Ps. 44:8). "For from him and through him and to him are all things. To him be glory forever. Amen" (Rom. 11:36). Whatever is well spoken of begins and ends in the Holy Trinity.

The mediator of all that is commendable and praiseworthy is Jesus Christ himself. In his own way he incarnates in his person the good, the beautiful, and the true. Whatever he incarnates he reveals, and what he reveals he imparts to the

---

80. Calvin, *Institutes* 1.1.1.
81. Calvin, *Institutes* 1.2.1.
82. *Works of Jonathan Edwards*, 2:181.
83. Barth, *Church Dogmatics* I/1, 13 (slightly modified).

world.[84] It is especially in his life of compassion that he embodies these marks of excellence, revealing them by grace to faith. He imparts them on earth as they are in heaven. They all find their defining center in him and his compassion. "When he went ashore he saw a great crowd, and he had compassion on them, because they were like sheep without a shepherd" (Mark 6:34). His heart for the lost is fulfilled in his death. "I am the good shepherd. The good shepherd lays down his life for the sheep" (John 10:11). The good, the beautiful, and the true are well spoken of as fulfilled in his merciful death.

Jesus Christ incarnates the good in himself. He is well spoken of as the goodness of the Lord. This goodness is revealed in his person and work. The incarnate Son would not be Goodness itself (*autoagathos*) if he failed to condemn all disobedience. As *this* goodness, he bears sin's condemnation vicariously in his flesh (Rom. 8:3) and bears it away (John 1:29). It is a goodness unlike any other that we know. It accepts bitter judgment to the point of dying on a cross, and its mercy is extended to all (Rom. 11:32). "He does not retain his anger forever, because he delights in steadfast love" (Mic. 7:18). In the mercy of Good Friday, goodness triumphs over judgment (Jas. 2:13). Christ in his goodness lays down his life, that the lost might be saved from ruin. "Surely goodness and mercy shall follow me all the days of my life, and I shall dwell in the house of the LORD forever" (Ps. 23:6). The goodness of Christ is the unexpected presence of grace. "And they were astonished beyond measure, saying, 'He has done all things well. He even makes the deaf hear and the mute speak'" (Mark 7:37). His goodness is met with thanks and praise. "O give thanks to the LORD, for he is good; his mercy endures for ever!" (Ps. 118:1). Goodness is the mercy well spoken of.[85]

Jesus Christ likewise incarnates the beautiful in himself. He is well spoken of as the beauty of the Lord. This beauty, too, is revealed in his person and work. And again, it is a beauty unlike any other that we know. Outwardly, as we have seen, "he had no form or comeliness that we should look on him, and no beauty that we should desire him" (Isa. 53:2). He is "despised and rejected . . . a man of sorrows, and acquainted with grief." He is like a monstrosity from whom we would turn our faces (Isa. 53:3). Beauty itself (*autokalos*) assumes the terrible form of

84. For the sake of convenience I will not try to elaborate on how the Holy Spirit operates from a Christic center in the work of revealing and mediating these transcendentals. In the time between the times, the Spirit of Christ reveals and mediates the good, the beautiful, and the true in many and various ways, not least in ways that are incognito.

85. To paraphrase what Calvin says about truth, we ought not to despise mercy wherever we find it, even in those who do not (yet) know the Lord, unless we wish to insult the Spirit of God. Cf. Calvin, *Institutes* 2.2.15.

unsightliness, that the unsightly before God (*coram Deo*) might be delivered in him from their spiritual deformity. Destined for total eclipse on Good Friday, Beauty itself is well spoken of, ahead of time, from above. "And he was transfigured before them, and his face shone like the sun, and his clothes became white as light" (Matt. 17:2). For a brief shining moment, the veil is parted on the holy mountain. "Behold, a bright cloud overshadowed them, and a voice from the cloud said, 'This is my beloved Son, with whom I am well pleased'" (Matt. 17:5). Loveliness incarnate is also well spoken of at the beginning and the end—by the Ground and Source of all beauty at his baptism (Mark 1:11), by the incongruous centurion beneath the cross (Mark 15:39), and by the mysterious figures in dazzling apparel at the empty tomb: "Why do you seek the living among the dead?" (Luke 24:5). The three Gospels that include appearance stories all depict the one who assumed disfigurement on the cross as the object of worship and awe (Matt. 28:17; Luke 24:52; John 20:28). Loveliness once blighted is made new. Beauty crucified is revealed as the mercy well spoken of.

Finally, Jesus Christ also embodies the true in himself. He is well spoken of as the truth of the Lord. The truthfulness of God is revealed in his person and work. It is again a truth unlike any that we know. The Son of God would not be the incarnation of truth if he failed to confront all falsehood—condemning and removing it once for all. "In him there is no falsehood" (John 7:18). Truth incarnate poses a threat to the forces of darkness, who recognize him for who he is. "What have you to do with us, Jesus of Nazareth? Have you come to destroy us? I know who you are—the Holy One of God" (Mark 1:24). Concealed in the flesh, the Truth itself (*autoaletheia*) proceeds to act with strange prerogatives, making himself "equal with God" (John 5:18). "He is blaspheming! Who can forgive sins but God alone?" (Mark 2:7). Truth so concealed cannot but pose the possibility of offense. "The possibility of offense is the crossroad," writes Kierkegaard, "or it is like standing at the crossroad. From the possibility of offense, one turns either to offense or to faith, but one never comes to faith except from the possibility of offense."[86] The offending truth stands condemned by loveless power. "'You have heard his blasphemy. What is your decision?' And they all condemned him as deserving death" (Mark 14:64). On Good Friday the truth is condemned for the offense of blasphemy, that even blasphemers might be restored to the truth. The ruses of falsehood cannot hold him. Crushed to the earth, he rises again. Truth is revealed as the mercy well spoken of.

---

86. Kierkegaard, *Practice in Christianity*, 81.

Whatever is well spoken of, therefore, finds its ground and source in the Trinity and its revelation in the incarnate Son. In his light, the ground and source of all that is commendable is made known. "The Lord is compassionate and merciful" (Jas. 5:11). "Every generous act of giving, with every perfect gift"—in this case the good, the beautiful, and the true, as manifest in the Son's generosity of compassion—"is from above, coming down from the Father of lights" (Jas. 1:17 NRSV). These are the qualities promised and imparted to the faithful from the Father through the Son and in the Spirit.

The good, the beautiful, and the true are well spoken of when the faithful, too, display them with compassion in their lives. They, too, may be called to do so in the midst of adversity. "We are afflicted in every way, but not crushed; perplexed, but not driven to despair; persecuted, but not forsaken; struck down, but not destroyed; always carrying in the body the death of Jesus, so that the life of Jesus may also be manifested in our bodies" (2 Cor. 4:8–10). When the faithful show compassion to others, as compassion has been shown to them (Col. 3:13), they too receive a commendation from above. "Well done, good and faithful servant. You have been faithful over a little; I will set you over much. Enter into the joy of your master" (Matt. 25:21, 23). In the end everything good, beautiful, and true is well spoken of when received in mercy from above.

⊹ ⊹ ⊹

This set of reflections began with Paul's injunction to "think on these things" (*tauta logizesthe*) (Phil. 4:8). When we consider them from their center in Christ and the Trinity, perhaps the most striking result is the necessity of adopting antithetical modes of thought. No mark of excellence commended by Paul can finally be grasped without resorting to some form of *coniunctio oppositorum*. In Christ each excellence is "spiritual" before it is "moral." Each one is placed in union with its diametrical opposite in order that its opposite might be overcome and abolished.

- "Whatever is true" (*hosa alēthē*) does not just point to the "moral" excellence of acting without hypocritical pretense, as it might have done for the Stoics. It points to the cross of Christ where the truth is crucified, that the deceitfulness of sin might be ended.
- "Whatever is honorable" (*hosa semna*) does not just denote the "moral" excellence of being above reproach. It points to the divine glory that is despised and rejected on the cross, that those who are dishonorable might be made honorable by the Lord of glory, who was crucified in shame for their sakes.

- "Whatever is just" (*hosa dikaia*) does not just signify the "moral" excellence of fairness and adherence to the moral law. When defined "spiritually" from a center in Christ, it points to the divine justice that ordains sin to be condemned in the flesh, that divine mercy might be extended to all.

- "Whatever is pure" (*hosa hagna*) does not just indicate the excellence of being untainted by impiety or wickedness. It points to the radical conjunction of holiness with unholiness by grace, that the unholy, the impious, and the wicked might be spared the judgment they deserve, while receiving the grace and holiness they do not deserve.

- "Whatever is lovely" (*hosa prosphilē*) does not just imply the excellence of being attractive or desirable, not even in the highest forms of beauty. It points to what Augustine calls being "beautiful under the scourge, beautiful on the cross, beautiful in the sepulchre." It points to beauty concealed under its opposite in the outwardly hideous aspects of a crucified love. "He had no form or comeliness that we should look on him" (Isa. 53:2).

- Finally, "whatever is commendable" or "well spoken of" (*hosa euphēma*) does not just suggest the "moral" excellence of having a good reputation. It points to the mercy well spoken of from above—as uttered at the Lord's baptism in the Jordan, at his transfiguration on the holy mountain, at his strange commendation by the centurion beneath the cross, at his silent vindication by the empty tomb. It points to the commendation of the One who became uncommendable (cf. Ps. 118:22), that in him those who are uncommendable might be commended with a commendation not their own.

What emerges when these marks of excellence are considered "spiritually" from a center in Christ—and therefore in patterns of *coniunctio oppositorum*—is again the primacy of cultic atonement modes of thought. They take precedence over other categories of discernment. Neither the moral nor the forensic, neither the apocalyptic nor the messianic, in themselves, can capture the full weight of whatever is true, honorable, just, pure, lovely, and well spoken of in Christ. They are all finally determined by the merciful substitution of the cross. Their significance can be grasped only through such cultic atonement categories as substitution, exchange, double transfer, objective and subjective participation, expiation/propitiation, and not least blood. Vicarious substitution means mercy, and mercy means *coniunctio oppositorum* with all its concomitant reversals and restorations. It is the mercy of vicarious substitution that determines whatever is true, honorable, just, pure, lovely, and well spoken of in Christ.

if there is any excellence, if there be anything worthy of praise—We arrive at the summation.[87] "Excellence" (*aretē*) is the objective side of the various qualities that have been proposed for reflection,[88] whereas "praise" (*epainos*) is the fitting response. Excellence serves, in other words, as a semantic marker for the first five qualities on the list: whatever is true, whatever is honorable, whatever is just, whatever is pure, whatever is lovely. Praise, in turn, honors everything in them that is commendable.[89]

It is God who determines all praise and excellence. Whatever is well spoken of by God is echoed by his people on earth.[90] God praises varieties of excellence in his people (1 Cor. 4:5), and his people praise God for providing them (Col. 1:12). Any spiritual excellence they may possess is received as a pure gift (1 Cor. 4:7). They receive it from God through Christ and in the Spirit. God brings about a variety of gifts in his people, even as he brings about their good works (Phil. 2:13).[91] If God implants any excellence in them, they are all the more indebted to his grace.

As with God, so also with his people, the center always resides in mercy. The mercy at the heart of the gospel is revealed in the excellency of Christ. It is present at the heart of the true, the honorable, the just, the pure, and the lovely. If there be any spiritual excellence, it is informed by the mercy of Christ. If there be anything worthy of praise, the same is true. "But the wisdom from above is

87. Here I follow O'Brien. Both phrases—"any excellence" (*tis aretē*) and "anything worthy of praise" (*tis epainos*)—are best taken here as "summarizing." O'Brien, *Philippians*, 507.

88. "The word rendered 'virtue' (*aretē*) occurs only here in St. Paul.... It is remarkable that a favorite word of Greek ethics should be thus avoided; but the reason is not far to seek. By derivation and in usage it is connected with ideas of manhood, courage, and so self-reliance. The basis of goodness in the gospel is self-renunciation, in order to the reception of grace, the undeserved gift of God." Moule, *Philippians*, 115. Lightfoot quotes Beza to the effect that the word *aretē* is too low for comparison with the gifts of the Holy Spirit. Lightfoot, *Philippians*, 160.

89. "A person may receive praise from those whose authority comes from God, from a congregation (2 Cor. 8:18), an apostle (1 Cor. 11:2, 17, 22), and from authorities appointed by God (Rom. 13:3–4; 1 Pet. 2:14). Usually the word group has to do with things that merit the praise of God." O'Brien, *Philippians*, 507.

90. There will be much excellence for the faithful to affirm in the world. Nevertheless, it follows that they must test carefully whatever is regarded as excellent and praiseworthy in the surrounding culture. Otherwise, what Fee calls "anti-gospel values" may all too easily be absorbed "through cultural osmosis" by the faithful themselves. Fee mentions "relativism, materialism, hedonism, nationalism, individualism, to name but a few." Anti-Semitism, militarism, the terrorizing of civilians, racism, torture, homophobia, patriarchalism, massive normalized abortion, sexual promiscuity, the sexual abuse of children by clergy, and more might be added to the list, not to mention indifference to indiscriminate killings in modern warfare, despoliation of the environment, and the production of nuclear weapons by one's own or any other government. Fee, *Philippians*, 421.

91. "Grace alone brings about every good work in us." *Omne bonum in nobis nonnisi gratiam facere.* Calvin, *Institutes* 2.3.13, paraphrasing Augustine, *Letter* 194.5.19.

first pure, then peaceable, gentle, open to reason, full of mercy and good fruits, impartial and sincere" (Jas. 3:17). The God of all mercy, incarnate in Christ, is honored by praise without end.

> O God beyond all praising,
> we worship you today
> and sing the love amazing
> that songs cannot repay.[92]

Transposed back into a more biblical idiom: "'Worthy is the Lamb who was slain, to receive power and wealth and wisdom and might and honor and glory and blessing!' . . . And the four living creatures said, 'Amen!' and the elders fell down and worshiped" (Rev. 5:12, 14).

4:9 What you have learned and received and heard and seen in me—The general exhortations of 4:8 are now anchored in the example of the apostle. Reflection (*logizesthe*) is now ordered to the deed (*prassete*).[93] The *vita contemplativa* is fulfilled in the *vita activa*. Contemplation is not perfected without action. Christ is the great object of contemplation, while bearing witness to Christ, in turn, is the great object of action by the faithful.[94]

The apostle offers himself as a witness to Christ. He is an example, sufficient in itself (regardless of any flaws), of those marks of excellence extolled as worthy of praise.[95] They are precisely the varieties of excellence he has taught by referring them to the mercy of Christ.[96] That mercy determines everything. It is what they have learned from his teaching (*emathete*), what they have received from his testimony (*parelabete*),[97] what they have heard in his sermons (*ēkousate*), and what they have observed in his conduct (*eidete*). The free grace of God in the mercy of Christ is to be practiced (and taught) by the faithful even as it has been

92. Perry, "O God Beyond All Praising."

93. "Meditation comes first, and then the deed follows." Calvin, *Philippians*, in *Calvin's New Testament Commentaries*, 11:291.

94. Cf. Edwards, "Heaven Is a World of Love," in *Works of Jonathan Edwards*, 8:366–97.

95. "The first thing in a preacher is that he should speak, not with his mouth only, but by his life, and procure authority for his doctrine by rectitude of life." Paul procures authority for his exhortation on these grounds. Calvin, *Philippians*, in *Calvin's New Testament Commentaries*, 11:291.

96. Paul's life and work serves as an illustration of the mind of Christ (Phil. 2:5–8): It "makes the truth visible" (cf. 2 Cor. 4:2). Moralizers need not worry about egotism here. The invitation to imitate one's teacher was standard practice in ancient communities, whether Greco-Roman or Jewish. Bockmuehl, *Philippians*, 254.

97. Cf. 1 Cor. 15:1, 3. "Paul portrays himself as 'a link in the chain of tradition' and implicitly charges the Philippians with the task of guarding and carefully passing on the tradition to others." Hellerman, *Philippians*, 250 (slightly modified).

practiced (and taught) by the apostle in their midst. "Paul is once again calling them to the kind of cruciform existence he has been commending and urging on them throughout."[98] It is the Christic form of life that they have learned, received, heard, and witnessed in him.

In short, unlike Aristotle and others, the apostle places the contemplative in the service of the active. Although the *visio Dei* cannot be separated from the *regnum Dei*, the emphasis falls on the divine activity and initiative. The divine initiative, in turn, is fulfilled in the mercy of Christ, and the mercy of Christ is exemplified in the witness of the apostle. The life and work of the apostle offers the faithful a model to be imitated.

To regard the *visio Dei* as the greatest good, observes H. Richard Niebuhr, is to make contemplation superior to action. It "is to make contemplation, however prepared for by activity and however issuing in action, the final end of life. To put the sovereignty of God in the first place, on the other hand, is to make obedient activity superior to contemplation, however much of *theoria* is necessary to action."[99] For the apostle, the mercy of Christ is made known through hearing (Rom. 10:17), internalized by reflection (Phil. 4:8), but attested most importantly in deeds (Phil. 4:9). The focus is eccentric—outward-oriented. If there be any excellence, or anything worthy of praise, it is rooted in the mercy of Christ *extra nos* and fulfilled by his mercy *in nobis*.

In short, whatever may be excellent and worthy of praise is continually dependent on Christ. It is established *extra nos* in him and made dynamically present in the Spirit. Whatever may be excellent is a gift before it is a task, and it remains a gift to be received ever anew (Phil. 2:13). All that may be intrinsic is radically dependent on the extrinsic. It never becomes an independent possession but must be sought continually from above. Whatever is excellent possesses its excellence through dynamic participation in Christ. On that basis it takes form through the Spirit.

the God of peace will be with you—The God of peace (*ho theos tēs eirēnēs*) is known in the bestowing of shalom, the messianic peace of God (4:7).[100] This peace is not merely inward but also outward, not just individual but also communal, not merely circumscribed but finally cosmic. It is bestowed through the mercy of Christ. Cornelius Plantinga describes shalom this way: "The webbing

---

98. Fee, *Philippians*, 420.
99. Niebuhr, *Kingdom of God in America*, 20 (slightly modified).
100. "Here *eirēnē* signifies the sum of all true blessings, including final salvation, effected in Christ." O'Brien, *Philippians*, 512.

together of God, humans, and all creation in justice, fulfillment, and delight is what the Hebrew prophets call *shalom*. We call it peace, but it means far more than mere peace of mind or a cease-fire between enemies. In the Bible, shalom means *universal flourishing, wholeness, and delight*—a rich state of affairs in which natural needs are satisfied and natural gifts fruitfully employed, a state of affairs that inspires joyful wonder as its Creator and Savior opens doors and welcomes the creatures in whom he delights."[101]

By bestowing shalom in this generous way, the God of peace makes himself known. In shalom he becomes present to the faithful.[102] His presence is a foretaste of the promised future. Peace, harmony, and communion are intrinsic to the divine presence in the world.[103] God himself is the peace (*interna Dei pax*) by which he acts peaceably in the world (*externa Dei pax*). Those who practice the mercy of Christ, attesting it in word and deed, will know the peace that passes all understanding. The God of shalom will be with them, and so they struggle and pray for peace against a world of warring madness.[104]

We may say, paraphrasing Bonaventure, that the God of peace is "a circle whose center is everywhere and whose circumference is nowhere."[105] This God is eternal, free, and immense. Revealed in the mercy of Christ, he is the mystery that makes all things new (Rev. 21:5). The God of shalom is present in mercy as the promised future of all things. Barth writes,

> He is free to be entirely unlimited over against the world: not bound by its finitude, nor by its infinitude; not confined to its time and space as a whole, nor to any one area of space or period of time.
>
> He is equally free to limit Himself: to be eternal in the tiny endlessness of our starry heavens, or of our human conceptuality, but eternal also in our finitude; to be shut up in the totality of our time-space universe, but also in all humility to be confined to this or that time and place as contrasted with other times and places.[106]

---

101. Plantinga, *Not the Way It's Supposed to Be*, 10 (italics original). "Shalom, in other words, is the way things ought to be" (10). Note: not only "ought to be" in the abstract, but *already are* in Christ and *will be* in the promised future. The divine *indicative* grounds every other modal contingency. Being-in-communion, a living communion of love, reveals itself as the ground and goal of all things.

102. "The gift of peace cannot be separated from his presence as the giver." O'Brien, *Philippians*, 512.

103. "What is striking is that in every [Pauline] instance, ["God of peace"] occurs in contexts where there is strife or unrest close at hand." Fee, *Philippians*, 420.

104. A sobering timeline of perpetual wars is available at "150 Years of Humanitarian Action," Magazine of the International Red Cross and Red Crescent Movement, accessed September 9, 2019, http://www.redcross.int/EN/mag/magazine2013_1/16-19.html.

105. Cf. Bonaventure, *Mind's Road to God*, chap. 5 (p. 36). Although this paradoxical image is sometimes ascribed to Augustine, it does not seem to appear as such in his writings.

106. Barth, *Church Dogmatics* II/1, 315.

He is free to be the God of peace in a mercy that triumphs over judgment.

> "For a brief moment I deserted you,
>   but with great compassion I will gather you.
> In overflowing anger for a moment
>   I hid my face from you,
> but with everlasting love I will have compassion on you,"
>   says the LORD, your Redeemer. . . .
>
> "For the mountains may depart
>   and the hills be removed,
> but my steadfast love shall not depart from you,
>   and my covenant of peace shall not be removed,"
>   says the LORD, who has compassion on you. (Isa. 54:7–8, 10)

Note that this promise in Second Isaiah contains elements of judgment, mercy, and peace. The prophet points indirectly to Christ. The type is fulfilled in the antitype.[107]

- The element of *judgment*—"for a brief moment I deserted you . . . for a moment I hid my face from you"—is fulfilled when God turns his face away from Jesus on the cross: "My God, my God why have you forsaken me?" (Mark 15:34; Matt. 27:46). The divine judgment is severe yet transitory in abandonment.

- The element of *mercy*—"with everlasting love I will have compassion on you . . . my steadfast love shall not depart from you"—is also fulfilled, no less profoundly, in Christ's death, with its *admirabile commercium*: "For our sakes he made him to be sin who knew no sin, that in him we might become the righteousness of God" (2 Cor. 5:21). The Lord's steadfast love is fulfilled in the wondrous exchange. Christ's vicarious death is an act of mercy.

- Finally, the element of *peace*—"my covenant of peace [*shalom*] shall not be removed"—is fulfilled in the risen Lord: "Peace be with you" (John 20:19, 21, 26). The risen Lord imparts the benediction of messianic shalom. He does so under many aspects. He embodies the peace that he imparts, he imparts the peace that he achieved (2 Cor. 5:19), he imparts it by imparting

---

107. Israel is included, not "superseded," in the fulfillment. Along with all other "justified sinners," Israel is embraced as the first among equals: "the Jew first and also the Greek" (Rom. 2:10). Contrary to Finlan, I do not believe that the type/antitype interpretive scheme is inherently supersessionist. See the thoughtful rejoinder by Patterson. Finlan, *Paul's Cultic Atonement Metaphors*, 185; Patterson, *Keeping the Feast*, 171.

himself, he imparts himself by means of his Spirit (John 20:22), and he appoints his Spirit to "unite all things in him" (Eph. 1:10). "For he himself is our peace" (Eph. 2:14).

In short, the "God of shalom" (4:9) exacts judgment, not as an end in itself, and not as a precondition to mercy, but that his mercy might be revealed as supreme, from beginning to end, and prevail.[108] The Lord of shalom is present in triumph on the cross. The Lord's exacting righteousness is fulfilled even as his far-reaching peace is established (Rom. 3:25–26). The "covenant of peace" is fulfilled in him. "Behold, I make all things new" (Rev. 21:5 RSV). The faithful cannot be witnesses to Christ without becoming a people of shalom who struggle against the culture of death in all its forms.

> [10]I rejoiced in the Lord greatly that now at length you have revived your concern for me. You were indeed concerned for me, but you had no opportunity. [11]Not that I am speaking of being in need, for I have learned in whatever situation I am to be content. [12]I know how to be brought low, and I know how to abound. In any and every circumstance, I have learned the secret of facing plenty and hunger, abundance and need. [13]I can do all things through him who strengthens me.

4:10 I rejoiced in the Lord greatly—It is perhaps astonishing that Paul returns to the theme of rejoicing. Yet that is the ray of hope which permeates his letter as a whole (cf. 1:4, 18, 22, 25; 2:2, 17–18, 28–29; 3:1; 4:1, 4).[109] Despite the severity of his sufferings, he misses no opportunity to rejoice.[110] Even in prison he lives above his adversities. He knows a Lord whom no prison can subdue.

The immediate occasion for rejoicing is his receipt of a gift from the Philippians. His joy in the Lord finds a special occasion in them. He sees their hand as the hand of the Lord. It demonstrates not only their fellowship with him but also the Lord's generosity through them. He cannot rejoice in the one without rejoicing in the other.[111] He rejoices greatly (*megalōs*).[112] "Paul rejoiced 'in the Lord,'"

---

108. In other words, again, the divine judgment is not a "precondition" but a concomitant aspect in the supreme outworking of divine mercy.

109. For an interesting table of linguistic parallels between 1:3–11 and 4:10–20, see Hellerman, *Philippians*, 254.

110. "This time it was not a summons to rejoice but a confession of his personal feelings." O'Brien, *Philippians*, 516.

111. "His expression of joy communicates his thankfulness." O'Brien, *Philippians*, 517.

112. "He tells them that he burst into joy at the arrival of Epaphroditus." Fee, *Philippians*, 428.

writes Fee, "the author of their common salvation, over the tangible evidence that they together belonged to the Lord and thus to one another."[113]

you had no opportunity—Perhaps communication between them had been cut off for some time.[114] But it was renewed with the arrival of Epaphroditus, who delivered their gift of material aid. Their concern for Paul had flowered at last (*ēdē pote*), like a seed long dormant in the earth. Paul reassures them that he understands the delay. It was due to circumstances beyond their control, he suggests, not to any lapse in their concern for him.

4:11 I have learned in whatever situation I am to be content—This can only be the remark of a person who is truly free. Paul has learned to be content in any circumstances. He can do so for the same reason that he is always ready to rejoice. His exuberance may be tempered by a measure of stoicism, but his stoicism is outstripped by a larger joy.[115] Both are grounded in the Lord. Paul rejoices when being assisted by another, while not complaining when he finds himself in want. He has learned through many ordeals that God's grace is sufficient for him (2 Cor. 12:9).[116] Neither his serenity nor his rejoicing is a matter of self-reliance. They are both dependent on the Lord. "He was not so much self-sufficient as 'God-sufficient.'"[117] He is a God-intoxicated man.

4:12 I have learned the secret—What is the secret into which Paul has been "initiated" (*memyēmai*)? Here are some possible aspects of his faith in divine providence:[118]

- Receive everything as from the hand of God.
- Keep your focus on the Lord.
- Cling to the promises of God.
- Be steadfast in prayer.

113. Fee, *Philippians*, 428.

114. "Explanations vary, none of which can be fully supported: (1) a lack of resources on the part of the Philippians; (2) no one to send on the long and difficult journey to Rome; (3) no need on Paul's part, until the imprisonment; (4) Paul's unwillingness to accept a gift." Hellerman, *Philippians*, 256. Given the greatness of Paul's rejoicing, the first two seem the most likely.

115. "The word translated 'content' expresses the goal of Stoicism, to live above need and abundance in such a way as to be 'self-sufficient,' not meaning that one is oblivious to circumstances, but that the truly *autarkēs* [independent] person is not determined by such." Fee, *Philippians*, 431–32.

116. "No reader of Philippians could fail to be struck by the powerfully Christ-centered redefinition of this 'contentment.'" Bockmuehl, *Philippians*, 261.

117. Bruce, *Philippians*, 150.

118. Paul's "secret" pertains not only to adversity but also to prosperity. He knows not only how to suffer want without bitterness but also how to enjoy plenty without adopting a sense of entitlement.

- Expect new life. A way will open out of adversity. Evil will be reversed into good.

Here are some corresponding dispositions:

- Thanksgiving in all things (*eucharistia*).
- Patience or perseverance (*hypomonē*).
- Freedom from anxiety (*parrēsia*, boldness).
- Freedom from anger and the root of bitterness (*chairō*, rejoicing).

Here is an account of the theological rationale: "In a wonderful and ineffable manner nothing is done without God's will, not even that which is against his will. For it would not be done if he did not permit it; yet he does not unwillingly permit it, but willingly; nor would he, being good, allow evil to be done, unless being also almighty he could make good even out of evil."[119]

4:13 I can do all things through him who strengthens me—A more literal translation would be, "I can do all things *in him* who strengthens me" (*en tō endynamounti*). Sadly, this verse is often taken out of context, but it needs to be read with reference to 4:11–12. For Paul, Christ is an end in himself, not merely an instrumental value. Christ the Lord cannot be reduced and manipulated as a source "through whom" arbitrary personal goals are to be sought and attained. Christ is rather the sustaining love in whose power and judgment Paul participates. *Participatio Christi* is the supreme good (*summum bonum*). It validates and relativizes all lesser goods. As an end in himself—"for me to live is Christ" (Phil. 1:21)—Christ is not only a possible means to secondary ends but also the absolute limit who infinitely judges and exceeds them. Because Christ is everything for Paul, in the end neither plenty nor want, neither security nor insecurity, neither esteem nor scorn, neither gain nor loss, as the world counts them, can be anything.

It is Christ by whose love Paul lives or dies, and Christ by whose power he is upheld. He can neither endure material deprivation nor escape the perils of prosperity apart from the one who empowers him. For Paul, Christ and his grace are as real and sufficient as they are necessary and tangible. They make possible what would otherwise be impossible. They make possible a life lived by grace alone.

With reference to this passage Augustine prays, "Paul had no power in himself because he was of the same dust as we, but he said these words [4:11–13], under

---

119. Augustine, *Comm.* on Ps. 111:2, quoted with approval by Calvin, *Institutes* 1.18.3.

the breath of [God's] inspiration, and I loved him for it." The bishop of Hippo then adds, "Strengthen me that I may have this power. Grant what you command, and command what you will. . . . That makes it clear, my holy God, that it is by your gift that your command is kept."[120] Whether in prosperity or in want, when Paul glories, he glories in the Lord (1 Cor. 1:31).

> [14]Nevertheless, you have done well to share with me in my affliction. [15]And you Philippians yourselves know that in the beginning of the gospel, when I left Macedonia, no church entered into partnership with me in giving and receiving, except you only. [16]Even in Thessalonica you sent me help for my needs once and again. [17]Not that I seek the gift, but I seek the fruit that increases to your credit.

4:14 You have done well—Paul's position is complex. On the one hand, he stresses the sufficiency of divine grace in itself. On the other hand, he welcomes human assistance from others with rejoicing. The sufficiency of grace does not make human assistance unwelcome, nor does the assistance make grace superfluous. Although the grace is sufficient in itself, the assistance is received gladly when it comes. Nevertheless, grace is necessary in a way that the other assistance is not. Paul can live without human assistance, if need be, but he cannot live under any circumstances without grace. Divine grace sustains his life, while human assistance (which itself comes from grace) is an added blessing.

The sufficiency of grace explains Paul's use of the word "nevertheless" (*plēn*). He knows from long experience that grace will supply all his needs. Nevertheless, the kindness of his friends is praiseworthy.[121] "You have done well" (*kalōs epoiēsate*).[122] Their gift is an act of fellowship (*koinōnia*) in the course of their common mission. It is in effect a sacramental sign, giving tangible expression to their partnership (*synkoinōnēsantes*) in the gospel.[123] It shows not only that Paul's Philippian friends have not forgotten him, but also that they share with him in his time of need. Paul uses the suggestive apocalyptic word "affliction" (*tē thlipsei*) to describe the

---

120. Augustine, *Confessions* 10.31.45 (Chadwick, 206). These, of course, are the famous words that offended Pelagius and continue to offend Pelagians of every stripe today.

121. "He is tender over their feelings, as he thinks how 'their deep poverty has abounded to the riches of their liberality' (2 Cor. 7:1, 2), in love to him and to the Lord; and not even his testimony to the power of Christ shall make him seem to slight their collection." Moule, *Philippians*, 118.

122. "It was a beautiful deed, true to the gospel ideal of *kalos*." Vincent, *Philippians*, 146.

123. "It was not the actual pecuniary relief, so much as the sympathy and companionship in his sorrow, that the apostle valued." Lightfoot, *Philippians*, 162.

distress of his imprisonment.[124] For the apostle, grace, *koinōnia*, and affliction go hand in hand.

4:15 no church entered into partnership with me in giving and receiving, except you only—The gift Paul receives from his Philippian friends is not without precedent. They have a long history of coming to his aid, their own poverty and affliction notwithstanding. They hold a special place in his heart. He will never forget that when he left Macedonia, no other church supported him besides them (*ei mē hymeis monoi*). Many had been blessed by the apostle, but few chose to follow through in that way.[125] Several features stand out.

First, the Philippians are aware of their special relationship with the apostle, probably because he has not neglected to mention it to them with thanksgiving in the past ("and you yourselves know," *oidate de kai hymeis*).

Second, the duration of their friendship stretches back to "the beginning of the *gospel*" (*en archē tou euangeliou*), an objective and implicitly Christocentric way of alluding to the course of his ministry in their midst. In the end, the apostle is nothing; the gospel is everything.

Third, the note of *koinōnia* is again sounded (*ekoinōnēsen*).[126] Their communion involves partnership in mission.

Fourth and finally, their mission is a matter of "giving and receiving" (*eis logon doseōs kai lēmpseōs*). Although the overt reference is financial,[127] at a deeper level Paul is not merely the receiver (of monetary aid), nor are they merely the givers.[128] Christ is the Giver whose Gift is himself. Having been joint receivers of the one Gift, both Paul and the Philippians have been drawn inexorably into the progress of the gospel. Together they collaborate in the matter of evangelical giving and

124. To borrow from Bonhoeffer, he was "participating in the sufferings of Christ in the world." Unlike some commentators, I see no reason to suppress the apocalyptic *connotations* of "affliction" here. The sufferings of the imprisoned and persecuted apostle, which his sympathetic friends had sought to alleviate, were sufferings for the sake of Christ and the gospel in the end time.

125. "For he had received nothing from certain ones, such as the Corinthians and Thessalonians, because the Corinthians were covetous and became annoyed when they ministered to him; and because the Thessalonians were given to idleness, he labored, giving them an example of work. Yet the Philippians were good, whether he was present or absent." Thomas Aquinas, *Philippians*, 120–21.

126. "*When I departed from Macedonia.* He refers to roughly the time of his advance into 'Achia,' or Roman Southern Greece; just before and just after he actually crossed the border. For the narrative, cf. Acts 18:1–15. This is a reminiscence after an interval of about ten years." Moule, *Philippians*, 119 (slightly modified). "The phrase likely refers to Paul's ministry in Corinth, when Christians from Macedonia supported Paul (2 Cor. 11:8–9; Acts 18:5)." Hellerman, *Philippians*, 263.

127. "The phrase 'in the matter' means that they have 'opened an account' with Paul, in which there is mutual 'credit' (giving) and 'debit' (receiving)." Fee, *Philippians*, 443.

128. At stake was "a three-way bond" that along with Paul and the Philippians included "Christ and the gospel." Fee, *Philippians*, 441.

receiving. They share in the great mission of passing on to others the Gift they have received and continue to receive day by day. That is why the Philippians have extended their generous aid.[129] Their financial gift acknowledges a greater Gift.[130]

4:16 Even in Thessalonica—Thessalonica was not greatly separated in distance from Philippi, only about a hundred miles to the west. But even there, shortly after he had departed, the Philippians began their practice of sending him financial aid. Paul had to work day and night in Thessalonica to support himself so as not to be a burden on the church there (1 Thess. 2:9). He would not accept support from others without paying for it (2 Thess. 3:8). Why not? For one thing he had to protect himself against foes who would impute mercenary motives to him (cf. 1 Cor. 9:11, 15).[131] Despite his policy of not accepting financial aid, however, it has been suggested, rather fancifully, that the wealthy women in Philippi supporting him would not take no for an answer![132] In any case Paul received support from the Philippians soon after he had arrived in Thessalonica.

The function of the sentence beginning "even in Thessalonica" (*kai en Thessalonikē*) is to express thanksgiving to his friends without causing them social embarrassment. Ancient etiquette frowned on more direct expressions of gratitude among friends.[133] Paul takes a more descriptive tack. By acknowledging that his friends have helped him again and again (*kai hapax kai dis*), from the very outset of their acquaintance, he communicates the thanksgiving that he feels. He reinforces what he said in 4:14–15.

4:17 Not that I seek the gift—We are back to the social complexities of Paul's position. A more overt expression of thanksgiving might make it seem as though he were fishing for financial aid.[134] He needs to find a way to thank his friends without leaving the impression of an ulterior motive. He thus expresses his thanksgiving in an oblique manner.[135] Another reason he is not fishing for aid is that in principle he believes he does not need it. He is convinced that God's grace is sufficient for him. What he can seek in good conscience is that the Philippians'

---

129. "Their giving to support Paul's gospel ministry was a response to receiving the gospel from Paul." Hansen, *Letter to the Philippians*, 318.

130. No conception of Christ as Gift can be adequate where the mercy of his substitutionary death is minimized or eclipsed.

131. For the complexities and shifts in Paul's personal policy about receiving financial aid from others, see Fee, *Philippians*, 448.

132. See Silva, *Philippians*, 205n7.

133. Fee, *Philippians*, 446–47.

134. He uses "the emphatic negative *ouch hoti*, 'I do not mean to say that.'" Bockmuehl, *Philippians*, 265.

135. It is unnecessary to read into this verse the apostle's supposed "nervous anxiety" to clear himself of ulterior motivations. Contra Lightfoot, *Philippians*, 164.

collaboration might bear fruit. If so, the financial aid would redound to their credit in God's eyes.[136] Under the circumstances, that is a fruit worth striving for. Paul desires not the gift (*to doma*) but the fruit (*ton karpon*) and its increase (*ton pleonazonta*), for the advance of the gospel (*eis prokopēn tou euangeliou*) (1:12) and for the good of his friends (*eis logon hymōn*) (4:17).

> **18**But I have all things, and abound. I am well supplied, having received from Epaphroditus the gifts you sent, a fragrant offering, a sacrifice acceptable and pleasing to God. **19**And my God will supply all your needs according to his riches in glory in Christ Jesus.

4:18 But I have all things, and abound—Because Paul has everything that he might need at the spiritual level, he also has whatever he might need at the material level. "I have all things" (*apechō de panta*).[137] He has enough, and more than enough, both spiritually and materially. "I abound" (*perisseuō*). Despite being in prison and facing a possible imminent death, not to mention his having to endure the bitter defection of other believers in Rome, he can say that he abounds.

I am well supplied, having received from Epaphroditus the gifts you sent— His material needs have been amply met, and more than met, by their gifts to him as delivered by Epaphroditus. "I am well supplied" (*peplērōmai*). He not only reassures his benefactors regarding his well-being, about which they are anxious, but also once again implicitly gives them a word of thanks, not least for sending Epaphroditus, whom he has previously praised very highly (2:25).

a fragrant offering, a sacrifice acceptable and pleasing to God—He interprets their gifts in a most favorable light.[138] Their gifts to him (*ta par' hymōn*) have a Godward direction. They are "a fragrant offering" (*osmēn euōdias*), "an acceptable sacrifice" (*thysian dektēn*), and "well-pleasing to God" (*euareston tō theō*). The vertical dimension is the secret to what happens at the horizontal level. Their God-relationship informs their interpersonal relations with the apostle.

Theologically, beyond the literal sense of the text, we may say that the generosity of the Philippians corresponds to the generosity of Christ. As the generosity of

---

136. Chrysostom interpreted the financial imagery here as suggesting an account that bore interest: "the interest that is accruing to your account." See Moule, *Philippians*, 120. "It suggests the figure of compound interest." O'Brien, *Philippians*, 539.

137. Although there might be a vague allusion here to Paul's possessing a financial "receipt" for having been "paid in full," it ought not to be inordinately stressed. His point is more personal and spiritual than narrowly financial. Interpreters ought not to allow the latter to obscure the former. Cf. Hellerman, *Philippians*, 266–67.

138. "No higher praise could be given." O'Brien, *Philippians*, 515.

Christ is profoundly sacrificial, so also is that of Paul's friends. The lesser sacrifice corresponds to the one Great Sacrifice, and attests it. At the same time it also mediates it indirectly in, as it were, a minor key. And what it mediates and attests it also partakes of as an aspect of *participatio Christi*. The sacrifice of Christ is the archetype that gives meaning to the Philippian gift.

The Pauline language of Eph. 5:2 parallels that of Phil. 4:18. "And walk in love, as Christ loved us and gave himself up for us, a fragrant offering and sacrifice to God" (Eph. 5:2). The great Gift of mercy confirms the lesser gift of mercy. In turn, the lesser gift attests, mediates, and shares in the greater Gift that has inspired it. Just as God is well pleased by the one great Sacrifice, so also is he well pleased by all such lesser sacrifices as this one. The Philippians with their gift are witnesses to the mercy of Christ. But it is Mercy himself (*autoeleos*) who is secretly at work, sacrificing through them in a self-attesting and self-mediating way. Without confusion or mix, the great Gift and the lesser gift are one.

4:19 And my God will supply all your needs—Paul can promise to others what he has experienced for himself. Above all, what he has experienced is the sufficiency of Christ. That has been his main point of emphasis throughout this section (4:10–19). Although Christ's sufficiency is primarily spiritual and not material, it does not exclude material benefits.[139] Like Paul, the Philippians will learn how to abound in any circumstances, whether in plenty or in want. The sufficiency of Christ will sustain them here and now, even through the ordeals of the present, under the aspect of the promised future.

This entire section has been framed by the themes of rejoicing and contentment. An overly narrow focus on the financial and material elements would be out of place when we come to 4:19.[140] "Supplying all your needs" (*pasan chreian hymōn*)

---

139. Calvin included material blessings in his account of divine providence: "No one will follow a better rule than to remember the end for which nature's gifts were created. If we consider the end for which God created food, for example, we shall find that he provided not only for our nourishment but also for our pleasure and delight. Likewise, the purpose of clothing, apart from mere necessity, was adornment and modesty. In herbs, fruits and trees, besides their various uses, there is beautiful appearance and pleasing fragrance. If these things were not so, the psalmist would not have included among the divine blessings, 'wine that gladdens the heart of man, oil that makes his face to shine' (Ps. 104:15). Nor would Scripture have reminded us repeatedly, in praise of God's kindness, that he gave all such gifts for our well-being." Calvin, *Institutes* 3.10.2 (trans. Battles, slightly modified), 721. Or to strike a more Pauline note: "He who did not spare his own Son but gave him up for us all, will he not also give us all things with him?" (Rom. 8:32 RSV).

140. It is astonishing how many modern commentators fall short here. They lose the forest for the trees. They amplify the bit about financial aid while neglecting the overall context about the sufficiency of grace. The underlying premise of Phil. 4:10–19 is Phil. 1:21: "For to me to live is Christ, and to die is gain." That is why Paul knows how to be brought low and how to abound (4:12) and how to be content in any circumstances (4:11). That is what governs not only his complex remarks about the gift of

is best interpreted as "ensuring your well-being in every aspect of your lives." It is as if Paul were saying (applying his words to our times): "Neither alcohol nor sex nor drugs, neither wealth nor power, neither fame nor status,[141] neither license nor apathy, neither self-indulgence nor social conformity,[142] nor any such thing, will serve, in itself, to ensure your well-being. In the end they will not meet your needs, whether spiritually or materially. Only one thing really suffices in life and in death: Christ and his grace as supplied by God."

according to his riches in glory in Christ Jesus—God acts with generosity toward the world according to the abundance of his own eternal being (*interna Dei abundantia*). "His riches in glory" (*to ploutos autou en doxē*) are made present and revealed "in Christ Jesus" (*en Christō Iēsou*). The phrase "in Christ Jesus" with its cognates runs throughout the Philippians letter like a red thread. I have argued that it is often best understood in terms of *participatio Christi*. In such cases, the instrumental aspect is secondary to the "mystical" and "apocalyptic" aspect. It indicates a spiritual relationship of union and communion with Christ, who makes all things new. The Christ-relationship remains hidden for the time being, apart from faith, but will be revealed for what it is on the last day. It will be revealed in its riches and glory. The Lord's transfiguration on the holy mountain, where he himself was revealed in riches and glory, becomes a foretaste of what is promised to all.

For the time being the faithful participate "in Christ Jesus" by grace through faith. In him they already share in the riches of God's glory. It is an active relation of mutual indwelling, of self-giving and receiving in love. They are in Christ even as he is in them. They act in and through him, even as he acts in and through them (and at times against them). Their union and communion with Christ is a function of his prior union and communion with them. The sustenance and mercy they receive from him anticipates the end of all things. It is a theme Paul continually adumbrates in a "mystical" and "apocalyptic" way. "And I am sure of this, that he who began a good work in you will bring it to completion at the day of Jesus Christ" (Phil. 1:6). "We . . . worship by the Spirit of God and glory

---

financial aid but also the promise he offers to the Philippians in 4:19. In the end, for Paul, Christ is not the ground and source of some sufficiency other than himself. He just is Paul's sufficiency, in life and in death. He is more nearly an intrinsic good than an instrumental value. He is the supreme good in himself.

141. Jockeying for status and power perhaps lay behind Paul's concern that adopting a mindset of humility and relinquishment is necessary for restoring harmonious relations within the Philippian community.

142. Self-seeking and social conformity seem to have been the two main temptations facing the Philippians as they considered how to get their material needs met with regard to the antagonistic outside world.

in Christ Jesus" (Phil. 3:3). "For I consider that the sufferings of this present time are not worth comparing with the glory that is to be revealed to us" (Rom. 8:18). "And the peace of God, which passes all understanding, will keep your hearts and your minds in Christ Jesus" (Phil. 4:7). "I press on toward the goal for the prize of the upward call of God in Christ Jesus" (Phil. 3:14). "But our citizenship is in heaven, and from it we await a Savior, the Lord Jesus Christ" (Phil. 3:20). "For his sake I have suffered the loss of all things and count them as refuse, in order that I may gain Christ and be found in him" (Phil. 3:8–9). "For in him the whole fullness of deity dwells bodily" (Col. 2:9). "Christ in you, the hope of glory" (Col. 1:27).[143]

20Now to our God and Father be glory forever and ever. Amen. **21**Greet every saint in Christ Jesus. The brothers and sisters who are with me greet you. **22**All the saints greet you, especially those of Caesar's household. **23**The grace of the Lord Jesus Christ be with your spirit.

4:20 Now to our God and Father—The Father of the Lord Jesus Christ is the "God and Father" (*theos kai patros*) of believers as well. That he should be their divine Father is a consequence of the incarnation. Whereas Christ is God's Son by nature, they are his sons and daughters by grace. As the *eternal* Son, his intimacy with the Father is immediate and direct. As the *incarnate* Son, it belongs to his office as the Mediator that his sonship might be shared, under a certain aspect, with others without losing its uniqueness.

Jesus mediates to others an indirect share in his unique relationship to God. He does so by transforming them from being fallen, shameful creatures into upright family members and heirs with him (Rom. 8:17). The language of adoption is unique to Paul in the New Testament,[144] but it has roots in Jesus's teaching about prayer and in the covenantal tradition with Israel. It is "in Christ," and only in

---

143. The relationship between (1) our being "in Christ" and (2) Christ's being "in us" is arguably governed by the Chalcedonian pattern. In other words, point (1) is related to point (2) through a pattern of unity-in-distinction: "without separation or division" (inseparable unity), "without confusion or change" (abiding distinction), and with the priority and precedence belonging to point (1) (asymmetry). The relation can thus be described as an asymmetrical relation of grace to faith, with the priority belonging to grace, on which faith is always completely dependent. In addition, it is finally a living relationship of *koinōnia* or mutual indwelling, of mutual self-giving and receiving, between Christ and us. The pattern of asymmetrical unity-in-distinction sets forth the formal structure of our union and communion with Christ. The mutual indwelling can be illustrated by the image of pouring water into a jar (Christ in us) and casting the jar into the ocean (our being in Christ). The water is in the jar, but the jar is in the greater water of the ocean. The relation is asymmetrical.

144. Hester, *Paul's Concept of Inheritance.*

that way, that believers are allotted their inheritance (Eph. 1:11). Through their active participation in Christ, they are conformed to him by his Spirit, not least in their prayers. It was commonplace in the primitive church for Christians, in conformity with Jesus, to address God as their Father (e.g., Rom. 8:15; Gal. 4:6). It was an immense blessing, one not to be despised or taken for granted. Apart from God's mercy in the cross of his Son, they would not have been delivered from the ruin of their sin and welcomed into the household of faith.[145] God is "my Father and your Father," said Jesus, "my God and your God," affirming at once the gift and the distinction (John 20:17).

be glory forever and ever. Amen—We have come to the end of Paul's letter. The transition from 4:19 to 4:20 is a transition from promise to doxology.[146] The faithful share in the promise of Christ's glory very largely through the practice of prayer. They can voice the prayers of adopted children because their "God and Father" is Mercy itself. As "the Father of mercies and God of all comfort," he is unlike any father we know. He is the holy Mercy who is moved to forgiveness when his wayward children call on him day by day. He comforts all who turn to him in affliction, that they might comfort others with the comfort received from him (2 Cor. 1:3–4). In their prayers they confess that "Jesus Christ is Lord, to the glory of God the Father" (Phil. 2:11). Lordship and divine mercy are acknowledged as one in inseparable unity "forever and ever. Amen."[147]

4:21 **Greet every saint in Christ Jesus**—Paul's letter ends much as it started. At the beginning he writes, "To all the saints who are in Christ Jesus at Philippi" (1:1). In conclusion he passes along greetings: "Greet every saint in Christ Jesus" (*Aspasasthe panta hagion en Christō Iēsou*). Paul sends greetings to the whole community—that is, to each and every Philippian who shares with him in Christ.

The brothers and sisters who are with me greet you—At the same time the apostle forwards greetings from his coworkers in Rome. While we can't be sure whether they included women, the possibility cannot be ruled out.[148]

Friends qua friends, wrote Aristotle, must be aware of "reciprocated good will." To be friends, persons have to feel good will toward each other, which means wishing each other's good. They also have to be aware of each other's good will, for "how could we call them friends when they are unaware of their attitude to each

---

145. See Davidson, "Salvation's Destiny." I have drawn freely from this essay.
146. Bockmuehl, *Philippians*, 266.
147. "The idea conveyed by the phrase here [*aiōnas tōn aiōnōn*, "for ever and ever"] is of circles of duration consisting of, embracing, other circles *ad infinitum*." Moule, *Philippians*, 122.
148. "Apparently the apostle's personal companions and fellow-travellers are meant, as distinguished from the Christians resident in Rome who are described in the following verse." Lightfoot, *Philippians*, 165.

other?" Finally, the cause of good will has to be a loveable quality in the friend.[149] While Aristotle has his own ideas about what those qualities might be, for Paul the cause of friendship with the Philippians is their shared participation in Christ (*en Christō Iēsou*). It is a shared condition and a shared vocation accompanied by a range of shared practices. Their practices of friendship in Christ include worship and service, self-giving and receiving, preservation and perseverance, mutual encouragement, rejoicing, and hope. These are largely the themes of Paul's letter.

4:22 All the saints greet you—Besides the inner circle of his coworkers, there is a larger circle of friends ("saints") around Paul as well. While it is fitting to mention the inner circle first, it would not have been fitting to leave the larger circle out. They all send greetings to the Philippians and share in the reciprocated good will.

especially those of Caesar's household—This reference comes as a surprise to the general reader. Did it also come as a surprise to the Philippians? It would probably have been taken as a sign of encouragement. The group in question, "those of Caesar's household" (*hoi ek tēs Kaisaros oikias*),[150] probably does not refer to Roman elites but to slaves and free persons who labored on the emperor's estate and in government administration.[151] But there is a subtext at work here as well. "Concealed behind this innocuous greeting," writes Markus Bockmuehl, "is a powerful symbol of the day when, even in Rome, the seat of imperial power, 'every knee shall bow' to Christ (2:11)."[152]

4:23 The grace of the Lord Jesus Christ—The letter to the Philippians is not so much about Paul as about the centrality of Christ and the sufficiency of his grace. Grace has accompanied Paul in his afflictions, and grace will accompany the Philippians in theirs.

be with your spirit—The indicative of grace therefore ends with a benediction of grace. It is the utterance of a blessing, a solemn invocation of the mercy of the cross, and a prayer of confidence that the grace of the Lord Jesus Christ (*hē charis tou kyriou Iēsou Christou*) will provide for them in life and in death.

---

149. Aristotle, *Nicomachean Ethics* 8.9.22 (Irwin, 210).

150. "The phrase *ek tēs Kaisaros oikias*, along with *praitōriō* ('Praetorian Guard' [1:13]) constitutes the strongest evidence for a Roman origin for Philippians. Both groups are especially 'at home' in Rome, while 'one must look under all kinds of "stones" to turn up evidence for their existence in Ephesus or Caesarea.'" Hellerman, *Philippians*, 276, quoting Fee, *Philippians*, 459.

151. Reumann, *Philippians*, 730.

152. Bockmuehl, *Philippians*, 270.

EXCURSUS 1

On the Phrase "in Christ"

"The primary meaning of *en Christo* is to be understood in a local sense," writes Udo Schnelle, "indicating a sphere of being." This sphere, he says, is at once "pneumatic" and "eschatological."[1] What Schnelle regards as "pneumatic," I am more loosely terming "mystical," and what he regards as "eschatological," I am more specifically calling "apocalyptic."

With regard to the term "mystical," I am following Calvin, who writes, "That joining together of Head and members, that indwelling of Christ in our hearts—in short, that mystical union—are accorded by us the highest degree of importance, so that Christ, having been made ours, makes us sharers with him in the gifts with which he has been endowed."[2] Over against Calvin, however, at least in this statement, I am suggesting that the term "mystical union" would apply not only to Christ's dwelling "in us" but also to our being "in Christ."

With regard to the term "apocalyptic," I am following John Collins, who defines the genre of "apocalypse" as follows: "'Apocalypse' is a genre of revelatory literature with a narrative framework, in which a revelation is mediated by another-worldly being to a human recipient, disclosing a transcendent reality which is both temporal, insofar as it envisages eschatological salvation, and spatial insofar as it involves another, supernatural world."[3] I would suggest that although

1. Schnelle, *Apostle Paul*, 481. I generally interpret *en Christō* in a local rather than an instrumental sense.
2. Calvin, *Institutes* 3.11.10 (trans. Battles), 737.
3. Collins, "Introduction," 9.

Philippians is not an instance of the genre of apocalyptic literature, Paul's term "in Christ," as used in Philippians, is apocalyptic in tenor insofar as it involves at least these elements: incorporation into a new, transcendent reality; revelation in hiddenness; and a drastic transformation from the old eon to the new, with an unresolved tension in this life between the "already" and the "not yet."

Being in Christ is "apocalyptic" insofar as it is premised on an eschatology in which revelation brings righteousness out of sin, new life out of death, blessing out of curse, and new creation out of the present evil age. Paul's apocalyptic eschatology is "disjunctive" insofar as the new—righteousness, new life, blessing, and new creation—is brought into being only as the old—sin, death, curse, and the present evil age—is destroyed. A disjunctive, apocalyptic eschatology would be one that posits continuity in the midst of radical discontinuity. The element of destruction is what makes it both drastic and disjunctive, while the element of continuity in the midst of discontinuity is what makes it redemptive.[4]

---

4. For an argument that this sort of disjunctive eschatology in Paul is not "apocalyptic" but merely "christomorphic," see L. Williams, "Disjunction in Paul." I would agree with Williams that Paul's eschatology is "disjunctive" and "christomorphic," but not that it cannot be described as "apocalyptic." I would say that a "disjunctive eschatology" is by definition "apocalyptic," in a certain sense of the term. Williams poses a false alternative, because he argues from too narrow a base. For a different base, see Hasel, "Resurrection." According to Hasel, "resurrection," which is disjunctive by definition, "is a principal element in the apocalyptic theology of the Hebrew Bible" (284). Williams would have been on stronger ground if he had argued that Paul reinterprets some existing ideas of apocalyptic, disjunctive eschatology in christomorphic terms.

EXCURSUS 2

On Ecclesial Hermeneutics (Philippians 2:7)

Modern scholarship has been much exercised over the question of whether the word "servant" or "slave" (*doulos*) in Phil. 2:7 carries any "reference" to the Ebed Yahweh passages in Isaiah.[1] Here (as elsewhere) the interpretation followed in this commentary departs from certain well-worn procedures, whether biblicist or historicist. It regards biblicism and historicism as siblings under the skin: both are "originalists" insofar as they tend to regard the original meaning (what it meant) as sufficient to establish the final meaning (what it means).[2] Although both biblicism and historicism have a contribution to make (each in its own way), they are arguably overly narrow insofar as they tend to prohibit intertextual scriptural hermeneutics. Too often they tend to focus on the part at the expense of the whole, at least as the whole would be understood through the lens of Nicene Christianity.

---

1. For a detailed survey, see R. Martin, *Carmen Christi*, 182–96.
2. By "what it means" I refer to the level of *explicatio* as opposed to *applicatio*. I do not wish to make a point about how a text might apply existentially to our lives. Rather, I wish to make a point about the content that is implicit in the literal sense of the text, but which in its original wording may be ambiguous or less than fully clear. Thus the statement that Christ Jesus was "in the form of God" (*morphe theou*) (Phil. 2:6) is explained and clarified, according to ecclesial hermeneutics, by the Nicene statement that the Son is of "the same essence" (*homoousios*) with the Father, just as the statement that "the Word became flesh" (John 1:14) is clarified by the Chalcedonian Definition. For the church, the final meaning of such biblical statements ("what it means") is authoritatively determined by the councils. The term *homoousios* and the language of Chalcedon (e.g., *physis*) are not to be rejected simply because they use expressions not found in Holy Scripture.

In denying any connection between *doulos* and Ebed Yahweh, as some would do here, it is as if they fixate on one small piece of colored glass in a mosaic, noting that it has clear and distinct boundaries when taken by itself, as well as a limited content, while missing its placement within a larger, loosely constructed intertextual whole. Discerning the relationship between the whole and the parts, as well as between the center and the periphery, is what makes the interpretive enterprise so delicate—being more nearly an art than a science, or a matter of the spirit, not merely the letter. For ecclesial hermeneutics, as here posited, it does not finally matter whether an Ebed Yahweh reference was *explicitly* "given," "presupposed," or "intended" by Paul's use of *doulos* in 2:7. The warrants for discerning *doulos* in relation to a larger scriptural whole do not necessarily rest only in the term itself when isolated or taken in abstraction, nor when looked at only from the standpoint of its possible historical origins.

For ecclesial hermeneutics the relationship between the various parts and the whole is more like a feedback loop than a one-way street (i.e., from an earlier to a later text). Biblicist, philological, and historicist denials that *doulos* in 2:7 can be read in connection with Ebed Yahweh in Isaiah seem to assume that no warrants for a connection are valid if they cannot be extracted from the corresponding points in Isaiah, so that they tally nicely with what is said about the term *doulos* in 2:7. One may certainly grant that the relevant hermeneutical whole (as posited by ecclesial hermeneutics) is established neither by the Ebed Yahweh passages alone nor by the immediate function of *doulos* in this verse, since the relevant whole is not derived narrowly from either one when taken by itself. There may be other warrants (broadly literary and theological) for placing a term in the context of a larger intertextual or scriptural network, even when the later term may go beyond important elements in the precursor.

Of course it is necessary not to become overly broad (or fanciful) while attempting to avoid being overly narrow, but after roughly three hundred years of restrictive modern criticism, it also seems necessary to be wary of an overly constricted hermeneutical imagination. It does not seem arbitrary to remember, for example, that, according to Mark's Gospel, "the Son of Man came not to be served but to serve, and to give his life as a ransom for many" (Mark 10:45). Here we have not only an evident allusion to the Isaianic Ebed Yahweh but also a clear connection between the idea of Jesus as servant and his saving death.[3] Affirming such an intertextual connection has nothing to do with "importing" something

3. The "Son of Man" element even adumbrates the idea of the *Lord* as servant.

alien *into* the Markan passage, as if one had no choice but to be bound by a certain biblicism with regard to the literal wording of the precursor.

Nor does it seem irrelevant to recall what we read in Luke: "I am among you as the one who serves" (Luke 22:27), even though no allusion occurs here to Jesus's death. Elsewhere Jesus's disciples are told a parable about a "master" (*kyrios*) who hopes to find his servants awake when he comes. He will dress himself for "service," bidding them to recline "at table," and he will "come and serve them" (Luke 12:37). Here we have an intimation of "the coming Lord" who not only assumes the role of a servant but also (more remotely) presents himself as their master, precisely in service to his servants, particularly at the (eucharistic) table.

Finally, in John 13, which is set, significantly, in the context of a Passover meal, and at the time when Jesus is soon to "depart from this world" (John 13:1)—that is, to die on the cross—he takes the form of a slave. Laying aside his outer garments and wrapping himself in a towel,[4] he proceeds to wash his disciples' feet. This washing arguably foreshadows the saving power of his death, whereby those who receive his service to them are cleansed of their sins. Note that the Father "had given all things into his hands. . . . [The Son] had come from God and was going back to God" (John 13:3). He enacts a mysterious pattern of descent and ascent.

The idea of the Lord as slave or servant, into whose hands all things have been given, yet who stoops down to humble himself for the good of others, even to the point of dying for them, on the way to his being highly exalted, is, according to this reading, adumbrated (loosely) in Isaiah and fulfilled (definitively) in Christ Jesus. The narrative pattern here (abasement/death/exaltation) is broadly parallel in the case of both the Ebed Yahweh passages and the Philippians hymn.[5] Like the hymn, the Johannine material also makes an ethical point. "If I then, your Lord and Teacher, have washed your feet, you also ought to wash one another's feet" (John 13:14). What is enjoined is a mindset of humility.

For ecclesial hermeneutics, the Ebed Yahweh in Isaiah is a type to which Jesus Christ as the *doulos* in Philippians (and elsewhere in the New Testament) can be read as the antitype. The type is not a blueprint, nor should we expect the antitype to be slavishly conformed to it. There need be no more than broad family resemblances. When viewed retrospectively from the standpoint of the antitype, the type will often seem like a partial or imperfect anticipation. The

---

4. Like a slave he "girded himself" (*diezōsen heauton*) (John 13:4). Cf. Luke 12:37: "he will gird himself" (*perizōsetai*). From a literary-theological point of view, these would be ways of adumbrating the (counterintuitive) idea of the Lord as servant.

5. Again, I use the word "hymn" simply for the sake of convenience.

antitype will characteristically add to, omit, or greatly reconfigure elements present in the type.[6]

Therefore clear differences between antitype and type need to be noted as carefully as any interesting similarities. It is a matter of loose (though not insignificant) conceptual and metaphorical resonances, not of literal, point-for-point replications. Differences within the typological pattern do not invalidate the similarities.

To look for a point-for-point "literary dependence" of the antitype on the type is a blind alley.[7] It can be, in effect, a way of overpowering exegesis with historical criticism and then confusing the latter with hermeneutics. What 2:7 meant, and where it perhaps came from, is not the same as what it means in and for the church.[8] For ecclesial hermeneutics, what it means cannot finally be understood apart from the normative conciliar decisions of Nicaea and Chalcedon.[9] It is a matter of reading the Philippians hymn in light of the ecumenical councils, as well as reading it intertextually as "scripture," by looking back from the antitypes to the types—and not merely the other way around (or only on that basis the other way around). It is thus, in both senses, a matter of "reading backwards."[10] In this commentary, reading backwards means reading the Old Testament in light of the New, and also reading the New Testament in light of the ecumenical councils of the undivided church as well as in light of the Protestant Reformation.

Historicizing and biblicizing exegesis can help us to see what the Philippians hymn may have meant, and perhaps where it came from. But from the standpoint of ecclesial hermeneutics, that would not be enough in itself to tell us what the

6. Jesus is said to be the "great high priest" (Heb. 4:14). Yet he is not only uniquely "without sin" (Heb. 4:15), but is himself also the "sacrifice" that was offered "once for all" (Heb. 10:10, 12). The "antitype" thus goes well beyond the anticipatory "types" without invalidating them as types. Much the same is true of *doulos* in Philippians and in the LXX of Isaiah. Note that in Isaiah's four servant songs, *ebed* is usually translated as *pais* (child), but is translated as *doulos* in Isa. 49:3, 5. In these cases the "type/antitype" relation would be more conceptual than strictly linguistic. For the LXX of Isaiah, see Harris, *Slave of Christ*, 174.

7. Most of the scholars discussed in the survey cited from R. Martin, *Carmen Christi*, seem to fall into this trap. They all make it harder than it has to be.

8. I think this is partly what Barth had in mind when he said that if he had to choose between biblical inspiration and modern criticism, he would opt without hesitation for inspiration, though he was glad not to have to make the choice. See Barth, *Epistle to the Romans*, 1. "No one has ever read Scripture only with his own eyes and no one ever should. The only question is what interpreters we allow and in what order we let them speak" (Barth, *Church Dogmatics* I/2, 649, slightly modified). I take this as an argument for the apostolic witness as read through the *sensus conciliorum*.

9. Here I agree with George A. Lindbeck. "Biblical conceptualities may be supplanted or displaced—as at Nicaea and Chalcedon—but only if this is necessary for the sake of greater faithfulness, intelligibility or efficaciousness." Lindbeck, "Church," 182 (slightly modified).

10. Figural interpretation of course already occurs extensively in the New Testament itself. See Hays, *Reading Backwards*. Prior to the ascendancy of modernity in the eighteenth and nineteenth centuries, it was standard hermeneutical practice in the church. See Frei, *Eclipse of Biblical Narrative*.

hymn finally came to mean (and what it was thought always to have meant implicitly) for the church as informed by later conciliar decisions.[11] Those decisions were themselves not merely "doctrinal." They were set forth as hermeneutical guidelines and normative rules for reading scripture.[12]

New light, of course, can always break forth from old texts. It may go beyond, but not *fundamentally* against, what the texts would first have meant or how they would have been originally (and at times perhaps only dimly) perceived. According to John's Gospel, new insight will be given to the church under guidance from the Spirit. "What I am doing you do not understand now, but afterward you will understand" (John 13:7). "The Holy Spirit, whom the Father will send in my name, he will teach you all things and bring to your remembrance all that I have said to you" (John 14:26). "But when the Paraclete comes, whom I will send to you from the Father, the Spirit of truth, who proceeds from the Father, he will bear witness to me" (John 15:26). "When the Spirit of truth comes, he will guide you into all the truth" (John 16:13).[13] Ecclesial hermeneutics is inseparable from both conciliarity and common prayer.[14]

For this kind of hermeneutics, only the church (or ecclesial communities) can finally assess the validity of any such proposed new light. Even if (as the Reformation argued) the prophetic and apostolic witness, as codified normatively in scripture, retains a higher authority than the conciliar tradition, in practice the

11. To repeat, with regard to the Philippians hymn, I am making a distinction between what it meant and what it means. Although I posit that the two exist in strong continuity, I resist any suggestion that what it means can be reduced merely to what it meant, when seen in narrow historicist or biblicist terms. What it means for the church is found in the *sensus communalis* as determined by the *sensus conciliorum* through authoritative interpreters under the guidance of the Holy Spirit. Academically trained biblical scholars, as wonderful as they can be, are not necessarily authoritative interpreters.

12. At this point I am in broad agreement with John Henry Newman. "Time is necessary for the full comprehension and perfection of great ideas.... The highest and most wonderful truths, though communicated to the world once for all by inspired teachers, could not be comprehended all at once by the recipients, but ... have required ... longer time and deeper thought for their full elucidation. This may be called the *Theory of Development*." Newman, *Development of Christian Doctrine*, 29–30. Over against Newman, however, I would distinguish more sharply than he does between developments that bring out the necessary implications of apostolic teaching and those that substantially add to it.

13. The term "you" in these verses is given in the plural and would seem to pertain primarily to the apostolate.

14. In other words, I am suggesting that *all* biblical hermeneutics, whether ecclesial or skeptical, is socially *and* spiritually situated, and that therefore *all* ecclesial hermeneutics involves a form of "soft perspectivalism" that is at once antifoundationalist and antirelativist, without needing to supply a purely neutral account of how ecclesial interpretation ought always to work out in practice. In the long run the church's *sensus literalis* about the unique identity of Jesus Christ—as normatively attested in Holy Scripture and as determined by the *sensus conciliorum*—will be indefectible, while still allowing for a range of acceptable diversity. For "soft perspectivalism," see Clark, Lints, and Smith, *101 Key Terms in Philosophy*, 66–67. For the idea of "indefectibility," see Küng, *Infallible?*, 151, 158, 182–90.

Reformation was loath to go very far, for the most part, in departing from the seven ecumenical councils of the undivided church, even the later ones (though even today issues still remain to be resolved). Normative hermeneutical decisions are, in any case, never to be left entirely in the hands of individual academic readers tucked away in their cubicles, contrary to a modern interpreter like the hyper-Protestant John Locke.[15]

---

15. Locke famously retired to his study in order to extract, by his more or less "evidentialist" lights, what he thought the New Testament really taught about Jesus. The result was *The Reasonableness of Christianity* (1695), an anti-trinitarian and Socinian-leaning treatise, which arguably read the "letter" by a different "spirit" than the one posited in the Gospel of John. From the example of Locke we may learn that the disciplines of modern exegesis are a necessary but not a sufficient condition for the conclusions of ecclesial interpretation. Locke represents what can happen under the conditions of modernity when biblical interpretation is severed from its ecclesial (and eucharistic) roots. For a spiritual connection between hermeneutics and the Eucharist, see Schmemann, *Eucharist*, 67–69.

EXCURSUS 3

On "Jesus as Lord" in Schleiermacher and Tillich (Philippians 2:11)

Friedrich Schleiermacher could refer to Jesus as "our Lord" only in a rhetorical or honorific sense. The closest he came to a literal ascription was to speak about "the purely spiritual lordship of his God-consciousness."[1] If God-consciousness was a predicate and the human Jesus was a subject, then it is of some importance that Schleiermacher ascribed "lordship" to the predicate but not the subject. In other words, lordship was ascribed to Jesus's "God-consciousness," not to Jesus.

Furthermore, although, for Schleiermacher, God may in some sense have been fully present in Jesus, there was no hypostatic union between the human nature of Jesus and the eternal Son. There was no "kenosis" of the eternal Son. There was therefore no "single-subject" Christology (in the patristic sense), and there was no literal ascription of deity to Jesus Christ. The connection of Jesus's "God-consciousness" to Jesus the human being was more nearly "spiritual" than "ontological." It thus tended toward a subtle form of Nestorianism. While it was certainly more nearly "spiritual" than "moral," it was not "hypostatic."

As David Law rightly observes, "Schleiermacher restated the two-natures doctrine in terms of 'God-consciousness.' Christ is the human being who is absolutely God-conscious. As such his entire existence is so focused on God that we can speak of this as a veritable existence of God in him. Schleiermacher, then, proposes an anthropological solution [to the christological question]. Christ does not share in the very being of God, but is a human being wholly centered in God.

1. Schleiermacher, *Christian Faith*, 473.

'Divinity' is a circumlocution for a quality of Jesus' human existence, rather than an ontological statement about the character of his being."[2]

Paul Tillich took a similar view. Because Jesus was not God incarnate, he himself could not be confessed as Lord, nor could he properly be worshiped. To say that "Jesus is Lord" was not to make a true statement about Jesus but only about "the New Being." "Jesus is Lord" was a "symbolic" statement about the New Being, affirming that "nothing can happen in history which would make the work of the New Being impossible."[3]

Tillich also argued that "the term 'divine nature' . . . cannot be applied to the Christ in any meaningful way."[4] Nor could Jesus himself be the object of prayer and worship. "We cannot pray to anyone except to God. If Jesus is someone besides God"—as he was for Tillich—"we cannot and should not pray to him. . . . But he who sees him sees the Father."[5] Prayer should not be addressed to Jesus but to "the Father" as disclosed through him.

Tillich felt that it would be "idolatrous" to pray to Jesus himself, who by nature was merely a human being. Prayer could be directed only to God as known through Jesus. An important difference between Tillich and the ancient Antiochenes was that the latter affirmed the Niceno-Constantinopolitan Creed, whereas Tillich did not. What Tillich shared with them was a strong emphasis that the human nature of Jesus had to be regarded as separable, in the end, from something divine and higher than himself, whether it be called "the New Being" or "God the Son." Tillich, however, could not say with Nestorius, "I separate the natures; I unite the worship."[6]

Neither Schleiermacher nor Tillich operated with a robustly trinitarian conception of God. What did they mean when they wrote about "God"? Despite all complexities, they seemed to mean something closer to a nontrinitarian monotheism than to Nicaea. Neither of them could ascribe lordship to Jesus without equivocation. Accordingly, neither could regard him as the incarnation of the eternal Son who is worshiped and glorified together with the Father and the Holy Spirit. In this regard they were typical of much modern theology.[7]

2. Law, *Kierkegaard's Kenotic Christology*, 36.
3. Tillich, *Systematic Theology*, 2:162.
4. Tillich, *Systematic Theology*, 2:148.
5. Tillich, *New Being*, 99–100.
6. See Bethune-Baker, *Nestorius and His Teaching*, 168.
7. No Christology can properly be regarded as "high Christology" if it hesitates to confess that "Jesus Christ is Lord" and thereby to embrace him as the object of worship. See Hunsinger, *Evangelical, Catholic, and Reformed*, 126–45, 146–68.

EXCURSUS 4

Kant's Rejection of Cultic Atonement on Moral Grounds

Working with a logic that was forensic or moral, and operating within the bounds of "mere reason," Kant argued that, in the case of sin, no innocent person could bear the guilt of another. Such an infinite guilt could only be borne by the person who was responsible for it. It could not be transferred to another, least of all to an innocent party. It could not be borne and borne away vicariously. To suppose otherwise would be "superstitious" or at least beyond rational comprehension. A debt of sins, that most personal of all liabilities, was something "which only the culprit, not the innocent, [could] bear."[1]

This implicit rejection of cultic atonement thinking represents an "anti-Judaic" element in Kant's thought (one of several) and in much modern theology after him. Nevertheless, it at least has the merit of perceiving, indirectly, that the logic of cultic atonement enters in at precisely the point where the logic of the court-room, or even of a good moral life, breaks down, if the sinner is to be spared from ruin. In the sacrificial religion of Israel, cultic atonement rituals, however severe, are rituals of mercy, designed by God to spare those who are otherwise condemned and without hope.[2]

It could be argued that whereas moral practices belong to one Wittgensteinian "language-game," cultic atonement rituals belong to another. To dismiss the rituals

1. See Kant, *Religion*, 89–92, 124–25, 144.
2. Kant of course proposes his own non-cultic solution for overcoming "radical evil," which at bottom is essentially Pelagian or semi-Pelagian. See Robert Merrihew Adams, introduction to Kant, *Religion*, xxi–xxv.

as "immoral" would perhaps be like rejecting the rules of chess on the grounds that they are contrary to the rules of checkers. The two sorts of practices, the moral and the sacrificial, are governed by different grammars and serve different purposes. They need to be assessed on that basis.[3]

The cultic atonement rituals, in particular, are embedded in a covenantal "form of life." They presuppose that moral rules—or, better, divine commandments— have been seriously breached. The rituals are designed to demonstrate the seriousness of the breach while still affording mercy to the guilty. Their validity is understood to be grounded in the irreducible singularities of revelation, election, and faith.

These remarks are not meant to resolve all questions of assessment. They merely suggest the terms on which assessment would need to take place. Wittgenstein arguably helps us to see that assessment is more complicated than Kant, and much "modernity" after him (including much modern theology), has realized. There is no such thing as a view from nowhere.[4]

---

3. To paraphrase Calvin, proposing a scheme of ethics without regarding the catastrophes of sin would be rather like "seeking in a ruin for a building" (*Institutes* 1.15.8). "*Nondum considerasti quanti ponderis sit peccatum*" ("You have not yet considered how great the weight of sin is"). Anselm, *Cur Deus Homo* 1.21. In the sacrificial religion of Israel, the gruesome severity of the cultic atonement practices is meant to bring home just how great is the weight of sin in the eyes of God.

4. I regard Stephen Finlan as an astute exegete but an unfortunate theologian. In subsequent theological writings he proceeds to repudiate cultic atonement thinking on modernist, moralistic grounds in a way that can seem uncharitable and reductive. He assumes, wrongly in my opinion, that vicarious atonement necessarily implies the appeasement of a vengeful Father. I reject the distorted view that cultic atonement in either Paul or Yom Kippur, respectively, has anything to do with appeasement through violence. See Finlan, *Paul's Cultic Atonement Metaphors*, 181, 188, 202, 222, but cf. 182. See also Finlan, *Problems with Atonement*; Finlan, *Options on Atonement*; Finlan, *Sacrifice and Atonement*.

EXCURSUS 5

On Righteousness as Grounded in "Merciful Substitution"

The ritual mystery of this "double transfer" or "wondrous exchange" is implicit in 2 Cor. 5:21: "For our sakes he made him to be sin who knew no sin so that in him we might become the righteousness of God." These words have been studied by Léopold Sabourin, SJ, with an eye toward the history of their interpretation.[1] As I read his results, neither the medieval scholastics nor the Post-Reformation Protestants were able, in various ways, to escape from being overly influenced in their exegesis by the prevailing forensic categories of the Latin West,[2] while to some extent the same was also true of the Protestant Reformers. The medieval scholastics could not allow Christ to be made sin,[3] and the Post-Reformation Protestants, as well as the Reformers themselves, could not break with an undue forensicism.[4]

1. See his contribution in Lyonnet and Sabourin, *Sin, Redemption, and Sacrifice*, 187–289.
2. "The great genius of the Romans," writes Torrance, "was for law and order. . . . These Latin modes of thought have left their mark in the legal structures, and social and political structures of the West." Torrance, *Theology in Reconstruction*, 14. "The development of penal and satisfaction notions in atonement," Torrance continues elsewhere, "owes a great deal to the Latin language and highly Latinised concepts as we can see when we compare the western development of these notions, either in Roman or Protestant thought, with the exposition of the penal and satisfaction aspects in the thought of Cyril of Alexandria especially. It was the penal-substitution notion, together with a narrowed understanding of justification, that became dominant in the centuries of so-called Protestant Orthodoxy and today in so-called Evangelical Protestantism." Torrance, *Atonement*, 57.
3. Admittedly a repellent idea. See, for example, in a contemporary instance, White, *Incarnate Lord*, 318n28, 332n57, 350n26, 406n86. See also Levering, *Christ's Fulfillment*, 64–65.
4. Lyonnet and Sabourin, *Sin, Redemption, and Sacrifice*, 237. Cf. Harnack, *Luthers Theologie*; Van Buren, *Christ in Our Place*; White, *Incarnate Lord*, 318, 389.

Renewed attention to the cultic atonement background of Pauline soteriology, as sometimes reflected in the Greek fathers,[5] would seem to hold promise for revising the excessively juridical and moralistic mindset of the Latin West, whether Catholic or Protestant, and whether "liberal" or "conservative." It might even be possible someday to lay aside the unhappy term "penal substitution," which has caused such enormous damage, in favor of a more biblically adequate term like "sacrificial substitution," or better still, as proposed here, "merciful substitution."

Salvation in Christ, for Paul, is not a forensic event with a merciful aspect, but precisely the reverse: a merciful event with a forensic aspect. It is a matter of "merciful substitution" with secondary penal elements as opposed to "penal substitution" with secondary merciful elements.[6]

Death is obviously a penalty by definition. The point here is not to deny that death is a penalty but to reject the unfortunate idea that punishment is a precondition of mercy. God's condemnation of sin is the concomitant of mercy, not its precondition. Paul places the accent on God's mercy, not on punishment. God is a God of mercy from beginning to end. He is never a vengeful Father. He does not need to be "appeased" in order to be made merciful. He is already merciful.[7] He needs only to carry out his mercy without compromising his righteousness, which is precisely what he does in the vicarious death of Christ (Rom. 3:25–26). It is of no small importance that in passages like Rom. 3:25; 5:8; and 8:3 the initiative is ascribed directly to God (as is also the case in Lev. 16:1–2, 34; 17:1–2), thus underscoring the primacy of divine mercy in the atonement and blocking any alien notions of appeasement. In short, God finds a way not only to be merciful without laxity toward human sin, but also to be righteous without undermining his mercy.[8]

5. See my comment on Phil. 3:9. See also the important citations from Gregory of Nazianzus, Cyril of Alexandria, and John Chrysostom in Thrall, *2 Corinthians 1–7*, 1:441.

6. Balthasar embraced a version of substitutionary atonement because he found it in the Greek fathers. At the same time, however, he rejected the more forensic idea of *penal* substitution, which is not much evident in the fathers, who were more attuned, so to speak, to the cultic and the ransom idea than to the forensic. See Balthasar, *Theo-Drama*, 4:240–54, 317, 337–38. For the disagreement between Balthasar and Rahner about substitutionary atonement, see Hunsinger, *Disruptive Grace*, 261–67.

7. The misguided idea that God must *first* satisfy his wrath *before* he can exercise his mercy has no basis in Holy Scripture, least of all when read from a center in Christ.

8. The idea that the Lord God (YHWH) tempers his justice by his mercy is not unknown in Rabbinic Judaism. In a Talmudic commentary on Isa. 56:7, for example, we read of God's benediction on Israel and the nations. In an eschatological act of blessing, God expresses his intention to overcome his wrath by his mercy, allowing his mercy to prevail; he will carry out his judgment with mercy "beyond the strict letter of the law." Babylonian Talmud, *Berakhot* 7a. I owe this point to David Novak, whose unpublished translation I am following. The passage implies that in the end, restoration prevails over retribution.

His mercy and righteousness are one in the atoning blood of Christ. "Christ's blood is a metaphor that stands primarily for the suffering love of God. It suggests that there is no sorrow God has not known, no grief he has not borne, no price he was unwilling to pay, in order to reconcile the world to himself in Christ. . . . It is a love that has endured the bitterest realities of suffering and death in order that its purposes might prevail. . . . The motif of Christ's blood signifies primarily the depth of the divine commitment to rescue, protect, and sustain those who would otherwise be lost."[9] Mercy and righteousness are distinct but not separate on the cross, with the priority and precedence belonging to mercy.

In his study of cultic metaphors in Paul's doctrine of the atonement, Stephen Finlan examines some relatively neglected themes in Paul's thought. He shows that it is characteristic of Paul to mix cultic metaphors with elements drawn from other domains, such as the juridical, the financial, the social, and the interpersonal.[10] At the same time, as we have seen, he suggests that it is not uncommon for cultic motifs to be "logically prior" in Paul, or at least logically basic, relative to the other motifs.[11] Finlan argues that Paul characteristically uses diverse elements in an eclectic way,[12] but that primacy is typically accorded to cultic metaphors and concepts, especially regarding the saving significance of Christ's cross. The primacy of the cultic, I would urge, is what ensures the primacy of mercy.

For Paul, writes Finlan, "salvation results from the death of Jesus, which functions as a cultic event."[13] He notes that in mixed and various ways "Paul uses sacrificial, judicial, and redemptive metaphors. No matter that these images cannot be perfectly harmonized; for Paul they capture a truth in that they picture Christ's death as a ritual act with universal saving consequences. Paul has an intuition that Christ's death fulfills a cultic pattern, perhaps all the basic cultic patterns, since he can equate [Christ] to the spotless sacrifice, the accursed scapegoat, or the Passover lamb."[14]

9. Hunsinger, "Meditation on the Blood of Christ," in *Disruptive Grace*, 361–62 (slightly modified).

10. As Dunn points out, Paul uses a wide range of metaphors to discuss salvation, including reconciliation, rescue, putting on new clothing or armor, being engrafted, being harvested, acquittal (being justified), being sanctified, victory, rebirth, and so on. Finlan's point is that although no one metaphor is dominant, cultic atonement metaphors—such as *hilastērion*, blood, sacrifice, substitution, cleansing, intercession, double transfer, and having access—are foundational to the rest at crucial points. See Dunn, *Theology of Paul the Apostle*, 328–31; Finlan, *Paul's Cultic Atonement Metaphors*, 102, 107, 117. I would suggest that priestly/cultic elements are generally presupposed by forensic elements, though not by royal/messianic elements (over which they are sometimes made superior). Both priestly/cultic and royal/messianic elements, in turn, can be read as being radicalized by the use of apocalyptic metaphors and concepts.

11. Finlan, *Paul's Cultic Atonement Metaphors*, 107, 117.

12. Finlan, *Paul's Cultic Atonement Metaphors*, 102.

13. Finlan, *Paul's Cultic Atonement Metaphors*, 216.

14. Finlan, *Paul's Cultic Atonement Metaphors*, 103.

Finlan's analysis helps us to see how "substitution" functions in Pauline so-teriology. "Substitutionary ideas," he writes, "underlie many of Paul's cultic and redemption metaphors."[15] It is crucial to see that "substitution" is fundamentally a cultic idea. It is *not* in the first instance a juridical or forensic idea. From a legal (or even a moral) point of view, there are instances, as Kant recognized, where no one can properly bear the guilt of another and its juridical consequences, particularly in capital cases. In a strictly forensic model there can be no place, under such circumstances, for substitution. The logic of the courtroom does not allow it.

Forensically, the prescribed solution to the problem of wrongdoing is *punishment*, whereas from a cultic point of view the solution is not punishment but *removal*.[16] Within a priestly/cultic scheme, therefore, substitution is not primarily "penal," despite the widespread currency of the almost blasphemous term "penal substitution."[17] It makes little sense to regard the sacrificial animal in the ritual practices of Israel as the object of vicarious *punishment*, even if that element may not be entirely absent in the background. In a cultic scheme the sacrificial animal is made to bear the dreadful consequences of sin vicariously, and to bear them away.

If sin means enmity toward God (as it does), its consequences mean estrangement from him. "The wages of sin is death" (Rom. 6:23). This estrangement could not be more dreadful. It means nothing less than spiritual death, however that may be conceived. It means being cut off from the holy source of all goodness and life. The seeds of spiritual death are inherent in sin itself. Sin is its own punishment. It leads inevitably to death, because God is of purer eyes than to behold evil (Hab. 1:13). God can have no fellowship with those who have corrupted themselves by sin. His condemnation of sin occurs when he abandons sinners to their self-chosen abandonment of him (Rom. 1:26, 28). His wrath is his necessary No to the sin that estranges his willful human creatures from himself (Rom. 1:18). But God does not give his No the last word. "He will not always chide, nor will he keep his anger forever" (Ps. 103:9). He is essentially a God of mercy whose No to sin is his rejection of everything that contradicts his love and that would prevent fellowship (*koinōnia*) with himself, the very fellowship for which his creatures were made.

15. Finlan, *Paul's Cultic Atonement Metaphors*, 169.
16. I take "removal" to be the core idea underlying such related sacrificial ideas as cleansing, covering, or transfer.
17. Cf. Marshall, *Aspects of the Atonement*, 59–75. Marshall's discussion is commendable except for his inability to shed the offending term. Apparently the idea of "merciful substitution," which better comports with his analysis, was unavailable to him.

In the New Testament Christ averts the death that would otherwise fall on the sinner by bearing our sin and bearing it away (John 1:29). The main point of such vicarious sin-bearing is not punishment but removal.[18] Finlan quotes Otfried Hofius to this effect: "It is the *cult* that rescues the sinner from a doomed fate: 'cultic atonement is to be primarily and decisively understood as the separation of the sinner from his sin—that means, as an event of sin-removal, which underlies the discharge of sin onto a substitutionary sin-bearer and the negation of the sin through the negation of the sin-bearer.'"[19]

In a characteristic move, Barth offers an essentially "apocalyptic" interpretation of how God separates the sinner from the sin. He writes, "What we cannot do, the forgiveness of sins, the separating of man [*des Menschen*] from his sin in the killing of the old and the raising up of a new man, God himself has done and revealed."[20] Several features of this remark are noteworthy. The phrase "what we cannot do" suggests a Reformational element (bondage of the will); "forgiveness of sins," an evangelical element (divine mercy); "separating" human beings from their sin, a cultic-atonement element (removal of guilt); and "the killing of the old and the raising up of a new man," an apocalyptic element (disjunction via destruction). What "God himself has done" points to an actual ontic occurrence, while its "revelation" points to a correlative noetic occurrence.

Reformational, evangelical, cultic-atonement, and apocalyptic elements are all at stake for Barth in explicating the mystery of how the sinner is separated from the sin. It is the atoning mystery of what God himself has done and revealed in Jesus Christ. Barth proposes that a merciful separation occurs (holistically) as the sinner dies and rises again in Christ. Just as the forensic (condemnation)

---

18. I should note that this interpretation of Yom Kippur as well as of Passover is retrospective and Christian. It is a matter of interpreting them by reading backwards from a center in Christ (e.g., John 1:29; Rom. 3:25; Gal. 3:13; Heb. 9:11–20; 1 Pet. 2:24; 3:18; 1 John 2:2, etc.). For Christian theology, Christ is the antitype who sheds light on the antecedent types. Stökl Ben Ezra suggests that by the time of early Christianity, as evidenced in the Gospel of John, Passover seems to have accrued some sort of atoning significance. Stökl Ben Ezra, *Impact of Yom Kippur*, 177nn147–48. Similarly, in an important article, Siker suggests that in New Testament Johannine literature, the distinction between the Passover lamb (which originally had no atoning or expiatory significance) and Yom Kippur is blurred: "In short, early Christians took the other most significant holy day in Jewish tradition, Yom Kippur, and imported its central emphasis on forgiveness of sins into the ritual imagination of Passover. Thus, early Christians engaged in a process of 'Yom Kippuring' Passover, a kind of recombinant theologizing of central Jewish rituals in the service of Christian efforts to make sense of Jesus' death in light of Jewish tradition." Siker, "Yom Kippuring Passover," 76.

19. Finlan, *Paul's Cultic Atonement Metaphors*, 182 (italics original), quoting Hofius, *Paulusstudien*, 41.

20. Barth, *Church Dogmatics* IV/1, 408. Jesus Christ "has borne the punishment that was rightly ours" (*CD* II/1, 152). Indeed he did so in an act of merciful substitution. In the cross of Christ the condemnation that must come upon us as sinners was at once carried out and removed in mercy by God himself. "This is the victory of grace over human enmity against grace" (ibid.). It is the victory of mercy over punishment.

is relativized by the cultic (mercy), so also is the cultic (expiation) relativized and radicalized by the apocalyptic (dying and rising again).[21]

The cultic method of dealing with sin is essentially merciful rather than retributory or vindictive. Given the peculiar logic of the cultus, "the supreme act of grace in salvation history [or, better, covenantal history] must be God's giving of the sacrificial cult. . . . [It is] the God-given method for removing sin."[22] This can only mean that the God-given cultus, instituted for the removal of sin and the restoration of fellowship, begins and ends in mercy and is merciful all the way through. *Hilastērion* at the center of the process means nothing less than "mercy seat."

Just as "expiation" (the bearing and removal of sin) and "propitiation" (the bearing and removal of wrath) are not mutually exclusive, but rather coincide, so also is neither of them incompatible with the cultic metaphor of the "mercy seat" (Rom. 3:25). "Mercy seat," in this interpretation, is the place where the cultic process of separating the sin from the sinner happens in the presence of the most holy God. "Mercy seat" is thus a metaphor standing for "expiation/propitiation." It can of course also stand for "covering" sins or "blotting" them out, but the central idea of removing sin through sacrificial blood remains broadly the same. All three—"mercy seat," "propitiation," and "expiation"—intersect. The "place" is a metonymy for the "process." There can be no reason to prefer any one of these terms to the exclusion of the others, as long as it is understood that "propitiation" has nothing to do with "appeasement."

It is a sad distortion to suppose that the purpose of the cultus is to "render" God merciful by a ritual sacrifice or to "appease" his wrath. God is never anything but merciful in his righteousness and truth. His mercy is already the source and ground of the cultus, not merely its eventual outcome. Nevertheless, when juridical modes of thought become blurred with cultic modes of thought—or, worse, when the juridical is granted precedence over the cultic (rather than the other way around)—any number of unfortunate consequences can occur.

It is interesting in this context that Paul writes in terms of "wrath," "judgment," and "condemnation," but rarely, if at all, in terms of "punishment" (a

---

21. Baptism would be the sacrament of separating sinners from their sin, insofar as it signifies dying and rising with Christ. Baptism, like resurrection, would therefore be an event of apocalyptic resonance.

22. Finlan, *Paul's Cultic Atonement Metaphors*, 182. My views are in line with Raymond Brown: "In cultic passages it is often impossible to distinguish propitiation from expiation. . . . God has appointed for his people means of removing evil [expiation] and turning away wrath [propitiation]. God is not manipulated by rites; he instituted the rites and always takes the initiative in pardoning. . . . God's love [mercy] is apparent in accepting the sacrifice after it was offered but even more in providing the priest and victim." Brown, *Epistles of John*, 219–20.

perfectly "forensic" idea).[23] It is not unjust of God, he says, "to inflict his wrath" (*ho epipherōn tēn orgēn*) on "our unrighteousness" (*adikia hēmōn*) (Rom. 3:5). The implication is that God would indeed be unjust if he allowed our sin to occur without condemning it.[24]

It seems that God finds a way to be merciful in Christ while upholding his righteousness, and therefore his wrath, against all human ungodliness and wickedness. I agree with Calvin that God acts righteously, in various respects, precisely because God is righteous in himself. "God is just, not indeed as one among many, but as one who contains in himself alone all the fullness of righteousness."[25] In other words, in interpreting Paul's idea of God, "being" ought not to be separated from "act." Divine being and action coincide in a pattern of unity-in-distinction. God acts righteously just because God is righteousness in and of himself. Righteousness, like holiness, is a predicate of God's being, not merely of his actions. God's righteousness, by definition, may overlap with his mercy but cannot be reduced to it.[26]

As should be clear, for Paul the divine wrath has absolutely nothing to do with revenge, vindictiveness, cruelty, or malice. The God who justly condemns sin is the God whose heart is a heart full of mercy. Although not without ambiguities, it seems that for Paul God's purposes in Christ are finally *restorative* rather than *retributive*, because forensic elements are tempered by cultic elements.[27] Declaring

23. I am referring mainly to the undisputed letters. As I note, however, an element of retributive justice cannot be expunged from Paul. It is not a question of its presence or absence but of the ordering of retribution to mercy.

24. "Condemnation" and "wrath" certainly imply divine *rejection*, but not necessarily divine *retribution*. The automatic conflation of "rejection" with "retribution" can be traced to the influence accorded to juridical over cultic modes of thought in Pauline interpretation. Here Travis is instructive: "Words which 'look retributive' are significantly rare in Paul's letters. . . . We have found reason to believe that a retributive significance is likely only in a small minority of . . . instances. . . . There is, therefore, a striking contrast between his own writings and the literature which forms a background to his thought." Travis, *Christ and the Judgment of God*, 205. Travis is especially good in extracting "retribution" from Paul's cultic understanding of the atonement (181–204). Nevertheless, I do not agree with him that divine judgment does not actually come upon sinners "from without" (i.e., from the will of God) but only in an "immanent" manner (automatically). For Paul sin is its own punishment, precisely because *the Lord God* abandons sinners to their sins (*paredōken autous ho theos*) (Rom. 1:28), and sinners "know that those who do such things *deserve* to die [*axioi thanatou*]" (Rom. 1:32)—an element of retributive justice. In Paul the retributive element is not absent but is tempered in Christ by the restorative element, which at once embraces the condemnation (vicariously) in order to transcend it (effectually).

25. Calvin, on Rom. 3:26, in *Calvin's New Testament Commentaries*, 8:77.

26. The idea that in key verses such as Rom. 3:5, 21–26 and 2 Cor. 5:21 "righteousness of God" means no more than God's "covenant faithfulness" has been extensively weighed and refuted by Irons, *Righteousness of God*.

27. If so, God's "wrath" would, depending on the context, finally tend toward being *purgative* rather than merely *retributive*. On Rom. 12:20, for example, Cranfield argues that the "coals of fire" heaped on an enemy's head, through acts of kindness toward him, would refer not to future divine punishment

that *our* sin was condemned in *his* flesh (Rom. 8:3), for example, makes little sense if the transfer of "condemnation" to (the sinless) Christ were not essentially vicarious. Recall that, according to Paul, we are justified not only by faith but also "by his blood" (Rom. 5:9). It seems that God's condemnation is fully carried out, only to be fully transcended by his mercy toward all (Rom. 11:32). The primacy of mercy suggests, in effect, that the forensic is not only included within the cultic but also subordinated to it.[28]

It seems that for Paul cultic atonement metaphors are finally more basic than forensic ones. Although his general use of metaphors is eclectic and mixed, those with a cultic background can be read as tending toward being foundational to the others. Although Paul deliberately mixes his metaphors, Finlan suggests that he makes the metaphor of expiation through blood "fundamental to the others."[29] "The cultic action is logically prior; there could be no participation in Christ's atoning death if atonement had not first been accomplished in that death."[30] Ac-

---

or retribution but to stirring up pangs of conscience and contrition, in the hope of provoking him to repentance. See Cranfield, *Epistle to the Romans*, 2:648–50.

28. The ambiguities that remain can possibly be traced to an unresolved tension in Paul's mind about how these elements work out regarding final salvation. The *forensic* element, with its focus on the individual under divine judgment, would point in one direction ("particularist," most especially for the unrepentant), while the *cultic* element, with its more corporate emphasis on sin's removal for the sake of restoration (even for the "ungodly"), would point in another direction ("universalist").

The "particularist" and the "universalist" strands in Paul regarding final salvation are left in an unresolved tension according to Eugene Boring, while Martinus C. de Boer and to a lesser degree Sven Hillert suggest that the universalist statements appear finally to receive the accent. See Boring, "Universal Salvation in Paul"; de Boer, "Paul and Apocalyptic Eschatology," esp. 1:374–78; Hillert, *Limited and Universal Salvation*, 251. Hillert is more cautious than de Boer. He is closer to Boring in *explicatio* but closer to de Boer in *applicatio*. See also now the very extensive study by Jens Adam, *Paulus und die Versöhnung aller*. Adam reads Paul as leaning strongly toward the hope of universal salvation. For a theological account that supports universalism, see Hart, *That All May Be Saved*. Hart, however, lacks a proper sense of reticence toward the texts.

Others of course see the particularist elements as prevailing. My point is that the tension between the "particularist" and "universalist" strands in Paul can be read as reflecting a prior tension between "forensic" and "cultic" elements in his thought. I agree with Cranfield, however, that the overall trajectory tends toward mercy. Rom. 9:11–18 can be interpreted in light of Rom. 11:32b. See, for example, Munck, *Christ and Israel*, and also Cranfield, *Epistle to the Romans*, 2:445–50, 477–89, 586–87. See especially Cranfield's final intervention, shortly before he died, "Note on Rom. 11:32," where, more decisively than ever before, he opts for a form of universal hope.

Even Calvin could commend a certain openness in Christian prayer to a wider hope. Christians, he says, ought to conform their prayers to this rule—namely, that they should pray not only for those who confess Christ by faith but indeed for all others as well. They ought to pray "not only for those whom they at present see and recognize as believers, but for all persons who dwell on earth. For what God has determined concerning them is beyond our knowing except that it is no less godly than humane to wish and hope the best for them." *Institutes* 3.20.38 (slightly modified). In this mood Calvin represents a reverent agnosticism.

29. Finlan, *Paul's Cultic Atonement Metaphors*, 214.

30. Finlan, *Paul's Cultic Atonement Metaphors*, 117.

---

cording to Rom. 3:25, Christ has become the "mercy seat" (*hilastērion, kapporet*) by which our sin is expiated and God's wrath is propitiated. Again, there can be no question of "appeasement" here, since the entire cultic atonement process is conceived from beginning to end as the gift of God's mercy.

The main sacrificial rituals of Israel are grounded in divine mercy. They are initiated by the mercy of God, carried out through the mercy of God, and come to rest in the mercy of God. What is true of Yom Kippur also applies to Rom. 3:25. "It is God himself," writes Markus Tiwald, "who atones for humankind. God is the acting *subject*, not the placated *object*, of atonement."[31] "You atone [*techapperem*] for our transgressions" (Ps. 65:3).

In the Day of Atonement rituals, God in his mercy is not a passive spectator but the principal acting subject. It is God in his mercy, acting in and through the high priest and the whole cultic process, who separates the sinner from the sin by means of vicarious sacrifice. Likewise, for Christian faith, it is God in his mercy who acts in and through his incarnate Son as he dies for us vicariously, and who is made to be, as Luther calls him, "the one great sinner" on the cross.[32] It is God who not only initiates the cultic atonement process in his mercy but also acts in and through it to accomplish his saving purposes. In short, the divine mercy is present in Yom Kippur not only at its conclusion but also at its inception and throughout the entire course of its enactment.

It is noteworthy that in Leviticus Yom Kippur is not associated with repentance. In that text the emphasis falls on the divine initiative through the surrogacy of the high priest, who restores the people to the Lord by separating them from their sins. Not until the book of Jubilees is there any suggestion that repentance is necessary to achieve mercy.[33] "Whereas in Leviticus and Numbers, it is the high priest who obtains atonement for the people of Israel," writes Anke Dorman, "*Jubilees* stresses that the people personally atone for their sins through repentance and mourning."[34] In Leviticus, by contrast, the divine initiative remains decisive throughout. The Day of Atonement is the day "when the sins of God's people were forgiven, and it was as though God had newly-created them."[35] At the same time, of course, God's kindness is meant to lead them to repentance (Rom. 2:4; cf. Lev. 5:5–6; 26:1–46).

In the book of Leviticus one textual strand states that the bloody sacrifices are offered "to God" and, in effect, "before God" (e.g., Lev. 1:14; 4:3), while another

31. Tiwald, "Christ as *Hilastērion*," 193 (slightly modified).
32. *Luther's Works*, 26:277, 280–81.
33. See Stökl Ben Ezra, *Impact of Yom Kippur*, 95.
34. Dorman, "'Commit Injustice,'" 57.
35. Thrall, *2 Corinthians 1–7*, 1:422.

states repeatedly that "I am the LORD who sanctifies you" (e.g., Lev. 20:8; 21:8). In the one strand God is the object, while in the other God is the key acting subject. Most importantly, the Lord God does not remain aloof or on high above the cultic process. "I will appear in the cloud upon the mercy seat" (Lev. 16:2). God is present in the holy of holies at the very heart of the atoning process. By separating the sin from the sinner, the cultic process is ultimately restorative. Its purpose is the purpose of mercy—namely, to "repair the broken relationship" between the Lord God and his people.[36]

Ambiguities remain about how Yahweh does so. Nevertheless, according to Roy Gane, on the Day of Atonement, it is precisely as Yahweh's representative that the high priest "effected purgation by performing the ritual." Yahweh operates, Gane suggests, through his surrogate, the high priest, in such a way that Yahweh's repudiation of evil is reaffirmed and his justice upheld, even as he divides his people from their sins and restores them to himself. The Day of Atonement, with its solemnity and slaughter and expurgation, is a dreadful expression of God's manner of working. It demonstrates that God is merciful in his severity and severe in his mercy.[37]

A similar line of thought is developed by Baruch J. Schwartz. When the priest is directed to splash blood on the altar, Schwartz suggests, the priest is acting as a surrogate of the Lord. It is as if the key text (Lev. 17:11) were saying, "When you place the blood on the altar, you do so at my command, because I have assigned it a role to play there." The direction of the sacrifice is reversed. It is not merely offered to God, but is also and primarily instituted—for the sake of mercy—by God.[38] "It is not you who are placing the blood on the altar for me, for my benefit, but rather the opposite: it is I who have placed it there for you—for your benefit. . . . I have assigned [the blood] to you for making expiation upon the altar. . . . It is *I* who have provided *you* with the opportunity 'to atone for your lives.'"[39] Schwartz agrees that the cultic sacrifice has everything to do with "removal" and nothing to do with "appeasement."[40]

---

36. Milgrom, *Leviticus 1–16*, 245. In Yom Kippur, "though the priest performs the rituals, it is only by the grace of God that they are efficacious. . . . God [is] the sole dispenser of expiation." Milgrom, *Leviticus 1–16*, 1084.

37. Gane, *Cult and Character*, 51, 104–5, 322–23 (slightly modified).

38. Mary Douglas writes about the "sanctity of blood" in Leviticus: "God protects the people of Israel, his rites give them covering, sacrifice is the means *he has given to them* for expiation. Sacrifice protects them from the consequences of their own behavior, even from his just anger." Douglas, *Leviticus as Literature*, 137 (italics added).

39. Schwartz, "Prohibitions," 50–51 (italics original).

40. Schwartz, "Prohibitions," 56.

On this reading, the central text of Lev. 17:11 not only defines what blood means in the sacrificial ritual but also carries resonances with the divine initiative in Gen. 22:8—namely, that "God will provide the lamb." Similarly, according to Jay Sklar, Lev. 17:11 suggests that the only use of animal blood that the Lord allows is "making atonement." Sklar goes on to argue that the blood of the sacrifice involves both "substitution" and "expiation" (ransom and purification), and not the one without the other.[41] Schwartz likewise finds that "expiation" and "substitution" are already inseparable in Lev. 17. The expiation is an act of ransom that occurs "as payment *in place of* your lives, which would otherwise be forfeit."[42] Mercy, substitution, and expiation, at the severe cost of sacrificial blood, go together.

In Christ as in Yom Kippur, the emphasis falls on sin's removal and only concomitantly on its condemnation.[43] Again, when the sin is borne and borne away (expiation), God's wrath is borne and borne away with it (propitiation). There can be no conflict between propitiation and expiation. They are two sides of one and the same atoning process not only as *divinely instituted* but also as *divinely effected*. This interpretation would hold even if the proper translation of *hilastērion* in Rom. 3:25 is simply "mercy seat." "Expiation," "propitiation," and "mercy seat" as interpretations of *hilastērion* are, as already suggested, intertwined ideas.[44] They are not mutually exclusive. They point to complementary aspects in a single complex process of removal. It is a process of atonement grounded in mercy.[45]

It is noteworthy that the Greek fathers in particular tend to grasp the primacy of the cultic over the forensic. "In New Testament writings," writes Romuald Mollaun, OFM, as interpreted by the Greek fathers, "*dikaioō* does not signify to declare righteous, but to make righteous by the removal of sin."[46] Mollaun

41. Sklar, *Sin, Impurity, Sacrifice, Atonement*, 177–78, 181–84.

42. Schwartz, "Prohibitions," 55 (italics added).

43. These conclusions are in line with the full-length study by Joshua M. Vis. "Leviticus 17:11 should be understood," he writes, "to describe how blood, due to the ['life' or animating spirit] contained within it, purges the [sin, guilt, or impurity in the spirit] of the offerer." Vis, "Purification Offering of Leviticus," 254. Vis translates Lev. 17:11 as follows: "For the spirit of the flesh is in the blood, and I have placed it for you upon the altar to purge your spirits; for it is the blood that purges by means of the spirit" (205). The emphasis is on purgation, not punishment.

44. See Cranfield, *Epistle to the Romans*, 1:208–18. For a good survey of the three terms, see Gundry Volf, "Expiation/Propitiation/Mercy Seat."

45. The Greek fathers discern a cultic atonement background at work in Rom. 3:25. As we may learn from Mollaun, they seem to pay more attention to it with respect to this verse (Rom. 3:25) than do the Latin fathers and the Protestant Reformers. In interpreting *hilastērion* in Rom. 3:25, the Greek fathers rightly assume that a choice does not need to be made between "mercy seat," "expiation," and "propitiation," for each contributes a nuance to the overall meaning. See Mollaun, *St. Paul's Concept of* Ἱλαστήριον, 25–42, 96.

46. Mollaun, *St. Paul's Concept of* Ἱλαστήριον, 113.

perhaps does not lay sufficient emphasis on the vicarious element in Christ's death and on the communication of his righteousness to faith by means of union with Christ. But when these "cultic" elements are taken into account, we may say with Calvin, in partial accord with Mollaun, that in Christ "we are entirely righteous before God."[47]

---

47. Calvin, *Institutes* 3.11.11. As sinners we have "no alternative but to flee to Christ alone, that we may be regarded as righteous in him, not being so in ourselves." Calvin, "On the Sixth Session of the Council of Trent," in *John Calvin: Tracts and Letters*, 3:116.

EXCURSUS 6

On *"Pistis Christou" as a Vicarious Term*

What follows is a brief consideration of T. F. Torrance.[1] Torrance is of interest in this connection for two reasons: first, because he translates *pistis Iēsou Christou* subjectively,[2] and second, because he nonetheless interprets it vicariously.[3] He thus serves to corroborate my point that the soteriology is more important than the translation.[4] While I believe Torrance is correct about the one, I think he is

---

1. For Torrance's complex and subtle reflections on *pistis Iēsou Christou* as involving a subjective genitive, see Torrance, "One Aspect"; Torrance, "Biblical Conception of 'Faith.'"

2. For a good summary of how Torrance interprets *pistis Iēsou Christou*, with extensive references, see Chiarot, *The Unassumed Is the Unhealed*, 181–83. See also the complementary material in Ho, *T. F. Torrance's Theology of Incarnation*, 79–90.

3. New Testament scholars who adopt the subjective translation for *pistis Christou* do not usually interpret it vicariously. Their idea of the "faithfulness of Christ" therefore tends toward becoming a new law even as their idea of salvation tends toward sanctification without justification. See, e.g., Hays, *Faith of Jesus Christ*. The idea of participation, for Hays, mainly means participating in a "pattern." This idea of participation is then merged with "justification" (206, 211–15). On the other hand, Hays elsewhere stresses that "rectification" (his alternative word for "justification") is "God's doing, not ours." The faithfulness of Jesus in dying on the cross is answered by the faithfulness of God, who raises him from the dead. Here Jesus is said to be the object of faith, not just the pattern of faith. God's act of faithfulness to Jesus, Hays states, creates a new world that liberates us from the bondage of sin. Although these statements are fine as far as they go, they seriously underplay sin as guilt, the Christian as *simul iustus et peccator* (Rom. 7:14–25), and the vicarious significance of Christ's saving person in his obedience and death. See Hays, "Letter to the Galatians," 246–47. In any case, it is not entirely clear in this material how Jesus is the object of faith. Moo suggests that for Hays faith seems more like believing "with" Christ than believing "in" Christ. Moo, *Galatians*, 42.

4. It might be worth noting, as an aside, that *pistis Christou* could possibly be interpreted as a genitive of source or possession. I have argued that Christ as our righteousness is essentially the object and content of faith. As long as that remains intact, the translation question, one way or another, is relatively *adiaphora*. I'm more interested in the soteriology than the translation.

mistaken about the other.[5] A better soteriology can therefore be combined with an unsatisfactory translation.[6]

Significantly, Torrance does not pit "faith *in* Christ" and "faith *of* Christ" against each other as mutually exclusive options at the level of substance. For Torrance, because Christ's "faithfulness" (*pistis Christou* in the subjective sense) is not only "representative" but above all "vicarious" and "substitutionary," the person of Christ in his subjective faithfulness is at once the "object of faith" and yet also the "object of participation." Those who believe in Christ by grace are given a share in his *perfect* "righteousness" or "faithfulness" (sinlessness) at the same time. Through his active obedience, Christ lived a life of unbroken faithfulness to God (and love toward others) for our sakes and in our stead. This is the very kind of life that we in our sinfulness have failed to live.

For Torrance, Jesus Christ is first of all the incarnation of God's faithfulness toward us. "God interposes *himself* between us and his judgment and takes the righteous infliction on sin upon himself, and so provides for its expiation in himself in the sacrifice of Christ."[7] Note that this statement represents the quintessence of what I have called "merciful substitution." It describes God's mercy as his interposing of himself between us and final judgment, in the sacrifice of Christ, for the sake of our deliverance. The mercy of Christ is the fulfillment of the cultic atonement rituals initiated by the grace of God in the history of Israel. For Torrance, that is how God's mercy is expressed in his faithfulness toward us.

At the same time, Christ also embodied and actualized in himself our human faithfulness in answer to God's. He entered into solidarity with us and offered to God, in our place, the human response of faithfulness that we had failed to provide. The "faithfulness of Christ" might be said to include "the fact that he believed for us, offering to God in his vicarious faithfulness, the perfect response of human faith which we could not offer."[8] This too—the vicarious faithfulness of Christ—is the mercy of God.

We are summoned to acknowledge and to participate in the faithfulness that Christ enacted for us vicariously in his mercy.[9] "The Gospel . . . holds out

5. Whether the reverse might be possible—a correct ("objectivist") translation with a weak ("emulationist") soteriology—is a moot point.

6. From this point of view, the famous critique of Torrance by James Barr may be regarded as philologically correct but theologically irrelevant. See Barr, *Semantics of Biblical Language*, 161–205. Torrance's judgments rest on a wider base than his mistaken philology.

7. Torrance, *Atonement*, 154 (italics original).

8. Torrance, *God and Rationality*, 154.

9. For a powerful account of how this idea can work out in pastoral care, see J. B. Torrance, *Worship*, 32–35.

to us free participation in the faithful response of Christ already made on our behalf. Hence our response of faith is made within the ring of faithfulness which Christ has already thrown around us, when in faith we rely not on our own believing but wholly on his vicarious response of faithfulness toward God. In this way Christ's faithfulness undergirds our feeble and faltering faith and enfolds it in his own."[10]

Participation in Christ means little, for Torrance, apart from this *vicarious* "faithfulness" as carried out on our behalf as the *pars pro toto*. Received as a gift through participation (by grace through faith), Christ's "active righteousness" in our stead makes an important contribution to our being made acceptable *in him* for the sake of fellowship with God. We cannot be conformed to Christ in his subjective faithfulness apart from this vicarious aspect. His perfect faithfulness in our place (both "active" and "passive") is a gift to be received before it is a pattern to be emulated. "The absolute measure of forgiveness is the absolute measure of the judgment of divine mercy. That is why we are saved not by the works that we do but by faith that flees from what we do to find refuge alone in what Christ has done for us."[11]

Participation also means little, for Torrance, apart from Christ's "passive obedience," whereby he bore our condemnation in his flesh.[12] He saved us from our sinfulness as the object of divine wrath by taking our plight to himself in mercy and dying in our place so that we might live. Here, for Torrance, our participation *in Christ* is objective before it can be actualized in us through faith. For him atonement, justification, and sanctification are not only substitutionary and Christocentric. They are also objective and significantly corporate.

> The individual is not left out of sight in the New Testament, but the emphasis is on the corporate union in Christ, and justification is expounded only within that corporate emphasis. In the widest sense, and in a very profound sense, Christ's death for all humankind means that all men and women are *already* [objectively] involved in God's act of justification—Christ died for them when they were yet sinners, and in that he died, all died, all were condemned, and all came under his substitutionary atonement. . . .

10. Torrance, *God and Rationality*, 154.

11. Torrance, *God and Rationality*, 66.

12. The proponents of the subjective translation for *pistis Christou* typically focus on its "active" aspect virtually to the neglect of its "passive" aspect. Despite allowing, for example, that Christ vicariously bears the curse of the law (Gal. 3:13), Hays makes little or nothing of it. Virtually all the emphasis falls on being "transformed" (i.e., sanctified) through our participating in the (active) "faithfulness" of Christ. Hays, *Faith of Jesus Christ*, 225n90.

Christ Jesus is himself our wisdom and righteousness and sanctification and redemption. He is our total justification *in himself.* That corporate justification in Christ—God's righteousness and our righteousness—finds expression in the church as the one body of Christ. Justification is extended in its actualization among all humanity through [subjective] incorporation into Christ by his Spirit, the operation and indwelling of people by the Spirit that is through faith. Thus the complete doctrine of justification is the doctrine of the church, the church of the "saints" or the *hagioi* in Christ.[13]

In his concept of the "vicarious faithfulness of Christ," Torrance goes on to embrace not only elements of "substitution" and "participation" (with objective and corporate aspects) but also the indispensable cultic element of "exchange."

This reconciliation took place through a "wondrous exchange" . . . in which Christ took our place, that we might have his place. . . . The Son of God substituted himself in our place, . . . taking all our shame and curse upon himself, . . . that he might stand in humanity's place and work out in himself humanity's reconciliation.

In that he thus *took* our place of sin and shame and death, he freely *gives* us his place of holiness and glory and life, that we through his poverty might become rich, that we through his being made sin and a curse for us, might be reconciled to God clothed with his righteousness and stand before God *in his person.* He came in our name, that we in his name might have access to the presence of the Father and be restored to him as his children.[14]

For Torrance our "participation in Christ" is essentially a participation in his *person* before it is a participation in a *pattern.* It means entering into union and loving communion with Christ himself as the object and content of faith. On the basis of his finished, fully sufficient, and unrepeatable saving work, faith receives Christ and his mercy as a free gift. Works of love, in conformity with Christ, are a consequence, not a cause, of salvation. The cultic atonement themes—expiation (blood), substitution, participation, exchange, and above all mercy—thus function as an antidote not only to mere moralism but also to the external relations of mere forensicism.[15]

In Reformational accounts of salvation, as previously suggested, forensic ideas are often accorded an undue prominence. This is what happens when Paul's cultic

13. Torrance, *Atonement*, 128–29 (slightly modified; italics added).
14. Torrance, *Atonement*, 151 (italics added).
15. For a thoughtful critique of Torrance, see Allen, *Christ's Faith*, 17–19, 195–200, 213–14. Allen thinks that Torrance underplays Christ's faithfulness and obedience as an ethical norm. Maybe so. But this is easily fixed.

atonement metaphors are marginalized. Removal is eclipsed by punishment, union with Christ is overshadowed by the idea of forensic declaration, the *admirabile commercium* ("imputation") is interpreted against a courtroom backdrop rather than a priestly/cultic one, and the focus becomes overly individualistic rather than corporate. Let us glance briefly at these concerns.

Removal is eclipsed by punishment. When the cultic is displaced by the forensic, punishment becomes the necessary solution for dealing with sin, and God's wrath needs to be appeased before his mercy can go into effect. God is wrathful first and merciful second. He is punitive before he is gracious. Such anti-evangelical distortions, which is what they are, can be avoided when Paul's cultic atonement metaphors receive their due.

Union with Christ is overshadowed by the idea of forensic declaration. When forensic metaphors are made to do too much work, it is claimed that the guilty sinner is "declared" to be righteous "because of Christ," on the premise that the sinner has faith. The sinner, who remains sinful in himself, is said to be "made righteous" by means of a declaration of acquittal ("not guilty"), which is regarded as "effectual" (effecting what it declares). It is hard to see, however, how righteousness by judicial declaration, in the face of ongoing sinfulness, can escape from seeming like a legal fiction.[16]

The mystery of union with Christ, on the other hand, as one side of the double exchange, allows for Christ's righteousness really to be communicated to sinners by grace. Having no righteousness of their own (Phil. 3:9), they are clothed with the righteousness of Christ. They can be acquitted (justified) because they are made righteous through their participation in him (*en autō*), not merely by divine fiat. The key ideas here—union (by grace through faith), exchange, transfer, and real predication—are cultic in their roots, not forensic. Moreover, in a legal declaration, the relationship of believers to Christ seems to be merely "external." Union with Christ, on the other hand, with its cultic roots, suggests that the relationship is more nearly "internal" and "participatory" (mutual indwelling of the faithful with Christ).

"Imputation" is placed against a courtroom backdrop rather than a priestly/cultic one. "Imputation" (*logizomai*) is a complex term. In Pauline soteriology it is arguably

16. "The doctrine of justification apart from union with Christ cannot avoid the charge of a legal fiction." Torrance, *Atonement*, 54. Leaving aside questions of subjective appropriation, the *logical* sequence for which I am arguing is expiation–justification–sanctification–glorification. They each depend, in various ways, on our union with Christ. That is, they each depend, both objectively and subjectively, on his union with us by grace and our union with him through faith.

an accounting metaphor ("reckoning") with priestly/cultic roots ("transfer") and a forensic function ("acquittal"). The "imputation," or "real transfer"—not only of our sinfulness to Christ but also of his righteousness to us—has no place within the logic of the courtroom. Its background lies in the idea of a cultic exchange.[17]

The exchange is mysterious but real. Neither Christ's having been made to be sin, though he knew no sin, nor our being made righteous in him, is a "legal fiction." The sinner can be acquitted because the sinner has been made to be righteous in Christ by grace through faith. Again, this happens through a process whose background is essentially cultic, not forensic.[18]

The focus becomes overly individualistic rather than corporate. The courtroom metaphor focuses on the individual offender, whereas the cultic atonement metaphors deal corporately with the people as a whole. Although both individual and corporate elements are important, the dominance of the forensic in soteriology can lead to a one-sided predominance of individualistic modes of thought, as is all too common in Reformational Protestantism.

If this analysis is on the right track, it suggests how even a correct translation of *pistis Christou* ("faith *in* Christ") can be combined with a faulty (excessively

17. The priestly/cultic roots of the idea of "transfer" may be traced back to Yom Kippur. In the cultic ritual the sins of the people are transferred to the head of the live goat by the action of the high priest in the laying on of hands. "A *transfer* thus takes place," writes Jacob Milgrom, "from Israel itself; its sins, exorcised by the high priest's confession, are *transferred* to the body of the goat, just as the sanctuary's impurities, absorbed by the purgation of blood, are (originally) *conveyed* to the goat." Milgrom, *Leviticus 1–16*, 1043 (italics added). Traditional Protestant attempts to explain imputation by resorting to forensic or banking metaphors, while neglecting Yom Kippur, are strained and implausible. Imputation is not well explained as a function of forensic "declaration," nor by the idea of a deposit of funds mysteriously landing in the sinner's bank account "because of Christ." For Paul, in 2 Cor. 5:21, the guilt of the guilty is *transferred* to him who knew no sin, even as the innocence of the innocent One is *transferred* to the guilty many by means of their union with Christ (*en autō*). The latter transfer is more nearly an internal relation (*in Christo*), by faith, than an external one (*propter Christum*). Certainly, of course, the two "transfers," the Hebraic and the Christian, are not identical. Yom Kippur as the type is reconfigured in Christ as the antitype of the Christian *admirabile commercium*. In any case, the idea of transfer, though mysterious, is what makes the idea of imputation intelligible—the imputation (or transfer) of sin to Christ, and the imputation (or transfer) of righteousness to those who are "in him." Yom Kippur forms the background for the "wondrous exchange." The one provides the grammar for the other.

18. The various statements about "imputation" in Rom. 4 can be read as a kind of shorthand for this more complex Christocentric account. Even in Rom. 4 the risen Christ is arguably the covert object of that faith which is said to be "reckoned" as righteousness (Rom. 4:22–25). Abraham is not justified by the act of faith so much as by the object of faith, though both are involved. (See note 35 in chap. 3 above.) "The crucial point," writes Gathercole, "is that Abraham's belief in the God who gives life to the dead is witness to the Christian faith in the same God, who is identified as the one who raised Jesus Christ from the dead." Gathercole, "Justified by Faith," 164–65. In any case, Christ is certainly not unknown as the object of faith in Pauline writings (e.g., Rom. 10:9; Phil. 1:29; Col. 1:4). "Imputation" needs to be read from a center in 2 Cor. 5:21, and therefore against a priestly/cultic template of merciful exchange in Christ.

"forensic") soteriology. When merciful substitution is eclipsed by the idea of penal substitution, when union with Christ is sidelined by the idea of forensic declaration, when the *admirabile commercium* is severed from its priestly/cultic roots, when imputation is reduced to a juridical declaratory act, and when salvation is invested with an inveterate individualism that is difficult to shake, the problems cannot be solved at the level of philology alone, because they exist mainly at the level of soteriology.

EXCURSUS 7

On the Pattern of Exchange

The "pattern of exchange" in Paul, as touched on several times in the commentary on Phil. 3:9, involves a two-directional transfer of predicates. The one vector moves from Christ to us, while the other moves from us to Christ. Christ stands at one pole even as fallen humanity stands at the other. The pole represented by Christ cannot be understood without the concepts of substitution and objective participation. It is important to underscore that for Paul there is no substitution without participation (under both objective and subjective aspects), and vice versa. The Christ who takes our place, and in whom we participate objectively by grace and subjectively by faith, is the Christ whom God made to be sin. The sin that is entirely ours is transferred vicariously (and truly) to him, who knew no sin, in order that in him it might be removed and abolished. That is one pole of the two-directional transfer.

The other vector is that the righteousness of the one who knew no sin is transferred to the faithful. Their objective participation in Christ by grace, which is logically prior,[1] is not fulfilled until he is acknowledged and received by faith. The faithful come to participate in Christ and his saving work by confessing him with their lips and believing in their hearts that God raised him from the dead (Rom. 10:9). Through union and communion with him by faith, his perfect

---

1. The idea that objective participation in Christ is logically prior to its subjective aspect is grounded in verses like Eph. 1:4 (pretemporal election in Christ) and 2 Cor. 5:14 (the death of Christ as the vicarious death of all, prior to its being humanly acknowledged by faith).

righteousness—as accomplished *extra nos* by his earthly obedience—is given by God and received through faith (*in nobis*) here and now.

In short, Christ takes our sin and gives us his righteousness, even as he takes our death and gives us his life. This is the *admirabile commercium*—the great and wondrous exchange—between Christ and the faithful, as it is posited in 2 Cor. 5:21. For Paul this is the heart of the gospel. Finlan argues, rightly in my opinion, that the scapegoat image of Yom Kippur underlies 2 Cor. 5:21. "In curse transmission there is an exchange. . . . The model for the exchange is the [Yom Kippur] curse transmission ritual. . . . In his whole corpus, this chapter is probably Paul's most moving metaphor. . . . One cannot adequately interpret this passage without noticing the cultic exchange that describes it."[2] The idea of exchange, Finlan continues, is grounded in Yom Kippur: the spotless goat takes on the sin or curse of the people, even as the sinful people are, in effect, accorded the goat's spotlessness. It is a "supernatural transference," effected by God, in both directions.[3] As applied to the gospel, Luther writes: "And this is that mystery which is rich in divine grace to sinners: wherein, by a wonderful exchange, our sins are now no longer ours but Christ's: and the righteousness of Christ is ours [author's note: the double transfer]. He has imparted that unto us, that he might clothe us with it, and fill us with it: and he has taken our evils upon himself that he might deliver us from them. So that now, the righteousness of Christ is not only ours objectively (as they term it), but formally also." In other words, it is both an ontological reality (no mere legal fiction) as well as the formal righteousness by which we are righteous before God.[4] "For in the same manner as he grieved and suffered in our sins, and was confounded," Luther continues, "in the same manner we rejoice and glory in his righteousness: and it is manifest that he did grieve and was confounded in them truly, as we here see [in Ps. 22:1]."[5] Our righteousness in Christ is just as objective and real as is his suffering and death in our place and for our sakes.

In interpreting 2 Cor. 5:21, I follow Murray J. Harris. Again, the verse runs as follows: "For our sakes he made him to be sin who knew no sin so that in him

---

2. Finlan, *Paul's Cultic Atonement Metaphors*, 99, 100. For a contrary view, based on philological considerations, see Stökl Ben Ezra, *Impact of Yom Kippur*, 173n129.

3. Finlan, *Paul's Cultic Atonement Metaphors*, 106. Exchange, participation, and substitution are linked together (115, 181).

4. See note 55 in chapter 3 above.

5. Luther, *Commentary on the First Twenty-Two Psalms*, 369. What we have here is the essence of the Reformation. Note that, remarkably, the gist of this passage was quoted favorably by Pope Benedict XVI, general audience, September 24, 2008, http://w2.vatican.va/content/benedict-xvi/en/audiences/2008/documents/hf_ben-xvi_aud_20080924.html.

we might become the righteousness of God."[6] I want to lift up four points for comment.

First, I agree with Harris that the phrase "he made him to be sin for us" (*hyper hēmōn hamartian epoiēsen*) implies "substitution," especially because it is said that he himself "knew no sin" (*ton mē gnonta hamartian*). Christ died the death deserved by sinners—in their place and for their sakes—in order that they themselves might be spared.[7] Harris is certainly correct that this is "one of the most profound mysteries" of the gospel.[8]

Second, I also agree with Harris that the phrase "in him"—"so that in him [*en autō*] we might become the righteousness of God"—entails participation and union with Christ. That is the context in which the faithful are made to be what they otherwise are not—"righteous." I would add that this is primarily (though not exclusively) a matter of what may be called "subjective" or "present tense" participation.[9] However, I would depart somewhat from Harris in suggesting that "righteousness" (*dikaiosynē*) indicates a real *condition* and not merely a relation, just as "sin" (*hamartian*) or "sinfulness" signifies a real *condition* and not merely a relation (or "disrelation").[10]

Third, I agree with Harris that the phrase "not counting" (*mē logizomenos*) from 2 Cor. 5:19—"not counting their trespasses against them"—can be carried over, not inappropriately, into the interpretation of 5:21, even though it is not used there. This is the term that underlies the "pattern of exchange" with its real transfer of predicates. Following tradition, Harris speaks of this transfer as "imputation." I do not object to this term, but as previously suggested, when "imputation" is interpreted merely as "declaration," it is unfortunately entangled with the idea of a "legal fiction"—an idea that has no place here.[11]

"Sin" (*hamartia*) and "righteousness" (*dikaiosynē*) are juxtaposed in 5:21 as opposites. Harris comments, "As a result of God's imputing to Christ something that was extrinsic to him, namely sin, believers have something imputed to them

6. The Greek: *ton mē gnonta hamartian hyper hēmōn hamartian epoiēsen, hina hēmeis genōmetha dikaiosynē theou en autō.*

7. Harris, *Second Epistle to the Corinthians*, 453.

8. Harris, *Second Epistle to the Corinthians*, 451.

9. Looking back to 2 Cor. 5:14, one could perhaps argue that the phrase also allows for a prior "objective" participation in which the faithful, who died when Christ died, are somehow "made righteous in him" by grace before they receive it and partake of it through faith.

10. Harris, *Second Epistle to the Corinthians*, 455. See my remarks in note 61 in chap. 3 above.

11. I am suggesting that "imputation" (*logizomai*) has "ontic" as well as "noetic" aspects in this context. It is not merely how God looks on us. God looks on us as righteous (noetically) because he has actually made us to be righteous (ontically) in Christ (*en autō*). Sometimes the noetic aspect is more in the forefront, however, as in 2 Cor. 5:19.

that was extrinsic to them, namely righteousness."[12] I believe this statement is correct as long as "imputing" entails a real transfer and real exchange of predicates. There is nothing fictional in this mystery. The transfer of righteousness to the faithful is just as real as the transfer of sin to Christ.[13]

Finally, Harris rightly notes that 5:21 speaks about the "righteousness of God" (*dikaiosynē theou*), not about the "righteousness of Christ." Therefore it might seem unwarranted to regard Christ's righteousness as being transferred (or imputed) to the faithful.[14] A solution to this dilemma, I suggest, might run as follows.

- First, when this verse designates Christ as the one "who knew no sin," that is functionally equivalent to describing him as "righteous."[15]

- Second, although God's righteousness and Christ's righteousness are certainly distinct, they ought not to be regarded as divided. They coexist, arguably, in a pattern of unity-in-distinction.

- Third, the righteousness by which the faithful are made to become (*genōmetha*) righteous (in this transfer) is the righteousness of Christ as grounded in his human obedience, especially his obedience to the point of death (Phil. 2:8). "By the one man's obedience many will be made [*katastathēsontai*] righteous" (Rom. 5:19). "The Righteous One, my servant, shall make many righteous [*dikaiōsai*], and he shall bear their iniquities" (Isa. 53:11b LXX).[16]

- Fourth, the faithful do not become righteous through a direct impartation of divine righteousness as such, but they do become righteous through the action of God. The very God who made Christ to be sin is the same God who made the faithful to become (*genōmetha*) righteous in him. God makes

12. Harris, *Second Epistle to the Corinthians*, 455.

13. The reality of the double transfer in both directions is grasped by Calvin, rightly in my view, though it is often rejected by modern commentators. See Calvin, *Second Epistle of Paul to the Corinthians*, 81–82. A similar reading is found in Barth. "In that he took our place, and was made sin for us, we are made the righteousness of God in him, because we are put in his place." Barth, *Church Dogmatics* IV/1, 75.

14. Harris, *Second Epistle to the Corinthians*, 455n207.

15. As Harris notes, the Pauline doctrine of the "sinlessness" or "righteousness" of Jesus Christ is in line with the rest of the New Testament, including the Johannine and Petrine traditions. In 1 John 2:1 we find the phrase "Jesus Christ the righteous" (*Iēsoun Christon dikaion*). In 1 Pet. 3:18 we read of him as the righteous one who suffers and dies for the unrighteous (*dikaios hyper adikōn*). Harris concludes, "In its testimony to the sinlessness of Jesus, the NT is uniform." *Second Epistle to the Corinthians*, 451; for further documentation, see 451n177.

16. Again, it is not merely a change in "status." It is a change in status grounded in an actual change of condition *coram Deo*. As previously suggested, Christ's righteousness *extra nos* is therefore what later tradition would call the "formal cause" of righteousness in the faithful, who (like Paul) have no righteousness of their own.

the faithful to become righteous through their participation in Christ and his righteousness (*en autō*).

• Finally, in this verse, the phrase "righteousness of God" (*dikaiosynē theou*) is best regarded as a kind of shorthand. The phrase "in him" (*en autō*) involves both the obedience and the mediation of Christ. By Christ's obedience, and through his substitutionary death, the faithful become righteous in him by the operation of God. They are made to be righteous through a righteousness not their own, which they receive through their participation in him who knew no sin, and who bore away their sins on the cross.

If this solution is valid, what would be the relationship between the righteousness of Christ and the righteousness of God? As far as I can see, the answer is that the righteousness of Christ, as grounded in his "obedience" (Rom. 5:19; Phil. 2:8), represents the righteousness of God and corresponds to it.[17] The righteousness that God requires of his human creatures originates from himself and is mediated to them through Christ. In Christ—who is Righteousness itself—the faithful receive and partake of the righteousness that God gives them in and through his obedience. Through union and communion with Christ, they receive the righteousness that makes them acceptable before God. It is a righteousness that originates from God and leads back to God, but only as grounded in the obedience of Christ and as received through faith in him (e.g., Rom. 3:22, 26; 5:17–19, 21; 1 Cor. 1:30; Eph. 2:8–9; Phil. 1:11).

The faithful thereby "become the righteousness of God" in the sense that God's righteousness is the ground, the source, and the goal of the vicarious righteousness of Christ as enacted in obedience on their behalf and in their stead, and which they receive as they are incorporated into him by grace through faith. In and through Christ, God not only removes their sins but also communicates to them the righteousness they need for eternal life in communion with himself. This train of thought, I would suggest, makes explicit the unity and the distinction between the righteousness of Christ and that of God implicit in this verse (2 Cor. 5:21).

Among New Testament scholars, the faith-*of*-Christ interpreters certainly have some conception of participation, but as a rule they lack any robust conceptions of expiation, substitution, transfer, and exchange. Their soteriology of participation is accordingly diminished. For them, as a rule, the faithful do not receive the gift of Christ's righteousness whole and entire in their union with him, but only

17. Again, we might say that the two coinhere in a pattern of unity-in-distinction.

gradually by means of their own striving as assisted by grace. Whether subtly or not, these are the seeds of works righteousness.[18]

For their part, the faith-*in*-Christ exponents are often encumbered by an unfortunate emphasis—or overemphasis—on forensic or juridical modes of thought. This imbalance tends to distort their conceptions of expiation, substitution, participation, transfer, and exchange all the way down. As already suggested, forensic modes of thought, when not held in due proportion, have a tendency to reduce Christ and the faithful to a set of merely external, legalistic, and individualistic relations. What both camps tend to lack, I suggest, is a sufficient grasp of how cultic atonement modes of thought operate in the background of Pauline soteriology as well as throughout the rest of the New Testament.

It should be noted that although the opposing views just sketched are not untypical, there is of course a diverse range of opinion that falls between such views and beyond them. In any case, my larger point is that, apart from *pistis Christou* translation questions, the significance of the cultic atonement metaphors in the background of Pauline soteriology would benefit from greater attention all around.

---

18. I am thinking here along the medieval lines of "God not denying grace to those who do what is within their power" (*facienti quod in se est Deus non denegat gratiam*). To ground salvation in "faithfulness" is to ground it in a human practice, disposition, or quality as assisted by divine grace. By contrast, salvation as grounded in the vicarious obedience of Christ, and as communicated through participating in his death and resurrection, is another matter. In the one case, the *saving* righteousness as such, by which we are righteous before God, is found wholly or partially in us (*in nobis*); in the other, it is found entirely apart from us (*extra nos*)—which is then "imputed" or transferred, whole and entire, to us as a free gift. It begins to be subjectively appropriated from there. Cf. Oberman, "*Facientibus Quod in se est Deus non Denegat Gratiam*: Robert Holcot O.P. and the Beginnings of Luther's Theology," in *Dawn of the Reformation*, 84–103. For Luther, according to Oberman, believers are no more than beggars who cry out for a salvation they cannot attain by their own efforts or faithfulness even when assisted by grace. The relevant actions of believers are their groans (*gemitus*)—the groans of those who know they can find salvation only outside themselves (*extra se*), in Christ (*solus Christus, solo Christo*). In short, it is not due to our faithfulness that we are saved, but solely to the mercy of God in Jesus Christ. Faithfulness (sanctification) is a consequence, not a cause, of our salvation. See Oberman, "*Wir Sein Pettler, Hoc Est Verum*," in *Reformation*, 91–115, esp. 112–13. Also Oberman, "*Simul Gemitus et Raptus*," in *Dawn of the Reformation*, 126–54, esp. 150–54. See also Seifrid, "Blind Alleys," esp. 92–93.

EXCURSUS 8

On the Eschatology of the "Wondrous Exchange"

An asymmetry may be noted regarding the two sides of the wondrous exchange (*admirabile commercium*) as set forth in 2 Cor. 5:21. Recall that the verse runs as follows: "For our sake he made him to be sin who knew no sin, that in him we might become the righteousness of God." Aspects of this verse have already been discussed above. For the sake of completeness, a further comment regarding eschatology may be in order.

Note that the exchange between Christ and the sinner is not completely symmetrical. When the eternal Son becomes truly human, he does not cease to be truly God. Similarly, when Christ is made to be sin for our sakes, he does not cease to be sinless in himself. He bears the full consequences of our sin, and bears them away, without literally becoming a sinner *simpliciter*. However, unlike his assumption of human nature, which is not transitory but permanent, his assumption of human sin is but momentary. In other words, his being made to be sin, though real, is temporary and functional, while his sinlessness remains constant and unimpaired. He is free to take our sinfulness to himself (*secundum quid*), that it might be condemned in his flesh, without ceasing to be righteous in himself. The mystery of his having been made sin for our sakes (*hyper hēmōn*) is beyond human comprehension. The one who is Righteousness itself (*autodikaiosynē*) is made to be Sin itself (*autoamartia*), without ceasing to be Righteousness itself, that in him the unrighteous might be delivered from death. Obscured by the cross, his righteousness is vindicated by his resurrection.

When the faithful are made to be righteous in Christ (*en autō*), the situation is different. For the time being, they still remain sinful in themselves even though they are righteous in him. Paradoxically, their sinfulness has already been abolished, and yet it still remains in force. Their righteousness is perfect in Christ, while remaining imperfect in themselves. Righteousness has been given to them once-for-all *coram Deo*, while remaining hidden in its fullness between the times. Sin's power has been broken for them (*posse non peccare*)—"for sin will have no dominion over you" (Rom. 6:14)—and yet they must continue to pray each day, "Forgive us our debts, as we also have forgiven our debtors" (Matt. 6:12 NASB). How can this complex situation be explained?

A rough analogy might be drawn from quantum mechanics. Under certain circumstances, an atomic particle will exist in two mutually exclusive states at the same time. It is said to be in "superposition." Superposition occurs when one self-identical entity is bound up simultaneously in two apparently contrary states for a period of time. It is not partly in one state and partly in the other, but in both at the same time. It continues in this perplexing situation until something changes. It then transitions into one of the two states or the other. The one is left behind as the other is actualized. Neither ordinary, Newtonian modes of thought nor Aristotelian logic is capable of grasping this contradictory situation as it exists prior to the resolution. Over against the phenomenon of superposition, Newton and Aristotle reach their categorical limit. What cannot be *explained* about one entity paradoxically existing in two mutually exclusive states at the same time can only be *described*.[1]

Leaving other complications aside,[2] we might say something similar about the faithful. They exist in two states at the same time, states that appear to be mutually exclusive. They are righteous in Christ, while remaining imperfect, and to that extent unrighteous, in themselves. *Simul iustus et peccator*. Moreover, in Christ they already have the gift of eternal life, while still being susceptible to death. *Simul vivus et mortale*. Neither their perfect righteousness nor their eternal life waits merely to be bestowed in the future, for in Christ each is already truly given and truly received under a particular aspect.

1. For the idea of a superposition, see Rosenblum and Kuttner, *Quantum Enigma*, 98–99, 145–66. Feynman acknowledges that quantum physics involves profoundly mysterious and paradoxical phenomena that cannot be explained but only described. See Feynman, *Feynman Lectures on Physics*, 3:1. The strangeness encountered at the "micro" or quantum level is thus not entirely unlike the strangeness encountered at the "macro" or theological level. The Newtonian world of ordinary experience is not normative for all of reality, and Aristotelian logic does not entirely work at the quantum level.

2. It goes without saying that many aspects of "superposition" bear no similarity to the paradox of righteousness here being explored.

These mutually exclusive states are essentially categorical; however, in a complicated wrinkle, they may also involve matters of degree. From a theological point of view, sin and righteousness are essentially categorical. "For whoever keeps the whole law but fails in one point has become guilty of all of it" (Jas. 2:10).[3] You can't be a little bit sinful any more than you can be a little bit pregnant or a little bit dead. That is the prior theological context for thinking about matters of degree (cf. Rom. 2:25; 3:20; Gal. 2:16; 3:10–14). You can drown in twelve inches of water, or you can drown at the bottom of the ocean, but if your head is not above the water, you drown.[4] Before God (*coram Deo*), the waterline represents the categorical; the depth of submergence, matters of degree. Something like this notion is apparently at stake when Reinhold Niebuhr writes about "the equality of sin" and "the inequality of guilt."[5] In any case, for the faithful, certain mutually exclusive states—perfection and existential imperfection, righteousness and ongoing sinfulness, life and susceptibility to death—will coexist until they are resolved on the day of the Lord. What will be true there and then, however, is already true, under a particular aspect, here and now: "Christ is our righteousness and our life" (Luther).

A complex eschatology is in play. It involves an apocalyptic event framed within a Christ-centered eschatology of participation. It is "apocalyptic" because the new comes into being through the destruction of the old. How the new humanity in Christ relates to the old humanity in sin is a matter of continuity in the midst of radical discontinuity. Baptism as the sacrament of dying and rising with Christ is the emblem of this radical transition (Rom. 6:3–4).[6] Grace has indeed perfected nature, in Christ, but only by way of destroying its old corrupted form. *Gratia perficit naturam, in Christo, sed destruit eius corruptam formam.* "If anyone is in Christ [*en Christō*], *the old things* [*ta archaia*] are passed away [*parēlthein*]; behold *they* have become new [*gegonen kaina*]" (2 Cor. 5:17, italics added). In other words, the old nature has been abolished in its corrupt form (*in eius*

3. For a discussion of Jas. 2:10, from a different point of view, see Jackson-McCabe, *Logos and Law*, 169–76.

4. The condition of righteousness, in turn, would be like breathing air above the waterline, regardless of how high above. The one would represent the categorical aspect; the other, matters of degree. (This is obviously only a rough analogy.) For the idea of matters of degree in heaven, see Edwards, "Heaven Is a World of Love," in *Works of Jonathan Edwards*, 8:366–97.

5. Niebuhr, *Nature and Destiny of Man*, 1:219–27. The equality would be categorical; the inequality, a matter of degree.

6. Baptism, according to Calvin, is, among other things, "a token and proof of our cleansing" in Christ. "It is like a sealed document to confirm to us that all our sins are so abolished, remitted, and effaced that they can never come to his sight, be recalled, or charged against us." *Institutes* 4.15.1.

corruptam formam). It has been miraculously abolished only to be made new in an unexpected way. The first verb is in the aorist ("passed away"), indicating a completed action of elimination, while the second verb is in the perfect tense ("have become"), suggesting a new ongoing reality, brought forth, so to speak, from the ruins of the old. A drastic, nongradual transition has occurred through the death and resurrection of Christ. The emergence of the new through the negation of the old has consequences for both the present and the future. The old has been abolished in Christ only to be recovered and reconstituted on a higher plane. The Crucified is risen from the dead.

The radical eschatology at stake is also a matter of "participation." The faithful, it is suggested, have died and risen in union with Christ. "We have concluded this," writes Paul, "that one died [*apethanen*] for all, therefore all died [*apethanon*]" (2 Cor. 5:14). Remarkably, in this statement both verbs, which differ by only one vowel, are given in the aorist, indicating a completed action in the past. When Christ died, all died with him. All died, it would seem, even those who in the ordinary sense are not yet dead. The scope of resurrection hope is left open. Meanwhile, "one died for all, that those who live might no longer live for themselves, but for him who for their sake died and was raised" (2 Cor. 5:15). Those who receive Christ and confess him for who he is will live for him—and through him for their neighbors—in love and gratitude.

A similar verse points in the same direction. "For you died [*apethanete*] and your life is hidden with Christ in God" (Col. 3:3). The verb is again in the aorist. The death of the faithful has already occurred in the death of Christ. His death is their death, his life is their life, and his righteousness is their righteousness. What the faithful are in themselves is transitory, while what they are in Christ is imperishable. What they are in him is real, hidden, and yet to come.

The asymmetry in 2 Cor. 5:21 would therefore be this: whereas Christ's having been made sin was momentary, the faithful's having already been made righteous in him is not transitory but enduring. In the eschatological interim, the time between the times, their perfect righteousness is hidden in the midst of their ongoing susceptibility to sin, just as their eternal life is hidden in the midst of their vulnerability to death. In Christ they are already truly alive notwithstanding their death, just as they are already truly righteous despite the sin that still clings so closely. Over against what they are in themselves, the living Christ—in whom they participate by grace through faith, and who gives himself to them continually in the sacrament of his body and blood—is himself the reality and the hope of their righteousness and life *coram Deo*.

EXCURSUS 9

On Destruction and Restoration

I then will destroy your high places, and cut down your incense altars, and heap
your remains on the remains of your idols, for My soul shall abhor you. (Lev.
26:30 NASB)

> Behold, the day of the LORD comes,
>   cruel, with wrath and fierce anger,
> to make the land a desolation
>   and to destroy its sinners from it. (Isa. 13:9)

From a Christian theological standpoint, it is not easy to interpret passages
like these. A whole strand of biblical material does not shrink back from severe
warnings and outcomes. Perhaps this strand may be regarded as the negative
and reverse image of God's holiness. God's holiness would thus be a "consuming
fire" (Heb. 12:29) standing in opposition to everything that contradicts God's
love—to all human "ungodliness" (vertical) and "wickedness" (horizontal) (Rom.
1:18). The absolute intolerability of idolatry and iniquity in God's sight would
be etched indelibly in the mind.

Seen from a center in Christ, however, where the cross is succeeded by the
resurrection, the severe passages might be taken as "vigorously one-sided"
(Kierkegaard).[1] They could be interpreted as belonging to a larger, if provision-
ally hidden, scheme. Holiness would be inseparable from God's grace, even if the

---

1. Kierkegaard liked to use this phrase to describe his work as a "corrective."

grace element, while finally destined to prevail, would often be hidden or suppressed. "To understand it [the explicit in relation to the tacit] there was and is needed what is called faith in the New Testament, namely, the perception either way of what is not said."[2] There would finally be a twofold template: no grace without holy judgment, and no judgment without holy, and therefore sanctifying, grace.[3] Faith would be the perception of the one even when only the other comes to expression. The element of judgment would finally be in the service of grace.

> Fear not, you worm Jacob,
>> you men of Israel!
> I am the one who helps you, declares the LORD;
>> your Redeemer is the Holy One of Israel. (Isa. 41:14)

> Our Redeemer—the LORD of hosts is his name—
>> is the Holy One of Israel. (Isa. 47:4)

> I will not execute my burning anger;
>> I will not again destroy Ephraim;
> for I am God and not a man,
>> the Holy One in your midst,
>> and I will not come in wrath. (Hos. 11:9)

Passages like these would bring out the other, more positive side of the overall twofold template. "For God has shut up all in disobedience, that he may have mercy on all" (Rom. 11:32). The tension in scripture between passages that intimate destruction and those that intimate restoration could be read, from a center in Christ crucified and risen, as tilting toward the hope of restoration—and prayers for mercy on all.

---

2. Barth, *Church Dogmatics* I/1, 180.
3. See introduction to Hunsinger, *Thy Word Is Truth*, xv–xix.

BIBLIOGRAPHY

Adam, Jens. *Paulus und die Versöhnung aller: Eine Studie zum paulinischen Heilsuniversalismus.* Neukirchen-Vluyn: Neukirchener Verlag, 2009.

Allen, Michael. *Christ's Faith: A Dogmatic Account.* London: T&T Clark, 2009.

Allison, C. F. *The Rise of Moralism.* New York: Seabury, 1966.

Anselm. *Anselm of Canterbury: The Major Works.* Edited by G. R. Evans and Brian Davies. New York: Oxford University Press, 2008.

Aristotle. *Nicomachean Ethics.* Translated by Terence Irwin. Indianapolis: Hackett, 1985.

Athanasius. *Athanasius on the Incarnation.* Crestwood, NY: St. Vladimir's Seminary Press, 1989.

———. *The Incarnation of the Word of God: Being the Treatise of St. Athanasius, De Incarnatione Verbi Dei.* New York: Macmillan, 1946.

Augustine. *City of God.* Translated by R. W. Dyson. Cambridge: Cambridge University Press, 1998.

———. *Confessions.* Translated by Henry Chadwick. Oxford: Oxford University Press, 1991.

———. *Expositions on the Book of Psalms by S. Augustine, Bishop of Hippo.* 6 vols. Library of Fathers of the Holy Catholic Church. Oxford: John Henry Parker, 1848–57.

———. "On Rebuke and Grace." In *A Select Library of Nicene and Post-Nicene Fathers of the Christian Church.* 1st series. Edited by Philip Schaff. 14 vols. New York: Christian Literature, 1886–89. Reprint, Peabody, MA: Hendrickson, 1994.

———. "On the Gift of Perseverance." In *A Select Library of Nicene and Post-Nicene Fathers of the Christian Church.* 1st series. Edited by Philip Schaff. 14 vols. New York: Christian Literature, 1886–89. Reprint, Peabody, MA: Hendrickson, 1994.

Balthasar, Hans Urs von. *Theo-Drama.* 5 vols. San Francisco: Ignatius, 1988–94.

Barclay, John M. G. "Why the Roman Empire Was Insignificant to Paul." In *Pauline Churches and Diaspora Jews,* 363–87. Tübingen: Mohr Siebeck, 2011.

Barr, James. *The Semantics of Biblical Language.* London: Oxford University Press, 1961.

Bartchy, S. Scott. "Slavery (Greco-Roman)." In *Anchor Bible Dictionary,* edited by David Noel Freedman, 6:65B–73B. New York: Doubleday, 1992.

Barth, Karl. *Church Dogmatics.* 4 vols. Edinburgh: T&T Clark, 1956–75.

———. *The Epistle to the Philippians.* London: SCM, 1962.

———. *The Epistle to the Romans.* New York: Oxford University Press, 1968.

———. *The Göttingen Dogmatics.* Vol. 1. Grand Rapids: Eerdmans, 1991.

Bauckham, Richard J. "Colossians 1:24 Again: The Apocalyptic Motif." *Evangelical Quarterly* 47 (1975): 168–70.

———. "Devotion to Jesus Christ in Earliest Christianity." In *Mark, Manuscripts, and Monotheism: Essays in Honor of Larry W. Hurtado,* edited by Chris Keith and Dieter T. Roth, 182–85. London: Bloomsbury, 2014.

———. *Jesus and the God of Israel.* Grand Rapids: Eerdmans, 2008.

———. "The Worship of Jesus in Philippians 2:9–11." In *Where Christology Began: Essays on Philippians 2,* edited by Ralph P. Martin and Brian J. Dodd, 128–39. Louisville: Westminster John Knox, 1998.

Bauer, Walter, Frederick W. Danker, William F. Arndt, and F. Wilbur Gingrich. *Greek-English Lexicon of the New Testament and Other Early Christian Literature.* 3rd ed. Chicago: University of Chicago Press, 2000.

Beard, Mary, John North, and Simon Price. *Religions of Rome.* 2 vols. Cambridge: Cambridge University Press, 1998.

Beeley, Christopher A. *The Unity of Christ.* New Haven: Yale University Press, 2012.

Bell, Richard H. "Sacrifice and Christology in Paul." *Journal of Theological Studies* 53 (2002): 1–27.

Belsey, Catherine. "The Case of Hamlet's Conscience." *Studies in Philology* 76 (1979): 127–48.

Berry, Wendell. *The Country of Marriage.* New York: Harcourt Brace Jovanovich, 1973.

Bertschmann, Dorothea. "Is There a Kenosis in This Text? Rereading Philippians 3:2–11 in the Light of the Christ Hymn." *Journal of Biblical Literature* 137 (2018): 235–54.

Bethune-Baker, J. F. *Nestorius and His Teaching: A Fresh Examination of the Evidence.* Cambridge: Cambridge University Press, 1908.

Bird, Michael F. *An Anomalous Jew: Paul among Jews, Greeks, and Romans.* Grand Rapids: Eerdmans, 2016.

———. *The Saving Righteousness of God: Studies on Paul, Justification, and the New Perspective.* Eugene, OR: Wipf & Stock, 2007.

Bloom, Harold. *Shakespeare: The Invention of the Human.* New York: Riverhead, 1998.

Bockmuehl, Markus. *The Epistle to the Philippians.* Peabody, MA: Hendrickson, 1998.

Bonaventure. *The Mind's Road to God.* New York: Prentice Hall, 1953.

Bonhoeffer, Dietrich. *The Cost of Discipleship.* New York: Macmillan, 1963.

The Book of Common Prayer. New York: Oxford University Press, 1979.

Book of Confessions. Louisville: Westminster John Knox, 2017.

Boring, M. Eugene. "The Language of Universal Salvation in Paul." *Journal of Biblical Literature* 105 (1986): 269–92.

Bradshaw, Graham. "Hamlet and the Art of Grafting." In *Hamlet: Bloom's Shakespeare through the Ages,* edited by Harold Bloom, 375–98. New York: Infobase, 2008.

Brown, Raymond E. *The Epistles of John.* Anchor Bible 30. Garden City, NY: Doubleday, 1982.

Bruce, F. F. *Paul: Apostle of the Heart Set Free.* Grand Rapids: Eerdmans, 2000.

———. *Philippians.* Peabody, MA: Hendrickson, 1989.

Calvin, John. *Calvin's New Testament Commentaries.* Edited by David W. Torrance and Thomas F. Torrance. 12 vols. Grand Rapids: Eerdmans, 1960–.

———. *Institutes.* Translated by John Allen. Philadelphia: Presbyterian Board of Christian Education, 1928.

———. *Institutes.* Translated by Ford Lewis Battles. Philadelphia: Westminster, 1960.

———. *Instruction in Faith.* 1537. Philadelphia: Westminster, 1949.

———. *John Calvin: Tracts and Letters.* Vol. 3. Edited by Henry Beveridge. Grand Rapids: Baker, 1983.

———. *The Second Epistle of Paul to the Corinthians.* Grand Rapids: Eerdmans, 1964.

Campbell, Douglas A. *The Rhetoric of Righteousness in Romans 3:21–26*. Sheffield: JSOT Press, 1992.

Chadwick, Henry. "The Chalcedonian Definition." In *Henry Chadwick: Selected Writings*, edited by William Rusch, 101–14. Grand Rapids: Eerdmans, 2017.

———. "Episcopacy in the New Testament and Early Church." In *Henry Chadwick: Selected Writings*, edited by William Rusch, 1–17. Grand Rapids: Eerdmans, 2017.

Chiarot, Kevin. *The Unassumed Is the Unhealed: The Humanity of Christ in the Christology of T. F. Torrance*. Eugene, OR: Pickwick, 2013.

Childs, Brevard. *The New Testament as Canon: An Introduction*. Philadelphia: Fortress, 1985.

Clark, Kelly James, Richard Lints, and James K. A. Smith. *101 Key Terms in Philosophy and Their Importance for Theology*. Louisville: Westminster John Knox, 2004.

Coakley, Sarah. "What Chalcedon Solved and Didn't Solve." In *The Incarnation: An Interdisciplinary Symposium on the Incarnation of the Son of God*, edited by Stephen T. Davis, Daniel Kendall, and Gerald O'Collins, 143–63. Oxford: Oxford University Press, 2004.

Cockerill, Gareth Lee. *The Epistle to the Hebrews*. Grand Rapids: Eerdmans, 2012.

Collins, John J. "Introduction: Towards the Morphology of a Genre." *Semeia* 14 (1979): 9.

Compton, Jared. *Psalm 110 and the Logic of Hebrews*. London: Bloomsbury T&T Clark, 2018.

Constas, Nicholas. *Proclus of Constantinople and the Cult of the Virgin in Late Antiquity*. Leiden: Brill, 2003.

Cranfield, C. E. B. *The Epistle to the Romans*. 2 vols. Edinburgh: T&T Clark, 1975, 1979.

———. "Note on Rom. 11:32." *Theology in Scotland* 20 (2013): 73.

Crisp, Oliver D., and Kyle C. Strobel. *Jonathan Edwards: An Introduction to His Thought*. Grand Rapids: Eerdmans, 2018.

Curran, John E., Jr. *"Hamlet," Protestantism, and the Mourning of Contingency*. Aldershot, UK: Ashgate, 2006.

Cyril of Alexandria. *On the Unity of Christ*. Crestwood, NY: St. Vladimir's Seminary Press, 1995.

Danby, Herbert. *The Mishnah*. Oxford: Clarendon, 1933.

Davidson, Ivor J. "Salvation's Destiny: Heirs of God." In *God of Salvation*, edited by Ivor J. Davidson and Murray A. Rae, 155–75. Burlington, VT: Ashgate, 2011.

de Boer, M. C. "Paul and Apocalyptic Eschatology." In *The Encyclopedia of Apocalyptic*, edited by John J. Collins, 1:345–83. New York: Continuum, 2006.

Dorman, Anke. "'Commit Injustice and Shed Innocent Blood': Motives behind the Institution of the Day of Atonement in the Book of *Jubilees*." In *The Day of Atonement: Its Interpretations in Early Jewish and Christian Traditions*, edited by Thomas Hieke and Tobias Nicklas, 49–62. Leiden: Brill, 2012.

Douglas, Mary. *Leviticus as Literature*. Oxford: Oxford University Press, 1999.

Dunn, James D. G. *Christology in the Making*. 2nd ed. Grand Rapids: Eerdmans, 1996.

———. *The Epistles to the Colossians and to Philemon*. Grand Rapids: Eerdmans, 2014.

———. *The Theology of Paul the Apostle*. Grand Rapids: Eerdmans, 1998.

Du Plessis, Paul Johannes. *Teleios: The Idea of Perfection in the New Testament*. Kampen: Kok, 1959.

Edwards, Jonathan. *The Works of Jonathan Edwards*. 26 vols. New Haven: Yale University Press, 1957–2008.

Elder Porphyrios. "Counsels." In *Precious Vessels of the Holy Spirit: The Lives and Counsels of Contemporary Elders of Greece*, edited by Herman A. Middleton, 165–75. Scotts Valley, CA: CreateSpace, 2011.

Fabricatore, Daniel J. *Form of God, Form of a Servant: An Examination of the Greek Noun μορφή in Philippians 2:6–7*. Lanham, MD: University Press of America, 2010.

Fee, Gordon D. *Pauline Christology*. Grand Rapids: Baker Academic, 2007.

———. *Paul's Letter to the Philippians*. Grand Rapids: Eerdmans, 1995.

Feynman, Richard P. *The Feynman Lectures on Physics*. Vol. 3. Reading, MA: Addison Wesley, 1965.

Finlan, Stephen. *The Background and Content of Paul's Cultic Atonement Metaphors*. Atlanta: Society of Biblical Literature, 2004.

———. *Options on Atonement in Christian Thought*. Collegeville, MN: Michael Glazier, 2007.

———. *Problems with Atonement: The Origins of, and Controversy about, the Atonement Doctrine*. Collegeville, MN: Michael Glazier, 2005.

———. *Sacrifice and Atonement: Psychological Motives and Biblical Patterns*. Minneapolis: Fortress, 2016.

Fitzgerald, Allan, ed. *Augustine through the Ages*. Grand Rapids: Eerdmans, 1999.

Fowl, Stephen E. *Philippians*. Grand Rapids: Eerdmans, 2005.

Frei, Hans W. *The Eclipse of Biblical Narrative*. New Haven: Yale University Press, 1974.

———. *The Identity of Jesus Christ*. Philadelphia: Fortress, 1975.

Gaffin, R. B., Jr. "Glory, Glorification." In Hawthorne and Martin, *Dictionary of Paul and His Letters*, 349.

Gane, Roy. *Cult and Character: Purification Offerings, Day of Atonement, and Theodicy*. Winona Lake, IN: Eisenbrauns, 2005.

Garrett, Stephen M. *God's Beauty-in-Act: Participating in God's Suffering Glory*. Grand Rapids: Eerdmans, 2008.

Gathercole, Simon J. "Justified by Faith, Justified by His Blood: The Evidence of Romans 3:21–4:25." In *Justification and Variegated Nomism*, edited by D. A. Carson, Peter T. O'Brien, and Mark A. Seifrid, 2:147–84. Grand Rapids: Baker Academic, 2004.

———. "'Sins' in Paul." *New Testament Studies* 64 (2018): 143–61.

Gilkey, Langdon. *Maker of Heaven and Earth: A Study of the Christian Doctrine of Creation*. Garden City, NY: Doubleday, 1959.

Gollwitzer, Helmut. *The Rich Christians and Poor Lazarus*. New York: Macmillan, 1970.

Gregory of Nazianzus. *On God and Christ: The Five Theological Orations and Two Letters to Cledonius*. Crestwood, NY: St. Vladimir's Seminary Press, 2002.

Gundry Volf, Judith M. "Expiation/Propitiation/Mercy Seat." In Hawthorne and Martin, *Dictionary of Paul and His Letters*, 279–84.

———. *Paul and Perseverance*. Louisville: Westminster John Knox, 1990.

Hansen, G. Walter. *The Letter to the Philippians*. Grand Rapids: Eerdmans, 2009.

Harnack, Theodosius. *Luthers Theologie*. 2 vols. Munich: Kaiser, 1927.

Harris, Murray J. *Jesus as God: The New Testament Use of "Theos" in Reference to Jesus*. Grand Rapids: Baker, 1992.

———. *The Second Epistle to the Corinthians*. Grand Rapids: Eerdmans, 2005.

———. *Slave of Christ*. Downers Grove, IL: InterVarsity, 1999.

Hart, David Bentley. *That All May Be Saved: Heaven, Hell, and Universal Salvation*. New Haven: Yale University Press, 2019.

Hasel, Gerhard F. "The Day of Atonement." In *The Sanctuary and the Atonement*, edited by Frank B. Holbrook, 107–22. Silver Spring, MD: Biblical Research Institute, 1989.

———. "Resurrection in the Theology of Old Testament Apocalyptic." *Zeitschrift für die alttestamentliche Wissenschaft* 92 (1980): 267–84.

Hawthorne, Gerald F. *Philippians*. Waco: Word, 1983.

Hawthorne, Gerald F., and Ralph P. Martin, eds. *Dictionary of Paul and His Letters*. Downers Grove, IL: InterVarsity, 1993.

Hays, Richard B. *The Faith of Jesus Christ*. 2nd ed. Grand Rapids: Eerdmans, 2002.

———. "The Letter to the Galatians." In *The New Interpreter's Bible*, edited by Leander E. Keck et al., 11:181–348. Nashville: Abingdon, 2000.

———. *Reading Backwards: Figural Christology and the Fourfold Gospel Witness*. Waco: Baylor University Press, 2014.

Hefner, Philip J. "The Creation." In *Christian Dogmatics*, edited by Carl E. Braaten and Robert W. Jenson, 1:269–362. 2nd ed. Minneapolis: Fortress, 2011.

Hellerman, Joseph. *Philippians*. Nashville: B&H Academic, 2015.

Hengel, Martin. *Son of God: The Origin of Christology and the History of Jewish-Hellenistic Religion*. London: SCM, 1976.

Herbert, L. Joseph. "Wings as Swift as Love: *Hamlet* and the Virtues (and Vices) of a King." In *The Soul of Statesmanship: Shakespeare on Nature, Virtue, and Political Wisdom*, edited by Khalil M. Habib and L. Joseph Hebert Jr., 37–55. Lanham, MD: Lexington Books, 2018.

Hester, James D. *Paul's Concept of Inheritance*. Edinburgh: Oliver & Boyd, 1968.

Hillert, Sven. *Limited and Universal Salvation: A Text-Oriented and Hermeneutical Study of Two Perspectives in Paul*. Stockholm: Almqvist & Wiksell, 1999.

Ho, Man Kei. *A Critical Study on T. F. Torrance's Theology of Incarnation*. Bern: Peter Lang, 2008.

Hofius, Otfried. *Der Christushymnus: Philipper 2:6–11*. 2nd ed. Tübingen: Mohr Siebeck, 1991.

———. "The Fourth Servant Song in the New Testament Letters." In *The Suffering Servant: Isaiah 53 in Jewish and Christian Sources*, edited by Bernd Janowski and Peter Stuhlmacher, 176. Grand Rapids: Eerdmans, 2004.

———. *Paulusstudien*. Tübingen: Mohr Siebeck, 1989.

Holloway, Paul A. *Consolation in Philippians*. Cambridge: Cambridge University Press, 2001.

———. *Philippians: A Commentary*. Minneapolis: Fortress, 2017.

Hooker, Morna D. *From Adam to Christ*. Cambridge: Cambridge University Press, 1990.

———. "Interchange and Atonement." *Bulletin of the John Rylands Library* 60 (1978): 462–81.

———. "Interchange in Christ." *Journal of Theological Studies* 22 (1971): 349–61.

Hopkins, Jasper. *A New, Interpretive Translation of St. Anselm's Monologion and Proslogion*. Minneapolis: Arthur Banning, 1996.

Hultgren, Arland J. "Paul and the Law." In *The Blackwell Companion to Paul*, edited by Stephen Westerholm, 202–15. Oxford: Blackwell, 2011.

Hunsinger, George. "After Barth: A Christian Appreciation of Jews and Judaism." In *Karl Barth, the Jews, and Judaism*, edited by George Hunsinger, 60–74. Grand Rapids: Eerdmans, 2018.

———. *The Beatitudes*. Mahwah, NJ: Paulist Press, 2015.

———. *Conversational Theology*. London: Bloomsbury T&T Clark, 2015.

———. *Disruptive Grace*. Grand Rapids: Eerdmans, 2000.

———. *The Eucharist and Ecumenism: Let Us Keep the Feast*. Cambridge: Cambridge University Press, 2008.

———. *Evangelical, Catholic, and Reformed*. Grand Rapids: Eerdmans, 2015.

———. *Reading Barth with Charity*. Grand Rapids: Baker Academic, 2015.

———. "The Sinner and the Victim." In *The T&T Clark Companion to the Doctrine of Sin*, edited by Keith Johnson and David Lauber, 433–49. London: Bloomsbury T&T Clark, 2016.

———, ed. *Thy Word Is Truth: Barth on Scripture*. Grand Rapids: Eerdmans, 2012.

Hurtado, Larry. *Lord Jesus Christ: Devotion to Jesus in Earliest Christianity*. Grand Rapids: Eerdmans, 2005.

Irons, Charles Lee. *The Righteousness of God*. Tübingen: Mohr Siebeck, 2015.

Jackson-McCabe, M. A. *Logos and Law in the Letter of James*. Leiden: Brill, 2001.

Johnson, Todd M., Gina A. Zurlo, Albert W. Hickman, and Peter F. Crossing. "Christianity 2017: Five Hundred Years of Protestant Christianity." *International Bulletin of Mission Research* 41, no. 1 (January 2017): 41–52.

Jordan, Clarence. *The Substance of Faith, and Other Cotton Patch Sermons*. Eugene, OR: Wipf & Stock, 2005.

Kalantzis, George. *Caesar and the Lamb: Early Christian Attitudes on War and Military Service*. Eugene, OR: Wipf & Stock, 2012.

Kant, Immanuel. *Religion within the Boundaries of Mere Reason*. Edited by Allen Wood and George Di Giovanni. Cambridge: Cambridge University Press, 1998.

Käsemann, Ernst. *New Testament Questions of Today*. Philadelphia: Fortress, 1969.

Kelsey, David H. *Eccentric Existence: A Theological Anthropology*. 2 vols. Louisville: Westminster John Knox, 2009.

Kierkegaard, Søren. *Practice in Christianity*. Edited and translated by Howard V. Hong and Edna H. Hong. Princeton: Princeton University Press, 1991.

Kim, Seyoon. *The Origin of Paul's Gospel*. Tübingen: Mohr Siebeck, 1981.

King, Martin Luther, Jr. *A Testament of Hope: The Essential Writings and Speeches of Martin Luther King, Jr.* Edited by James M. Washington. New York: HarperCollins, 1986.

Koperski, Veronica. *The Knowledge of Christ Jesus My Lord: The High Christology of Philippians 3:7–11*. Kampen: Kok Pharos, 1996.

Küng, Hans. *The Church*. New York: Sheed & Ward, 1967.

———. *Infallible? An Enquiry*. New York: Doubleday, 1971.

Law, David R. "Kenotic Theology." In *The Cambridge Dictionary of Christian Theology*, edited by Iain MacFarland et al., 261–62. Cambridge: Cambridge University Press, 2011.

———. *Kierkegaard's Kenotic Christology*. Oxford: Oxford University Press, 2013.

Levering, Matthew. *Christ's Fulfillment of Torah and Temple: Salvation according to Thomas Aquinas*. Notre Dame, IN: University of Notre Dame Press, 2002.

Lightfoot, J. B. *St. Paul's Epistle to the Philippians*. London: Macmillan, 1873.

Lindbeck, George A. "The Church." In *Keeping the Faith*, edited by Geoffrey Wainwright, 182. London: SPCK, 1989.

Loke, Andrew Ter Ern. *A Kryptic Model of the Incarnation*. Burlington, VT: Ashgate, 2014.

———. *The Origin of Divine Christology*. Cambridge: Cambridge University Press, 2017.

Luther, Martin. *Commentary on the First Twenty-Two Psalms*. Vol. 2. Translated by Henry Cole. London: Simkin and Marshall, 1826.

———. *Luther's Works*. 55 vols. Edited by Jaroslav Pelikan and Helmut T. Lehman. Philadelphia: Muehlenberg and Fortress; St. Louis: Concordia, 1955–86.

———. "Preface to St. Paul's Letter to the Romans." In *Martin Luther in His Own Words*, edited by J. D. Kilcrease and E. W. Lutzer, 49–69. Grand Rapids: Baker Books, 2017.

Lyonnet, Stanislas, SJ, and Léopold Sabourin, SJ. *Sin, Redemption, and Sacrifice: A Biblical and Patristic Study*. Rome: Biblical Institute, 1970.

Marshall, I. Howard. *Aspects of the Atonement*. Colorado Springs: Paternoster, 2007.

Martin, Dale B. *Slavery as Salvation: The Metaphor of Slavery in Pauline Christianity*. New Haven: Yale University Press, 1990.

Martin, Ralph P. *Carmen Christi*. Cambridge: Cambridge University Press, 1967.

Martyn, J. Louis. *Theological Issues in the Letters of Paul*. Nashville: Abingdon, 1997.

Massey, Isabel Ann. *Interpreting the Sermon on the Mount in the Light of Jewish Tradition*. Lewiston, NY: Edwin Mellen, 1991.

Matheson, George. *Sacred Songs*. Edinburgh: Blackwood & Sons, 1890.

McAuley, David. *Paul's Covert Use of Scripture*. Eugene, OR: Pickwick, 2015.

McGinnis, Andrew M. *The Son of God beyond the Flesh*. London: Bloomsbury T&T Clark, 2014.

McGowan, Andrew. *Ancient Christian Worship: Early Church Practices in Social, Historical, and Theological Perspective*. Grand Rapids: Baker Academic, 2014.

McLelland, Joseph C. *The Visible Words of God*. London: Oliver & Boyd, 1957.

Migliore, Daniel L. *Philippians and Philemon*. Louisville: Westminster John Knox, 2014.

Milgrom, Jacob. *Leviticus 1–16.* Anchor Bible. New Haven: Yale University Press, 1998.

Minow, Martha. *Between Vengeance and Forgiveness.* Boston: Beacon, 1998.

Mollaun, Romuald. *St. Paul's Concept of Ἱλαστήριον according to Rom. III, 25: An Historico-Exegetical Investigation.* Washington, DC: Catholic University of America Press, 1923.

Moltmann, Jürgen. *Theology and Joy.* London: SCM, 1973.

Moo, Douglas J. *Galatians.* Grand Rapids: Baker Academic, 2013.

Morris, Leon. *The Gospel according to John.* Grand Rapids: Eerdmans, 1995.

Moule, H. G. C. *The Epistle to the Philippians.* Cambridge: Cambridge University Press, 1890.

Munck, Johannes. *Christ and Israel: An Interpretation of Romans 9–11.* Philadelphia: Fortress, 1967.

Murphy, Colleen. *The Conceptual Foundations of Transitional Justice.* Cambridge: Cambridge University Press, 2017.

Newman, John Henry Cardinal. *An Essay on the Development of Christian Doctrine.* 1845. Reprint, Notre Dame, IN: University of Notre Dame Press, 1989.

Niebuhr, H. Richard. *The Kingdom of God in America.* 1937. Reprint, New York: Harper, 1959.

Niebuhr, Reinhold. *The Nature and Destiny of Man.* 2 vols. New York: Scribner's, 1941.

Oakes, Peter. *Philippians: From People to Letter.* Cambridge: Cambridge University Press, 2007.

Oberman, Heiko A. *The Dawn of the Reformation.* Grand Rapids: Eerdmans, 1992.

———. *The Reformation: Roots and Ramifications.* Grand Rapids: Eerdmans, 1994.

O'Brien, Peter T. *The Epistle to the Philippians.* Grand Rapids: Eerdmans, 2013.

———. *God Has Spoken in His Son: A Biblical Theology of Hebrews.* Downers Grove, IL: InterVarsity, 2016.

Outka, Gene. "Following at a Distance: Ethics and the Identity of Jesus." In *Scriptural Authority and Narrative Interpretation,* edited by Garrett Green, 144–60. Philadelphia: Fortress, 1987.

Owen, John. *An Exposition of the Epistle to the Hebrews.* Vol. 6 of *The Works of John Owen.* Edinburgh: Banner of Truth, 1967.

Pardue, Stephen T. *The Mind of Christ: Humility and the Intellect in Early Christian Theology.* London: T&T Clark, 2013.

Patterson, Jane Lancaster. *Keeping the Feast: Metaphors of Sacrifice in 1 Corinthians and Philippians.* Atlanta: SBL Press, 2015.

Perry, Michael. "O God beyond All Praising." In *Singing to God: Hymns and Songs, 1965–1995.* Carol Stream, IL: Hope Publishing, 1995.

Pitre, Brant. *Jesus and the Last Supper.* Grand Rapids: Eerdmans, 2015.

Plantinga, Cornelius. "Deep Wisdom." In *God the Holy Trinity: Reflections on Christian Faith and Practice,* edited by Timothy George, 149–55. Grand Rapids: Baker Academic, 2006.

———. *Not the Way It's Supposed to Be: A Breviary of Sin.* Grand Rapids: Eerdmans, 1996.

Prejean, Helen. *Dead Man Walking.* New York: Random House, 1993.

Prestige, G. L. *Fathers and Heretics.* London: SPCK, 1040.

———. *God in Patristic Thought.* 1936. Reprint, London: SPCK, 1981.

Prosser, Eleanor. *Hamlet and Revenge.* 2nd ed. Stanford, CA: Stanford University Press, 1971.

Reumann, John. *Philippians.* Anchor Yale Bible 33. New Haven: Yale University Press, 2008.

Richards, Irving T. "The Meaning of Hamlet's Soliloquy." *PMLA* 48, no. 3 (1933): 741–66.

Rivière, Jean. *The Doctrine of the Atonement: A Historical Essay.* Vol. 1. London: Kegan Paul, 1909.

Robertson, A. T. *Paul's Joy in Christ: Studies in Philippians.* 1913. Reprint, Nashville: Broadman, 1979.

Rosenblum, Bruce, and Fred Kuttner. *Quantum Enigma: Physics Encounters Consciousness.* New York: Oxford, 2011.

Rowe, C. Kavin. "Biblical Pressure and Trinitarian Hermeneutics." *Pro Ecclesia* 11 (2002): 295–312.

Rudolph, David J. *A Jew to the Jews: Jewish Contours of Pauline Flexibility in 1 Corinthians 9:19–23.* 2nd ed. Eugene, OR: Pickwick, 2016.

Sanday, William, and Arthur C. Headlam. *The Epistle to the Romans.* International Critical Commentary. Edinburgh: T&T Clark, 1902.

Sandnes, Karl Olav. *Belly and Body in the Pauline Epistles.* Cambridge: Cambridge University Press, 2002.

Schleiermacher, Friedrich. *The Christian Faith.* Edinburgh: T&T Clark, 1928.

Schmemann, Alexander. *The Eucharist: Sacrament of the Kingdom.* Crestwood, NY: St. Vladimir's Seminary Press, 1988.

Schnelle, Udo. *Apostle Paul: His Life and Theology.* Grand Rapids: Baker Academic, 2012.

Schwartz, Baruch J. "The Prohibitions concerning the 'Eating' of Blood in Leviticus 17." In *Priesthood and Cult in Ancient Israel,* 34–66. Sheffield, UK: JSOT Press, 1991.

Scott, John, and Gordon Marshall. *A Dictionary of Sociology.* 3rd ed. Oxford: Oxford University Press, 2009.

Sechrest, Love L. *A Former Jew: Paul and the Dialectics of Race.* London: Continuum, 2009.

Seifrid, Mark A. "Blind Alleys in the Controversy over the Paul of History." *Tyndale Bulletin* 45 (1994): 73–95.

———. "Paul's Turn to Christ in Romans." *Concordia Journal* 44 (2018): 15–24.

———. "Romans 7: The Voice of the Law, the Cry of Lament, and the Shout of Thanksgiving." In *Perspectives in Our Struggle with Sin: Three Views of Romans 7,* edited by Terry L. Wilder, 111–65. Nashville: B&H, 2011.

Sergienko, Gennadi A. *Our Politeuma Is in Heaven!* Carlisle, UK: Langham Monographs, 2013.

Shapiro, James. "The Question of Hamlet." *New York Review of Books* 65, no. 7 (April 19, 2018): 20, 22–23.

Sider, Ronald J. *Rich Christians in an Age of Hunger.* 6th ed. Nashville: Thomas Nelson, 2015.

Siker, Jeffrey S. *Jesus, Sin, and Perfection in Early Christianity.* Cambridge: Cambridge University Press, 2015.

———. "Yom Kippuring Passover: Recombinant Sacrifice in Early Christianity." In *Ritual and Metaphor: Sacrifice in the Bible,* edited by Christian A. Eberhart, 65–82. Atlanta: Society of Biblical Literature, 2011.

Silva, Moisés. *Philippians.* 2nd ed. Grand Rapids: Baker Academic, 2005.

Sklar, Jay. *Sin, Impurity, Sacrifice, Atonement.* Sheffield: Sheffield Phoenix, 2015.

Smith, Mitzi J. "Slavery in the Early Church." In *True to Our Native Land: An African American New Testament Commentary,* edited by Brian K. Blount, Cain Hope Felder, Clarice J. Martin, and Emerson B. Powery, 11–22. Minneapolis: Fortress, 2007.

Stead, Christopher. *Divine Substance.* Oxford: Oxford University Press, 1977.

Stökl Ben Ezra, Daniel. *The Impact of Yom Kippur on Early Christianity.* Tübingen: Mohr Siebeck, 2003.

Stuhlmacher, Peter. "Isaiah 53 in the Gospels and Acts." In *The Suffering Servant: Isaiah 53 in Jewish and Christian Sources,* edited by Bernd Janowski and Peter Stuhlmacher, 150–51. Grand Rapids: Eerdmans, 2004.

Tannehill, Robert C. *The Shape of the Gospel.* Eugene, OR: Wipf & Stock, 2007.

Tappenden, Frederick S. *Resurrection in Paul: Cognition, Metaphor, and Transformation.* Atlanta: SBL Press, 2016.

Thérèse of Lisieux. *Story of a Soul.* Translated by John Clarke. Washington, DC: ICS Publications, 2005.

Thielman, Frank. *Paul and the Law.* Downers Grove, IL: InterVarsity, 1994.

Thomas Aquinas. *The Aquinas Catechism.* Manchester, NH: Sophia Institute, 2000.

———. *Commentary on Saint Paul's First Letter to the Thessalonians and the Letter to the Philippians*. Albany, NY: Magi Books, 1969.

———. *Summa Theologiae*. Translated by Fathers of the English Dominican Province. Benziger Bros., 1947. Available at https://dhspriory.org/thomas/summa/index.html.

Thrall, Margaret. *2 Corinthians 1–7*. Vol. 1. London: T&T Clark, 1994.

Tillich, Paul. *The New Being*. New York: Charles Scribner's Sons, 1955.

———. *Systematic Theology*. 3 vols. Chicago: University of Chicago Press, 1951–63.

Timmins, Will N. *Romans 7 and Christian Identity: A Study of the "I" in Its Literary Context*. Cambridge: Cambridge University Press, 2017.

Tiwald, Markus. "Christ as *Hilastērion* (Rom. 3:25): Pauline Theology on the Day of Atonement in the Mirror of Early Jewish Thought." In *The Day of Atonement: Its Interpretations in Early Jewish and Christian Traditions*, edited by Thomas Hieke and Tobias Nicklas, 189–209. Leiden: Brill Academic, 2012.

Torrance, James B. *Worship, Community, and the Triune God of Grace*. Carlisle, UK: Paternoster, 1996.

Torrance, Thomas F. *Atonement: The Person and Work of Christ*. Downers Grove, IL: IVP Academic, 2014.

———. "The Biblical Conception of 'Faith.'" *Expository Times* 68 (1957): 221–22.

———. *The Christian Doctrine of God: One Being, Three Persons*. Edinburgh: T&T Clark, 1996.

———. *God and Rationality*. Oxford: Oxford University Press, 1971.

———. "The Mind of Christ in Worship: The Problem of Apollinarianism in the Liturgy." In *Theology in Reconciliation*, 139–214. Grand Rapids: Eerdmans, 1975.

———. "One Aspect of the Biblical Conception of Faith." *Expository Times* 68 (1957): 111–14.

———. *Theology in Reconstruction*. Grand Rapids: Eerdmans, 1965.

———. *The Trinitarian Faith*. Edinburgh: T&T Clark, 1988.

Travis, Steven. *Christ and the Judgment of God: The Limits of Divine Retribution in New Testament Thought*. Grand Rapids: Baker Academic, 2009.

Trigg, Joseph, trans. *Origen*. Early Church Fathers. London: Routledge, 1998.

Turretin, Francis. *Institutes of Elenctic Theology*. 3 vols. Phillipsburg, NJ: P&R, 1994.

Van Buren, Paul. *Christ in Our Place: The Substitutionary Character of Calvin's Doctrine of Reconciliation*. Edinburgh: Oliver & Boyd, 1957.

Van Zyl, Paul. "Dilemmas of Transitional Justice: The Case of South Africa's Truth and Reconciliation Commission." *Journal of International Affairs* 52 (1999): 647–67.

Vincent, Marvin R. *Epistles to the Philippians and to Philemon*. International Critical Commentary. Edinburgh: T&T Clark, 1897.

Vis, Joshua M. "The Purification Offering of Leviticus and the Sacrificial Offering of Jesus." PhD diss., Duke University, 2012.

Wagner, J. Ross. *Heralds of the Good News: Isaiah and Paul in Concert in the Letter to the Romans*. Leiden: Brill, 2003.

Walker, Peter. *In the Steps of Saint Paul: An Illustrated Guide to Paul's Journeys*. Oxford: Lion Hudson, 2008.

Webster, John. "The Holiness and Love of God." *Scottish Journal of Theology* 57 (2004): 249–68.

Weinandy, Thomas A. *Does God Suffer?* Edinburgh: T&T Clark, 2000.

Wesley, John. *Sermons II*. Vol. 2 of *The Works of John Wesley*. Edited by Albert C. Outler. Nashville: Abingdon, 1985.

Weymouth, Richard J. "The Christ-Story of Philippians 2:6–11: Narrative Shape and Paraenetic Purpose in Paul's Letter to Philippi." PhD diss., University of Otago, 2015.

White, Thomas Joseph. *The Incarnate Lord: A Thomistic Study in Christology*. Washington,

DC: Catholic University of America Press, 2017.

Williams, Logan. "Disjunction in Paul: Apocalyptic or Christomorphic? Comparing the *Apocalypse of Weeks* with Galatians." *New Testament Studies* 64 (2018): 64–80.

Williams, Sam K. "The 'Righteousness of God' in Romans." *Journal of Biblical Literature* 99 (1980): 241–90.

Witherington, Ben, III. *A Week in the Life of Corinth*. Downers Grove, IL: IVP Academic, 2012.

Woolever, Frank. *Gandhi's List of Social Sins: Lessons in Truth*. Pittsburgh: Dorrance, 2011.

Wright, N. T. *The Climax of the Covenant: Christ and the Law in Pauline Theology*. Minneapolis: Fortress, 1992.

SCRIPTURE INDEX

SUBJECT INDEX

Abraham, 140, 202n18
Adam, 54–55, 56–57, 59, 61, 63
Adams, Jens, 192n28
admirabile commercium, xviii–
   xvix, 59, 102, 202n17, 203,
   204, 210. *See also* Jesus Christ:
   exchange; pattern of exchange
Allison, C. F., 106n55
Anselm, 58–59, 137n36
anxiety, 130
apocalyptic, 6–7, 173–74,
   189–90, 212
Aquinas, Thomas, 8, 39n14, 76
Aristotle, 10, 211
Athanasius, 6, 108n60, 131n19
atonement
   blood, 142, 195
   cultic, 102–5, 154, 183–84,
      189–90, 200–202
   Greek fathers, 59
   Latin, 185n2
   Paul, 200–201
   and righteousness, 100
   Yom Kippur, 194–95
Augustine, 76, 154, 162–63

Balthasar, Hans Urs von, 186n6
baptism, 71, 92, 190n21, 212
Barr, James, 198n6
Bartchy, S. Scott, 2n2
Barth, Karl, 50n41, 58–59, 70n93,
   105, 150, 158, 178n8, 189
Bauckham, Richard, 63n76
beauty, 145, 146–47, 148, 149,
   150, 151–52, 154
belly worshipers, 119
benevolence, 32
Bird, Michael F., 97n24, 137n37
bishops, 4
Bockmuehl, Markus, 87, 171
Bonhoeffer, Dietrich, 75
Boring, Eugene, 192n28
bride and bridegroom, 8–9
brothers and sisters, in Christ, 89,
   170–71

Caesar, 31, 124, 171. *See also*
   emperor cult
Calvin, John, 59, 74n104, 150,
   167n139, 173, 184n3, 191,
   192n28, 207n13, 212n6
causality, 106n55
Chalcedon, Council of, 49n37,
   49n39, 53n50, 169n143,
   175n2, 178
Childs, Brevard S., xvii
Christology, 45, 48–49, 65
Chrysostom, John, 116–17
church, the, xiii–xiv, 4, 35, 66,
   88n164, 96, 144, 178–80
   Philippian, 2n1, 33, 121–23,
      164–66. *See also* Paul: and
      Philippians
circumcision, 91–93, 94
citizenship, 29–31, 120, 122–23
civic association, 122
Collins, John, 173
communion, 9, 146. See also
   koinōnia
compassion, 153
contemplation, 157
Cranfield, C. E. B., 104, 191n27
Cranmer, Thomas, 9n16
creation, 41
cross, the, 138, 147, 148, 149,
   153–54
   enemies of, 118–20
   See also Jesus Christ: death
cult
   atonement, 102–5, 154, 183–
      84, 189–90, 200–202
   and Christ, 195–96, 201–2
   and covenant, 78
   emperor, 121–22, 123
   exchange, 103–4, 201–2
   and forensic, 103–5, 109
   Paul, 187, 188, 192–93,
      200–202
   sacrifice, 82

sin, 189–90, 193–94
substitution, 188–89
Cyril of Alexandria, 47–48

Day of Atonement. *See* Yom
   Kippur
deacons, 4
de Boer, Martinus C., 192n28
discord, 33
double transfer, 101–2
doulos, 2, 175–76. *See also* Jesus
   Christ: servant/slave; servant
   of Yahweh; slave
doxology, 170
Dunn, James D. G., 187n10

earthly things, 120–21
Ebed Yahweh. *See* servant of
   Yahweh
ecclesial hermeneutics, xvii–xviii,
   5n10, 35, 69–70, 175, 176,
   178–80
Edwards, Jonathan, 75–76, 132,
   148–49, 150
Eliot, T. S., 19
emperor cult, 121–22, 123
enemies of the cross, 118–20
Epaphroditus, 85–88, 161, 166
Ephesus, Council of, 53n50
eschatology, 113, 173–74, 212–13
ethics, 37
Euodia, 128–29
evil, 17–18, 147–48
excellence, 131–32, 153–55, 157
exchange, saving. See *admirabile
   commercium*
expiation, 105, 195
explicatio, 175n2

faith, 130–31, 197–99
faithful, 77–80, 138, 148, 208,
   211, 213
Father (God)
   of believers, 169
   and Christ, 67

229